A Bittersweet Season

A Bittersweet Season

Caring for Our Aging Parents—and Ourselves

Jane Gross

ALFRED A. KNOPF · NEW YORK · 2011

THIS IS A BORZOI BOOK
PUBLISHED BY ALFRED A. KNOPF

Library of Congress Cataloging-in-Publication Data
Gross, Jane.
A bittersweet season : caring for our aging parents and ourselves / Jane Gross.
p. cm.
Includes index.
ISBN 978-0-307-27182-2
1. Aging parents—Care—United States. 2. Adult children of aging parents—Family
relationships—United States. 3. Gross, Jane—Family. I. Title.
HQ1063.6.G74 2011
306.8740973—dc22
2011007079

Jacket design by Barbara de Wilde

Manufactured in the United States of America
First Edition

For Michael: "The eagle has landed"

I have seen in you what courage can be when there is no hope.

—MAY SARTON, *As We Are Now*

CONTENTS

AUTHOR'S NOTE

This book reflects the experiences of an upper-middle-class family, blessed with financial and professional resources that made our journey easier. I have tried to direct readers in different circumstances to affordable services but am mindful that I am not capable of fully understanding how difficult their experience may be. I have purposefully not delved into Alzheimer's disease in more than a glancing way because, of all aspects of aging and caregiving, it has the richest literature of its own, written by those with firsthand knowledge, which I do not have.

The places where my mother lived in the final years of her life are all identified by name. If I could locate the professionals who took care of her in her final years and obtain their permission to use their real names, I have done so. I interviewed most of them to confirm, or correct, my memory of events. Where quotation marks are used, these sections come from verbatim conversation. Where quotation marks are not used and dialogue appears in italics instead, this reflects a reconstruction based on my best recollection.

Portions of this book have been vetted for accuracy by experts in the field. My brother has read the sections about our family. Where our memories differ, he helped me figure out whose was accurate. He often views events through a different emotional lens and had different relations than I did with the dramatis personae. This is my version, but never factually at odds with what he experienced.

—J.G., January 2011

A Bittersweet Season

Finding Our Better Selves

The day I started writing this book, I spent hours commiserating by telephone with three friends who were being turned upside down by the needs of their aging parents.

One lived a short distance from her mother, who was in precarious health, bouncing back and forth between home and hospital, unwilling to consider a retirement community or nursing home. For months, without time to rest and regroup, my friend, herself nearing the end of a fatal illness and keeping it from her mother, had managed a series of medical and home care emergencies. She was running on empty.

The second friend, rocked by the financial strains and childrearing conflicts that often follow divorce, had largely abdicated to his siblings the demands of long-distance supervision of two increasingly disabled parents, one lost in the fog of Alzheimer's disease and the other plagued by stress pain and the broken bones of osteoporosis. When my friend tried to do his fair share of the work, he was overwhelmed. When he didn't try, he was conscience-stricken.

The third friend was considering making a cross-country move to be closer to his mother, who was then past ninety and losing her customary verve. Driving had become risky, and her once-daily walks to the store or the library were just too much sometimes, now that simply dressing or preparing meals took so much energy. My friend knew his mother needed more from him than three-times-a-day phone calls. And he wanted more from her as their time together dwindled.

Before that day was over, I had also spoken to each friend's mother, as I do regularly, since all of them are dear to me. What they had to say, unbidden, was the flip side of my earlier conversations with their children. These three strong-willed old women were grateful for their children's devotion but resistant to giving up the reins. They were embarrassed by their own diminished capacity and frightened of what lay ahead, but nothing was worse, they said, than being a burden. Like my mother, who died in 2003, they fought dependence, even as it became inevitable.

All of my conversations served as a fitting reminder that we stand at an unprecedented demographic crossroads. Never before have there been so many Americans over the age of eighty-five. Never before have there been so many Americans in late middle age, the huge baby boom cohort, responsible for their parents' health and well-being. Most often, neither the aged parents nor the adult children are prepared for this long, often tortured, time in life, or for these role reversals, which are unanticipated, unwelcome, and unfamiliar. How do we become our parents' parents without robbing them of their dignity? How do they let us? How do we collaborate with our siblings, leaving behind any baggage we may have with them, or manage on our own if we are only children?

The task is to get through it with grace, mindfulness, and good sense: to do the very best we can for our parents without sacrificing the lives we've built for ourselves—our families, our jobs, and our own financial future, which is the last thing they'd want us to do. But how do we know when it's still appropriate to aggressively pursue medical care, try to fix everything that's broken, and restore our parents to a measure of health, vitality, and dignity? How do we know when, logistically and financially, we must break a solemn promise not to "put them away" (and how do we forgive ourselves for doing it, if we must)? How do we know when the time for heroics has passed? Our parents may have escaped earlier threats to their health—strokes, cardiac events, cancer—and lived longer than any generation before them, but eventually some things are just going to wear out. Their death certificates will say they died of heart failure or diabetic complications or respiratory failure, because the government has decreed that "old age" is not an acceptable cause of death. I beg to differ. At a certain point, the wheels simply fall off the bicycle.

So here we are, not just with a herculean job but with a front-row seat for this long, slow dying. We want to do all we realistically can to ease the suffering, smooth the passing, of our loved ones. But we also have the opportunity to watch what happens to our parents, listen to what they have to say to us, and use that information to look squarely at our own mortality and prepare as best we can for the end of our own lives. In fact, we have the opportunity to become better people, wiser and stronger, not simply older and grayer. We can make something of this crisis, or we can endure the experience until it's over and then escape back into the daily buzz of our lives until suddenly it's our turn.

That is what this book is about: how we get through this time, no matter how long it lasts. It is written from the far shore of caregiving, an all-consuming and life-altering experience that wrings you out, uses you up, and then sends you back into the world with your heart full and your eyes open, if you let it. First and foremost it is my own story—mine, my mother's, and my brother's—the one I know best. But it will be amplified and enriched, at every turn, by the people I've interviewed on this subject over the years as part of my job for *The New York Times*—the elderly, their adult children, professionals in the field—and more recently by the hundreds of thousands of monthly readers of the blog I launched for the *Times,* called *The New Old Age,* the first such forum for two intersecting generations finding their way through a timeless challenge but never before experienced in these daunting new ways or in these numbers.

Although my caregiving days are behind me, they are vivid still. In the space of three years, between 2000 and 2003, my mother's ferocious independence gave way to utter reliance on her two adult children. Garden-variety aches and pains became major health problems; halfhearted attention no longer sufficed, and managing her needs from afar became impossible. The time had come for my mother's reverse migration, from a retirement community in Florida to another in New York, and in short order to a nursing home. By the end of her life, at eighty-eight, she was paralyzed, incontinent, could not speak, was losing the ability to swallow, and wanted nothing so much as a dignified way to die.

Those are the bare-bones facts. Missing is the panic of being in charge; and the shock to my brother, Michael, and me when our competence and resources proved all but useless in the face of America's incoherent and inadequate safety net for the frail elderly. We were flattened by the enormous demands on our time, energy, and bank accounts; the disruption to our professional and personal lives; the fear that our time in this parallel universe would never end and the guilt for wishing that it would. I can tell you now that it was worth every dreadful minute, a transformative experience. But at the time, living in the eternal present tense, all we could manage was muddling from one day to the next.

My brother and I were late children, so we reached this juncture before our friends and colleagues, who, innocent of experience, telegraphed the belief, painful to us, that we were exaggerating how awful it was. Only occasionally did they say it out loud, but in the silence between sentences I could hear judgment: *This can't be as hard as you're making it sound. Old people get sick and die all the time. This isn't your child, or your spouse, or yourself. It's inevitable.*

It was a lonely time. I was too tired and too sad for socially appropriate chitchat; I emptied the room at cocktail parties with gloom-and-doom stories nobody wanted to hear and quickly found it easier to just stay home. My brother, luckily, seemed to cross more easily between these disparate worlds in which we found ourselves.

At work, I tried to keep pace with my job while fielding my mother's incessant phone calls, chasing down doctors, phoning in prescriptions, hiring geriatric care managers and aides, arguing with my brother, fighting back tears, and dashing out of the newsroom for emergencies. Had I been a parent, I might have been just as stressed, but part of my energies would have been invested in a child's bright future. Old people may have good days, and it was my job to maximize those for my mother, but they don't have bright futures.

Among my somewhat younger friends and colleagues, the fear and confusion I remember has now become commonplace. I hear it from behind the partitioned cubicles at work, in weary discussions on the train platform or in the supermarket checkout line, at business meetings with people I barely know. A total stranger confides his feelings of guilt at letting his sister do all the heavy lifting. Another, ashamed, says he recoiled when shaving his father for the first time. A third is at her wit's end because her parents, usually frugal coupon clippers, have for months been paying rent at an assisted living facility but still refuse to leave their home. A fourth cannot afford home care for his mother and wants her to end her days in his house but wonders at the effect on his children.

The same day that I tried to console my three friends, and their mothers, I had an appointment with my internist, who spent half the visit telling me about her mother's ups and downs since her move to a continuing care retirement community. When I spoke to my literary agent, whose father was in failing health and would die within months, she was passing the caregiver's baton to her brother on the eve of an overseas vacation. Colleagues wanted to know the cost of a home health aide, an explanation as to why adult diapers fit women better than men, and product reviews for medical alert pendants and staircase chair-lifts. I also bumped into a neighbor whose mother-in-law, recently widowed, was no longer talking to her. With the best of intentions and a clear head, my neighbor had invited a geriatric social worker to help open a difficult family dialogue. Her mother-in-law was enraged. The list goes on.

So what did I have to offer the dozen-plus people who had shared their heartache with me in the space of a single day (and not an atypical one in that regard)? And, more pertinent, what do I have to offer you? Alas, not a comprehensive rule book for being your parent's parent; I don't believe there is such a thing, not one that tells the truth. If there had been, I assure you I would have found it and read it when I needed it most.

But I can share with you my hard-earned list of tips that you won't find in the growing collection of how-to books and websites. I can describe my mistakes and triumphs—I hope in a constructive way—as well as make other suggestions, things for you to do or at least think very hard about, regardless of the fact that no two families face the same issues.

I can tell you, from experience, that if you take charge too soon, you will patronize and humiliate your parents, but if you step in too late, their manageable problems will have turned unmanageable. I will try to give you advice for determining when the right time has arrived. I can tell you how to initiate family discussions if your parents or siblings prefer to avoid them and how to participate in such conversations even if you'd rather not. I can tell you that most bad decisions are made in the heat of a crisis, when alarm and ignorance collide. I can tell you that it is usually possible to slow things down—refuse to be rushed by doctors, discharge planners, and others who have different agendas than yours—and demand the time to consider alternatives calmly and deliberately.

I can tell you how to work out a fair division of labor with siblings whose hearts are in the right place but who are not hardwired to help in certain ways. I can tell you how to appreciate assistance when you get it, how to conserve energy by avoiding unproductive resentment when you don't, and how to relax exacting standards that guarantee nothing anyone else does will be good enough. I can make suggestions about looking after yourself so you don't fall apart when someone else needs you, having learned the hard way. And I can ask uncomfortable questions about whether your insistence on doing everything, your way and with less help than is available, is about solving real problems, satisfying your ego, or settling old scores.

I can tell you what various entitlement programs pay for, and what they don't; which situations are covered by long-term care insurance, and which aren't; and why workplace accommodations designed for child care don't help much when you're caring for an elderly parent. I can tell you when it might be wise to avoid specialists, who are trained to cure and consider anything less a failure, and instead search for a primary care doctor with an interest in geriatrics—the biology, physiology, sociology, and psychology of the elderly. Among other things, geriatricians know the difference between quality of life and quantity of life, and can explore with an elderly parent, and with you, where to draw that line.

I can tell you to stay out of emergency rooms and hospitals to the extent possible and never to leave your parents there to fend for themselves. I can tell you that taking an elderly person for a single test—say, an MRI—is generally an all-day affair, so it's a bad idea to tell your boss you'll be back after lunch. I can tell you to leave a spare pair of glasses in the car; to keep the gas tank full and the driveway shoveled; to always carry your cell phone charger; and to maintain an updated list of your parents' medications. All of this will prepare you best for dealing with inevitable emergencies.

I can tell you not to be impressed by grand marble staircases in assisted living communities, which are too slippery and steep for the elderly ever to use; these decorative flourishes are there to reassure *you* that you've moved Mom or Dad to a nice place and needn't feel bad about it. Better you should ask if there's anyone with medical training around after six at night. And I can tell you that the rude sounds and smells of a nursing home, which assault you the first time you cross the threshold, will likely become less depressing over time, and that they count for less than the number of registered nurses or the turnover among aides; more important, they will be less disturbing to your parents than to you because old people are at a different, more accepting place, or will be soon.

I can tell you all of these things and more. But the most important thing I can tell you is that being clueless—utterly clueless—is the central and unavoidable part of this experience, perhaps the greatest challenge to those of us who pride ourselves on knowing what we're doing, who like being in control. That's because every decision—medical, residential, financial, personal—is contingent on the particular trajectory of your parent's decline. I can't tell you how your mother or father will die, how long it will take, how much suffering it will involve, what it will cost, how you will pay for it, what will happen to your career or your marriage in the meantime, or whether the experience will bring your family together or pull it apart. All of that depends on imponderables, things you can't know or prepare for no matter how smart you are, how organized, or how loving and attentive.

So even more important than seeking and dutifully following prescriptive advice, in my experience, is learning to roll with the punches, to play without a net. To some, improvisation comes naturally. To me, it didn't. I hated it when my elaborate plans went awry. And I beat myself up over "bad" decisions when there really was no such thing, given the situation. Forgive the New Age–speak, but this is all about the journey, not the destination, because we all know the final outcome.

My brother, who flies by the seat of his pants better than anyone I know, found my obsessive strategizing exasperating and a waste of energy, my own and his, when I tried to force his participation. I found what I considered his la-di-da approach infuriating and irresponsible. With the benefit of hindsight, we've come full circle. He says he's grateful for the plans I made that actually worked, and I'm grateful for his nimbleness when they didn't. So consider, if you must, possible if/then scenarios. But try to avoid woulda-coulda-shouldas, except as a guide for the next crisis or as hard-won wisdom to pass along—gently, very gently—to friends.

My mother's lament, that we live too long and die too slowly, has become more common, with impact on two generations, as medical science has made it possible to keep very sick and very old people alive longer. The typical eighty-five-year-old, geriatric researchers say, can expect more than two years at the end of his life when he is totally dependent on others for the most basic daily activities: getting out of bed, getting dressed, going to the bathroom, eating. And the eighty-five-and-over group, by far the fastest growing in America, is expected to more than double by 2035, according to census projections, to 11.5 million, from about 5 million as I write. By then the youngest of the baby boomers, 77 million strong, will be celebrating their seventieth birthdays. This is a demographic Category 5 hurricane bearing down on weak levees.

These alarming numbers were not at my fingertips until my mother was face-to-face with the serial humiliations of advanced age; nor, for the most part, were they at my friends' or colleagues'. So what I took for judgment I now see as ignorance or denial. That denial—the widespread notion that our parents, and by extension ourselves, will beat the odds, play tennis at eighty or ninety, and then drop dead with no fuss and bother—has been fed by the mainstream media, which until very recently offered little or no information to help two generations through this unprecedented and arduous passage. Why is the coverage of old age mostly happy talk—wizened mountain climbers or marathoners; nursing homes that permit, even celebrate, consensual sex; weddings on the far side of one hundred? Uplifting? Sure. Possible? Of course. Typical? Hardly.

No wonder we're so ill prepared.

When my mother, Estelle Gross, became my brother's and my responsibility, we knew nothing about entitlement programs. (*What do you mean Medicare doesn't cover the cost of home care or assisted living or a nursing home?*) We knew nothing about the advantages and disadvantages of hiring aides through agencies or word of mouth. (*What do you mean the agency aide needs permission from a supervisor before picking up my mother from the floor if she falls?*)

We knew nothing about hospital discharge planning. (*What do you mean she has to leave tomorrow when we have no satisfactory place to take her?*) We knew nothing about geriatric medicine. (*What do you mean emergency rooms and intensive care units can cause a form of psychosis in the elderly or that a catheter can lead to an undiagnosed urinary tract infection and even death?*)

We knew nothing about Medicaid spend-downs, in-hospital versus out-of-hospital "do not resuscitate" orders, Hoyer lifts, motorized wheelchairs, or assistive devices for people who can neither speak nor type. We knew nothing about "pre-need consultants," who handle advance payment for the funerals of people who aren't dead yet, or "feeders," whose job it is to spoon pureed food into the mouths of men and women who can no longer hold a utensil.

Obituaries and paid death notices tell stories of the dead and those who loved them, generally chronicle lives of accomplishment, cite cause of death, and list survivors. But they rarely include any mention of suffering other than the occasional reference to a long illness. What was that long illness like? Who did the messy work that often surrounds dying? Did some family members go missing when the going got tough? Did the dying man or woman know or care? Did he or she hear the bedside squabbles about end-of-life decisions? And what happened next, after the donations-in-lieu-of-flowers, the wake or the shiva, the graveside service? Did the grown children fight over their inheritance or, by then, was there nothing left?

My aim here is to give more precise and vivid meaning to the platitude that old age isn't for sissies. I want to try to make sure that adult children, our ranks growing, are not as isolated and ignorant as my brother and I were, lurching from crisis to crisis without enough reflection, information, or support. Maybe I can help other sons and daughters empathize with the growing mountain of loss in their parents' lives, make peace with an unwelcome role reversal, and adjust to the changed architecture of their families. Maybe I can set an example for how to finish unfinished business with parents, find a more peaceful place in relationships with siblings, and lay a foundation for a mature relationship with brothers and sisters once all the "grown-ups" are gone.

Even before I understood how desperate people were for this kind of information, my editors at the *Times*—many of them entering the time of life when responsibility for their own parents was a daily concern—embraced the line of reporting I'd initiated. The demographics trumped the old notion that nobody would want to read such depressing fare over breakfast. Most of my stories wound up on the front page, the precious real estate usually reserved for war, politics, and natural disasters. The reader response was overwhelming, and the stories invariably rode the top of the "most e-mailed" list.

Between 2004 and 2008, *Times* readers learned, along with me, about the astronomical cost of advanced old age for all but the wealthy and the destitute, an unintended consequence of government programs that date to the mid-1960s, when life expectancy was seventy. They learned, along with me, the difference between Medicare and Medicaid, between assisted living and continuing care retirement communities, between home health aides hired from agencies and those recommended over the back fence, between slow medicine and comfort care.

In the summer of 2008, I launched a blog, *The New Old Age.* The introductory post, "Our Parents, Ourselves," drew 710 comments; the first month there were 907,000 page views. Readers were hungry for information and grateful for a place to vent. Mostly they were overwhelmed adult children, but their parents chimed in, too, usually saying that they yearned for a legal and graceful exit when frailty or dementia trapped them in lives that no longer had meaning for them. The generously shared comments, like the findings of my earlier reporting, sometimes confirmed and sometimes contradicted my personal experience, and filled in many of the gaps.

I am not an only child or a member of a large extended family, so I've called on the experience of others who have walked that path, amateurs and professionals alike. I am childless, as is my brother, so I've turned to those who are themselves parents for stories of the daily choices they made between cheering at a child's Little League game and bringing dinner to an ailing parent. I've compared my own good fortune to the experience of adult children who, unlike my brother and me, have no savings to dip into.

I've distilled advice I've heard and read on taking away a parent's car keys or on begging them to leave a beloved home. I've done the same for guidance on caring for two failing parents in tandem or one right after the other, or moving a frail parent into your home or relocating to theirs. I'll discuss, in a very limited way, the special rigors of Alzheimer's disease and the unenviable task of taking care of someone who no longer knows who you are. And I'll review disputed end-of-life decisions—say, when one sibling wants a feeding tube and the other doesn't—as well as squabbles over inheritances.

My family's story began at a moment of crisis, when my mother's routine medical problems ceased to be routine, her relatively independent life was threatened, and all three of us were reeling at the time when a clear head mattered the most. This is the way it often happens, a before-and-after event, the day when everything changes.

Like so many in her generation, and legions more to come in ours, my mother had lived into her eighties without succumbing to cancer, a sudden heart attack, a disabling stroke, pulmonary disease, severe diabetic complications, or other diseases that once killed people, often swiftly, and generally before the long, slow ravages of dementia or frailty. That is not to say there wasn't plenty wrong with her: arthritis, obesity, high blood pressure, an inner ear disturbance that caused extreme vertigo, mild diabetes, hearing loss, cataracts, and lifelong depression. All of it was unpleasant but not life-threatening.

Widowed at fifty-eight and justifiably proud of her self-sufficiency, she asked little of her two adult children and mostly took matters into her own hands. *She* told *us* when it was time for her to stop driving, sell the house on Long Island, and move to a more supported environment. She figured out which of many Florida retirement communities suited her best, what size apartment she wanted, and which furniture to take and which to leave behind. The proceeds from the sale of her house would cover the rent in Florida for years to come. Taking no chances, she hired a financial planner once she got there to guide the process. She had a living will, a health care proxy, a durable power of attorney—all without any prodding. My mother was a realist. She neither expected to live forever nor wanted to.

During the seven years in Florida, when she declined but not dramatically, my mother was glad for the emergency call button in her apartment, the meals she didn't have to prepare, the grass that somebody else cut. My brother and I were glad we could call the front desk if she didn't answer the telephone and someone would check on her. Her cane gave way to a walker, but she continued to ride a van to the grocery store and shop for herself, bringing home a few small bags after each trip. She enjoyed a regular bridge game, occasional dinners out with her sister-in-law who lived nearby, and several visits a year from her two children and daughter-in-law. Michael and I were not terribly attentive, except for weekly phone calls. That was fine with her. Our lives were still mostly our own, as was hers. Then came the bombshell from her Florida internist. Our mother, we were told, had a benign tumor sitting on the outer surface of her spine. Without surgery she would wind up paralyzed from the waist down and incontinent.

Was this the "after" moment?

Now, nearly a decade later, I see all the mistakes we made. I had never even met her Florida doctor or talked to him on the phone until this diagnosis. What had prompted him to give my mother an MRI? Had she complained to him of some new symptom she had kept from us? I would have known all this if I'd bothered to develop a relationship with the doctor, joined my mother at appointments when I was there, and talked to him on the phone when I wasn't. My mother wouldn't have welcomed my intrusion, but I should have been pushier. I should have paid more attention. But I liked our family's rules of (dis)engagement because they made my life easier.

Thus the diagnosis left me totally unprepared. My heart raced. My stomach was an elevator falling down the shaft. My head was noisy with static. I made fast decisions rather than good decisions, partly because the sooner we could take care of everything, the sooner we'd be done and back to normal. This was just another to-do list, and I'd work my way from top to bottom, as would my brother.

Maybe this was the moment for my mother's inevitable reverse migration, back to the embrace of her children. Perhaps this was the time to shut down her Florida apartment and move all her worldy goods to another residence near us, I said to myself, time to close bank accounts at one end and open new ones at the other. Go-visit-Mom weekends would be replaced with quick visits on the way to work. And Michael and I had the skill and metabolism to make it all happen quickly, which was better for us. I didn't stop to think that the pace would be dizzying, exhausting, and ultimately traumatic for her.

I sprinted when I should have cautiously watched my step, rushed when I should have ruminated, barked orders when I should have discussed things with my mother. I heard what I wanted to hear, not what doctors or admissions directors of long-term care facilities were actually telling me. Does any of this sound familiar to you? If it does, slow down. Get your bearings. You can't bulldoze your way through this like a work project. Still, you can take comfort in knowing that this precipitating crisis, for many of us, is the hardest part, because you probably still think you can make it right, that you can stop the clock.

It takes a while to learn that some decisions are far more important than others; some things are actually in your hands and some not. What is vital, and well within your control, is being present in a consoling way and respectful enough to bear witness to the inevitable. This, too, is about slowing down. At first it's hard to walk at a snail's pace beside your mother or father when they can no longer keep up, at least without impatiently rolling your eyes. Or to kneel at their level if they're in a wheelchair. But the pace and the vantage become more natural and annoyance softens into tenderness, if you let it.

I keep saying that this experience can become something other than desperate and bleak, *if you let it*. It really is a choice. We all know grown children who have bolted when the moment arrived. You aren't one of those, or you wouldn't be reading this book. But imagining running away doesn't make you a bad person. I fantasized, usually in the hypnagogic space between sleeping and waking, facing another day of ignorance and exhaustion, about pointing the car west and driving, driving, driving. I'm glad that I didn't, because instead I learned what I was made of; I found my better self. I found my mother. I found my brother. But all of that came later.

CHAPTER 1

The Early Heroic Rush

Maybe I sensed something was brewing. Maybe it was a coincidence. Maybe I'd simply had it with sleeping on my mother's couch during visits to the euphemistically named Horizon Club in Deerfield Beach, Florida, where she kept the air-conditioning on full blast, the television at peak volume, and the mother-daughter sniping coming fast and furious.

I was grateful my mother lived in an assisted living community—far enough away that I wasn't at her beck and call—and had for more than six years, making the move from the family home on Long Island, as I've said, of her own accord. She was spared the isolation of snowy winters; she was mobile with a cane or a walker, played a mean game of bridge, read voraciously, and told hysterical stories about the neighbor ladies on the prowl for new gentlemen friends before the last ones were cold in the ground. She was also relatively healthy and fiercely independent, exactly as I wanted her to stay, even if it meant keeping my eyes squeezed shut at early evidence to the contrary.

For example, for many years my mother's most essential piece of furniture was one of those cheesy 1950s TV tables, the plastic kind, with a mottled finish designed to look like marble, which folded up, stacked vertically in a stand, and got pulled out when a *Leave It to Beaver*-type family gathered in the den to eat dinner. This particular TV table first came to my adult notice after my mother was widowed and still living in my childhood home. Back then, her attachment to it, instead of buying herself a proper piece of furniture to place next to the chair where she watched television, played solitaire, and took some of her meals, was a matter of frugality. But by the time I was visiting her in Florida, the table had become an early indicator of how disabled she was.

Its top, a mere twelve inches square, held my mother's address book, the *TV Guide*, the day's mail, the telephone, the remote control, her eyeglasses, an emery board, a deck of cards, whatever she was reading, and a pad and a pencil. Each of these objects was always in the identical place. My mother liked and enforced order in her orbit. But this was something else. This was survival. Because my mother's shoulders were crippled by arthritis, she had figured out the exact spot for each object so it would cause her the least pain when she swiveled and reached for it. And she rarely got out of the chair, because that would require a push with those very same ruined shoulders. Everything she needed had to be on that table, accessible with no help from anyone.

Once in a while I'd put something down carelessly, slightly out of place, without understanding that the rules were necessary, not arbitrary. Only now do I see that her insistence that I return the object to its original location wasn't peevish or unwelcoming but rather pragmatic. This was comparable to adapting, while still on Long Island, when she could no longer open or close the door on the driver's side of her car with her left hand because that shoulder was killing her. She couldn't rotate her body in order to use the other hand, unaided. So she took the belt from a terrycloth robe and tied it to the door handle, making the right-handed movement possible.

My mother wasn't going to burden me or my brother by explaining any of this, ask our assistance, or even welcome it if we offered it unsolicited. All of these were problems she preferred to solve on her own. But how could I not have seen that this independence was really stoicism in the face of considerable pain? Why wasn't I more careful with the objects on the table? Why didn't I pay more attention to her suffering, notice what was going on sooner? Why didn't I realize that her refusal to ask for help was the natural reaction of a proud woman seeing her control slipping away, as it so often does in advanced age? This was still the in-between stage. The parent says "Everything is fine," and the adult child is desperate to believe it. It's a dance: a different person now leads but must use a light touch, which required more wisdom and kindness than I yet knew how to muster.

Today, the how-to books, websites, and blogs about elder care wisely advise pushing elderly parents to do as much as they can for as long as they can—not to infantilize them. "Use it or lose it" is the mantra of healthy longevity. A regular routine of walking extends mobility. Weight-bearing exercise fends off broken hips. Balancing the checkbook keeps the brain sharp. All of that, I have no doubt, is true. Indeed, many of my mother's health problems—overweight, arthritis, depression—might have been avoided had I pushed her harder in her sixties and seventies. But long after that point had passed and the damage was done, I wanted her to be fine so badly that I pretended she still was, until shortly before this visit, employing a commonly used combination of denial, laziness, and attachment to the very convenient status quo.

My gut, eventually, told me that this long-distance, low-maintenance arrangement had about run its course. I'd already quietly put her on the waiting list for two proposed retirement communities not far from my home in the New York City suburbs. Now I flew down for a typical visit. It lasted twenty-eight hours, during which time I bought her a 1.56-gallon jug of laundry detergent (she couldn't lift it from the grocery store shelves with her arthritic hands) and a twelve-pack of toilet paper (too unwieldy to carry from the Horizon Club's van to her apartment, even with the help of the solicitous driver). I drove from supermarket to supermarket in a rental car until I found the brand of artificial sweetener she preferred.

I stacked her night table with novels: *Evening* by Susan Minot, *Plainsong* by Kent Haruf, Sue Miller's *While I Was Gone,* and *The Hours* by Michael Cunningham. Best of all, since my mother loved good food, we ate fresh fish within sight of the Atlantic Ocean, at Charley's Crab, her favorite local restaurant, where she got to go only when my brother or I visited. I'd hoped we could squeeze in a movie, but we ran out of time.

No doubt her bridge partners whispered about the failings of a daughter who came for such a short visit, giving me no extra credit for six hours in the air and three additional hours due to airport delays. Or maybe I thought they were tut-tutting because I was, indeed, stingy with my time with her and felt guilty about it. Still, my mother and I were equally peculiar about our privacy; two days sharing her one-bedroom apartment were a strain, and these quick visits worked for both of us. We talked on this occasion, for the first time, about whether it was time to think about a reverse migration. I told her about the two places I was considering and that I wanted to send her information when I got home.

Instead of the balking I anticipated, she agreed it would be nice to move to a comparable assisted living community in Westchester County, where I could drop in for a cup of coffee, stay for an hour, and head back home. She agreed it would be reassuring if I could accompany her to outpatient cataract surgery and still go to work the same day, pleasing for the three of us to spend a few good years close to one another before her inevitable decline. This was wishful thinking for so many reasons, but none more so than that we had missed the moment. The crisis was already upon us. We just didn't know it yet.

My father, Milton Gross, was a sports columnist for the *New York Post,* followed into journalism by both of his children—me, the obedient daddy's girl, and my younger brother, Michael, the insouciant rebel. Only my mother didn't participate in what she called "the family business." She had come to New York after high school from a dot on the map in upstate New York, near the Vermont border. She graduated first in her high school class but was never encouraged to apply for a college scholarship. Instead, she came to the big city to study nursing and escape a childhood with a stepmother she had never warmed to, a mother who had died when she was a toddler and she barely remembered, and several step- and half-brothers to whom she felt no particular attachment. Only when I was an adult did my father reveal that she suffered from depression severe enough to warrant several hospitalizations. Belatedly, I understood her emotional distance, the way she literally recoiled when hugged and responded to "I love you" with a mumbled "Uh-huh."

She had always been stoic in the face of hardship, inventive at solving problems, and totally unsentimental. She discussed her end-of-life wishes long before it was necessary. Each move she made to a more protected environment, until she'd settled in, raised her anxiety level substantially, but she pushed through it, resolute. We never had to force these painful decisions on her as most of our friends have had to do with their parents. She spared us the experience of other adult children who were left with no choice but to disable the battery of a parent's car, sneak an aide into their home under the guise she was a graduate student doing research or desperate for a place to live, or practically push a parent from his own home, because he was no longer safe there, to a group facility. I think that for my mother, making such decisions on her own was a matter of control more than consideration. Still, when I hear the more common stories of parental resistance, I'm grateful for her grit.

My mother's career, running the nursery for premature babies at New York City's Lenox Hill Hospital, ended with my birth in 1947, a first child after three miscarriages and a pregnancy spent largely bedridden. My brother was born five years later, an age gap that contributed to our spending little time together as children. In a tract house on Long Island, a few notches up from Levittown, my mother raised a family and tended to a husband who worked nights, slept late, wrote at home, traveled frequently, basked in his own fame, and was demanding of all of us. For my mother, that meant no noisy vacuuming until he awoke at ten or eleven, no morning bowling league because he needed her at home to heat the maple syrup for his pancakes. Friends who came over for lunch wondered about a grown man still in his pajamas at noon, eating breakfast and reading the newspapers, back when they could be stacked high enough to consume several hours. Playdates took place elsewhere so my father wouldn't be disturbed while writing in his basement office. We lived by the ominous dictum "Daddy's downstairs working."

He treated my mother dismissively, took my brother's rebelliousness as a personal affront, and alternately adored me and raged at my failings. He was a force of nature, charismatic, gifted, temperamental, very ambitious for me and less so for Michael, who was just twenty, a college junior, when my father died in 1973, at the age of sixty-one, following misdiagnosed pneumonia and a cascade of other medical blunders. I was bereft, just beginning a career as a sports journalist myself, the beneficiary of his considerable connections. Michael was emotionally unreadable, often stoned. But he wrote his first book while still in college, both admiring of and in competition with an accomplished but bullying father.

My mother, bred for solitude, thrived as a widow, even so prematurely. She was intelligent, resilient, thrifty, resourceful, and better than my father with both money and power tools. She had low expectations ("Where did you get the idea you were supposed to be happy?") and solved problems without imposing on her children or behaving in a way that inspired guilt.

When she could no longer open or close the garage door, she left the car in the driveway, snow or no snow, rather than accept our offer of an electronic opener. She was as low-maintenance as my father had been high-maintenance.

Eventually Michael simply showed up one day with a garage door opener; ditto a telephone answering machine and a VCR. He had figured out not to ask her what she wanted but simply to shower her with gifts, the more extravagant the better, and she loved it. I bought her books that she read eagerly but certainly made no fuss about receiving, while carrying on nonstop about the latest bauble from him. On the other hand, I was the one my father had taken to Toots Shor's and Jilly's to mingle with star athletes and entertainers, my little legs dangling from a bar stool at the age of ten. I was the one who rode with him to Western Union late at night, long before fax machines, let alone computers, doing the final edit on his column by the light of the glove compartment. While in some ways rarefied, ours was not an atypical family architecture in its mother-son, father-daughter configuration.

Had my mother died first, she and I often joked, once joking became a belated but delicious part of our repertoire, my father would have moved into my house without a by-your-leave, and I'd have welcomed him. He likely would have been a handful, not knowing how to make coffee or where the dry cleaner was located. She reminded me, all things considered, how lucky I was, and she was right. I won't pretend I found her a demonstrative, coochy-coochy-coo kind of mother. But amid the mortifications of old age, her clear head and courage were something to behold. If only I had appreciated her sooner.

My brother and I, while never close, collaborated more effectively than I'd have guessed during my mother's decline, bringing useful skills to our new roles. We are both journalists, skilled at information gathering, at cajoling or intimidating people whose help we need, whether to get an elusive interview for ourselves or a coveted nursing home bed for our mother. When making decisions about her, we generally showed up in tandem, each with a reporter's notebook and several backup pens in case one went dry. We asked lots of questions and took copious notes. I had the added credential of having cared for a dying friend during the last ten months of his life, an invaluable education. And my brother has an easy charm and happy-go-lucky disposition that naturally wins people over, working its magic on strangers as it always had on my mother. In other words, we seemed a formidable pair, acting like we knew what we were doing even when we didn't.

My mother was dizzy. There was nothing new about that, since she had long had Ménière's disease, an inner ear disturbance that sometimes left her so woozy that she had to take to her bed and hold her head perfectly still. Compared to a raging Ménière's attack, this episode sounded routine. Her right leg (both knees had long ago been replaced because of arthritis) was weak and tingly, but that didn't sound so awful, either. I doubt she did more than mention these symptoms in passing to me or Michael, and she didn't tell either of us about a recent fall (which I learned about much later from medical records) that raised concerns of a possible brain bleed. She was always stingy with information and rarely complained, sometimes at the expense of what good sense would dictate.

The first glimmer of trouble came when my mother's internist—I didn't even know his name after all those years—sent her to see a neurologist, who referred her for an MRI. With a retired nurse's lifelong disdain for doctors, she told me, expletives deleted, that "I don't intend to do anything he told me to do. Anyway, I'm feeling better the last few days." Even unwary me knew the second part was a lie, a way to get me off her back. Somehow we persuaded her to keep the MRI appointment. Or rather Michael did, since only Michael could persuade her to do anything when she'd dug her heels in against it.

On the day of the test—November 15, to be precise—I bought stamps, D batteries, Pledge furniture polish, and kitty litter, and arranged for the gutters to be cleaned. Life goes on. I'd been on the waiting list for Thanksgiving week at a spa in Mexico, and a room opened up. Michael and his wife were headed to London for the holiday weekend. Both of us were eager for a break from work.

In the meantime, my brother, sister-in-law, and I had gone to take a look at one of the assisted living places nearby, open less than a month and very much a work in progress. When Michael called the Meadowview— oh, those names! no meadow, no view—for driving directions from the city, an employee said, "I don't know. I take the train." Should that have raised our antennae? Instead of noticing a rude and ill-informed employee, I was concerned whether my mother would be okay without a full kitchen, which she was used to. What we looked at was a deluxe studio, 460 square feet for $2,893 a month, with a two-burner stovetop, a microwave, and an under-the-counter refrigerator. The three of us agreed she'd do just fine in that space.

I didn't notice the sign at the entrance to the Meadowview that said A LUTHERAN MINISTRY SINCE 1866. Surely that would have caught my eye if I'd been serious about my mother living there. We were Jewish, and my mother, raised in a mostly non-Jewish world, had always preferred mixed communities. But now she was old. Religion mattered to her, whether she wanted to admit it or not. She would hate this place.

The Meadowview was sparkling clean, with no institutional smells. The residents didn't look too sick or too dotty. I hated the lack of greenery—in Florida there'd been a swimming pool and lush gardens—but the plantings would fill in with time. And once inside, all these assisted living places look alike: the same pastel landscapes on the walls, the same communal kitchens on the main floor for snacks and socializing, the same vast two-story living rooms mimicking suburban mega-mansions—all boring and antiseptic. But you wouldn't be wracked with guilt if your mother lived here. You could tell yourself it was a lifestyle decision, a way for her not to have to cook or drive but still be a regular person. So after our visit, Michael and I figured the Meadowview was a possibility if at some point Mom moved.

"We saw what we wanted to see," Michael said much later, refusing to join my second-guessing of dubious decisions made under pressure. "Understand the context. It was very short-term thinking. We just wanted to find a place where she'd be happy. Potemkin façade . . . Shiny happy faces of the other 'inmates' . . ." (That was my mother's word, coined in Florida, and a family favorite, to this day.) "The people seemed caring. There was access to medical facilities. Our motives were good. What we should have done, and didn't, is talk to other people who had been through this."

Back then I didn't know any.

Soon we had the MRI results, and they were scary. We were told by my mother's Florida doctor that she had a benign tumor, a meningioma, on the outside of her spine, in the high thoracic region—T-3, to be exact. As the tumor pushed on the spinal cord, the doctor said, the compression would cause paralysis in her legs and both bladder and bowel incontinence. Surgery would be straightforward in a younger person; for someone my mother's age, it would be riskier, and so it might be advisable to hold off until she was more symptomatic.

Distrustful of her Florida doctor, we were determined to bring my mother to New York for a second opinion. So Michael and I went into overdrive. This is what Nell Casey, in the introduction to her anthology *An Uncertain Inheritance: Writers on Caring for Family*, calls the "early heroic rush." Calamity can be exhilarating. Anything seems possible. Only later, much later, do you "settle in for the long, earthbound haul. Some cross this threshold and maintain a sense of purpose; others don't."

Riding the early rush, Michael and I made that daunting to-do list, divided up the tasks, and attacked them as if we had a crushing deadline. We would try to outrun our fear, a desperate, debilitating, and dangerous approach to what we should have known was an inevitable downward trajectory.

Based on some jottings and assorted e-mails, here is what happened in the two weeks that followed the MRI report from Florida.

November 21: Michael got referrals to two premier New York City neurosurgeons, at Memorial Sloan-Kettering Cancer Center and Weill Cornell Medical Center. He arranged for my mother's MRI films to be sent from Florida. I canceled my trip to Mexico and, pleading "family emergency" to both spa and airline, got some of my money back. I forgot to pick up a pie I had ordered for Thanksgiving.

November 22: Michael dropped off the films at Sloan and e-mailed me the name, phone number, fax, pager, and beeper number of the head nurse in the neurology service there and comparable information for the second neurosurgeon across the street at Cornell. He passed along which elevators to take to the respective offices in case I would be the one picking up the films when they were finished reviewing them. I waited, after work, buffeted by the wind, on the annual Thanksgiving eve whatever-is-left-over line at the Little Pie Company on West Forty-fourth Street so I didn't arrive at a friend's holiday table empty-handed.

November 23: It was Thanksgiving, and Michael and his wife were on a dawn flight to London for the weekend, the sort of trip I'd never have been able to enjoy under these circumstances. Michael is hardwired differently and later told me, "I know how to protect myself, find pleasure where I may." My assignment was to track down my mother's Social Security information and insurance policies—Medicare, supplemental Medigap, and John Hancock long-term care. Those—and the phone, fax, beeper, and pager numbers for the Sloan-Kettering and Cornell doctors—were the first entries on a computerized list of "Mom Info" that we would update, share, print, reprint, and carry with us everywhere. I left messages for both neurosurgeons, reminding them to call me on Friday. I canceled all nonessential activities for the next few days.

November 24: I spoke to the nurse at Sloan and e-mailed my brother an account of our conversation. The neurosurgeon and several neuroradiologists there had read my mother's MRI. Taking into account that the Florida scan was a "bad film, lots of motion in it, hard to read," it seemed my mother did indeed have a spinal meningioma, and "as it grows it will press against the cord, causing all kinds of deficits" in the lower half of her body. The good news, I told Michael, was that it was "a slow-moving tumor. . . . In other words, she might die of something else first." The nurse wanted to know if my mother, by telephone, could give the New York doctors an oral report of her current condition. I replied that she'd "lie, leave stuff out so it didn't sound that bad." In that case, the nurse advised, we needed to bring her to New York for an evaluation. Only if her symptoms were progressing rapidly would they operate immediately; otherwise, as the Florida doctor suggested, they would watch and wait.

It amazes me how quickly and accurately my brother and I had gathered, interpreted, absorbed, and communicated this medical information, but otherwise we were stupefied. We knew my mother was headed to New York, sooner rather than later, yet we had only the vaguest idea of where she would live and no internist to manage her care here. We were crossing tasks off our list, but we had no long-term strategy. Nowadays I think only long term, perhaps to a fault, and cringe when I see others heading down the familiar just-put-out-today's-fire path. When a colleague recently asked me for a referral to a reliable company to install a lift on the staircase at her parents' house, I thought to myself: *Today they need a lift. Tomorrow they might need a round-the-clock nurse.* I thought this but didn't say it, because it was too scary for her to hear and none of my business. But I did suggest that a geriatric care manager would help, first with the lift and later with other problems if they cropped up. My colleague, who clearly knew otherwise or she wouldn't have called, said that wasn't necessary; her parents were fine, *really* they were.

Michael replied on the twenty-fifth, responding to my report that surgery for my mother was likely not imminent, saying that it "seems strange to call this good news, but it is. Nice to wake up to . . . You did good,

Sis." He advised including my mother in the conversation immediately, as she was already primed to move north, and this might be the time to address everything at once. Both of us would be happiest if she could stay in Florida—he if we could find a top-of-the-line doctor to follow her there, me because I was concerned she'd wind up living in my house, which, to put it mildly, would not go well for either of us. But both Michael and I saw the sense and convenience of having her closer. I suggested we "fast-track" the Meadowview process, without realizing the wisdom of slowing things down by delaying the medical appointments. We could have consolidated a neurosurgical consultation and a permanent move north without this intemperate haste. Neither needed to happen that second.

Michael ignored most of the doom-and-gloom hand-wringing in my messages to him. He had just one agenda item, he later told me—to "find the best medical care on earth"—and he wasn't thinking about what we might have done differently in the past or what could happen in the future. "We're spoiled, full-of-ourselves New Yorkers," he said years later. "The best of everything is two or three phone calls away. I had ultimate faith in our ability as reporters to find what we needed. We're forceful professionals trained to get what we want. It was goal-oriented behavior, unexamined beyond that." (Are we all reporters? Of course not. But most of us in successful careers learn, during this painful time of life, that we are very skilled at running our own affairs and less so our parents'.)

Still, in his London hotel, Michael reported that he had "snapped awake at five a.m. with a full-blown anxiety attack." Why did his anxiety comfort me? Perhaps for the same reason I had reacted so badly to some of his earlier messages that invariably included the social details of his day: Drinks with this friend. Dinner with that one. What art he and his wife had seen or shopping they'd done. Now I admire his dexterity. Women can be harsh about the way men compartmentalize at times like this. Maybe that anger is really envy. Would that more of us—I know very few—were like them.

The next day, November 26, Michael crossed the Atlantic again, homeward bound. The morning after his return, he e-mailed his magazine editor that "things have now clarified a bit." He would go to Florida in the morning to supervise additional tests that the New York neurosurgeon had ordered for my mother. Then he would bring her north, where she'd be examined at Sloan-Kettering. Michael reassured the editor that he'd do phone reporting about the French fashion photographer he was writing about while in Florida, which was utterly unrealistic. Those of you caring for elderly parents have written dozens of these e-mails to bosses. You want it both ways, to gain their sympathy and to buy some time with heavy-duty words like *neurosurgeon* and to reassure them that your problems will not get in the way of what they are counting on you to do.

November 28: My brother boarded a 6:35 a.m. plane to Florida. "I won't whine yet about sleep deprivation," he e-mailed, "but might at some point." I suspected he was being so agreeable as a way of compensating for going to London while I had canceled my spa plans. Regardless, I was grateful for his stamina and good cheer. My mother had a 10:45 a.m. appointment for a new, and hopefully clear, MRI of her thoracic spine, and scans of her chest and abdomen looking for primary-site cancer, unlikely with this particular diagnosis but always a possibility when a tumor is found. While Michael was in the air, I coordinated a phone call between the Boca Raton radiologist and the New York neurosurgeon. We were on a very tight schedule, and our whole plan (was it a plan, and if so, when did we make it?) would fall apart if some inattentive lab tech did the wrong test or another blurry one. When Michael hit the ground, he called me to report he'd make it to the lab on time. My mother was to be transported there from the Horizon Club in an ambulette. All parties reached their destinations on schedule. Michael and I all but high-fived each other across the phone lines.

In New York, I filled out a financial statement for admission to the Meadowview. It required that I know my own and my brother's real estate equity, each of our combined assets in cash, stock, and bonds, and each of our monthly incomes from salary, royalties, and contracts. I also needed to know how much money my mother had. Oh, did I forget my brother's Social Security number? As I made many, many phone calls, gathering this information, since Michael and my mother were otherwise occupied, I wondered if other people knew this about their siblings and parents and had it tucked in a safe place for just such an eventuality. (If not, they should, like a list of their own credit card numbers in case a wallet is lost or stolen. As hard as it is to reassemble one's own information, it is many times harder to gather from scratch all this information on family members.)

I also sent cloying e-mails to the important people at the Meadowview. "I'm impressed beyond words by the amount of help you folks are giving us to make this happen both quickly and pleasantly," I wrote. "I feel so secure and my mom seems so excited." (As I look back, these words are both embarrassing and pointless. Why wouldn't they happily rush her through the process when they'd rented only one-third of the units? I totally missed the point that I was an eager customer in a buyer's market, not a supplicant. I wanted them to like me.)

On November 29 I took the financial statement to the director of the Meadowview. Between us, Michael and I were well enough off to cover my mother's expenses for a good long time if we needed to. She still had approximately $175,000, the remains of nearly three decades of frugal widowhood. We were very fortunate people. But let me hasten to add that people with resources similar to ours can go broke if our parents live a long time and die of garden-variety old age, frailty, or dementia rather than the acute illnesses covered by Medicare. Long-term care—whether assisted living, home health aides, or nursing homes—is, overwhelmingly, not covered by government health insurance, except for those who are impoverished, regardless of age. Unless and until our parents reach the point of indigence (or are enrolled in a tiny number of pilot projects), families must pay their own way, two generations essentially abandoned with hundreds of thousands of dollars in bills for which few of us are prepared because we never knew or thought about whether they'd be our responsibility. "What do you mean Medicare doesn't cover it?" may be the most frequently asked question among elder care novices. Just assume that whatever it is you need, Medicare won't pay for it. Let any other outcome be a pleasant surprise.

On November 30, after a lot of back-and-forth consultation with my mother, I sent Michael a list of what to pack for her return trip to New York. She had luggage, bought for the move to Florida in 1994, but no winter coat. We'd worry about that later. I told him to bring all her insurance cards, her living will, and her health care proxy; also her pearls, the only valuable jewelry she had. I was giddy about how fabulous it was going to be at the Meadowview, partially to convince myself. I'd taken the furnished model apartment, at $145 a day, where she would stay until her furniture came north. Renting furniture would be a hassle and, I'd learned, a wash financially with her own soon to be en route, and this was a practical alternative in the meantime. After she was up north, had seen the neurosurgeon, had or not had surgery, and then pitched up in the model apartment, I'd go to Florida to pack up her old life, and discard much of it. Eventually she'd have a new home in apartment 321, the room closest to the pool table. Michael recently told me he had been "enchanted" by that, enough to put to rest his sadness that this place "looked like a just-built urban renewal project compared to Florida."

December 1: I bought groceries, trying to imagine what she ate. Nonfat or 1 percent milk? Golden Delicious apples or Anjou pears? What kind of cereal? I made up what passes for a guest room in my tiny nineteenth-century carriage house and plugged in a nightlight. My sister-in-law was the only one who had stopped to think how totally wrong a warren of tiny rooms was for an old lady with a walker. The bedrooms were up a steep flight of stairs, so I couldn't put her there; she'd have to sleep on a fold-out sofa, and would be miserable. The doorways were narrow. There were lots of dangerous small rugs. The tub and shower required that she climb over a ledge. I didn't know if she could still do that, since the Florida apartment had a shower designed for the handicapped. I remembered to cancel her Florida newspapers. I did some work. I went out to dinner with friends. I must have been one dreary companion, able to talk only about the situation with my mother.

December 2: Michael tried to get a bulkhead seat for my mother on the flight north but couldn't. She did fine sitting on the aisle. What mattered more, so much that we each reconfirmed it separately, was a wheelchair at the gate, where I would meet them on arrival. That was vital: by then my mother would be frayed and ready to strike out if there was any delay. Michael was justifiably eager to head home and let me take over, which was more than fair.

When she arrived, my mother and I drove north, both of us desperately cheerful in the car. The mood, a mask of sorts, didn't last. I wanted her to love every nook and cranny of my house, where she had never been. She saw it only as a dangerous obstacle course. Not a single chair was the right height and depth for her, or had the armrests that she needed to hoist herself up. I later learned from geriatric doctors that inability to rise from a chair without using one's hands is a signal of imminent immobility. A major red flag. Maybe it was a blessing not to know that then.

The meal I had planned with such care was an utter disaster in her view. I must have forgotten a starch. Or a salad. Maybe I made lamb stew, forgetting that she hated lamb. I flashed back to her critique of my first dinner party, fresh from college and recently moved to New York City. There weren't enough courses, she told me. I was missing essential food groups. Not everyone ate like a bird. I'm a woman in late middle age and still hear those old echoes. I suppose everyone labors under some form of this. Even if it has been an easy ride throughout adulthood, old grievances will likely weigh you down again during this time of role reversals. I have no useful suggestions other than to expect it. If you're seeing a therapist, talk about it. If not, now might be an excellent time to go.

After the table was cleared, I sneaked onto the side porch and called Michael. It was bitterly cold outside, and I was sobbing. I told him that her constant criticism stung. I asked him to promise me we were all going to get through this just fine. He couldn't, or not with enough conviction to satisfy me. He might have been as fearful as I was but simply wore it differently. He might even have been looking for the solid shoulder of his big sister. To think that a few months ago I had been fantasizing about the three of us living happily ever after, maybe having Thanksgiving together at my dining room table. Dreams die hard.

On Sunday, December 3, we all visited the Meadowview. They'd received my mother's medical and functional evaluations, and she was deemed "completely independent and appropriate" for the facility. That was our goal, to get the Florida doctors to make her sound like a perfect candidate. The internist "does it all the time and never gives details of underlying medical conditions," Michael had e-mailed during his Florida trip. The form was completely honest, as far as it went, and also totally obscuring. She had hypertension, hypothyroidism, frequent cellulitis (an infection of the bloodstream, usually from a tear in the skin), and that thoracic meningioma. (Yes, the information was there, but buried among the rest and unamplified in terms of potential consequences.) There were no restrictions on her activities, the form continued. She was mobile with a cane or a walker and was fully weight bearing. She took Prinivil and Lasix (for high blood pressure), Glucophage (diabetes), and Synthroid (thyroid). She had no mental health history that she had told the Florida doctor about (a blatant omission), severe hearing loss in her left ear, was routinely constipated, wore dentures, was five feet one inch tall, and weighed 180 pounds.

Recently, talking with the current management of the Meadowview about my family's experience there, the residency coordinator told me doctors routinely rush through these evaluations, not because adult children have explicitly requested that they lie but because of their pushy insistence that "this is the form we need, and we have to get it to them right now!" Then places like the Meadowview find themselves accepting "people who sound healthier than they are." Like the Florida internist, and like me and Michael, the coordinator was obscuring the facilty's complicity in this shared deception. My mother's doctor, however inconspicuously and without clarifying detail, had cited her spinal tumor. Nobody at the Meadowview, under its original management, had ever asked us a single question about the tumor's likely impact. Nor did we volunteer what we knew very well by then. This collusion of silence helped nobody, except perhaps a salesperson on commission or gunning for employee of the month.

December 4, the day of our Sloan-Kettering appointment, Michael and I were manic with our own efficiency. We knew where the hospital parking garage was. We knew which elevators to use. Should the neurosurgeon decide to operate on my mother the next day, we knew she could spend the night at the Helmsley Medical Tower next door for $140 rather than travel back and forth to Westchester. By now I could effortlessly fold and unfold the walker and buckle and unbuckle her seat belt. I brought a small plastic kitchen stool so she could get in and out of the car. We were to see the neurosurgeon at 11:30 a.m.—and were expected at the Meadowview by 4:30 p.m.! Nobody there had a clue that my mother might be headed for surgery or had a condition that would likely leave her paralyzed, incontinent, and entirely inappropriate for their facility. This kind of terrible mismatch happens often.

After the neurosurgeon saw my mother that first time, he repeated pretty much what the nurse had already told us, based on the Florida reports, about watching and waiting unless she became very symptomatic. Striking to me in the records I later got from Memorial Sloan-Kettering Cancer Center is that the neurosurgeon, alone among all the specialists there we would consult about my mother, made no mention of her age in his official documentation of this visit—which was how I remembered the conversation. They discussed, and he recorded, her light-headedness, unbalanced gait, and long-standing arthritis. The Florida doctor had already noted small-vessel changes in her brain, raising the possibility of more than one cause for her symptoms. The neurosurgeon agreed and said in his written report that the "patient would probably benefit" from removal of the tumor, "although other diagnoses are possible." He told her this was the most common procedure he did, with a 1 percent or less chance of paralysis and a 1 to 2 percent chance of infection. (These data came from research that explicitly excludes the elderly because of their multiple diagnoses, but this fact went unmentioned to us.) The worst-case scenario, he said, was that the tumor would eventually extend upward along her spine and affect her diaphragm and lungs, but it was highly unlikely. He then referred her for another, clearer, MRI of her thoracic spine, as well as consultations with a pulmonologist and a neurologist, and various tests to determine her suitability for surgery, should her symptoms worsen or the new MRI reveal anything alarming.

I remember nothing about moving her into the Meadowview that day or returning to my now-tranquil home. I do recall that we sent floral tributes to the surgeon and the director of admissions at the assisted living facility, wanting both to think us a model pair of children, worthy of present admiration and future attention. Now I could plan my trip to Florida, inform the Horizon Club of my mother's checkout date, cancel her Bell South and Florida Power & Light accounts, and book a mover. With a floor plan of the Meadowview apartment, but only guesses as to the dimensions of her furniture in Florida, my mother and I made a list of what she wanted shipped to New York, what should go to Goodwill, and what I should hand-carry home. I took lots of cash for tips, keys to the apartment and storage shed, a tape measure, grungy work clothes, a nightgown, and a bathing suit. I never had time for a swim.

The trip to Florida and the move itself are a blur, except for a five a.m. burst of anxiety in my mother's bed in her empty Deerfield Beach apartment. The packing part was easy. Physical work is distracting in a healthy way, silencing the spiral of rumination. The nights, on the other hand, allow for negative thoughts, as you try to resolve the unresolvable. Be prepared for that. In the morning, the mover loaded the truck. I paid him $3,589 and left the apartment broom-ready for its next occupant. Then it was back to New York and the unknown rigors, and unexpected rewards, that lay ahead.

CHAPTER 2

The Myth of Assisted Living

My mother took a fall in the bathroom and cut her head, and the overnight receptionist at the Meadowview, a dim bulb, phoned me to say an ambulance was on the way. So often these calls came in the middle of the night. I wanted, more than anything, to roll over and go back to sleep. I knew exactly how awful the next however-many hours would be: enduring my mother's crankiness, masking my own with brittle good cheer, struggling with the medical people, and then fighting the effects of my fatigue the next day. The emergency room ordeal would leave my mother, and to a lesser extent me, limp for days.

The gash on her head was, to use my mother's phrase, "a big nothing." As a former registered nurse, she knew the difference between a cut and a *cut* and had no patience for what she called the "cover your ass" policy—standard in assisted living facilities—of calling 911 at the drop of a hat rather than risking the wrath of a resident's litigious family. All three of us had offered to sign a waiver releasing Meadowview from any responsibility, in exchange for their agreement not to ship her off to an emergency room without notifying us first. They declined our offer without explanation, and all of us were too weary to argue.

After six p.m., when the facility's limited medical staff left for the day, there was nobody on-site, unless you counted my mother, who had the training to know what qualified as an emergency. She tried to explain to the gum-cracking receptionist that minor scalp wounds produce alarming amounts of blood but don't necessarily warrant a trip to the emergency room. But at her advanced age and in this environment, my mother was no longer a respected professional, her intellect and judgment intact; she was that cranky old woman in apartment 321. Old, sick, and helpless, she had no say in what would happen next, or she had lost the confidence to put up a fight.

The ambulance workers, too, saw right away that the wound didn't need a single stitch. But their job, now that they'd been called, was not to determine if the summons was warranted but to get her on a gurney and whisk her to the nearest emergency room. And by now, a few months after her arrival in New York, my brother and I had this ER drill down pat. He lived in Manhattan, his car was in a garage, and thus I was the logical person, living just a few minutes away, to speed to my mother's side at the Meadowview. His job was to call the emergency medical technicians, or EMTs, and jawbone them until I got there from my house in Hastings-on-Hudson, a ten-minute dogleg across Westchester County.

Why couldn't I just meet her at the emergency room? That's a reasonable question for the uninitiated. But Michael and I had become connoisseurs of ERs in lower Westchester. (A *Zagat,* anyone?) We knew the paramedics had the option of taking her to either of two equidistant hospitals, one in Bronxville, a tranquil suburb, the other in Mount Vernon, serving a down-trodden community and sure to be bedlam. This was no time for political correctness. If you'd been to both hospitals, you'd know that a very hard night, for my mother and for me, would be a little less hard at Lawrence Hospital in Bronxville. The EMTs wouldn't care, but I had to get there fast enough to call the shots.

That winter we spent so much time in emergency rooms that I wished they gave frequent-flier miles. It was a snowy few months, so with travel time crucial, I made sure the driveway was always shoveled. Heading out the door, I alerted Michael to this latest emergency, and he stayed on the phone with me to track my progress and jolly me on the short drive. I complained to him this night about a dirty windshield, then gulped and raised my hands to my face. No glasses. He ordered me back home to get them, although I'd have preferred to forge ahead, squinting. When I'm scared, I hurry, even though I understand the slowing-down-when-you're-frightened thing. Michael often saved me from myself at times like this, his hand up, metaphorically, like a school crossing guard, stopping me before I hurtled into worse trouble than we were already in.

I knew that whichever emergency room we wound up in would be too noisy and too bright. The rooms would be windowless, like a casino, so there's no way of telling day from night. People would be running all over the place, screaming, some in lab coats and others not. Orders would crackle over the public address system. Sometimes there would be blood (more likely in Mount Vernon than in tony Bronxville). The coffee would taste burned and the vending machines eat quarters. ERs are dreadful places at any age, but for the elderly they're depleting and disorienting, sometimes permanently. The reaction of the aged population to this environment even has a name, I later learn: emergency room psychosis. Experts in the field do whatever they can to keep their own parents out of this cruel chaos; their patients, too. On my short list of ironclad rules for elder care is *stay out of emergency rooms to the extent possible.*

Michael's chitchat with the EMTs had kept them occupied long enough for me to get to the Meadowview and request the calmer hospital. With the destination problem out of the way, I was then free to fixate on the fact that my mother's "do not resuscitate" order was useless in an ambulance in New York State. If my mother were to go into cardiac arrest, by law the emergency team would have to paddle her back to life unless she also had an out-of-hospital DNR. But even if she had one, how preposterous to think she'd remember to bring it with her, as a bunch of uniformed strangers, moving quickly and explaining nothing, loomed over her, took her pulse, tightened a blood pressure cuff, ran an intravenous line, covered her nose and mouth with an oxygen mask, strapped her onto a gurney, and jostled her down the corridor, as nosy neighbors peered through their peepholes, gathering gossip for the next day. Ridiculous.

Ignorant of the out-of-hospital DNR until years later but aware of the medics' legal obligation to keep her alive at all costs, I was hell-bent that some well-meaning, hunky EMT didn't paddle her back to life. She'd be enraged. This, after all, was a woman who had her end-of-life paperwork in order long before it was fashionable. She liked to call herself a card-carrying member of the Hemlock Society, an exaggeration, but not by much.

Unwanted ambulance heroics simply were not okay. Once, my brother asked me how I intended to prevent them. I hadn't thought it through but had faith I'd improvise. Maybe, from behind, I'd ram the ambulance long enough to at least distract the paramedics. We never had to try.

I arrived at the assisted living place in plenty of time, even after back-tracking for my glasses. The early frenzy, when every synapse seemed to be firing at once, had ebbed but not entirely gone away. It eventually would, as always, but on its own schedule, and I could rarely summon the will to do much about it until it passed. My mother had now been wheeled into the ambulance and strapped in with what looked like yoga belts. If I rode with her, held her hand, and talked about nothing in particular, I knew we'd be stranded at the ER later, since the EMTs do only one-way transport and I was certain she wouldn't be admitted to the hospital. Then we'd have to call a commercial ambulette company, wait, probably for quite a while, our nerves already frayed and tempers short.

Instead, I got in my own car and drove close enough to the ambulance that my mother could see me. I didn't bother trying to look cheerful. She'd never fall for that. But her eyes held mine. How could my presence be so calming when my hands were shaking, partly in fear and partly in anger at having to endure these emergency room trips over and over again? She trusted this thin veneer of calm and confidence because she wanted so badly to believe I knew what I was doing and everything would be fine. Faking it had become one of my most valuable functions.

Alone in the car, I focused on calming myself down before we pushed through the ER doors, because that was when I must not just pass as but *be* the imperturbable daughter ready for the long night ahead. Even if my mother got nasty, as she often did when scared, I'd turn the other cheek. *"You're right, Mom," that guy could have been gentler when he pitched you from the gurney to the bed. "You're right, Mom," you shouldn't have to have two sets of X-rays because some idiot can't find the first set. "You're right, Mom," we didn't need to be here in the first place.*

In the ER, no one knew anything about my mother except her vital signs and a few scribbled notes from the EMTs. We hadn't yet found her a new primary care physician, so the ER docs had nobody to call for a medical history. I had notes on her preexisting conditions and medications. Another rule: *Carry that information with you at all times.* But it's no easy task, even in a relatively tranquil suburban ER, to get a doctor or nurse to stand still long enough to hear the medical history. Their job, you must remember, is to save lives, not to know all the details about the people they're trying hastily to take care of. Your job, hard but not impossible in these surroundings, is to be as soothing as possible, perhaps holding your parent's hand, talking to the medical personnel calmly, and not adding to the chaos with your own behavior.

My mother couldn't walk without help or see without her glasses, which were left behind in the tumult. So every time she had to go to the bathroom, I helped her off the table, steadied her as far as the ladies' room door, backed off respectfully, and resumed helping only when she'd finished. We didn't make eye contact, a tactic for pretending she wasn't really this helpless. My brother called every half hour, or so it seemed, looking for reassuring updates. *Let him come next time,* I fumed to myself, not acknowledging how inefficient it would have been for him to drive up here. Our division of labor mostly made sense, but I forgot that fact when my hands were full (and shaking).

My mother was hungry. My mother was thirsty. My mother wanted an extra blanket. She used to be more "martyred saint" than "demanding old lady." I hated "martyred saint" because it gave me no role to play. Now I hated "demanding old lady" because I was at the other end of all the demands.

Sometimes I remembered to bring a book, or work that wasn't too taxing, even snacks and bottled water, though she couldn't eat or drink until all the tests were done and I couldn't have swallowed if my life depended on it. The concentration necessary for reading even *People* magazine was beyond me. Who were those families in the waiting room wolfing down McDonald's burgers, checking the sports scores or the stock tables, making normal conversation?

I paced, badgered anyone wearing a white coat, sneaked a look at her chart, paced and badgered some more. (This, by the way, is not helpful behavior. You can't let the staff ignore you, but neither should you run around like the proverbial chicken without a head.) I imagined the comfort of calling one of my close friends and dialed the first few digits of the number, then hung up when I realized that if she answered, I'd have to talk to her. The effort would be too great for the solace it might provide.

My mother, who wastes no energy twitching like I do, was still a wreck by the time we left, despite getting a clean bill of health. She not only understood she hadn't needed to be here; she also knew, as a medical professional would, that each of these ER runs was a disaster waiting to happen. A tear in her paper-thin skin, while moving her from gurney to wheelchair, could lead to cellulitis. A catheter, should they decide to insert one to avoid her trips to the bathroom, might cause a urinary tract infection. Either can be a potential killer in old people. But even a "routine" ER visit (and there really is no such thing) would leave a little less of her than there was before, draining my mother's dwindling supply of energy. Aware of this loss of resilience, she would compare herself to an old brassiere that has been washed so many times that the elastic just gives out.

Even in this "nice" emergency room—the one without gunshot victims being rushed to the head of the line—we'd spent hour upon hour waiting for X-rays and blood tests. Time crawled. It was impossible to relax into this ER experience, unless you happened to be a true Zen master. Utter boredom alternated with spikes of panic, plus clock watching. I knew that tomorrow would be a struggle. The adrenaline was pumping. It was essential now, but useless later, and would leave a toxic residue. The morning would bring a queasy stomach, a low-grade headache, and raw nerve endings. And it was worse for my mother than for me. For at least a day or two after one of these emergency room outings, she'd be spent and desolate.

The sky was pink when I took her back to her apartment and put her to bed. Upon leaving, I made a mental note to add one more item to the "Caregiving for Dummies" list: *Always keep a spare pair of glasses in the glove compartment.* It was only because of this expanding and evolving list that I found my car in the ER parking lot. I already knew that, when anxious, I must write down its location—three rows to the left of the revolving door, halfway up the file of cars, directly under the dented light post— otherwise I'd be wandering, aimless and clueless, Mom in tow, looking for a silver Subaru. My list also guaranteed I had a working phone all night long: *Never leave the house without a charger.*

The car was my sanctuary. Before heading home from the Meadowview, with my mother snug in bed, I slumped over the steering wheel, sobbing. Across America, in parking lots like this one, middle-aged daughters do this all the time. I never noticed until I became one of them.

In all those years in Florida I don't think my mother ever got sent to the emergency room. A few vertigo attacks were severe enough for her to use the pull cord in her apartment. Once, walking to the elevator along an out-door breezeway, the dizziness and nausea were so extreme that she lowered herself to the ground and waited for someone to come to her aid. Later, seeing her old medical records, I would learn of one hard fall. But the staff there never felt the need to call 911, even though there were no doctors or nurses on duty. My hunch is that's because she had a local primary care physician of her own, and everyone knew her so well.

But once we moved her north, despite our belief that she would be safer close to her children, emergency room visits became regular events. Indeed, the first 911 call from the Meadowview came just ten days after my mother moved in, during my overnight trip to Florida to shut down her apartment there. Michael got the summons that the ambulance was on the way. He'd had too much wine with dinner, and the weather was treacher-ous. So rather than drive to Westchester, he chose to have the ambulance take her, all by herself, to Mount Vernon, as it turned out. The experience was dreadful, she told me, although she spared me the details. Later, more than once, she said how grateful she was that she was never again in an emergency room alone.

At the time, I thought my brother selfish, derelict, and ignorant of what such an experience would be like for an old woman alone. He could have hired a car service. If necessary, my mother would have reimbursed him from her still-more-than-adequate checking account. Years later, he told me that that emergency room incident was, for him, "the big flashing light," the "serious wake-up call," the moment when he realized that "everything was going to change." He was a few weeks behind me in this realization, but he was more shook up than I had guessed at the time. Still, he had made his decision—in my view, the wrong one. There is no way you should allow your parent to spend a night alone in an emergency room if you can pos-sibly avoid it.

Until that moment, Michael had been an exemplary collaborator; he'd done more than his share of the work, not complaining and exercising excellent judgment—consistently better than mine because he is calmer and not inclined to feeling guilt and other beside-the-point emotions. This was the first sign that we wouldn't always agree about what was necessary or appropriate. Those differences didn't yet loom large, but they would: sometimes a quiet undercurrent of tension, sometimes a source of seeth-ing anger or harsh recrimination. Sometimes the cause was reasonable resentment on my part, but often it was the residue of old sibling discord.

I wouldn't have chosen to be an only child during the years of my mother's decline, but I could make a compelling argument that it might have been easier, both because of the ability to make unilateral decisions and because of the absence of that particular form of tension.

Frequent emergency room adventures are an experience shared by many families who elect assisted living as the residential option for an elderly parent, and they come up regularly when experts comment on that option's deficiencies. Most gerontologists (physicians and other professionals in the field of aging) say that having a parent in assisted living is a crushing and unexpected burden for adult children, especially daughters. I know from blog readers, friends, and colleagues that caring for a mother or father at home—especially for the sandwich generation juggling elderly parents and children simultaneously, and for those who can afford neither to quit their jobs and be full-time caregivers nor to hire help—is more crushing. But everyone knows ahead of time that moving a parent into your house, or vice versa, will mean total immersion. By contrast, experiencing the shock of assisted living's limitations is like being hit between the eyes with the proverbial two-by-four. We assume, incorrectly, that a good assisted living facility will relieve us of day-to-day labor and responsibility. Instead, we find we must do our parents' grocery shopping, pay attention to whether they eat, take them to religious services, buy their clothes and make sure they're clean and mended, supervise their medications, keep them supplied with books or videos, accompany them to doctor appointments, and show up for anything that might be construed as an emergency. I never worked as hard or worried as much as I did during my mother's second assisted living experience.

This yawning gap between expectation and reality is what makes assisted living problematic for so many families. Even the term is meaningless, since each state defines it differently and providers vary greatly within states. So, some basics: at its core, assisted living is a social, rather than a medical, model of long-term care. Your parent is a tenant, not a patient. An assisted living resident has the privacy and comfort of an apartment, the autonomy to come and go as she pleases, the congeniality and ease of congregate meals in a well-appointed dining room, light housekeeping, social activities, transportation, and some amount of supervision and assistance with daily activities. The last one costs extra. We were unaware of that when we moved my mother north, as she had never needed assistance before; nor was it even offered, with a younger clientele, when she first moved to Florida. But my hunch is that absent some major overhaul of the industry, which took hold in the United States in the mid-1980s and exploded a decade later, no list of questions will ever be thorough enough to prevent people from misunderstanding what they're getting into and what it will cost as their parents' needs increase, given the wild variability.

Some assisted living facilities have doctors, registered nurses, or licensed practical nurses on staff. Some don't. Some have LPNs on duty 24/7. Some have only a receptionist or doorman on the premises at night. Some provide, at an additional cost, a graduated number of hours of help per day with daily living activities, like bathing, dressing, toileting, and eating. Some don't. Some allow families to hire private-duty help. Some don't. Some are regulated to varying degrees, and others not at all. If a parent moves from another state, as my mother did, make no assumptions based on past experience. If you are totally new to this issue, understand, first and foremost, that Medicare and Medicaid do not pay for room and board because an assisted living facility is a provider not of health care but of housing.

Medicare (federal health insurance for those sixty-five and over) and Medicaid (the combined federal and state program that subsidizes long-term care for the indigent elderly) may pick up the tab for some of the à la carte services—those deemed medical, not residential, including help with personal care tasks like bathing and toileting. This coverage is but a tiny portion of the total cost, most of which comes from rent. In other words, assisted living is for people with money. In 2010, the average annual cost nationwide was $39,516 compared to $74,270 for a semi-private nursing home bed (or $83,585 for a private room); the fees for both were far higher in major metropolitan areas. But in a nursing home—by definition a medical, not a residential, setting—Medicare pays certain limited costs for everybody past sixty-five, and Medicaid foots the *entire* bill for the indigent, for those originally from the middle class who have exhausted their resources, and for the rare elderly who have fabricated indigence by giving away their money to protect their children's inheritance (which is legal but, to many, questionable ethically and harder to pull off than it once was).

Add enough à la carte services to make assisted living a viable alternative for increasingly infirm residents, and the bill quickly mounts. At the Meadowview, for instance, as I write, a resident in a $4,200-a-month studio apartment would pay an additional $1,000 a month for daily help taking his medications and for assistance with one activity of daily living—for instance, showering. If that resident needed both medication assistance and help with multiple daily activities, the extra fee would be $1,600 a month, for an annual bill of $62,400 in the first case and $69,600 in the second. Need more help than that? The Meadowview now has its own agency that provides private-duty aides, at $22 an hour. If you are a thousand miles away and you need to be sure Mom's personal bills are getting paid and her prescriptions filled, you can hire someone to supervise (usually called a geriatric care manager), at upward of $150 an hour. Do that, and the cost far exceeds that of a skilled nursing facility. If a resident runs out of money while in assisted living, in most cases they are thrown out, usually with advance warning, but that doesn't change the fact that they must relocate to a nursing home that has no choice but to house people with or without money. Still, if a nursing home is your next stop, it is advisable to arrive before you are penniless and can pay your own way, however briefly. It is legal for nursing homes to put paying customers at the front of the waiting list. But once residents are there, a nursing home can't evict them if they run out of assets.

Every decent guidebook, website, or expert on the subject of long-term care begs those of us considering assisted living for a loved one to understand, first and foremost, what it is *not*. Here are some pithy examples.

- It is "not a nursing home with fancy furniture," says the respected *Gilbert Guide* to long-term care, which urges the "hidden consumers"—adult children—to consider whether "nursing care or constant supervision" will likely be needed in the "near future," because "moving an elder twice in a short time can be very hard on both of you."

- It is "neither fish not fowl, the grayest of options," said Dr. Robert L. Kane, a geriatrician, health policy expert, and author at the University of Minnesota, who adds that "most assisted living facilities do not view themselves as health care providers and . . . respond to medical problems by sending the resident to the emergency room." He should know; his mother had a dreadful experience in one that he and his sister, Joan C. West, wrote about in a book called *It Shouldn't Be This Way: The Failure of Long-Term Care* (Nashville, Tenn.: Vanderbilt University Press, 2005).

• It is "not designed to deal with the realities of aging," said Paul R. Willging, onetime president of the Assisted Living Federation of America, who learned this only after his own mother moved into one such facility. He found it better at providing hospitality than health care and ill prepared to "deal with a frail and declining clientele."

Aging in place, everyone's fantasy, is all but impossible in assisted living, these experts agree, since most people get progressively worse and are not fortunate enough to die a sudden rather than a protracted death. To have the best chance at remaining in one facility, you can consider, instead, a continuing care retirement community (CCRC), which offers a range of options on one campus, from independent-living apartments to assisted living to a full-scale nursing home. But CCRCs require large up-front payments, vary both in quality and in long-term solvency (no small consideration and all but impossible to predict), and are feasible only for those far richer than the typical assisted living resident.

Also, based on my experience, freestanding assisted living facilities and many CCRCs (quite a few of which are part of large for-profit corporations, with mighty propaganda machines) hit you with a very hard sell. They understand that potential customers are guilt-ridden, frightened, and thus fuzzy-headed adult children who would do just about anything to avoid putting their parent in a nursing home. In fact, those that advertise pitch their product to the childen, not the elder.

Is this judgment harsh and one-sided? Perhaps. I have a strong bias against this model of long-term care, and I know that many readers of my *New York Times* blog agreed wholeheartedly. But others took a different viewpoint. Here is a representative guest post from Brian Weiss, a freelance medical and marketing writer in Pasadena, California, whose late mother thrived in assisted living as she hadn't at home. Weiss is a thoughtful commentator on the trade-offs inherent in assisted living.

I do not feel there was either illusion or deception about the fact that [the facility] offered minimal medical support. They DID have an

R.N. on duty (days only), and I always knew that if anything serious were to arise (day or night), the answer would be calling the paramedics. I had zero problem with these conditions, since they represented a considerable IMPROVEMENT over what my mother had when she lived alone in her own home.

My [widowed] mother's life prior to assisted living was one of increasing isolation, and constant fear . . . [and] the move to assisted living came with considerable resistance. . . . Once in assisted living my mother got an instant "restart" on life. Suddenly, she had people to talk to and care about, nutritious meals served in a pleasant setting, no worries about physical safety, and the assurance that if something was wrong she could pull a cord and help was on the way. . . .

Was I aware that [she had] serious maladies that required monitoring and care? Yes. Did I think the assisted living facility was giving her medical care? No, except to the extent that I knew she got a weekly blood pressure check and that if something didn't feel right, she could go to the nurse in the facility a LOT more easily than to the doctor, which meant more little things got looked at and evaluated than if she'd had to make a doctor's appointment and go to an office. . . .

I do not think the industry should object to full disclosure of what they DO and DON'T offer. . . . Consumers should clearly know what they are and aren't getting. But I also think that forcing ALL assisted living facilities to add costly medical options would drive the prices up and make it accessible for an even smaller percentage of the population.

When my mother first moved to the assisted living facility in Florida, hotel companies like Marriott were the developers and managers of these communities, and the residents were on average a decade younger and in much better physical and cognitive shape than their counterparts today. It was a lovely setup for older people—overwhelmingly women—who didn't want to be bothered managing a big house, who elected or needed to stop driving but then faced isolation in suburban homes, especially those in snowy climes. My mother and her Florida neighbors cooked many of their own meals in full kitchens and managed fine with weekly maid service, making their beds and tidying up for themselves the rest of the time. How convenient that a bridge game or an evening movie was only an elevator ride away and that when a lightbulb needed changing, the concierge was at your service. Lots of people needed a cane and some used walkers, but I don't recall seeing a single wheelchair except on the veranda of what I took to be a nursing home kind of place, located on the far side of the lush campus (out of sight, out of mind). Some of *those* people had aides, but there were none in my mother's building, which was called "assisted living" but today would likely be considered "independent living."

As the assisted living clientele changed, so did the purveyors. The newer ones, like Sunrise and Atria, adopted a more medical model to attract older residents, those with multiple chronic conditions, complicated medication regimes, and often serious health problems. At sales-pitch time, along with information about the apartment size, amenities, cuisine, and activities, you began hearing about various "personal care plans"—some euphemistically called "bronze," "silver," and "gold"—based on how much one-on-one attention a resident needed from an aide. The escalating fees at certain places are calculated according to hours per day; at others, according to the number and nature of the activities that require assistance—with a degree of specificity that differentiates among wheeling a resident to the dining room, keeping her company at mealtime, cutting her food into bite-size pieces, keeping watch so she doesn't choke, or actually spooning food into her mouth; and at still others, in some hybrid form.

In their book *It Shouldn't Be This Way,* Dr. Kane and his sister write that their mother's money (and blessedly she had plenty) was "hemorrhaging not dwindling" in assisted living because of the ever-increasing add-ons. One of my blog readers, who was footing a parent's bill herself, wrote to me of "nightmares about running out of money." While I was visiting a geriatric medical practice in New York, I met an adult daughter who was about to move her mother from a well-appointed assisted living facility to a shabbier place because funds were low. Ironically, I was familiar with the place her mother had to leave and also the one where she was going and shared that the "nicer" place actually provided inferior care.

Most assisted living residents will need more help as time goes on, but there's no way of predicting how much, what kind, or for how long. That makes budgeting impossible. But even if it weren't impossible, budgeting means thinking ahead, contemplating decline, and not assuming that your aged mother, for example, will be one of the tiny minority of people who die suddenly, without extended disability or dependence, as Weiss's did of a massive stoke. (Could this be why assisted living worked so well for him?)

Extended and progressive disability is hard to consider in advance, and many adult children making the long-term care decisions for their parents choose denial. They refuse to even consider that a parent might require attention, financial support, and eventually custodial care for years and years and maybe decades. Lacking any sense of what the future might hold, adult children in denial may also promise parents they will never put them in nursing homes. I never made such a vow, although many of my friends have. My mother did not ask for such a promise and rejected one when offered. *Don't be ridiculous; you can't guarantee that,* she said, or words to that effect. *You'll do what you have to do when you have to do it,* she told me. Her lack of sentiment, once disturbing, had by now become a blessing. Still, I was determined not to "put her away." That would be the most unforgivable decision a daughter could make, or so I thought.

I have notes and handouts about all the care plans and add-ons from my first visit to the Meadowview, but I might as well have had my fingers in my ears and my hands over my eyes. My mother had a long-term care insurance policy, purchased in 1993 from John Hancock at an annual cost of $7,000, with a $150-a-day benefit. (Long-term care insurance has an annual premium based on age at the time of purchase and extent of benefits. It is activated once the policyholder meets certain criteria of disability, pays a fixed amount per day, specifies what kind of care is covered, has or does not have cost-of-living adjustments, and includes other add-ons, such as the cost of home modification. Policies have evolved over time, with a greater array of benefits to choose from but stricter eligibility standards since the product was new to the market, as it was when my mother's policy was purchased. Lately, some companies have stopped issuing new policies or dramatically raised premiums, finding their original assumptions about future claims way off the mark.)

At the Meadowview, because she had a policy, I chose a studio apartment with a sleeping alcove, an additional space for a foldout sofa, with the expectation that some nice West Indian lady, whom I would hire and John Hancock would pay, could live with my mother if the need arose.

I didn't understand that, at the time, the Meadowview's license did not permit this kind of arrangement. I didn't even know enough to ask. My brother calls it "double ignorance. We didn't know how it worked. And we didn't know that we didn't know. You're absolutely ignorant about what to ask, and nobody will tell you fully."

Now, with a different kind of license, the Meadowview permits live-in aides, part of what Dr. Kane calls the continual reinvention of the assisted living concept "until almost every level [of care] can be included under the same term." When I visited nine years after my mother had lived there, lots of residents had live-ins, the residency coordinator told me. But a privately hired aide was not *instead* of one of their enhanced care plans, she said. You could buy one-on-one time, from one of *their* in-house aides, under the assorted plans, and also hire *another* of your own. I didn't bother to calculate what that redundancy would cost—residents surely didn't need both—but I did ask her why it was required. "We need accountability as the ones responsible for care," she explained. I did my best not to raise a cynical eyebrow. (Unlike nursing homes, which can be either for-profit or not-for-profit, assisted living is always a business.)

Back when I was a frantic daughter who cared solely about getting my mother into the Meadowview, I was prepared to resort to the kind of dirty tricks that a certain class of New Yorkers use to gain acceptance into the right nursery school. I had to clear the financial hurdles. I had to make sure my mother got all A's on the functional and medical assessment tests. I had to hurry because she was arriving from Florida in just a few days. My goal was to sweet-talk my mother's way into a facility—one I would quickly discover had neither the expertise nor the staff to care for her. Compounding the problem, they were in start-up mode—something to be avoided, even current officials there agreed. A new facility with lots of empty units, the residency coordinator explained, can't afford to hire adequate staff, and until they have adequate staff, they can't properly care for the residents who are there. So the salespeople, unlike those at a mature and fully occupied facility, like my mother's in Florida, are under pressure to fill apartments. They ask no probing questions and maybe even think they are being kind when they accept borderline residents. Surely my brother and I appreciated the Florida doctor, who did us a favor by dashing off a hasty evaluation that made no mention of the kind of help my mother would need either during postsurgical rehabilitation (if she had the spinal tumor removed) or because of gradual immobility and incontinence (if she didn't). And we appreciated the similarly hasty admission, with no questions asked.

Arguably none of this is venal, yet the results can be a disaster. Lots of families must be making the same mistake, which explains the traffic jam of ambulances outside assisted living facilities everywhere and, in the parking lots, the daughters slumped, weeping, in their cars.

Do not kid yourself: despite a flurry of politically correct news coverage about the growing number of men caring for aging parents, this is not an equal-opportunity job. It is the daughters who fetch and carry, who miss work or give it halfhearted attention, when a parent is in assisted living, except when there are only sons. There is no shortage of examples I could offer about the division of labor between male and female siblings, no shortage of rants from readers of my blog. But few capture the dynamic as well as a family telephone conference that I was invited to eavesdrop on by Dr. Cheryl E. Woodson, a geriatrician with a solo practice amid the strip malls of Chicago Heights, Illinois. Her patient was an eighty-seven-year-old woman in steep decline at an assisted living facility; the phone consultation was with an adult son and daughter.

Dr. Woodson had already told me, and had written in a guidebook, that she considered assisted living a "myth," "a place for people who don't exist." What did she mean by that? I asked. Residents are supposedly people who "just need a little help," Dr. Woodson said, a catchphrase she finds ridiculous. "If they just needed a little help, they'd be living in the community." But families are told that Mom or Dad will be looked after, so the grown children can "focus on jobs and family," which is exactly what they want to hear. Their parents will be fine, and their own lives will be uninterrupted. Then, before you know it, a parent requires "more than meals you don't have to cook, grass you don't have to cut, and socialization." Taking care of all the services not provided falls to one sibling, she said, in this patient's case, as in most, a daughter.

The daughter of Dr. Woodson's patient lived nearby; her brother lived on ritzy Central Park West in New York City. The daughter made several trips a day to her mother's apartment to make sure she took an array of medications on schedule, including one that required a nebulizer, and to help her into compression stockings for her swollen legs, all of which was beyond the level of service the facility provided. Throughout the half-hour phone conversation, the son was defensive, argumentative, and did all the talking. He interrupted repeatedly as Dr. Woodson proposed solutions:

adding private-duty help for their mother several hours a day; hiring a geriatric care manager (a profession Dr. Woodson, in private, refers to as "a rent-a-daughter") to take some of the burden off the sister; or moving their frail and medically complicated mother into a nursing home. The son balked at the first two because they were too expensive and at the third because he preferred the appearance and amenities of assisted living to the institutional surroundings of a nursing home. Dr. Woodson pressed on. *Your sister,* she told him in no uncertain terms, *is overwhelmed and sacrificing more than should be expected of one person.* The call ended with no resolution. The daughter, through it all, had spoken not one word.

No matter how many times she told the son, Dr. Woodson said later, that there was "no level of care between assisted living and a nursing home," he did not believe her. He didn't seem to take seriously her repeated warnings that more and more services would be necessary as his mother's condition worsened and that eventually he'd be spending more money than he thought possible. As for his beleaguered sibling, Dr. Woodson said, "One person can't handle this and I think he's giving only lip service to the amount of work his sister is doing."

Several of my mother's all-too-frequent trips to the emergency room might have been avoided if she had had a geriatrician like Dr. Woodson, or a local primary care doctor, for that matter. But she didn't, for four months—no quarterback, no doctor in charge of her health rather than her individual body parts (in this case, her thoracic spine). This was partly due to our ignorance and neglect, and partly because such general physicians had begun closing their practices to new Medicare patients, as Dr. Woodson did a few years back, because of the gap between the cost of caring for them and the government's reimbursement rates, a problem that would soon reach crisis proportions. So there was nobody who might have been able to put two and two together when my mother started going downhill rapidly. She didn't tell us what was going on, and we didn't probe.

The Meadowview now has an LPN (a licensed practical nurse) on duty twenty-four hours a day, but even she would have lacked the expertise or authority to keep my mother out of the emergency room as the falls became more frequent. Clearly her legs were giving out, as predicted. Plus, older people's bladders don't work like yours or mine—although I didn't understand that then. They are slower to send the brain a signal that it's time to get to the bathroom, and they don't do as well at holding it in. So needing to urinate, with no time to spare, my mother would rush to avoid soiling herself and thus not use her walker properly or be deliberate enough transferring to the toilet seat. Sometimes she'd slide to the floor in a gentle and harmless tumble. Sometimes she'd slam her head on the porcelain sink or the tile floor and wind up back in the ER.

We brought her back to Sloan-Kettering once in January and again in February for consultations with the neurosurgeon, pulmonologist, and cardiologist, those "best that money can buy" kind of doctors that my brother and I still thought had the magical solutions to all our problems. ("I wanted to believe in Tinker Bell," Michael said later. "All we had to do was clap louder and it would be okay.") All the specialists agreed that the deterioration in her legs was likely to be irreversible, given her advanced symptoms, but that surgery might slow its progression. When my mother asked, "Do I get anything back?" Dr. Mark H. Bilsky, the best in the business, equivocated but emphatically told her that "down the line you'll get into trouble" if the tumor wasn't removed. Again, as at her original consultation, he and the other specialists noted that a lot was going on besides the tumor, including numbness in her hands, shortness of breath, and lightheadedness.

The three doctors' reports overlap in many ways and diverge in others, which I now understand is why having too many specialists without a generalist in charge is such a dreadful prescription. It's confusing and thus leads to potentially dangerous or unnecessary interventions; it imposes duplicative or pointless costs on the health care system, whether public Medicare or private insurance; and it sometimes produces too much, but not necessarily better, care. In my mother's case, besides the spinal meningioma (which would affect her mobility only from the waist down because of its location), this latest round of tests and examinations revealed a possibly cancerous liver mass, less ominous lesions on her kidneys, further small-vessel disease in the brain, deconditioning as the result of inactivity, and—less likely but not impossible—congestive heart failure. In addition, the doctors disagreed as to whether my mother actually had hypothyroidism or even Ménière's disease.

Some of these symptoms were news to me and Michael. My mother didn't want to worry us, and we were accustomed to her withholding information. But surely she should have understood that, at this stage of the game, we needed as much information as she could give us so that we could help her. Surely we suspected but ignored what was playing out before our eyes, if not all the details, either to protect her pride or to avoid more responsibility. Need I point out how common this phenomenon is? How well intentioned but ill advised? Elderly parents who don't "bother" their children today are setting the stage for a crisis tomorrow. Adult children who pretend they don't see trouble brewing are doing the same. At this point in a parent's decline, it ought to be against the rules for anyone to indulge in wishful thinking or to keep secrets, because everyone else will pay the price, whatever it is. Like it or not, this is now a family affair.

The emergency room trips were the worst of it, but they were not the only signal that we were in deep trouble. My mother could no longer get to the facility's community dining room with her walker, so she prepared Stouffer's Lean Cuisine dinners in her microwave. Or she did for a while. Then, one day, I went to reheat a cup of coffee for myself—and opened the door to a whoosh of black cinders, the remains of one of those Lean Cuisines that she had burned to a crisp. For the first time we discussed that she might need a wheelchair instead of a walker to get to the dining room. (It never crossed my mind, nor had we discussed at admission, that wheelchairs were not allowed at this facility. Residents who needed them were relocated to the affiliated nursing home.) We discussed paying for meals to be brought to her apartment. That was another service not provided that I'd never bothered to ask about.

Most important, we discussed hiring a part-time aide, maybe even a live-in. We called John Hancock to review the criteria for activating her long-term care insurance policy, which she easily met—the inability to perform a certain number of "activities of daily living" without help—and the details of exactly what it would cover. My brother, who had considered the policy a terrible waste of money all these years, was suddenly grateful that I was programmed to anticipate disaster.

But my self-righteousness was short-lived. The policy was useless at just the moment when we needed it most. Among the many things I didn't ask about, didn't hear, or didn't understand was this: in the crazy-quilt world of assisted living, I had fast-tracked my mother into a facility that neither provided nor permitted private-duty aides, John Hancock or no John Hancock. My mother, who could barely walk, get to the bathroom without help, make her way to the dining room, or prepare her own meals, was essentially on her own, a decade after she'd had the good sense to buy a policy rare in her age group and to move out of her house before living there became dangerous. My mother, who had had a doctor until we uprooted her from Florida, still had no medical professional to guide her—and us—through whatever nasty thing was going to happen next. She was now dependent on her adult children to get this right, and so far we were congratulating ourselves on our energy and enterprise while making a mess of it.

CHAPTER 3

The Vestiges of Family Medicine

Of all those early messes—once we calmed down, began asking better questions, and listened to the answers, we stopped making quite so many—few had more far-reaching or damaging consequences than our failure to find our mother a primary care physician immediately upon her relocation from Florida to New York (or, better yet, before the move). Instead, we rushed her to a specialist, a recipe for misunderstood or ill-advised decision-making and medical treatment.

Only much later did we discover that finding a new internist or family doctor for someone past the age of sixty-five, and thus insured by Medicare, is no easy task, despite the myth that the elderly are the one group of Americans with universal health coverage. Shocking to me, when I went looking for a new doctor for my mother, was that nobody was willing to see her, and I gradually realized that it was simply because she was old, time-consuming to treat, and thus inadequately insured by a fee-for-service health care system that reimburses doctors and hospitals for doing things, not for talking about them; for ordering tests and procedures, not for discussing their advisability. All American health insurance, harnessed to the fee-for-service model, works this way, but Medicare, in general, pays 15 to 20 percent less than private insurance, and the elderly, with multiple acute and chronic conditions, and other complicating and time-consuming issues, can't be whisked in and out of the office in fifteen minutes. So general practitioners, who are paid by the visit (as hospitals are paid by the day and specialists by the procedure), avoid them when their conscience allows.

These days the desperate shortage of primary care physicians is a well-known and much-discussed phenomenon. They are not easy to find, even if you are young, healthy, and well insured. But I assumed that the Medicare set, unlike the rest of us, didn't have to worry about this problem. It never crossed my mind a decade ago, nor do I see or hear much talk of it even now, that elderly people—those lucky folks with Medicare—are regularly told that a doctor's "practice is closed," even when it isn't. When I called around, seeking a doctor for my mother, and heard this door-slamming phrase over and over, should I have been suspicious? I could have tried a controlled experiment: contact the same doctors and ask for an initial appointment for myself rather than for my mother. (I was then fifty-two, in fine fettle, and with medical insurance from my employer.) *Nah,* I told myself. *You're being paranoid.*

Since the introduction of Medicare in 1965, we have believed that health care coverage for the elderly is an inalienable right, one of the few things nobody has to worry about in their not-so-golden years. But unanticipated at the time of that historic promise (an adjunct, three decades later, to the Depression-era Social Security system) was the explosion of life-prolonging medical technology. The dramatic changes in life expectancy eventually placed a financial strain on Medicare. The oldest of the old became budget-busters, making Medicare much closer to insolvency than Social Security. So, at the most inopportune moment, I was to learn that Medicare—which all of us, and our employers, pay for throughout our working lives, largely through FICA payroll taxes—depends on people staying in the same place, seeing the same doctor, so that when they get old, the doctor is less likely to refuse to see them any longer, although he is legally entitled to do so. (How scary is that?) Looking for a replacement internist late in life is a terrible thing to have to do.

But staying put from sixty-five onward is no longer the norm. Old age, in the twenty-first century, generally lasts for two decades past Medicare eligibility. A sixty-five-year-old American woman, on average, will live past the age of eighty-five; a man past the age of eighty-two. Often, those with the means to do so will move twice during those years: first south or west to the golf courses and palm trees of Florida, Southern California, Arizona, or some other soothing retirement climate; then, with the onset of illness, frailty, or dementia, in a reverse migration, back to the embrace of family in the Northeast and Midwest. We want our parents near us when they're eighty-plus and failing, to reassemble as a family and to spend time together before it's too late but also to avoid the inconvenience, expense, and worry connected with long-distance caregiving. Usually, despite the trauma of relocation, our parents (especially if widowed) want to be closer to us, or at least are realistic enough about their own situation to see the wisdom in the move. They need us, no matter how badly they wish otherwise, and even as they protest that they are doing just fine on their own and don't want to be uprooted again. Eventually, in my experience and that of my friends, even stiff resistance is eventually trumped by necessity or fear. The last resort, but sometimes an unavoidable one, is for adult children to lay down the law (or try to) to the very same parents who once laid down the law to them.

And so they come home, as my mother did. I wish I could say that the reason she wound up stuck for nearly four months in the clutches of high-tech specialty care—a neurosurgeon, no less—was that I was working day and night to find her a new primary care physician and failing at the task in the face of America's perverse health care system. But the explanation was that I simply wasn't thinking clearly. Adult children often don't think clearly when the crisis first arises; they are ill prepared, reluctant to take on this new (and mostly unwelcome) responsibility, and are hoping against hope that after a brief period of unpleasantness and inconvenience life will return to normal. I'm not sure what Michael and I thought "normal" would look like, once we had wrested our mother from a familiar but faraway place back into our day-to-day lives after so many years of distance, both physical and emotional. But we were too busy doing it to think beyond the tips of our noses. I had always been the family disaster planner, and, as I've said, for more than a year had been secretly scouting places for her to live up north, mindful that her odds of having a quick and easy death were small. I should also have been scouting a replacement doctor, but didn't know enough to.

In retrospect, it's easy to see that what my brother and I perceived as a crisis, requiring instant action, wasn't a crisis at all. My mother could have stayed where she was in Florida, quite happily and safely, while we took the necessary time to make medical, residential, financial, and other decisions with care, deliberation, and professional guidance. My mother wasn't in the midst of a sudden cardiac event or anything of that sort. She wasn't facing the decision of whether to be put on a ventilator. She had, if the Florida diagnosis was accurate (and we were hoping it wasn't), a slow-moving and nonmalignant tumor on her spine that did not require instant attention. Still, we pushed the panic button prematurely, plain and simple.

Our reaction, it is consoling to know even in retrospect, is common. Rosanne Leipzig, a geriatrician at Mount Sinai Medical Center, sees this hectic response among adult children all the time and says it invariably leads to a cascade of bad decisions. "What feels like a crisis rarely requires such a big rush, and you have a much better chance of getting it right if you slow everything down," Dr. Leipzig said. "It may feel like something that requires instant action because you have a life and you have to get back to it. But you never get that life back anyway, and ten days later you see what you've gotten yourself into, and it's a mess. It's important to realize that where your parent is at the moment, for the most part, is a stable enough environment to get through the beginning parts. You have time on your side."

But I didn't meet Dr. Leipzig, or anyone with expertise in the care and tending of aged parents, until I was deep into the process. Denial runs deep, and the odds that you are reading this book to prepare for something that hasn't yet happened are slim, no matter how much I wish otherwise. More than likely, you're already in the thick of things, as I was, and have already made your share of panicky mistakes. There's little to be gained by going back down the pointless highway of second-guessing yourself. I, you, most of us do the best we can, just as our parents did the best they could with us when we were children, getting tons of things wrong, or just a few, some because of omission and some commission, but guided, except in rare instances, by good intentions. Relax, even if you've already made some bad decisions, because it will still, give or take some rough patches, mostly come out okay.

But here my mother was, in the wrong assisted living community, being rushed to the emergency room so often I lost count, and in the hands of a specialist, Dr. Bilsky, the *über*-doctor, which was exactly what my brother and I wanted (or thought we did back then). Dr. Bilsky's job was to worry about one specific body part—my mother's thoracic spine, the tumor sitting on it, and what to do about it. That meant he would perform tests, consult other specialists, perform more tests, and have more consultations. He had never seen her, or us, before the day we wheeled her into his office for that first appointment, and he didn't know enough about her, or us, to guide good decision-making. Nor did he try very hard to figure her out, except in the narrowest medical sense, just as we didn't push him in that direction. She was a short-timer in his life, Dr. Bilsky readily acknowledged years later, not a whole person with a past, present, and future; a value system; emotions and aspirations; strong opinions; and two adult children, who (like it or not) were now part of her day-to-day decision-making.

"A surgeon can do a very good job [at what he is trained to do] but not give good advice," said Dr. Beatriz Korc, hired by Sloan-Kettering from Mount Sinai in 2009 to run its geriatric service. "You need someone else to put it all together, someone you trust. Even a brand-new primary care doctor is better than none."

As the American medical system is constructed, specialists rarely consider any of that touchy-feely, family-meeting stuff as part of their job description. Among specialists, moreover, it's a good bet the least touchy-feely end up as neurosurgeons. "Physicians are trained for mastery, and specialized skills are revered," wrote Dr. Christine K. Cassell, president and CEO of the American Board of Internal Medicine, in the foreword to a book called *The Cultures of Caregiving: Conflict and Common Ground Among Families, Health Professionals, and Policy Makers* (Baltimore: Johns Hopkins University Press, 2004). That translates, Dr. Cassell wrote, into a "dominant medical culture [that] places a high value" on "certainty, technology, scientific evidence, and hierarchy," churning out of its medical schools "physicians [who] are too often ill equipped to give reassurance and, instead, give impersonal statistics." But "family priorities, especially in chronic or terminal illness, are weighted toward actions that build or sustain relationships. When technological expertise has limits, communication, compassion, and consideration become even more paramount."

That is what skillful primary care physicians do: build a relationship over time with patients and their families, communicate with them, and treat them with compassion. In a perfect world, for elderly patients, with multiple medical problems and enough medications to fill a gallon-size Ziploc bag, that primary physician would have the extra training and expertise of a geriatrician. But those are even harder to find. I, of all people, should have known the risk of relying solely on specialists, a lesson I'd learned the hard way, or thought I had, as the main caregiver for a friend and contemporary who was diagnosed with brain cancer and died ten months later. He had no primary care doctor coordinating his treatment, someone who might have given us unbiased advice about the pros and cons of an array of experimental and conventional, but all likely hopeless, treatments—or discussed with us the alternative of no treatment at all, given the grim prognosis. Instead, each specialist we encountered had a personal investment in his particular approach, argued for it passionately, put my friend through tortuous protocols, and then, when one after another didn't work, handed us off to someone else, never to be heard from again. By the end, all the specialists had peeled off, abandoning us. I vowed such a thing would never happen again to anyone I loved.

That dress rehearsal was what taught me to write down where I'd parked the car in hospital parking lots, to keep a running list of useful phone numbers and other essential information, and never to leave the house without the cell phone charger. But at the top of the list should have been: find a Marcus Welby–type doctor, a caring generalist. In the scramble of an emergency, real or imagined, common sense can fly out the window. Not only was I slow to begin the search, I was seduced—as my late friend had been, and as my brother also was—by the idea that the fancier the specialist, the better the result. I find this attitude especially common in New York City and Los Angeles. The faith in the specialist, subspecialist, and subsubspecialist runs deep in certain cultures and infects the decision-making of adult children who want only the best for their aging parents, especially those with the means to provide it and the expertise or connections to find it.

Alas, some of the most expensive care is also some of the least effective. A small corps of researchers, primarily affiliated with the Dartmouth Medical School, have been documenting this subject for years, without much attention or regard, and also with some open dissent. In a geographic ranking they call a Health Care Atlas, the Dartmouth researchers found that high-spending regions have no better survival rates than others for colon cancer, rectal cancer, hip fractures, and heart attacks. The patients don't function better; nor are they happier with the medical care they receive. They are also less likely to get preventive services, like flu shots, and they have longer waits both at doctors' offices and in the ER. The authors of the Health Care Atlas hypothesize that higher spending correlates, in part, with an oversupply of specialists, razzle-dazzle diagnostic equipment, and hospital beds. (If you build it, they will come.) New York City, for instance, with 186 specialists per 100,000 residents in 2009, spent $12,114 a year on each Medicare recipient. Albany, the state capital, with 93 specialists per 100,000 residents, spent $5,950.

The Dartmouth work, and other research like it, entered the broad public policy dialogue in the early months of the Obama administration, which was attempting to rein in health care costs. The reasons for the disjuncture between spending and outcomes were many: the way health care is financed in this country; the way it rewards specialists rather than generalists with both money and prestige; powerful lobbying interests, like the insurance and pharmaceutical industries; physicians' vulnerability to malpractice claims if they leave any stone unturned; and Americans' abiding faith in technology, to name a few. The administration, talking of flattening this "cost curve," proposed that a panel of experts do "effectiveness research" to determine what works and what doesn't and allocate scarce resources accordingly. The underlying notion is that just because medical technology has made certain things possible doesn't mean they are necessarily useful, wise, or worth doing. The administration also proposed reimbursing doctors for the time spent engaging families in ongoing, evolving conversations about end-of-life care, something previously not covered except for those enrolled in a hospice upon certification that they had but six months to live and were not engaging in curative therapies—or some in tiny pilot projects.

The proposal that the government pay for such conversations, especially for the aged, created a firestorm. Paying for care at the end of people's lives uses up the lion's share of Medicare dollars, is often ineffective and even unwelcome, and sometimes is more attractive to the adult children and physicians than to the aged themselves. Yet angry words flew about "rationing," "killing Granny," and "death panels." It was scary stuff for some elderly patients and their families, especially those inclined toward aggressive care, irrespective of age; it was scary, too, for politicians to explicitly defend the proposal, or even to talk openly about it. Discussion of end-of-life care is the third rail of health care reform but is essential to control costs. To those with insurance, the costs are all but invisible, yet they make health coverage of the uninsured essentially unaffordable and could bankrupt Medicare. During the heated rhetoric that began in late 2009, and continues as I write, calmer voices were drowned out or got limited attention. Among the calmer voices was that of Peter B. Bach, senior adviser to the administrator for Medicare and Medicaid Services from 2005 to 2006, who said in a *New York Times* op-ed piece that wasteful and ineffective Medicare spending could add up to as much as $700 billion a year, enough to provide insurance for everyone who didn't have it then.

Also documenting the "broad overuse of medicine" in ways that were bad for both the budget and people's health was Atul Gawande, physician and author of an article called "The Cost Conundrum," which appeared in *The New Yorker* in June 2009. Dr. Gawande zoomed in on McAllen, Texas, which, according to the Dartmouth Institute for Public Health Policy and Clinical Practice, is home to Medicare recipients who each cost the government $15,000 a year. That's more than recipients in New York, almost twice the national average, and more than twice the annual cost per enrollee in neighboring El Paso. People in McAllen undergo lots of tests and operations; they see a lot of doctors and take a lot of pills. Practicing medicine this way just seems to be the norm there, not the result of different demographics or cultures. Dr. Gawande, echoing and narratively expanding the Dartmouth data, concluded that the McAllen enrollees "got more of the stuff that cost more but not more of what they needed. . . . Americans like to believe that with most things, more is better. But research suggests that where medicine is concerned it may actually be worse."

During those months when my mother had no primary care doctor, she nevertheless received lots and lots of medical attention, arguably too much. Most of it was delivered in emergency rooms; the rest was in laboratories and radiology offices, where the specialists at Memorial Sloan-Kettering tested and retested her, first to confirm her Florida diagnosis and then to determine her suitability for surgery. The ER trips, of course, I considered excessive, usually unnecessary, and the result of unskilled after-hours staff at the assisted living facility, who lacked the expertise to make informed decisions and simply followed a rule book designed to protect the facility from litigation, not to promote the health and well-being of residents. The tests ordered by Sloan were objectionable to me for other reasons: they were necessary for accurate diagnosis and future decision-making but all too often were duplicative. Insurance coverage hides the financial costs of such duplication from the patient and family, who might otherwise balk if they were paying out of pocket. The professionals, too, are not concerned about duplication, because insurance mostly covers it. The fact that it all seemed free, to us as a family though not to the larger society, made it no less tortuous for my mother or by extension for me. She had to live through all those tests, and I had to live through them with her.

The neurosurgeon seemed oblivious (as I had been during my mother's years of independence) that an MRI is a huge deal for someone as old and crippled as she was by then. She'd had them before, but I'd never been with her; I'd asked afterward only about the awful banging and claustrophobia inside that tube. But once I became her MRI escort, I learned that there was much more to it than that for her. It came as a revelation that these tests are far different for someone in her eighties than for someone in her fifties. People my age certainly don't beg for diagnostic tests, be they mammograms, blood work, or MRIs. They are unpleasant, scary, and cost us time at work or with our families, but they're bearable. We can usually go for all of them by ourselves. Not so for my mother. First, since her arthritis was worst in the morning, she had to rise at dawn and wait to dress until her joints had loosened. Then, at the Meadowview, I'd go up to her apartment and help her downstairs to the car, fold the walker and put it in the trunk, settle her into the front seat, and fasten her seat belt, since she could no longer swivel from the shoulder and waist or manipulate the buckle. These were among my early lessons in how hard it is to be old, how long everything takes, how much some of it hurts, and how a loving caregiver must stop moving at the warp speed of a New York minute and adapt to the pace of someone who is disabled, making it look natural and effortless. Don't shame your mother into rushing to keep up with you. First, it's not nice. Second, both of you will have to cope with her broken hip if rushing leads to a fall. And, if you have a mother as observant as mine, simply slowing down isn't sufficient: if your face reflects impatience, she will see it; it will make her feel guilty or shame her.

At the radiology center (we used one in Westchester, with Sloan's okay, to avoid exhausting trips to the city), I'd drop her off in the lobby, get her settled into a chair, go and park the car, get out the walker, and return to the building to meet her. Then, upstairs in the MRI suite, we'd wait, and wait, and wait some more. Every time she had to go to the bathroom, I'd be on the alert. I forgot to bring bottles of water, not realizing she wouldn't be able to use the fountain. I forgot to bring snacks, assuming there'd be a cafeteria or vending machines. The uncomfortable plastic chairs had no armrests and no contoured backs, and thus were painful for her to sit in.

It was easier to read there than in the emergency room but not by much. There was no TV. My mother was scared, miserable, and alternately whiny and snappish. I ricocheted between jolly and sullen, with occasional bursts of genuine kindness. Maybe I was kind more often than that, but what I recall is hating it, hating myself for hating it, and hating her for making it all necessary. It's okay, sometimes, to hate your mother or father in these moments when their needs are devouring. Thoughts are only thoughts, and there is nothing terrible, or exceptional, about having them. But they sure make you feel like a bad person when they're happening.

What is not okay is to hurt them. While neglect and financial abuse of the elderly are much more common than we'd like to think, flat-out black-and-blue-mark abuse is very rare. It amazes me more that it happens infrequently than that it happens at all, given the level of frustration and exhaustion that sometimes overtook me. Somehow, very, very few of us lose control in that way. If the news coverage of elder abuse, like everything else, weren't built upon man-bites-dog rather than dog-bites-man— the exceptional, not the more common, however heroic, self-control—we would see stories about wrung-out daughters (or wrung-out mothers of tantrum-throwing toddlers) who thought terrible thoughts but acted on none of them. That we hear only of the rare cases that actually lead to abuse is both a misrepresentation of what is really going on and an implied insult to all the caretakers, especially of people with Alzheimer's, who hold it together under circumstances that might well sink them.

As we waited for the MRI, my mother's name was finally called. Together we squeezed into one dressing room so I could help her out of her clothes and into the paper gown. We learned quickly that on test days she'd do better without a brassiere, because it was so arduous to get in and out of, and venturing into the world without one was for her one small humiliation among many. The second-hardest thing for my mother was her socks— unavoidable in winter. She resisted assistance in taking them off, but watching her struggle both saddened and annoyed me. When we finally finished undressing her—both of us by then embarrassed and testy— I accompanied her into the MRI room. There, the young technician acted as if he expected her to hop up on the table, like a gymnast. I explained that she needed help. He, like the other technicians we met along the way, was nice about that once asked but seemed surprised by the request, as if she were the first person of her age and degree of immobility he'd ever seen, which seemed somewhere between unlikely and impossible. Ever the stoic, my mother never uttered a word of complaint, either during the test or during the reverse process—dressing, getting settled into the car, being driven home and then helped upstairs. One MRI, door-to-door, generally consumed a full day for me and two for my mother, since she was physically spent for twenty-four hours afterward, rather like the aftermath of an ER visit. Blessedly, I had an employer who simply let me skip a day of work, knowing I'd make it up on my own time. How many adult daughters, in blue-collar or pink-collar jobs—or white-collar jobs with mean bosses—would lose a day's pay, and eventually a job, because of these frequent disappearing acts? Ironically, many of the adult daughters so penalized are the very home health aides who are caring for their own parents, and ours.

These tests, emergency room visits, and the like "use up time and sap energy and morale" that the aged don't have to spare, according to Dennis McCullough, a geriatrician and author. Dartmouth Medical School, where he teaches, is the home of what has come to be known as "slow medicine," a standard of care that assumes that the very old need not be subjected to every test and procedure in a physician's arsenal because, as Dr. McCullough said, "then there's nothing left for anything beyond a medicalized life" and "the designated benefits do not match the needs of this group." These are tough individual decisions, balancing arduous but possibly life-extending medical procedures against the quality of daily life and ability to function.

We, as a family, were near the far edge of the bell curve, much more interested in quality than quantity of life, and in certain ways that simplified matters by eliminating much confusion and dissent. My mother had long refused mammograms and Pap smears because she had no intention of undergoing cancer treatment, so why bother knowing? Many of my friends were horrified by my acquiescence to that choice. But as the geriatrician Cheryl Woodson told me long after my mother's death, she admired her refusal of so many tests: "There's no need for a road map to where you're not going." At a later point in the process, my mother had no problem saying a fierce no to MRIs and the like, as if defying anyone to argue with her, but at this point she, like me and Michael, was still too disoriented to assert herself in her characteristic way. Once the tumor was diagnosed, we were all out of our comfort zone and would have benefited from more discussion of the pros and cons of intervention.

I knew my mother's general stubbornness and attitudes toward certain kinds of medical care in old age, and I knew her deep distrust and dislike of doctors, dating from a time when nurses were treated more like domestic servants or flight attendants than like fellow medical professionals. So I guessed from day one that she would refuse the spinal surgery, even if it was indicated. Her primary care doctor in Florida most likely knew that about her, and I might have shared the information with a new one, since I certainly would have been less intimidated by an internist than I was by the hotshot neurosurgeon. A primary care doctor might have advocated less testing, less duplication, or at least have asked my mother more pointedly whether she ever intended to go forward. All three of us might have made the identical decisions in the end, but we would have done so intelligently, not by blundering around like a trio of drunks.

I want to explain a bit more about why replacing a primary care doctor for a Medicare patient can be so difficult. America's aforementioned fee-for-service medical care system does not properly reimburse doctors for the extra time it takes to treat elderly patients, many of whom have visual, auditory, or cognitive impairments or who come to doctors' visits accompanied by family members with lots of questions or aides who don't speak English. Even for a relatively healthy elderly person, there is no such thing as a fifteen-minute office visit. Just ask your mother a simple question and see how long it takes her to wend her way to an answer. Also, under our fee-for-service system, a doctor gets paid only by performing a billable procedure, not by advising against one. That's why so few medical students are choosing primary care and fewer still are choosing geriatrics, and many of those already in general practice (family doctors, internists) rather than procedure-driven specialties are retiring early. It simply doesn't pay for them to do this kind of old-fashioned medicine.

Yes, we tend to think of doctors as raking in the big bucks, and compared to many of us they do, so it is easy to dismiss their financial complaints as something akin to Marie Antoinette's "let them eat cake." But there are doctors, and there are *doctors*. Anesthesiologists, for example, earn $400,000 a year. Do any of us even know the names of the people who put us to sleep before surgery? We generally don't even choose or interact with them. Meanwhile, general practitioners make $150,000 a year. Between 1998 and 2006, according to an article in *The Journal of the American Medical Asso-*

ciation, the number of residents studying family medicine dropped by 51 percent. In the same span, 150 percent more medical students chose anesthesiology. The Medicare Payment Advisory Commission (MedPac), an independent federal panel, has warned of a crisis in primary care, pointing out that more primary care means better outcomes, less unnecessary treatment, less duplication of service, greater patient satisfaction, and lower costs. Still, the specialists proliferate, and the ratio gets more and more skewed. In a 2008 report, MedPac said a third of the Medicare beneficiaries it had surveyed had a problem finding a doctor to treat them. The Texas Medical Association, the same year, found that 58 percent of the state's doctors overall took new Medicare patients, but only 38 percent of primary care doctors did.

The reasons prospective doctors choose prestigious specialties over family or internal medicine are mostly financial. The average medical student graduates with upward of $200,000 in debt; doctors are often in their thirties before they complete their years of internship and residency and can begin repaying their loans. Their earnings depend on insurance payments. Medicare is the standard-bearer, determining reimbursements for 7,500 individual medical procedures: which ones to pay for and which not, and how much to pay doctors for each of the approved ones. These decisions, which favor specialists, not generalists, are made anew annually and are based on a formula that includes the time, training, supplies, availability of providers, and other resources each procedure requires. It's a zero-sum game, by law a fixed pool of money, so that when Medicare adds a new reimbursable procedure to the list, an existing one has to go. The ripples spread well beyond the government entitlement, since by custom, not law, employer-based and other private health insurance companies generally align their coverage decisions with Medicare's, which insures some 45 million Americans. When colonoscopies were approved for cancer screening, for instance, first by Medicare and then quickly by private plans, gastro-enterologists, virtually overnight, became the nation's richest doctors, and that specialty became the most popular internship for doctors in training.

So the anesthesiologist and gastroenterologist prosper while the generalist, who both lowers health care costs and increases its quality, suffers. And generalists, in our aging society, are seeing more and more old people. One study published in 2004 said that four in ten internal medicine patients were over sixty-five and one in four for family doctors. By 2015, according to another study, health professionals of all kinds will spend half their time with people of Medicare age. By 2030, when the last of the 77 million baby boomers turn sixty-five, there will be more than 70 million Americans in that age cohort. The mind boggles.

Other aspects of the current fee-for-service system boggle the mind as well. Suppose a doctor spends time dissuading a very old woman from having a Pap smear, because the patient has made clear she wouldn't elect treatment if cancer were found. The doctor doesn't get paid for that time. Suppose he discusses with a family a possible hip replacement for an uncle with advanced Alzheimer's disease. The procedure would be pointless, he explains, because the uncle would not be able to follow a physical therapist's instructions and thus would never walk again anyway. That discussion—which some have labeled a "death panel"—also is not billable. And joint discomfort can be handled in other ways, like pain medication, that would not leave the patient wheelchair- or bed-bound as surgery with no physical therapy would. Educating people to say no, when saying yes is human nature, would save millions of dollars, but it doesn't bring a doctor one penny in income or to pay for office space, staff, or new technology.

As I write, according to MedPac, one-third of Medicare-age patients have difficulty finding a new physician if their existing one retires or dies before them, or if they relocate. While it is legal to do so, few doctors "fire" long-standing patients who reach the age of sixty-five, because of anticipated opprobrium from their fellow doctors and medical societies. That said, Peter Strauss, one of New York City's leading elder care lawyers (he was still practicing and teaching in his mid-eighties), was told not too long ago by his dermatologist that he was being dumped along with all the other Medicare patients. Strauss was unperturbed—but said he'd be raising the roof if it were his cardiologist.

Doctors can legally opt out of Medicare altogether, avoiding the difficult decision of keeping or disposing of those who reach the age of sixty-five. According to its website, New York–Presbyterian Hospital in New York City, in 2009, had ninety-three internists, fifty-six of whom did not accept Medicare. (To find out which doctors take Medicare patients, check the government's website, your state medical society, or the site of an individual hospital, although that will not reveal who rejects *new* Medicare patients.) Other than opting out, doctors can also choose to participate in a secondary category of Medicare, in which they accept a 5 percent lower reimbursement rate from the government; the extra cost comes out of the patient's pocket. Another way for a doctor to avoid the Medicare shortfall is to set up a boutique practice, where patients pay an annual fee in exchange for more time with and greater access to the doctor. Sometimes insurance covers their actual care and sometimes it doesn't, but either way the doctor gets a tidy up-front fee. Older people able to afford it, as my mother was, often have so-called Medigap policies, supplemental insurance to cover deductibles and copayments, but those policies are available only if Medicare remains the primary insurer. So, no Medicare, no Medigap.

Anecdotal evidence of old people losing their doctors abounds. In 2008, the *AARP Bulletin* told the story of Donna and Larry Bry, who moved after the age of sixty-five from the Oregon coast to Salem and for two years couldn't find a doctor there willing to take Medicare. Also in 2008, the *Anchorage Daily News* reported that Primary Care Associates, the largest family practice in the state of Alaska, had opted out of Medicare. The doctors there reduced their fees by 25 percent for existing elderly patients, but absent any Medicare coverage, they had to pay the remaining 75 percent themselves. The poorer existing patients got even bigger price breaks, although they were still left paying for a portion of the care presumed to be guaranteed by the government. But no such offer was made to new patients. "Every neighborhood in the country is one doctor away from a crisis," Fred Ralston Jr., an internist in Fayetteville, North Carolina, told the *AARP Bulletin* in 2008. "If I go away and my 2,000 patients [that year he saw twenty a day in the office and others in hospitals and nursing homes] are let loose on the market, there are not enough doctors to absorb them."

My mother had a trusted doctor when she lived on Long Island, found a so-so substitute in Florida, and now had none. My belated efforts to find her one began with my own doctors, themselves mostly specialists who saw a limited number of internal medicine patients. How I wound up in their care is beside the point, but none was willing to see my mother. Then I reached beyond my immediate circle, not quite to the yellow pages, but to this friend's doctor and that friend's doctor. It was a labor-intensive exercise, like so much of family caregiving. Yes, more information is available now than I had then—blogs and websites, caregiving classes at the local recreation center or nearby hospital. But I've never seen a site, or been to a class, that warns about the "Mom moved and now has no doctor" dilemma.

The drill goes something like this. Suppose a friend or a friend-of-a-friend suggests a doctor. You call. The first unpleasantness, in a large group practice, is the diabolical telephone system. Press 1 if you're a patient, 2 if you're a doctor, 3 if you're a pharmacist, 4 if you're an insurance company, 5 if you want the appointments desk, 6 for a real person. Then a recorded voice apologizes that "all of the clerical associates are busy, but please stay on the line." Music alternates with health tips—*Wash your hands! Get your flu shot!*—while you wait. Then it's back to the recording apologizing for the busy clerical associates. Eventually, if you haven't hung up or gone mad, someone answers. You explain about your mom and ask for an appointment. The clerk tells you someone will call you back. The only way I ever found to get that callback was to remember that a watched pot never boils. I'd leave my desk, and my telephone, for a trip to the water fountain or the supply closet. The call would come in my brief absence. So I'd start all over. The reward, should that second call ever be returned (and often it isn't), is being told that "the practice is closed." Many times, exasperated, I'd just give up.

My mother considered using the health clinic on the grounds of the Meadowview, which had a regular cast of visiting doctors. But she decided, and I agreed (both of us still doctor snobs), that they'd likely be inferior to someone in private practice. We'd also had a few emergency room experiences by then and so were looking for a doctor affiliated with one of the hospitals where ambulances from the Meadowview were required to go, which meant those within a certain radius. If my mother was admitted to the "wrong" hospital, she'd be attended by strangers or by hospitalists—a growing category of doctors who see just hospitalized patients, often in lieu of their regular internists. Only when she was stable enough would she be transferred to the institution where her own doctor practiced. That would be bad for her, obviously, since moving her from place to place would extract a great physical and emotional toll. It would also be bad for me and Michael, because it would require so much follow-up, phone calls, and driving here and there. Our paying jobs were already suffering. He was in the midst of writing a book and often unable to work. I was getting less sympathy than I had at first at my office and, although rarely, outright hostility or punitive treatment in certain quarters. The two of us, in a mirror image of my mother, were ever more worn out by what seemed the endless list of "Mom tasks." Thus, we stopped being so fussy about hospital affiliation. We'd take whoever would have us, which turned out to be a lovely young female internist, Lori Saltzman, the sister of Michael's longtime doctor. My mother's first appointment was in March.

The desperate shortage of general practitioners, the frontline providers in all age groups, has captured the attention of policy wonks, who have a slew of ideas about how to reorganize the fee-for-service system, thus leveling the playing field. Many of the ideas are part of the Obama health plan, at first as local experiments; quite a few others were already being tested, before the new law, among Medicare patients, who drive the system because they are the only ones immediately under the control of the federal government and because of their sheer numbers. Historically, the two alternatives to fee-for-service medicine have been some form of capitated payment (a doctor gets a certain amount of money per patient rather than per procedure) or salary (the way effective HMOs, like Kaiser, and rare hospitals like the Mayo Clinic, pay their doctors). The main objection to these approaches is that the doctors potentially have a financial incentive to withhold care or cherry-pick healthier patients.

Other, more arcane ways of curbing the ill effects of fee-for-service, using the jargon of health care reformers, are "pay for performance," "episode-based payment," "accountable care organizations," and "patient-centered medical homes." The first, "pay for performance," involves compensating individual physicians for overall outcomes, using defined measures of effectiveness; so, say, a patient whose diabetes is well controlled through diet and frequent self-testing is worth more to the doctor than a patient with uncontrolled disease whose toes need to be amputated. "Episode-based payment" involves reimbursing a doctor for a bundle of related services, say, everything connected to a patient's heart attack, whether that be inserting a stent or implementing preventive strategies like diet and exercise. "Accountable care organizations" are groups of fee-for-service doctors who get paid for individual procedures but also get bonuses for overall outcomes. "Patient-centered medical homes" bring together fee-for-service doctors from various specialties who are led by one "quarterback" physician, who is paid extra for coordinating care.

Some cutting-edge providers are already combining and tweaking several of the above ideas into a hybrid system. In addition, many public policy experts endorse loan forgiveness for medical students who choose general practice; greater use of nurse practitioners and physicians' assistants;

increasing overall medical school enrollment; and/or the creation of more federally funded neighborhood health centers, in which doctors are obliged to serve every Medicare-eligible patient.

All of these ideas are interesting in the way science fiction is interesting. But visionaries couldn't get me through this time in life when I was the daughter on duty. Each day—and the next, and the next—was all I cared about. So I recently asked Rosanne Leipzig, who has trimmed her clinical practice to help reinvent geriatrics for the next generation, what she would advise someone to do *today*, not in the hypothetical future she is boldly imagining. Suppose your mother is about to move to a place near you. You've heard that finding her a new doctor won't be easy. You don't want to get lost in the scrum of specialty care without a primary physician. What can you do to improve the odds you will find a doctor, now, who will accept your mother, despite what Dr. Leipzig calls the unspoken "cap" on "complex and time-consuming" new Medicare patients? Here are her suggestions:

- Get a referral from the existing internist wherever Mom or Dad lives now. That doctor is likely to know someone wherever your parent is moving, and, fair or not, the doctor at the receiving end is far more likely to take a new Medicare patient as a favor to a colleague than over the transom. Do this *before* the move, not during or after. (Dr. Leipzig's idea shows the importance of taking the time and trouble to build a long-distance personal relationship with the original doctor. I highly doubt that my mother's Florida doctor would have helped two adult children whom he had never even met until she was halfway out the door, and I don't blame him.)

- The doctor at the receiving end will be more likely to welcome a new elderly patient who is arriving with records in an easily digestible form. Dr. Leipzig urges you to get tightly crafted summaries from the current general practitioner, and from all the specialists involved, not "piles and piles of records, especially handwritten and illegible." Less is more, she said, since doctors "don't get paid by the hour like lawyers." If all the former doctor does is Xerox everything and send it, the chances are it won't get read or your family will be rejected.

- Failing a referral, scout the area where a parent is relocating before—not during or after—the move. Don't contact individual doctors, as we did, after the fact. Rather, before the move, call local aging agencies, senior centers, medical societies, and the like. State and local budget cuts mean they may not be staffed five days a week, but they are also less likely to have elaborately annoying phone systems and thus may be easier to reach. (In acknowledgment of this problem, the new geriatric service at Sloan intends to offer its entering cancer patients a list of internists who will accept new Medicare cases.)

- One of doctors' disincentives to taking on new Medicare patients is that they will have to spend additional time, usually not reimbursed, dealing with squabbling, demanding, and often long-distance adult children. Physicians welcome the increased role of adult sons and daughters, Dr. Leipzig said, provided they thoughtfully organize themselves before walking in the door. So approach the doctor with a plan already in place for which sibling will be running the show medically. Don't expect each of you to have your own pipeline to the doctor, and don't show up en masse at appointments and waste the doctor's time fighting with one another in the office.

- Except for designated family meetings, the same sibling, whenever possible, should accompany the parent to medical appointments and be the point person for passing along information to sisters and brothers. Some doctors these days, with everyone's permission, send e-mail bulletins to all family members and other physicians on the case, to avoid fielding duplicative phone calls and to ensure that everyone is in the loop and getting the same information, unfiltered. A family that by and large manages its own dysfunctions (and few families are free of them) is more likely to find, keep, and get the best service from a doctor. In other words, act out on your own time. "You figure it out," Dr. Leipzig said, "or get over it for now. This is about what's best for your parent."

CHAPTER 4

A Job for Professionals

It was one of those days of too many doctors' appointments and too many tests. The early dark of that bitter winter was already upon us when I brought my mother back to the Meadowview, to an apartment that didn't yet feel like home to her and, we both wordlessly understood, probably never would. There was no welcoming greeting from the receptionist stationed at the front desk, no "How did your day go?" as we would have gotten in Florida. The "gathering room," as these common living rooms are known in assisted living facilities, was empty even during the pre-dinner hour, when "gathering" is the likeliest to occur, so we made our way silently to the elevator.

Exhausted and dispirited, neither of us was in the mood for friendly chitchat anyway. All my mother wanted was to go to bed, and all I wanted was to go home and recover from the sort of day that by now had become all too typical and none too productive. For months now, my mother had been dizzy much of the time, in the clutches of what we assumed was Ménière's disease, and thus she was moving around as little as possible. The vertigo attacks came in bunches, related (or so it seemed to me) to how anxious she was, and then fed on the anxiety. They had *always* subsided within days, with blessed months of remission in between. But "always" was how it used to be; "always," I was coming to admit, was a thing of the past. The tumor was the wild card. All three of us were anxious about it. None of the doctors seemed to know what to do next; hence the frequent medical appointments, the same tests repeated over and over—and the emergency room visits when she fell. She fell a lot because she was dizzy. She was dizzy because she was anxious. She grew ever more anxious as the dizziness, and the falling, took over her life. We were caught in a feedback loop that I understood but was powerless to change.

I suppose in that context this day counted as a good one, at least so far, as there'd been no trip to the emergency room. I commented on that to my mother, darkly, since it was her kind of mordant humor, which I was coming to appreciate. All I got back was a wan smile as we rode upstairs, she with a shaky hold on her walker and me with my hand inches from her back, so she didn't know it was there, but ready to steady her if she wobbled. We rarely bickered that winter, as if understanding that things were so bad, we owed it to each other not to make them any worse. Not once, that I recall, did we give in to easy recriminations. She never asked, *Why did you bring me here?* and I never asked, *Do you have any idea what this is doing to my life?* A gentleness had crept into our interactions, and a growing acceptance of the fact that she needed help with once-private tasks like dressing and undressing, and that I was the one best able to provide it. And so it was, by the light of her bedside lamp, that I helped her into a nightgown, persuaded her to have some soup and an English muffin, and literally tucked her in for the night.

Only then, in the corridor as I was leaving, did I notice how cold it was, almost see-your-breath cold. At the front desk I inquired politely and was told the furnace was broken, as it had been several times already since my mother's arrival in December. The new facility, it seemed, was still working out the kinks. But the absence of heat in the dead of winter, when your residents are mostly in their eighties, is not a "kink." Why had the young woman at the front desk, who a half hour before had watched me all but carry my mother through the door, not warned me of this "little inconvenience," as she now phrased it? Had she mentioned it when we were on our way in, I remarked to her, my voice flat and low even as anger rose in my throat, I could have taken my mother to my house, mere minutes away, where she'd have slept in a warm bed.

The rejoinder—*Well, take her there now*—turned my incipient anger to fury. Did this girl, at most twenty-five and essentially running the place after five p.m., have any clue what was involved in getting a frail old woman out of bed, changing her from nightclothes into slacks and a sweater, socks and shoes, a coat and hat, then taking her back downstairs on her walker and helping her into my car? This is a frustratingly slow process. And only if you make it look effortless, unconditional, is it seen as a kindness. Achieving that illusion, regardless of what might be going on inside my head, was more important to me than most of the things I actually "did."

The substantial time and effort that put-her-to-bed, take-her-out-of-bed, bring-her-to-my house required is all too familiar to anyone who has read this far. You're already doing this for someone. But the sentry at the Meadowview, the same gum-cracker who was in charge of calling the EMTs at night, was as clueless as a Valley Girl. I glared. She glared back. In schoolmarmish tones, I told her I would speak to her boss in the morning. By then I was pretty sure my mother was already asleep because my cell phone was not ringing. Gentleness between mother and daughter has its limits, and if she were cold and awake, I would have been hearing from her, justifiably complaining.

That night, lacking her knack for instant and deep sleep, and enraged by the experience, I tossed, turned, and worked myself into an insomniac snit. I'd picked this place in haste, mostly for my own convenience. My brother had concurred. But in the early division of labor, he'd done so many more and harder jobs—meeting with the Florida doctors, locating specialists here, transporting my mother to New York; my one task had been to find a decent place for her to live. I had known in my bones it was a bad choice even as I was making it, which compounded my culpability manyfold. Guilt, shame, anger, and sleeplessness are a combustible mixture. By nine a.m., when I called the facility director, I was braying.

The young woman at the front desk was a moron, I began, making no effort whatsoever to be diplomatic. Leaving her in charge overnight was a questionable management decision under the best of circumstances, I said, and a broken furnace was hardly the best of circumstances. The "little inconvenience" of no heat—multiple times—how dare that be permitted in what is essentially an old age home! People my mother's age die from the cold! You read about it in the newspaper every winter! I was nasty, condescending, and hectoring. The director gave not an inch. She seemed almost gleeful at my total loss of self-control. She accused me of overreacting, of being a hysterical daughter.

That last phrase made something inside me snap. Not a screamer, I was now screaming at her—which of course proved her point that I *was* hysterical. That huge tactical error would come back to haunt me. I was giving power to this person who had so much power over my mother and thus over me. You can go ballistic every once in a while, but you must pick your spots. It works best if the "tantrum" is planned, if you are actually in steely control and only sound like you aren't. You can also effectively orchestrate a good cop/bad cop routine with a sibling in which one of you goes nuts and the other brings cookies. But this morning, I had a raw explosion and in the process poisoned the well.

Those were my opening words—*I poisoned the well*—when I went many months later for a consultation with a geriatric care management agency, Fine Newcombe & Winsby, a benefit offered by my employer that I'd known nothing about. That this generous perk, a godsend, really, was so poorly promoted—one might say willfully hidden—is noteworthy but not an excuse. What *The New York Times* offered for free would have cost me $500. I could have afforded that; I didn't go out of a misguided sense I had things under control. Indeed, after my complimentary ninety minutes, I was so impressed by the wide-ranging knowledge and clearheaded advice I received, and so soothed by passing the baton of control (or at least sharing it) with people who knew what they were doing, that I spent thousands of dollars for additional help, all in the space of one whirlwind month when every mistake we had made, one at a time, caved in on us simultaneously.

In a perfect world, before a crisis, I would have found—and urge you to find—an internist, or better still, a geriatrician, or a geriatric care manager. The first two professions are shrinking under the pressure of increasing costs and decreasing Medicare reimbursement, and thus they are a challenge to locate. The third, on the other hand, is a growth industry, a bonanza for companies serving families of means in certain areas of the country. Carol Levine, director of the Families and Health Care Project at the United Hospital Fund, notes that geriatric care management is an urban luxury. She was a long-distance caregiver for her mother, in a small rural town in western New York, where "no one had even heard of the term," and all she could find on the association's website was someone in Buffalo, "seventy miles away and not likely to make home visits, especially in winter. That is a big gap for families in rural areas." The danger in metropolitan areas, where geriatric care managers are putting up shingles on every street corner, is that they must be vetted carefully. The manager's website, and the association's, is the place to start, although word of mouth from friends who have been though this and who know enough about your family to gauge if the person who helped them will be helpful to you is particularly useful. I have recommended one geriatric care manager to one friend and a different one to another, not because one is more skilled than the other but because I thought the fit would be better. As with most things, money helps, but anyone poor enough to be eligible for means-tested government services has access to similar (although far from equal) services. They are better than nothing, sometimes excellent, often free, and can be located through your county or local agency on aging.

Those in the vast middle of the financial spectrum—not rich enough to comfortably pay for private services and not poor enough to meet the government's definition of poor—have the most limited choices and think geriatric care management is beyond their means. Often it seems like it is, but these families need to find a way to pay or seek guidance on services that charge on a sliding scale from local agencies and senior centers. A comprehensive consultation, even just ninety minutes with no follow-up services (which many high-end agencies offer for free as a marketing tool), is likely to save far more money than it costs, both in misguided expenses and in physical and emotional wear and tear from trying to master this arcane universe. If you try to do everything by yourself, despite the best of intentions, you will get much of it wrong. Between the complexities of government entitlements, primarily Medicare and Medicaid, and the medical, residential, legal, and financial decisions that you must make when you are responsible for a frail elderly person, you can't learn what you need to know in time to put it to good use. Each aspect of elder care exists in its own silo, and experts in one often know little about the others. A good geriatric care manager is the closest thing there is to one-stop shopping, given the dearth of geriatric medical practices. The manager would have a referral network to additional professionals not in their in-house system, sparing you time-consuming legwork. Taking care of someone in old age isn't a job for an amateur, especially if you want some time at the end of your parents' life to enjoy them, learn more about them, and be a good son or daughter. To do that, delegate some of the expert tasks to professionals.

Geriatric care management was one of the earliest, and most reputable, cottage industries to spring up to help adult children understand, coordinate, and monitor the affairs of aging relatives—originally those who lived at a great distance from their families, and before long also those in the same state, city, or town. These agencies, or solo practitioners, first joined forces in 1985 as a trade group, with fifty members; by 2007 they had grown to a professional association of more than two thousand, with credentialing and certification requirements, a code of conduct, a headquarters and staff in Tuscon, Arizona, and a website with a search feature that enables families to punch in their zip code and find practitioners in their area.

Members of the National Association of Professional Geriatric Care Managers come from an array of fields, including, but not limited to, nursing, social work, psychology, and gerontology. They must have expertise in issues related to aging, several years of supervised experience in geriatric care settings, and certification by one of four organizations that require testing and continuing education. Claudia Fine, originally the co-owner of Fine Newcombe & Winsby and now executive vice president of Senior-Bridge, was the association's president in 2002, the year of its greatest expansion, from 1,575 to 1,717 members.

The tasks of geriatric care managers are many and varied. They conduct assessments, like my initial ninety-minute meeting with one of the firm's owners and a social work supervisor, to identify problems and propose solutions. They screen for, arrange, and monitor in-home help and other services. They review financial, legal, and medical issues and offer referrals to experts in those fields, who increasingly are making reverse referrals, as when a geriatric physician or elder care lawyer suggests that new patients or clients also see a care manager. They oversee long-distance care on behalf of faraway adult children. This can mean organizing services for an elderly person in the immediate area, regularly communicating with distant sons and daughters, and quickly alerting them to changes in status or other problems. Conversely, if the adult child resides nearby and the elderly parent elsewhere, the geriatric care manager locates and collaborates with service providers out of town and stays on top of the situation from afar.

They assist with moves from one part of the country to another and from one level of care to the next—say, from home to assisted living—in the same general location. (A much newer cottage industry of so-called move managers will do the same thing, but they have yet to develop the certification and practice standards of the geriatric care managers.) They evaluate options for where an elderly person might best live: if home care is appropriate, they suggest how to create and manage a team to provide it

(often using their own employees) and determine what physical modifications to the residence would add safety and comfort. (There are now specialists in this arena as well.) If a congregate setting is advisable, geriatric
care managers help identify which kind and which one, then supervise the
application, relocation, and often difficult transition. If private-duty aides
are warranted in a congregate facility, they screen, arrange for, and monitor those employees as they would at home. If two generations are living
together and the adult child is overwhelmed, they suggest and locate respite
care, adult day care, or other means of providing breaks for the caregiver.

They provide counseling, as needed, to the elderly person and family
members, and work with the entire "client system," meaning the elderly
person, family, paid caregivers, friends, neighbors, local agencies, other
professionals, including doctors and lawyers, and even a housekeeper.
They convene family meetings, help siblings divide responsibilities (often
with elaborate task and time schedules), referee disputes, and provide an
opportunity to vent to a dispassionate third party (as do uncertified elder
care mediators, yet another unregulated cottage industry). They also have
one-on-one relationships with both the aged parent and each of the children, often learning about issues that family members keep to themselves,
out of privacy, desires to protect one another from unpleasantness, ineffective communication, or deep-seated conflicts.

Pat Mulvey is a geriatric care manager who has worked in many settings,
including the Jewish Home Lifecare System, a consortium of hospitals and
nursing homes in the New York metropolitan area. She took questions
about her profession a while back on the *New Old Age* blog at *The New York
Times*. One of the things that most interested me was the family therapist
hat she must often wear. (This is so as well for the geriatrician or the elder
care lawyer, but it's more likely to come naturally to a social worker.) Pat
talked of "coming into a story at the last chapter," long after the relationships between mother and daughter, mother and son, son and daughter
have calcified into whatever they now are. Summoned after "a lifetime of
experiences" and without knowledge of "the depth and intricacy of those
relationships," Pat said, the care manager must figure out the origin of
"Mom always liked you best"—and many other old family dysfunctions—
by "listening carefully to what everyone is saying, and, as important, what
they're not." If a care manager can understand why a daughter might feel
compelled to be in charge of everything, regardless of how competent her
brother is, for instance, it may be possible to change that dynamic. "We can

weave the story together and provide the interpretation of the tale in a way that will help the family in the here and now," Pat said.

The formal relationship begins with a contract, which includes a fee schedule and, in a separate document, a written and itemized plan of care—a list of what the family needs that the care manager says he or she can deliver. Most of the larger care management agencies employ their own aides and take a percentage of their earnings, which is their primary source of profit. At SeniorBridge, which bought Fine Newcombe & Winsby, for instance, fees for aides and for hourly care management have gone up considerably in the years since my family was a client. But the original consultation fee remains $500, a way to introduce prospective families to the services (or to lure them in, depending on your level of cynicism). This is a high-end operation, but cheaper alternatives are available through local area agencies on aging and other nonprofits dedicated to seniors. There are also pilot programs, like one run by Medicaid, called PACE, or the Program of All-Inclusive Care for the Elderly, with geriatric clinics for the poor nationwide; they offer care management as part of a holistic and cost-effective approach to long-term care. In other words, finding something like the help my family got for lots of money is not out of your reach, although it is surely harder and its services will be less sleek.

Being neither very rich nor very poor, I thought this sort of service was a luxury that I couldn't afford, as do many friends and colleagues. Time and again I suggest it, and time and again I get the same answer: *We don't have that kind of money.* No doubt she's an interested party, but I asked Claudia Fine whether people's reluctance to pay for these services, until they're knocked to their knees, is common. "This is what I run up against every day," she said. "In fact they do [have enough money], but they'll wait until the cost is astronomical rather than put the money in initially. The biggest problem is that people think this isn't special knowledge." She amplified, "If you got a letter from the IRS that you'd screwed up your taxes, you wouldn't say 'I can't afford an accountant.' Even if you're putting a kid through college, and your mom just had her first stroke, and she's on Medicare in a subacute facility, you need to know 'What next?' To spend a thousand dollars to figure out a game plan . . . It's completely out of touch with reality not to do it."

Like Claudia, Pat Mulvey stressed the value of seeking advice before you need it, "when things are going well—the elder is managing on his or her own, with little help or oversight, but the family is noticing slight changes or the physician has indicated a change in status or diagnosis." Pat said that "this would be the time to know what resources are available to them, how much they would cost, how to access these resources, and what options are available." For example, she cited adult day care, short-term rehab, respite for caregivers, home care, long-term care insurance, and how to deal with sudden hospital discharges. Do families have that information in hand when they need it? Mine surely didn't. Experts say people put it off, inevitable though it might be, out of denial, just as people who are dying wait until the last twenty-four hours of life to seek the vast array of hospice services, covered by Medicare and most private insurance, that could have been beneficial for many months or longer.

The common misconception that Medicare pays for long-term care will also be quickly laid to rest by a geriatric professional, who will then help you figure out, one hopes, how to cover the costs. As I said in the prologue, the question I hear most often, when a parent first needs what is commonly known as custodial care—someone to run errands, fix meals, help him or her to the bathroom—is *What do you mean Medicare doesn't cover it?* Knowing that fact in advance is arguably *the* foundational lesson from which everything else follows.

Pat also advises that you learn about Medicaid sooner rather than later. Every case is different, particularly the so-called spend-down— the byzantine but legal process of depleting remaining assets and thus qualifying for government assistance—when a parent is nearing the bottom of his or her private piggy bank. It is a process full of nooks and crannies, where one can get lost, as in a maze of tall corn.

This is complicated stuff, all but impossible to master; a series of disconnected puzzle pieces without expert help. Most of us can muddle through the isolated task of hiring home health aides, or retrofitting a house with wider doorways and a chair lift on the stairs. We can choose an assisted living facility or a nursing home. We can even figure out who pays for what. But mostly we're putting out fires, with no long-range plan, hoping we won't need one, surely not one that culminates with a Medicaid application. We are clapping as loud as we can for Tinker Bell. Once a parent has passed eighty-five, easy and affordable passings are few and far between. Believing you're going to get one is magical thinking. Geriatric care managers, as Claudia says, can be "the brains of the operation."

·   ·   ·

"I'm beginning to feel more and more like I'm in the wrong place," my mother said to me as that harsh winter dragged on and on. As was so often the case, she was the first to say something so meaningful out loud, although Michael and I knew it and were alternatively pretending otherwise and making random stabs at solving the problem, one little bit at a time. The first of those pieces, better late than never, was finding her the internist, Dr. Saltzman. She never did the sort of assessment a geriatrician would have and actually saw my mother only once, but she became ever more involved and helpful, via phone and fax, as my mother's condition deteriorated, her living situation became more inappropriate, and we required notes from the doctor, literally, to get what we needed.

While Dr. Saltzman was ordering up echocardiograms and chemical stress tests, searching for the cause of the unrelenting vertigo, Michael was seeking information and answers of other kinds. Online, and in consultation with an elder care lawyer who had done my mother's will, financial power of attorney, and health care proxy back in 1993, my brother tried to make sense of New York State Department of Health regulations involving assisted living facilities, enriched housing, and adult care homes. Which was my mother actually in? We didn't have a clue. And why were they prohibiting us from hiring private-duty help for her or even providing her with a wheelchair so she could get to meals and to the bathroom without a high risk of falling?

It turned out, unbeknownst to us, that we had chosen a facility licensed to provide additional care to my mother in only one way: we could sign a new "enriched housing" lease, at a monthly price ranging from $150 to $1,150, on top of her rent, and buy her up to ten hours a week of personal care, but never more than four consecutive hours. In other words, she could have four hours of one-on-one care on Monday, four hours on Tuesday, and two on Wednesday. Otherwise she was on her own or one of us had to be with her. Anyone needing more one-on-one attention than that was expected to move to the on-campus nursing home, a dreary establishment that I visited during this period. There were crucifixes and religious statuary everywhere, which might be objectionable to some residents; no natural light; and a waiting list of more than a year for a single room. The place made me shudder and prompted yet another of my epiphanies on elder care:

When you are shopping for an independent living, assisted living, or continuing care retirement community, focus on the nursing home that is either affiliated with or part of the facility. If you can't imagine your mother or father winding up in that nursing home, look elsewhere. This requires you to imagine the worst-case scenario, which nobody wants to do. But only by doing it can you be sure your parent will be spared moving every time his or her condition deteriorates. "Aging in place" is the mantra (and mostly the myth) of elder care, ideally at home or else in one facility that will serve the person's needs forever. That rarely happens. Things change. In the trade, moves are known to cause "relocation trauma," physically and emotionally, for the frail elderly person, already sick and scared, and for the adult children, who must orchestrate everything.

The most dramatic example of relocation trauma occurred during Hurricane Katrina and a subsequent series of Gulf Coast storms, when long-term mortality and morbidity was significantly worse for the elders "successfully" relocated than those "sheltered in place." In other words, those who survived by being bused out of the eye of the storm to higher ground died subsequently at rates much higher than those who remained behind. The main causes of death were twofold: deadly urinary tract infections from catheters inserted for the long bus journey; and falls, leading to broken hips and their cascade of health risks—for instance, if a previously healthy nursing home resident took a tumble while looking for the bathroom in an unfamiliar place or while wearing ill-fitting slippers borrowed after fleeing without all her own belongings.

It is heresy, I know, to tell friends, colleagues, blog readers, and the like that a parent over eighty-five is not likely to die quickly, easily, or without full-time assistance with the activities of daily living. The data confirming this fact, however, are compelling and uncontested by the experts. Deny that data and make avoiding a nursing home your goal, and the odds are you will subject your parent to excessive, pointless, and damaging relocations. That was the case with my mother.

As she deteriorated in assisted living, I got her three hours a week of "personal care." It wasn't nearly enough. (The Meadowview has come to realize it, too, in subsequent years, as a series of new managers have revised and expanded its costly menu of options.) Many nights my mother couldn't make it to the dining room with her walker. But getting her the wheelchair she needed would have put her on the fast track to the on-site nursing home, which was unthinkable to all of us. Was there a chair we could borrow on especially difficult days? I asked. The facility had two, I was told. One had to be kept in the office at all times for emergencies, and the other could be borrowed by signing up for it during regular business hours, a day in advance. So I would have to know by five p.m. Tuesday that my mother was going to need the chair to get to dinner on Wednesday. Or maybe Wednesday's dizzy spell counted as an emergency? But no. The emergency chair had to stay in its place, unused, waiting for an emergency of a different magnitude. I didn't ask what that might be since I already knew it wasn't a trip to the emergency room; for that, paramedics took people from their room to the ambulance on a gurney. It all had a catch-22 quality.

During these months, assisted living seemed to mean *Call your daughter for whatever you need.* Most days I was there at least once. I brought her frozen dinners or sandwiches so she could skip the meals we were paying for in the dining room that she couldn't get to. I replaced the microwave, which was mounted high on the wall and was hard for her to reach without falling, with a countertop toaster oven. But that wasn't safe, I'd soon learn. I made sure her prescriptions were filled before she ran out of something since she could no longer write herself notes of reminder, and the staff nurse, long my favorite person there, seemed less attentive once I was labeled a hysterical daughter. I sneaked my mother over-the-counter seasickness medicine, which worked better for the vertigo than any of the prescriptions; she was not permitted it under the licensing requirements because it came from the outside, not approved by the Meadowview nurse. I paid her bills because her right hand was no longer strong enough to allow her to write. I put on, and took off, her compression stockings when the three hours a week of help had been exhausted. I had no idea what to do next and was too tired, depressed, and frightened to think about anything beyond the next ten minutes.

I didn't sign up for more hours of help because I was worried about money, but even the maximum ten hours wouldn't have fixed much of anything. The idea of going broke haunted me. At this point my mother had about $160,000 left, from a small investment portfolio, Social Security, and my father's pension. Today, as then, even with a long-term care insurance policy, she would have been responsible for her own rent in assisted living. Current long-term care insurance, depending on its provisions, and thus its cost, might have paid for the extra personal care services, but way back when she got her policy, a new product to the market in the early 1990s, it covered nothing associated with assisted living, so we were totally on our own financially.

At night, when I couldn't sleep, I did calculations in my head as to when she would run out of money, then further calculations as to when my brother and I would run out of money if we had to pay all the bills. Michael told me he was never plagued with such worries. "Cross that bridge when we come to it," he said. "I was dealing with today, not three weeks from today."

I believe this kind of remark is often a gender difference, and also a matter of temperament. When some angry adult daughters commented on the blog about their brothers' deficiencies, I suggested, with wisdom that came to me years too late, that this was no time for a feminist hissy fit, which they obviously found politically incorrect and so turned their anger on me. I didn't mind. But having done my time, so to speak, and wasted a ton of energy wanting Michael to worry in the same way I worried, and to be good at the same things I was good at, I have come to believe it is not sensible to be mad that someone else has a Y chromosome and you don't. Put him in charge of the checkbook, not compression stockings. And certainly don't fume because you're obsessing and he isn't. If you can find it in your heart, and at the time I couldn't, be glad one of you is sleeping at night rather than worrying about running out of money.

As March turned to April, work was the one safe place—but only if I wasn't at my desk, where the phone rang incessantly. My sturdy, independent mother was now in perpetual meltdown. She was petrified, losing control of everything at once, humiliated, enraged. The mood swings from sweet-and-grateful Mom to it's-all-your-fault Mom destabilized me as nothing ever had before. Even my brother, less vulnerable to this sort of thing than I, was rocked by her constant calls and wild mood swings. The best moments of my days were calls from him, or e-mails, commiserating about my mother's latest tantrum. Only to each other could we say the really awful thing: *Why doesn't she just die?* We said it often.

Relief came in other ways, too. I went to a yoga class or to the gym almost every night. I was too agitated to read and discovered books on tape. Especially in the dark, coming home from my mother's apartment, they soothed me, like being read to as a child. I spent a fortune on manicures, less because it improved my appearance and more because I preferred talking to people I hardly knew in the nail salon to lifelong friends who were sick of hearing my tales of woe. I struck up a nail salon friendship with a woman who was taking care of both her parents, plus a husband and teenage son, and herself had breast and ovarian cancer—a deadly combination, she knew. She never said "Buck up" or its equivalent. Trouble is trouble, she told me. It's not a contest.

On my mother's birthday, in June 2001, Michael, his wife, and I took her out to dinner. We pored over the Westchester County *Zagat* guide and chose the restaurant with more care than we had chosen the assisted living community. We were desperate for her to love it, to eat with her usual gusto, to celebrate her day and the fact that we were all together. But as we knew but didn't consider amid our wishful thinking, Ménière's disease makes noisy places intolerable, a babble of voices with no distinction between foreground and background conversation. The tables were close and the chairs uncomfortable. My mother, who loved nothing more than eating, picked at her food, winced in discomfort, and all but begged to leave before dessert. In my car afterward, she cried. I had never seen my mother cry, not even at my father's funeral.

By late June, my mother had essentially taken to her bed, overcome by vertigo and the accompanying fear of falling. On the rare occasions when she got up, her legs were clearly weakening. Medically, all three of us understood that something was terribly amiss, but we were immobilized. Was the tumor advancing? Had weeks of immobility taken a toll? Was anxiety exacerbating the Ménière's disease? Was she suffering small strokes? Was the tingling in both feet and hands diabetic neuropathy or a combination of anything and everything? Dr. Saltzman was at a loss. She upped the Antivert, for the dizziness, and added Valium. We talked of checking my mother into a local hospital, under Dr. Saltzman's care, for yet another battery of tests. Michael called the neurosurgeon to report her deteriorating condition and ask if we should return. My mother, who hated doctors, alternated between wanting to pursue a fresh diagnosis, by one route or another, and refusing more poking and prodding.

Days before I was to go on vacation in August, I realized that under these conditions there was no way I could leave my mother with my brother solely responsible. My vacation spot, for many years, had been a cabin in Martha's Vineyard, with no telephone and no cell reception. Being off the grid, remote, and unreachable had always been the appeal of the place. If I wanted to talk to someone, I drove down a long dirt road to the nearest pay phone or to the crest of a nearby hill, where I could pick up a hit-or-miss cell signal. But to go there now, given my nature, would mean twitching every waking moment I was in the cabin and spending the better part of two weeks searching out a telephone to make sure everything was okay or to hear the many ways in which it wasn't. My mother and Michael said all the right things: I needed a vacation. They'd be fine. They'd find me if they needed me. They probably even meant it. But I knew my own anxiety would overwhelm the trip, that I'd be worse off away than home. It was Monday, August 6, 2001. I had a ferry reservation for Sunday, August 12. I called my employer's human resources department.

Surely I had no right to expect someone to fix in less than a week a situation that had been deteriorating for months. But within hours, I was in a conference room at Fine Newcombe & Winsby. At the table with me was Nick Newcombe, one of the original principals, and Barbara Clark, the social work supervisor. I told them our story, of choosing an assisted living facility that could neither fill my mother's needs nor let me hire someone to fill them. I told them I saw no hope of negotiating a workable solution because I had "poisoned the well" with management, by then more than once. I told them I was coming unglued. I told them Michael and my mother were insisting I go on vacation but that that seemed impossible and counterproductive.

Nick agreed that I'd mishandled my dealings with the director, but that was water under the bridge, especially since it was clearly not where my mother belonged. The immediate task was to get her to an appropriate facility. He told me I needed to go away as planned, that he and Barbara would make that possible, and he laid out how. First, they would ask Dr. Saltzman to instruct the facility that my mother's changed status required twenty-four-hour care and a wheelchair, thus putting medical muscle behind what had so far been the requests and ravings of someone (me) who had long ago been pigeonholed as hysterical. Then, dispassionately and with the heft of her own professional credentials, Barbara would negotiate with the Meadowview about how to make that happen for an interim period until we could find a suitable placement. They would hire two aides, each on a twelve-hour shift. One of Barbara's junior social workers would visit my mom regularly during the transition. In the few days remaining before my vacation, Michael and I would go look at two alternative places nearby: a highly regarded nursing home and also an assisted living facility that Nick and Barbara already knew accepted residents with live-in aides and wheelchairs.

Nick and Barbara expected to help us decide which place was preferable, guide us through the application process, and in the meantime, with the junior social worker as their eyes and ears, supervise the aides and monitor what was going on at the Meadowview. If we wanted to go forward, their case management fee was $150 an hour, plus the hefty (but at that point incalculable) cost of the aides. Nick explained the pros and cons, financial and otherwise, of a nursing home as opposed to an assisted living apartment with 24/7 help. He seemed to be leaning toward the nursing home, largely because there, should my mother run out of money, as she likely would, her care would be paid for by Medicaid. In an assisted living facility, as I've said, someone who can't pay out of pocket must leave, forcing another move.

Should we choose another assisted living apartment, Nick said, we would need to monitor my mother's finances closely, because it was best to apply to a nursing home before she was broke. In other words, we should make that move when she still had, say, $30,000 and could pay her own way for a few months, he said, thus improving the odds of admission at the best and most competitive places. I didn't understand the whole Medicaid thing, and I wouldn't, except in the most rudimentary way, until long after my mother was dead. But my free ninety minutes were exhausted, so I didn't have to delve into its mysteries. Plus, my top priority was discussing the plan, and the cost, with my mother and brother. Nick and Barbara were ready to go to work the next morning, Tuesday, August 7, if we were all on board.

This was a no-brainer, and none of us even knew yet that the cost of all these services—hourly case management, the aides, and the initial consultation (had it not been an employment benefit)—would count toward my mother's Medicaid spend-down. We had finally acknowledged that we needed professional help, and we would have robbed a bank to get it.

Now, when friends protest that they can't afford geriatric care management for their parents or in-laws, who have very limited assets, I try to explain that this is an expenditure doubly worth making: it will solve problems, often more economically, than you could solve them yourself in hit-or-miss fashion, and it accelerates the Medicaid spend-down. A few months back, Michael, without realizing it, had already launched the spend-down when he consulted an elder law attorney, Gregg Weiss, who had handled earlier legal work for my mother, about our rights, under the lease we had signed, to hire care for my mother at the Meadowview. It turned out we had none. Now we had, instead, the third-party diplomacy of a care manager, who, we hoped, could cut a deal.

Over the next five days, things moved quickly but without that heady, anything-is-possible rush I remembered from the weeks surrounding moving my mother to New York. The past nine months had chastened all three of us. I wouldn't say we were smarter, only that we knew how much we didn't know. Also, we were well on the way to changing our definition of success. My mother was never again going to have the life she had in Florida—narrow, to be sure, but not without its small pleasures. She was never again going to be self-sufficient, independent of her children's interference, and we were never again, until her death, going to be free of responsibility for her well-being. Three people who had been family more in name than in fact, not estranged but certainly distant from one another in our day-to-day lives, were now working in harness, toward finding a safe harbor for my mother to live out her dwindling and increasingly difficult days.

On Tuesday, at Barbara Clark's request, Dr. Saltzman faxed a current medical evaluation to the director at the Meadowview. The goal was to kick-start a process that required the facility, under state regulations, to temporarily meet a resident's safety and personal needs while a discharge plan was being put into place. Dr. Saltzman, with no need to embellish, described my mother as "quite incapacitated," requiring twenty-four-hour-a-day assistance with some of the so-called activities of daily living. She did not need to be in a skilled nursing facility, Dr. Saltzman wrote, which we hoped would forestall any attempt to solve the problem by moving my mother to the on-premises nursing home. My brother faxed the doctor thanks for "artful" help in "crafting a short-term solution."

All day Wednesday the director at the Meadowview was unresponsive, contacting not Dr. Saltzman, the care managers, Michael, or me. I was leaving Barbara multiple messages but keeping my word that I would attempt no contact with the Meadowview myself. My mother was a mess, dizzier with every passing hour, and calling me with a play-by-play of another day of neglect: struggling to prepare her own food and to get dressed without help, afraid that every trip to the bathroom could lead to a fall. Her agitation, as if contagious, fed my own. Neither of us trusted that anything would go as planned.

In one note I faxed to Barbara from my office, mentioning the "deafening silence," I wrote of my own state of mind and my mother's. "She grows increasingly agitated by their inattention, and even asking her who has done what sends her into a Ménière's attack," I wrote of my mother. "She calls and calls and calls and then tells me that talking to me about it makes her upset and dizzy." As for myself, I told Barbara, I "need desperately, more than desperately," to get away, but didn't think Michael "really understands how much running back and forth he'll have to do if she is still unattended. So anything you can say about the vacation issue would be helpful, even if it's not what I want to hear. I'm struggling to untangle everyone else's needs, my needs, guilt, obsession, etc. I'm sure none of this is original to you."

Aware that the Meadowview was giving her the brush-off, Barbara sent the young social worker over there first thing on Thursday. She succeeded both in calming down my mother and in assuring the director that we were hard at work finding a new place for her to live. Surely the management there didn't want a big fuss on their hands by refusing a legal request that my mother be safe in the meantime, not when they would otherwise soon be rid of us. Barbara and the director played phone tag through the day, but it was clear we would have the rotation of aides in place by Friday. They would wind up caring for my mother for twenty days at a cost of $3,679.50, based on a weekday rate of $180 per day and a weekend rate of $189.

On Friday, Michael and I went to see the Hebrew Home for the Aged, on the banks of the Hudson River in Riverdale, the most prestigious nursing home in the New York City metropolitan area. We intended to look at the small assisted living building on the main campus, even now clinging to our reluctance to "put our mother away," and thinking we could later transition her to the skilled nursing facility if necessary. But River West, as it was called, was already inadequate to her needs. Instead we toured six nursing floors, each with forty-eight residents, two RNs, and six CNAs, or certified nursing assistants, on duty at all times. The admissions director, unbidden, told us the ratio of aides to residents was "never enough." Her honesty was appealing, as was the fact that they gave us no hard sell. The Hebrew Home, with a roster of celebrity residents, or residents with celebrity children, does not need to market itself in that way. It always has a waiting list. It helps to know somebody, and I did, a childhood friend on the board of directors. I counted as a player, and in this family crisis my usual scruples about using connections took a backseat.

Our next stop, on Saturday, was an Atria assisted living facility, also in Riverdale. Atria was an up-and-comer in the field, after the hotel companies bowed out, and I'd heard good things about the chain. This was one of its newer properties, with a capacity of 220 and 100 current residents, as the pushy salesperson told us. We could have a one-bedroom apartment, with room for a live-in aide on a pull-out sofa in the living room, for $3,295 a month, discounted from the list price of $3,650. Warning bells went off in my head. Michael and I made pointed eye contact. The spiel continued, but we weren't listening. Our minds were made up: our mother would go to the nursing home. Michael's decision, he later said, was based on "reluctantly realizing we were way past" assisted living and needed a "multitrack place" that could offer increasing support as my mother, inevitably, needed it. My certainty came from the fact that I'd already been on one shakedown cruise in a brand-new, half-empty facility, and I wasn't prepared to go on another. I was also hungry for the kind of support I knew we'd all get at the Hebrew Home. Michael and I might have had different reasons for our certainty, and maybe even overlapping ones, but this was the most important decision we had made so far, and we were in utter harmony.

When I tracked Barbara down eight years later, she explained that a new assisted living facility often works fine for less disabled residents, who bond more easily because they are all newcomers together. But my mother needed the peace of a well-oiled operation. And I was so worn out from the Meadowview experience that I craved the security blanket of a nursing home, with dense staffing that included social workers, psychologists, physical and occupational therapists, and clergy, all of them ready to support me, too. "Once she was there," Barbara recalled, "it was such a tremendous relief for you, and probably for your mom, too. You were tired and resentful. With the luxury of other people caring for her, you could go back to being her daughter."

Hard on myself as I am, I don't think I chose a nursing home over another assisted living facility because I longed for the embrace of all those caring people. I think it was in my mother's best interests. But it is certainly a question worth asking yourself, as is asking the opposite—whether you're choosing assisted living over skilled nursing for the chandeliers and spiral staircases. Guilt-ridden, overburdened adult children are generally the consumers, the ones making these decisions. But this isn't about us—it's about them. How easy that is to say, and how hard it is to live!

For sure, my neediness was real, and instantly apparent once I had someone other than Michael helping me; his cool competence had been both a comfort and a rebuke. Now I had Barbara, a stranger whose job it was to look after me. Finally, I was free to fall apart, and so I did. The night before I was to leave on vacation, already packed for my trip but roiled by ambivalence, I called her for another round of reassurance that it was okay to go, that I wasn't a bad daughter, that the world wasn't going to come to an end while I was away.

Later she told me that this obsession with controlling every aspect of an aged parent's care, this false belief that only you can do it right, is common among daughters. "Whether it's a positive or a negative relationship, you are so emotionally connected," she said. "Then the role reversal comes, and you set a certain standard. Sometimes it's because she took such good care of you as a child, and sometimes it's because she didn't and you want to show her up."

We spoke on the phone for two hours and forty-five minutes that steamy August night in 2001. The bill was $400.50. I suspect it was the most expensive telephone call I've ever made. Until now, I've never told my brother either its length or its cost. He would not have needed that much handholding. Neither would many, if not most, of you. But I did. Without it, I would not have been capable of driving to Woods Hole on Sunday, boarding the 3:45 p.m. ferry, settling into the cabin, taking a swim at dusk in Great Tisbury Pond, falling into bed while it was still light, and sleeping for fourteen hours.

CHAPTER 5

The Best Doctors Money Can Buy

My two weeks away were as restorative as intended. I imposed on a local Realtor and friend so Michael would have an emergency phone contact, since I was so far off the grid. Otherwise, when I was in cell phone range, we must have spoken every day or so, and I must have spoken to my mother, because I recall both of them describing their visit to the Hebrew Home and their shared conviction that it was the right place for her. But my customary anxiety that something would go wrong, that I shouldn't be so out of reach, didn't plague me. I didn't spend hours scouting places where my cell phone had at least two bars, or waiting on pay phone lines, or beeping my home answering machine. I wasn't fretful, distracted, or feeling guilty morning, noon, and night. Maybe I was worn past the point where I could sustain that kind of constant worry; maybe I trusted that Nick and Barbara would make everything all right.

Regardless, what stays with me from that trip—along with many more nights of deep slumber after that first one—is long days swimming with the college-age daughter of a childhood friend, who came for a week's visit. Even now, when the world closes in, I conjure us in that cool water, our only companions in Great Tisbury Pond a pair of swans. Sometimes we swam great distances. Other times we dog-paddled and yacked about the things women yack about. Afterward, some nights, we ate s'mores instead of dinner and fell into bed with our faces still sticky from melted chocolate and burned marshmallows. At no other time in the last few years of my mother's life are the pages of my daily calendar utterly blank, one after another, with not a single jotting.

Returning home was a jolt, literally an assault on my senses. I had been living steps from a tidal pond, down the road from the pounding ocean, amid wild rosa rugosa and rustling oak; I took my nightly shower outdoors, facing into the sunset, ate lobster fresh off the boat, and generally let myself go limp after what seemed like months of relentless crises. The dread didn't even descend on the long drive home, and I still had sand in my shoes when I got to my mother's apartment. Then I opened the door and was hit in the face by the unmistakable stench of urine. Surely this must have been a sudden, one-of-a-kind accident. My brother had been in and out many times while I was away. An aide had been there around the clock, or so I thought. My face surely reflected my shock, even before I was fully inside. Then my mother and I locked eyes. We didn't speak of it, beyond her uncharacteristic and just-above-a-whisper words, "I'm so relieved you're back."

Instead, we talked of my trip, her pleasure that I'd been able to relax and enjoy myself, her impressions of the nursing home—so much more accepting than Michael and I had been on our initial visit—and her astonishment at its cost. A single room (our goal, given her solitary nature) cost $14,000 a month, she reported, then quickly turned to the kind of macabre commentary for which she was famous. "By the time you push me through the revolving door, I'll be spent down," she said, having quickly mastered the lingo of Medicaid and, more important, the inevitable and irreversible nature of this next move. She had always had this unsentimental sense of humor, although until recently I didn't always appreciate it, choosing instead to be aggrieved by some insult, real or imagined, in that way that, between mothers and daughters, can drown out what would otherwise be simple banter. But this was an unambiguously funny remark, even to me: my mother at her very best.

That was Monday, August 27. I had taken an extra vacation day to spend time with her, unpack, pay bills, and otherwise get settled before returning to work, to be swept back into the maelstrom. My mother waited until Wednesday—tight-lipped as always? considerate in a way I never gave her credit for? silenced by fear of a special magnitude? Then, without elaboration or self-pity, she told me that she was incontinent, in pretty much those words. She said nothing about how long it had been going on, whether my brother knew, or why the aide hadn't attended to it. She said nothing more, except that I should take some money out of her wallet and go buy her adult diapers. And, oh, by the way, while I was at the store, she could also use some oatmeal—the instant kind—and Sweet'n Low in the individual packets. She relayed the information like the nurse she had been, clinically and matter-of-factly. There was nothing matter-of-fact about it to me.

As soon as I heard the word *diapers,* my mind went blank. The next thing I remember is being in a local supermarket. I know that market as well as the age spots on my own hands, but now I was lost, foreign-country kind of lost, blundering up and down the aisles, as if I were there for the first time. In my daze, I all but bumped into a neighbor. "Oatmeal?" "Sweet'n Low?" "Diapers?" I was incoherent. But the neighbor, blessedly herself a caregiver for two aged parents, sized up the situation instantly and led me, like the scared child I suddenly was, from aisle to aisle, product to product. On the checkout line, she silently squeezed my hand, and we went our separate ways. At that point, again, I went numb. I remember absolutely nothing of the next thirty-six hours.

Parenthetically, a friend offered her interpretation as to why my mother seemed so unfazed while I found the diaper purchase so traumatic, a rubicon of such significance that I still can't walk down that aisle of the supermarket without tearing up. For me, the friend ventured, it was an abrupt, disorienting change, a bright white line, while to my mother it was incremental. She had for many months been caught between the rock-and-hard-place of risking a fall on the way to the bathroom or soiling herself, a common scenario among the frail aged. Only in retrospect did it become clear to me that the flurry of emergency room visits that winter and spring had been a result of her choosing the dangerous rush to the toilet rather than the diaper. (This is what geriatricians call functional incontinence, to distinguish it from disease, and they have practical suggestions, which I'll itemize later, to avoid it.)

By now the diapers were probably a relief for my mother, my friend hypothesized, one less thing to worry about, surely preferable to the falls, head wounds, and nights in the ER. The lesson in my friend's observation is that the line moves. What had once seemed unendurable to an aged parent, and still does to us, the adult children, changes. They come to tolerate the formerly intolerable and to surprise us with their forbearance. Diapers, it turned out, were not the end of the world. Nor was a wheelchair, despite initial resistance. Millimeter by millimeter the line was moving, as it would many times more.

This is one reason professionals regard living wills as misguided documents without the added protection of a health care proxy. The living will sets out the general premise that heroic treatment is unwelcome, that you do not want your life prolonged in certain ways past a certain point. But who can say, years ahead of time, what treatment is welcome and unwelcome, or when the time has come to say "enough"? Not wanting "heroic" measures, the standard language in a living will, means one thing at fifty and another thing at ninety. Your definition of quality of life can change to encompass previously unthinkable things, like paralysis. No living will can account for that, can itemize all contingencies across the great arc of time and circumstance, unless its writer were to do little else but update the document. It is the proxy's job to understand this, to grasp both the abiding principles of what a loved one would want and the ever-changing details and attitudes. A well-chosen health care proxy appreciates that the line will move and decisions must intuitively move with it.

My mother now decided to return to Sloan-Kettering for the surgery she had avoided nine months earlier, not wanting it back then but never having to say so because the doctor preferred to wait and watch. Had she been mulling this over for a long time, in that slow and silent way she made all big decisions, without discussion or even a hint of what was going on inside her head? Had her precipitous recent decline scared her enough to prompt a hasty, even impulsive, change of mind? Was it the impending move to a nursing home and all that that implied? I have no clue. All I am sure of is that one Wednesday afternoon at around two o'clock I was out buying diapers for my mother, and that a week later, almost to the minute, she was on an operating table about to be anesthetized for surgery.

Even now, what I know is limited to the contents of 270 pages of medical records acquired from Memorial Sloan-Kettering Cancer Center and an interview, more than six years later, with Dr. Bilsky, her surgeon there. Only after seeing those records, not because of anything Michael or I remember, do I know that she was admitted to Sloan on Friday, August 31. Whether my mother's thought process had been deliberative or sudden, we had not been in the decision-making loop in any meaningful way.

My mother, as I've said, had always been a private person, not one to share her thoughts or fears, either with me or with the tiny number of women she counted as "friends" but held beyond arm's length. She had returned to New York, not only for convenience and necessity, but presumably with the understanding that the time had come for us to function as a family, to make decisions together. That had seemed to me such a promising sign. We had planned and carried out the move together, considered the pros and cons of various scenarios, and now, suddenly, my mother had again retreated into secrecy. Before Michael and I knew what had hit us, my mother, with Dr. Bilsky's acquiescence if not approval, had commandeered the train, and it was hurtling in a direction we had not discussed, considered, or had the skill, presence of mind, or right to stop. Wise or not, fair or not, my mother's life was her own to manage as she wished, despite the fact that her decisions would affect all three of us.

The only light Michael could shed on my mother's unilateral behavior (and he generously spared me this information while I was gone so I could have the real vacation he said I deserved) was that during my absence she had already gone off the family reservation once, "firing" the overnight aide on her first night of duty, presumably for tardiness, without consulting him either before or afterward. She had also declared to the geriatric care team and the Meadowview supervisors, again without bringing Michael into the conversation, that she didn't want a replacement, disliked having someone watching over her while she slept, and was perfectly capable of getting to the bathroom or using a bedside commode. When Michael figured out that she was alone at night (after thinking she'd had a brief tantrum over a late-arriving aide and then resumed the planned schedule), he was alarmed enough to reach out to Dr. Saltzman. "What this signifies to us," he told her in a fax, "is the need to move even faster." By that he meant rush the admissions paperwork to the Hebrew Home, since my mother wasn't safe all by herself overnight.

Did Dr. Saltzman talk to my mother, and did they together decide on the belated surgery? I don't know, Dr. Saltzman doesn't remember, and it seems unlikely. She had seen my mother only once, at the start of a potentially rewarding doctor-patient relationship but not one yet. Dr. Bilsky, in retrospect, also had no idea what had changed my mother's mind; he had met her only twice himself before her hospital admission and probably spent more time reviewing the case with me recently than he'd spent with our family during the nine months my mother was his patient. In our limited time with him in 2001, he had seemed to me arrogant, callow, and too cavalier about the prospect of surgery on someone my mother's age, with multiple chronic conditions.

I no longer trust my memory, or the completeness of my notes on our initial consultation with Dr. Bilsky. I know we had questions galore, as journalists would, and wrote down the answers. But we were too overwrought to ask everything we should have or to process what Dr. Bilsky told us intelligently. Even geriatric professionals, as I've read in their personal narratives in the journal *Health Affairs* and elsewhere, have found a lifetime of professional skills useless when faced with responsibility for an aged parent. Their stories have made me feel less foolish: if geriatricians can't manage this situation, I ought to stop beating myself up for feeling both stupid and overwhelmed. But I'm sure about one thing, because it's in my notebook multiple times, flanked by quotation marks, and its syntax is so distinctive. Dr. Bilsky told us at our initial consultation, and again in identical words in subsequent conversations: "I can pop that sucker out, easy!" Technically, he was true to his word.

According to my mother's hospital records, on the day of her admission, various interns and nurses—but not Dr. Bilsky—began their initial entries by noting her age and multiple medical problems, or "co-morbidities." She had had progressive weakness on her right side over the previous two months. Her right leg, their notes say, was all but useless; her right arm less so, but she could no longer tie her shoes, write, or reliably hold objects, including a cup of water that she dropped while answering questions during the admissions process. The right side of her face was drooping, and she drooled from that side of her mouth. She had been incontinent, in more than the "I can't get to the bathroom in time" sense, she told them, for the previous two or three days. She reported a recent spike in neck and back pain, as well as a marked increase in depression and anxiety, along with decreased appetite, concentration, and interest in normal activities like watching television. All who examined her attributed the symptoms above her waist to "ischemic brain changes," or minor strokes, since the location of the thoracic tumor would not account for them.

She was alert, fluent, and oriented; she passed with flying colors the cognitive tests of naming objects, recalling them later, and following three-step commands. She refused many medical tests, like a mammogram or Pap smear, not immediately related to her complaints, as she had declined them for many years. (In this she was well ahead of her time. Testing without regard for whether the patient would choose follow-up treatment, as I touched on earlier, is one factor in America's health care inflation and in the dangerous depletion of the Medicare trust fund.) She also refused a visit from a social worker, a chaplain, or any other psychosocial service, and none was forced on her despite her mental health history and her acknowledgment of escalating depression and anxiety.

The surgeon's brief entry, upon admission, notes the condition of my mother's right leg ("practically useless") and right arm ("progressively weak") without any elaboration. He then disappears from the written record until the day of surgery. We never spoke to him during the time she was at the hospital or heard from him again afterward. I'm sure many specialists at Sloan, and probably Dr. Bilsky is among them, are more involved with their patients and families, especially those with malignant or complex cancers. My mother's tumor was neither. Her procedure was, for Dr. Bilsky, routine, and her rehab would be conducted at a well-regarded facility that he knew was more than up to the task. In retrospect, my expectations of forming a working relationship with him were not reasonable. Our mistake was to expect a neurosurgeon to play the role of family doctor for an old, sick, and frightened woman and to guide us, her children, through the medical decision-making process.

As I did with so many other things, I discussed my mother's situation, the mistakes I thought we made as a family, and what we might have done differently many times over the ensuing years with Dr. Leipzig at Mount Sinai, who became first a source and eventually a friend. "A surgeon sees what he's going to operate on, not the person around it," she explained. "You needed an advocate, somebody working for you, to go up against the specialists, to ask what medical care *should* occur in this situation, not merely what was possible." The consulting specialists at Sloan, I told her, had consistently seemed far less persuaded than Dr. Bilsky that my mother would benefit from surgery. Could or should they have been more forceful in their dissent? Dr. Leipzig said the question was essentially moot, as he would not have listened to them, absent life-or-death reasons.

Other experts I spoke with over the years found this characterization unfair. Our family had *started* at a specialty hospital; had we had a good internist or family practice doctor, my mother's care would likely have been handled more holistically. When a patient shows up at a cancer hospital, these experts argue, the assumption is that she wants aggressive treatment. Why else would she be there? Moreover, Sloan pioneered the practice of psycho-oncology and has long had a psychiatrist on staff whose expertise is cancer patients and their loved ones. We never sought, and indeed my mother rejected, that kind of guidance. "It was your initial decision to go there that set things off on the wrong track," Carol Levine, at the United Hospital Fund, told me. On the basis of multiple experiences at Sloan, she agreed about only one of my criticisms, that they "don't do as well with older patients" as they might—or didn't before the introduction of the geriatric service.

Dr. Beatriz Korc, the head of that geriatric service, is now trying to introduce a less-is-sometimes-more mind-set. She agreed that, in dealing with the elderly, surgeons fail to see the wider picture. Her team's brief is to identify patients based on age and the number of overlapping, chronic, and acute illnesses, and to ask about each of their tests and treatments, "To what purpose?" The answer is generally clear, she said, for the "very fit or the very vulnerable." With the intermediate group, on the continuum between life and death, where my mother fell, "it's hard to know if you're doing more harm than good," Dr. Korc continued, and explained that a test or treatment is likely to have an impact—brief or lasting the rest of their lives—beyond the disease it was intended to diagnose or cure.

The decision about whether an older patient is an appropriate candidate for surgery is often made in the context of what some call "binary thinking" ("I'm healthy and I'm fine" or "I'm dead"), with little recognition or acknowledgment of the potential—no, the likelihood—that the patient will experience a lengthy period of deepening disability and dependence between those two extremes, often exacerbated by surgery. Families commonly fail to plan for this protracted, tortured, and expensive in-between state until faced with it, whether because the elderly person refuses to discuss it, the adult children shy away from the subject, or everyone tacitly agrees to remain silent. Whichever is the dominant reason, the results are uniformly bad. We, unlike many families, had all my mother's end-of-life paperwork in order, but we had no strategies for what could be the long haul between "well" and "gone."

The *New Old Age* blog, responding to one daughter's struggle to discuss that in-between time with her father, who was well prepared for death but not for extended infirmity, asked Dr. Muriel Gillick, a palliative care specialist at Harvard Medical School, about the psychology of what she identified as binary thinking. Why is it less threatening, Paula Span, one of the blog's authors, asked, "to plan one's memorial service than to consider a move into assisted living?"

Dr. Gillick, author of *The Denial of Aging: Perpetual Youth, Eternal Life, and Other Dangerous Fantasies* (Cambridge, Mass.: Harvard University Press, 2007), said it's easier to confront death than to confront dying: "People at some level do recognize that they're not immortal," but they do not consider "a period of decline and disability" as inevitable, perhaps because "it's painful to think about."

This blind spot, shared by many physicians, Dr. Gillick told *The New Old Age,* can have unwelcome results. "We typically tell [families] what the odds of [the patient's] dying on the table are, and they're pleased to learn they're pretty low," Dr. Gillick said. "What they're not told is the likelihood of spending six weeks in the hospital having one complication after another, following which they're so de-conditioned they aren't able to go home and have to go to a nursing home, and they'll be there for several months and may not get better. That's the scenario we don't present."

This is one way of explaining why we were racing toward surgery with almost no discussion of its potential aftermath—between my mother and her children, between me and Michael, or between our family and Dr. Bilsky. We had the intellectual, financial, and professional resources to do this right, and eventually we would. We had a mother who had made so many parts of her aging easy: no car-key struggles, no whining, no interest in having every test and procedure medical science had to offer. But she also was secretive, and my brother and I, at the seemingly oddest moments, were incurious, almost passive, beneath our competent exteriors, while at other moments we let hectic forward motion replace thoughtful decision-making.

"You fed it, I fed it, you fed it," Michael said later, comparing the sensation to being on a runaway train. "It did kind of take over."

Both Michael and I, at the time and also with hindsight, found my mother's decision to have surgery when she did mysterious and Dr. Bilsky's willingness, even eagerness, to perform it suspect, but did not speak up. Various attending and consulting physicians, and Dr. Bilsky himself, doubted that removing the tumor would result in any improvement in her current condition, given the advanced stage of her symptoms. But all held out the hope of arresting further loss of function from the waist down. Did they mean preventing complete failure of her bladder? Avoiding bowel incontinence, too? Did they mean keeping her right leg from becoming totally useless instead of almost totally useless? But wouldn't the assault of major surgery make everything else that was ailing her worse, perhaps accelerate the incidence of the small strokes that she was already having? It wasn't like everything was hunky-dory except for that pesky tumor. What was the risk-benefit ratio here? To me it seemed foolishly late in the game, a Hail Mary pass at best—surgery done because that's what surgeons do.

During my recent meeting with Dr. Bilsky, he did not, to my surprise, defend the decision to operate with the vigor I expected. He was neither defensive nor as arrogant and callow as I remembered. He said that this type of surgery is gratifying because 98 percent of people improve, sometimes dramatically, and perhaps my mother would have been one of them had he done it months earlier. He reiterated that his original hope was that her condition would never deteriorate to the extent it did and his goal, when he finally operated, was to halt further degeneration, not get her up on her feet again. "Bowel continence alone is worth preserving," he said. But when so many other medical problems exist, it's a "roll of the dice," and "it's hard to know where all the symptoms were coming from."

"There is no right and wrong here," Dr. Bilsky said. "It's all about judgment. And in hindsight it's very clear we intervened too late."

In fairness, my mother not only kept secrets from me and Michael during this interlude, as she always had, and as she did with her internists in Florida and with Dr. Saltzman. At Sloan, she withheld information from the doctors and nurses at her two early consultations and then subsequently let so much deterioration occur without telling anyone. I'm not sure how, during the two weeks I was away, she managed to keep from the social workers at Fine Newcombe & Winsby that she had become increasingly symptomatic and finally incontinent, or that she had only a day aide, not an overnight aide. But my hunch is that Barbara's arrangement with the Meadowview included using their employees as aides, and that they were not transmitting information as they should have been. Within weeks of my mother's move to a nursing home, all this subterfuge would be beside the point, thanks to a loving cast of nurses and social workers who slowly gained her trust, required us to attend and then delicately managed regular family meetings, and came, over time, to know us both as a family unit and as three very distinct individuals. But this is not what specialty care hospitals like Sloan-Kettering are best at, and a strong argument can be made that they shouldn't be.

In short-term relationships with doctors, Dr. Bilsky told me, patients commonly fail to provide accurate information—that is, in less gentle parlance, they tell lies, whether of omission or commission. They do so either to get treatment if they want it or to avoid it if they don't. "Everybody tells you what they want to tell you as a way of directing their own care," he said, adding that doctors do something similar when they quote prognostic data, to encourage procedures they are eager to do and discourage those they aren't. His honesty was bracing. It made me like him better than I had but feel even less secure that we adult children have much influence in our aged parents' medical care, absent a place where geriatric physicians, social workers, psychiatrists, physical and occupational therapists, pharmacists, and who knows who else are all managing the case as a team. Alas, such situations are the exception, not the rule, except in palliative care units, which more than doubled in number between 2000 and 2008.

Even with the explosion of palliative care in recent years—at this writing, 1,300 physicians are certified in the specialty—a "culture of rescue" still dominates American medicine, according to Sherwin B. Nuland, in a 2010 update to *How We Die: Reflections on Life's Final Chapter.* Dr. Nuland writes, in a coda to his sixteen-year-old best seller, that physicians continue to get their "psychic reward" in end-of-life "heroics," however hopeless and even tortuous; are schooled in "conquering" disease rather than "comforting" the dying, even when the results are "carnage"; and, all these years after he first took them to task, have failed to "demedicalize death."

Recently I had a conversation with Dr. Leipzig about concrete ways others could avoid these pitfalls. It ended with me crying in regret for all the now-obvious things I could have done differently. Some might characterize remaining so overwrought all these years later as a sign of what experts call "complicated grief," which extends long past the normal duration. I disagree, since my emotions were never before this close to the surface—not during her actual dying, her death, or its immediate aftermath, nor during the years I wrote about these topics as a journalist—because I was writing about strangers, not myself, and was shielded, actually and metaphorically, behind a notebook. Now, in choosing to guide others through this process by revisiting my own family's experience, the old dust was flying and tears came easily and often. This was one of those moments.

"I didn't ask any of the right questions," I said to Dr. Leipzig.

"That's because you didn't know what questions to ask," she answered. "You thought the doctors would lead the conversation, and they didn't."

"I did the best I could. I did the best I could, and it wasn't good enough."

"That's because of the system," Dr. Leipzig said. "You can't do better than you did in this system. Hold on to that."

In the days following my mother's admission to Sloan, scans taken of her heart and lungs showed nothing that would preclude surgery. These same tests had been done many months earlier, but were justified because her condition had changed in important ways. No tests were ordered to reassess the liver mass, probably because she refused them; nor is the original finding mentioned in any of the daily hospital notes. What is noted, for those five days, are several bouts of extreme vertigo (some of the doctors accepted the long-standing Ménière's diagnosis and others disputed it) and a marked deterioration in mood and demeanor toward the staff (as at admission, no psychological or social work consultation was ordered or even encouraged). Michael and I were unaware of the episodes of vertigo but were painfully aware of her mood and demeanor as our daily visits became dreaded occasions. Garden-variety crankiness had become verbal hostility that I would consider abusive in almost any other setting or situation; often she sullenly turned away and refused to even acknowledge us when we entered the room.

We had seen this a dozen years before, during my mother's two knee replacements. My brother attributes it to a former nurse's intense dislike of doctors and to her shock at the deterioration in nursing care since her era. I don't disagree but would add the utter loss of control that comes with being a hospital patient—surely more stressful for someone as set in her ways as my mother. Medical professionals have subsequently told me that extreme behavior is an especially common reaction to hospitalization among the elderly, even those without my mother's lifelong temperament: they come unglued psychologically and/or cognitively, entering the hospital in what seems to be a fully intact state, only to become delirious while there.

The research on hospital-related delirium is growing. Among the findings: about one-third of hospitalized patients over seventy will experience it, and the percentage is higher among those who have had surgery or spend time in an intensive care unit, according to the American Geriatric Society. Research at Harvard Medical School and its affiliated hospitals and at Indiana University's Center for Aging have shown that delirium extends the length of hospitalizations, delays scheduled procedures, and requires extra attention from staff, all costly to the health care system, as well as to the patient and family. Those who suffer hospital-related delirium, the research shows, wind up placed in nursing homes 75 percent of the time—five times as often as those without it. Nearly one in ten elderly with the condition die within a month and 35 to 40 percent within a year. The condition is often misdiagnosed, sometimes belittled as mere confusion or labeled as more serious dementia—Alzheimer's or one of its related fatal diseases—even when it isn't (although those who suffer hospital-related delirium seem more likely, later on, to develop full-blown dementia).

As I write, the causes for hospital (and emergency room) delirium among the elderly are only speculative. They include infection; adverse medication reactions; constant light and noise; being without eyeglasses, hearing aids, or dentures for extended periods; and the feeling of anxiety and entrapment that may accompany catheters, intravenous lines, and other confining equipment.

According to Dr. Patricia Bloom, a geriatrician at Mount Sinai Medical Center, 4 percent of elderly patients show complete resolution of these symptoms at discharge and 18 percent at six months. (My mother fell into the second category.) Dr. Bloom says she is unaware of data tracking patients beyond that point or of research on progression from hospital delirium to actual dementia. But, she said, based on anecdotal observation, undiagnosed early-stage dementia is often "unmasked" by a hospitalization, in sudden symptoms of paranoia that require treatment with a mild antipsychotic medication. Such a patient "rarely goes back" to normal, Dr. Bloom said, suggesting that the delirium may have dramatically hastened the inevitable. I have several friends whose parents, perhaps a bit forgetful but nothing worse than that, entered the hospital following a stroke or a broken pelvis and afterward seemed to have acquired serious dementia, as if overnight, never to recover. This was not the case with my mother.

The doctors would have initiated no discussion of my mother's hospitalization with my brother or me unless one of us effectively captured them by coming at dawn and staying well into the evening to talk with them, and even then our opportunities were limited to a few minutes. Yes, I know these are busy people, white coattails flying as they make rounds. But still. Not taking the time to talk to us, in my view, was a serious misunderstanding of how to provide good care to the elderly whose family members should be included as their responsibility grows, absent an outright declaration from the patient to exclude them. (Such a declaration would have been noted in the record for purposes of legal adherence to HIPAA, the federal law involving patient confidentiality; hospitals are rigidly obedient in this area, often going beyond what the statute requires in terms of privacy rather than risking sanction.)

On Wednesday, September 5, at 2:13 p.m., a week after my mother's bland announcement that she was incontinent, she was wheeled into the operating room. There Dr. Bilsky made an incision in her thoracic spine and performed a laminectomy, an intradural exploration and resection of the tumor. It was 1.5 by 1.1 centimeters in size. The surgery was completed at 5:52 p.m., with "minimal blood loss" and "no complications"; "the patient tolerated the surgery well," the medical records say. "Disposition: To the recovery room in good condition." The walk-on-water surgeon my brother and I had successfully set out to find had, as promised, "popped that sucker out, easy."

In the recovery room, when my mother's eyes fluttered open, Michael, in relief, wept great torrents. I stood by, emotionless, and studied the expression on her face, which shifted from wide-eyed surprise to tight-jawed anger. Even before my mother spoke, I knew she was pissed.

"I only had the surgery because I thought I'd die on the table." This, I was sure, was not one of my mother's black jokes but the absolute truth, and the explanation for her otherwise bewildering decision to have the surgery at this late date.

Great, Ma, I thought, not saying those words or any others aloud, as I was too enraged to trust myself to speak. *You lost your bet, and now all three of us get to live with whatever happens next.*

I never for a moment doubted that dying on the table was her plan— "suicide by doctor," as Michael calls it now. A long life, for its own sake, never appealed to my mother. A cake with one hundred candles wasn't her idea of an accomplishment or even a necessarily welcome celebration. She was smart and funny and wise and resourceful and brave; she loved good talk and good books and good food; and she cared deeply about justice in the world. But I would never call her a happy or an optimistic person. Her harsh childhood hadn't predisposed her to that, nor had her difficult marriage or unnaturally long and lonely widowhood. She had no grand-children to watch grow up. She didn't live in the embrace of a large, loving, multigenerational family. She had few friends, none of them intimate. For the last year she'd had a nasty preview of advanced old age, which was nei-ther a reversible process nor a curable disease, and in recent months she'd experienced a new level of disability and dependency.

I don't believe the depression that had dominated my mother's middle age was a particular factor now. You don't have to be clinically depressed to want to avoid needing someone else to clean your bottom and spoon food into your mouth. All the very old people I know, and the vast majority of those who commented on my blog, see long life as a blessing only if they are reasonably functional and not at the mercy of others to get through the day. Once they reach that point of helplessness, with only the rarest excep-tion, they want out. Many speak of the elderly Alaskan natives who drift out to sea on ice floes or of the ancient Japanese whose children dutifully carry them to the top of a holy mountain to die peacefully in the freezing snow. "Shoot me" is their long-term care plan.

My mother's misguided surgery was, arguably, a twenty-first-century version of that snowy mountaintop, and not all that crazy if you think about it in those terms. Unlike me, my brother, who did not hear the remark at the time, doubted that she was serious. What she said in the recovery room was clearly intended for my ears only, and he has always seemed disbeliev-ing, or at the very least queasy, whenever I've referred to it in the years since. He'll joke about it, as with the "suicide by doctor" remark. But the closest he's come to acknowledging that she might have meant it has been to say, "It's a fair speculation, but you can't prove it. And I can't prove it wasn't. But there was an element of 'Mom the comedienne.' The humor was often dark, but when she had a good line, she used it."

The next few days in the hospital were a terrible time, as bad as any I can recall, and my brother concurs. My mother was relentlessly surly to both of us, no matter what we said or did. Rather than visit separately, to give her twice as much time in the company of her children, we went together, or at least made sure we crossed paths on the way in or out, for moral support. A Post-it scribbled to myself at the time says, "Cuz it's the right thing to do and to stand by Michael." I must have been considering bailing out and reminding myself why I couldn't do that. I do believe these moments of wanting to run as far and as fast as you can are common, though they're rarely discussed even among siblings. Maybe it's easier to admit them to strangers, at caregiver support groups or in chatrooms on the Internet. (Such venues were rare during my caregiving years. Even today, to my surprise, they are barely used, according to recent research, as well as my own random visits in person and online.)

A few readers of *The New Old Age* have told me that some adult children, after lifetimes of severe abuse or abandonment, at this stage make thoughtful decisions not to reenter or remain in an elderly parent's life. I don't presume to judge. From the day we decided to move my mother to New York, I made a careful calculation that the awfulness of caring for an emotionally withholding, difficult mother was preferable to the guilt of living the rest of my life knowing I hadn't. For me, it was a deliberate choice between the lesser of two evils. But if I was going to take on this devoted-daughter role, it wouldn't be halfhearted. Every ounce of energy, enterprise, and empathy I could muster would go to the task.

As for my mother's postsurgical meltdown, the hospital records make clear that my brother and I were not imagining or exaggerating her behavior. She reported her mood as "lousy" and refused to participate in the first two days of physical therapy. She resisted medical exams, hospital records say. One nurse reported that my mother was complaining of "inattention," and an intern wrote that the "patient has not been able to cope with anger at staff." After a series of vertigo attacks, which did not match the usual Ménière's symptom pattern, my mother was given significant doses of anti-anxiety medications. Later in the records, a nurse wrote that the "patient is anxious about all changes," and an intern reported "her mood is progressively depressed." Later that day, my mother told another member of the house staff that she didn't "want to talk to anyone, including her family," and that she wished "she had died during the operation."

When I told Dr. Bilsky, during our recent interview, of my mother's remark in the recovery room, he said that that is not uncommon, and generally means nothing— people say lots of strange things right after surgery under the disinhibiting influence of anesthesia and heavy-duty pain medication. But it was an "earth-shattering lapse," he said, that she repeated it days later to a medical professional and he didn't pass it up the chain of command, prompting a psychiatric consultation, or at the very least inclusion in the discharge report that went with her to the Hebrew Home.

Yet in the same five days that she was driving us all to distraction, doctors and nurses were also reporting that my mother was progressively gaining strength, doing well from a neurological standpoint, and walking for the first time, with help, from bed to chair. That raised the possibility that continued rehabilitation, against all odds, would restore some measure of mobility. I'm sorry I missed that brief hospital walking episode, because I never again saw her stand on her own two feet unassisted.

She was officially cleared for discharge to a rehabilitation facility, which would be the Hebrew Home, where she had been accepted for admission before the decision to have surgery. The two facilities, cooperating with each other and with us, had agreed she would remain in the hospital until a bed became available at the nursing home. Because of the surgery and hospitalization and the necessity for skilled nursing care and/or rehabilitation, her first hundred days in the home, in what is known as a subacute facility, would be paid for by Medicare. On the 101st day she would become a permanent resident, paying her own way and no longer covered by Medicare, which, to reiterate, does not pay for long-term care; that is, for meeting the menial day-to-day needs of elderly people who cannot walk, feed, clothe, bathe, toilet, or otherwise take care of themselves, whether in an institution or at home.

Long-term care was not part of the original 1965 Medicare legislation, which backers of the historic social insurance program anticipated would evolve and expand over time, possibly all the way to a government-run universal health care system, like those common in Europe. In small ways it has expanded, as with the introduction of the Medicare prescription drug benefit in 2006. But Medicare (far more than its model, Social Security, passed three decades earlier) proved dangerously vulnerable to changing demographics, advances in technology, and rampant health care inflation, leading not to further growth but rather to fears for its insolvency. So the absence of long-term care protection for the aged, even in the Obama health care plan, remains a glaring gap; it is not covered by any other government entitlement program unless the recipient is impoverished. In the words of Theodore R. Marmor, author of *The Politics of Medicare* (Hawthorne, N.Y.: Aldine, 1970), the benefits of the Great Society program proved, in time, to be seriously mismatched with "the special circumstances of the elderly," its very constituents, who often had "medical conditions that wouldn't improve" and hoped to "maintain independent function rather than triumph over discrete illness and injury." Medicare, between its inception and the demographic tidal wave of the twenty-first century, failed to "adjust its benefits to the most distinctive circumstances of the group—namely chronic ailments." That remains true today.

CHAPTER 6

September Eleventh

Iawoke early and filled with relief on September 11—yes, *that* September 11—which also happened to be Primary Day in New York City. My assignment for the *Times* was to spend the day in a polling place to be sure there were no hanging chads or other irregularities, this being the first election after the disputed Bush–Gore debacle. It gave me an excuse not to visit my mother for the entire day. The prospect of standing for hours on end, probably with nothing interesting going on, in a dreary polling place— think peeling green walls, metal folding chairs, gum forever embedded in the linoleum floor—seemed by comparison a holiday. I knew my mother was in capable hands medically. She knew I was working from eight a.m. to nine p.m., and we had mutually agreed there was no need for me to come see her afterward, when she'd more than likely be asleep.

Given what we now know—what we knew less than an hour after I left my suburban home, heading toward both my assigned midtown polling place and, coincidentally, the World Trade Center downtown—it's hard to imagine relief as anyone's prevailing emotion that morning. But I had spent the last two weeks consumed with my mother's condition, at her side for many hours every day, living in a soup of fear, guilt, heartbreak, resentment, loneliness, and exhaustion from bearing the weight of so much responsibility. Now the sun was shining, and the cloudless sky was blue in a way that none of us will ever forget. The sunroof of my car was open. I had no premonition of what was to come, just the belief that the day, whole, wide open, was my own.

Even as the cataclysm unfolded, as the day's developments heaped one upon the next, as all of us at the *Times* worked the story, I didn't give my mother a second's thought other than once in a while to mentally thank the powers-that-be at Sloan-Kettering for keeping her cleared for discharge until a bed opened up for her at the Hebrew Home. The social workers at the two facilities were working in perfect synchrony, mindful and considerate of our family's needs. This was how things were supposed to work but rarely did, given the economic pressure on hospitals to get people in and out in the shortest time possible, regardless of whether the transition was smooth or the family satisfied or ready for the next step. I saw no reason why the events of the day would alter our plan and so was grateful to the professionals, confident I could carry out my work responsibilities with my concentration uninterrupted.

At Sloan, too, the historic events seemed unrelated to the matter at hand, which was caring for four hundred–odd very sick people. My mother's hospital records contain not one word about the attacks on the Twin Towers. This stunned me, although most medical professionals, and even "civilians," commented later that there would have been no reason to do so, and indeed it would have been inappropriate to refer to any of the wrenching details unless they directly affected my mother's care—say, if there had been a power failure, a water emergency, or even if she had expressed special anxiety about my safety or Michael's.

I had no idea at the time if she was aware of what was unfolding outside the hospital's cocoon. Were the ceiling-mounted televisions turned on in patients' rooms? Surely they were at the nurses' stations and in the doctors' break rooms. But I never even wondered, assuming that her universe was hermetically sealed, as if nothing had happened, while mine was the opposite. It had split wide open and was filled to the brim with the world and work and worry about everything—except her. So, too, my brother's world: the smell of death would linger for months in his Greenwich Village apartment. For several days, he says, he was paralyzed; for weeks, depressed. Facing, along with my mother's deterioration, a book deadline on a topic that now seemed beyond trivial, he found himself unable to work.

Daily journalism permits no paralysis, so that first day, for me, is a blur caused less by fear or sorrow than by coursing adrenaline, the collegial swirl of activity that took over the newsroom. I was not among those at Ground Zero, but I worked through the night, oblivious to all else, and began the next day on First Avenue, where strung like beads were the New York City morgue, Bellevue, and New York University Hospital Center. Along with my colleague Janny Scott, we were expecting the arrival of thousands upon thousands of injured who had been pulled overnight from the rubble of the Twin Towers. Instead, what Janny and I found was a parade of relatives of lost firemen and bond traders, lost fathers and sons, mothers and daughters, trekking from hospital to morgue to police precinct to Red Cross missing-persons site. They wore comfortable shoes, carried water bottles and cell phones, and passed out homemade flyers, hurried one-page scrapbooks about their loved ones, pasted together during the longest night of their lives and copied at the local Kinko's or Staples the second it opened. They forced these flyers into the hands of anyone wearing official garb, be it medical scrubs or a clerical collar, and to anyone like Janny or me carrying a reporter's notebook and pen. They posted them on lampposts alongside others for missing cats, apartments for rent, and movers for hire.

Never was it less awkward as a reporter to interview the grief-stricken. They thronged us, with stories of their loved ones, multiple phone numbers where we could reach them should we hear of a John Doe arriving dazed in an emergency room or calling out from the rubble. They described birthmarks, scars from cesarean sections, and tattoos. It would take days to realize that these lost souls would never be found.

But on September 12, nobody knew they were all dead. Nobody even knew what verb tense to use when speaking of them and thus toggled from past to present. In the space of a sentence, someone would tell Janny or me that his brother-in-law *works* on the 102nd floor, then say that that was where he *worked,* only to switch back again. Those of us squinting into the preternatural sunshine on First Avenue knew in our guts by late morning that if anyone were left alive there would be at least a few sirens, ambulances, or gurneys in our line of sight. But New York City wasn't functioning, nor could it, on gut instinct or anecdote, so preparations were being made for a monumental triage operation.

Unbeknownst to me, my mother would be a tiny footnote in that operation. Weill Cornell Medical Center, across the street from Sloan-Kettering, was readying itself for the onslaught that never came. Emptying a general hospital, so it could function as one huge emergency room, meant moving its patients across the street, where the expertise was cancer and no one was trained in triage. That meant making room for them at Sloan.

Thus, at some point, my cell phone rang. Surely it would be the office. But this wasn't a work call. Instead, a strange voice told me, simply, that my mother was being discharged, and why, and that I should come get her. I had no idea who I was speaking to or what else she said. I had no idea where my mother was supposed to go, since she did not yet have a nursing home bed, the Meadowview was out of the question, and I wasn't set up at home with skilled nurses, physical therapists, equipment, or any of the things necessary to safely and competently take charge, even briefly, of someone who had just had spinal surgery. The only remotely realistic option was for the Hebrew Home to somehow find a temporary bed until a permanent one materialized. Maybe they'd make room for her in the hall, as in overcrowded emergency rooms. Maybe they kept a bed in reserve for unexpected contingencies. Even then, how would I get her there? Lying on the backseat of my Subaru? What about work? Could I simply walk off the job? These questions hadn't yet fully formed in my mind. I just knew I was in deep trouble.

I also had no idea that the hospital could not simply put her out on the curb, possessions in hand, like a bag lady. That would have been illegal, I would later learn. Should you be faced with a discharge process that you feel is unsafe or improperly organized, you can slow it down: by negotiating, by having a doctor or outside advocate negotiate for you, and then, if necessary, by making a formal appeal. You must understand your legal rights but also the most effective way to get what you need without resorting to them, because if you lose the appeal, you will not be reimbursed for extra time in the hospital. I wish I'd known that, although even if I had, I wouldn't have tried to play that particular game at that moment. New York on September 12 was as close to the end of the world as I'd ever seen in my lifetime. My mother was, in fact, cleared for discharge, and discharging her was the right thing to do. But how was I supposed to handle that?

I quickly grasped that walking off the job to deal with the problem was not a possibility. The day before, the *Times*'s metropolitan editor, Jonathan Landman, managing the paper's largest and most crucial department, did not know the whereabouts of his teenage daughter, a student at a high school within sight of the Twin Towers, until she found her way to the

Times's midtown office in midafternoon. Never did his personal agony affect his behavior toward us, or disrupt the most important workday of his life. I doubt he was the only one in similar straits. We all had personal lives bumping up against public catastrophe. I wasn't about to be the one who left my post.

Why tell this story in a book about elder care? On its face these extraordinary circumstances have no place here, are so sui generis as to have no relevance to your life. On the other hand, the quotidian experience of an adult child responsible for an aged parent, like a parent responsible for a child, or a well spouse for an ill spouse, regularly involves the collision of public and private duties; on many days a family emergency disrupts work responsibilities and vice versa. You're on the airport check-in line, bound for a business trip, when a call comes from the hospital that your mother has fallen and broken her pelvis. A long-planned appointment with a lawyer to discuss estate plans, health care proxies, and powers of attorney collides with the necessity of making an unexpected presentation to a new client. Dad, who has dementia, wanders off, and the home care attendant can't find him and calls you at work; her cell phone number pops up on your caller ID while you're meeting with your supervisor. A job interview and your mother's cataract surgery wind up scheduled on the same day. You've been in the emergency room all night long with an ailing parent and need nothing more than a day to recover, but you must brush your teeth, throw on some clean clothes, and catch the 7:49 a.m. train.

Like the parents of young children (although I would argue with less institutional support), we are constantly trying to inconspicuously fit our caretaking duties into our work lives; to deflect attention from our problems, our absences from the office, our time on the phone unrelated to our jobs, our reduced concentration and productivity. Those of you in the professions, or with compassionate bosses, have it easy. What about the single mother with ailing parents who stocks shelves at Walmart, or who works in a call center or on a factory line where even bathroom breaks are scheduled? What about the home aide, earning barely a minimum wage, with no health insurance, taking care of *your* mother and worrying about her own and her children besides? These women aren't *juggling* jobs and families; they are *choosing between* jobs and families. They aren't, in their minds, members of the "sandwich generation," because they can't afford the time or the money to read the magazines that tell them that their lot in life has a catchy name.

It was Janny, in fact, with both teenage children and aging parents, who persuaded me that 9/11, albeit extreme, was a "striking single-case example" of the work-life conflict that is routine for women, and increasingly men, and that some, like the two of us, had it easier than most. Within days of my call from the hospital, one of her children's schools summoned her to "come get your kid" after a bomb scare. "We're lucky to be able to slip out and deal with things," she said. Both of us, thanks to our privileged employment, could receive and make private phone calls from work, and we could leave if we had to deal with an emergency. We didn't have the kind of jobs that studies characterize as "high demand and low control," with no ability to regulate one's own schedule. Those, Janny reminded me, are the most pressured of all.

The changes wrought by the women's movement have transformed how we care for our aged parents, a social dimension that exacerbates the current demographic one. In earlier generations, few women worked outside the home, and elder care was their responsibility, daughters and daughters-in-law alike. A woman took care of her frail mother or mother-in-law at home—no easy task. But she would have been home anyway. Also, families were larger and less likely to be scattered, so an ailing parent would have had more hands on deck. (A friend of mine with two sisters, all three living in Northern California, ably took turns caring for their dying mother in her own home without needing an iota of professional help. Another friend has *seven* married siblings, all but one of them nearby. Her mother died in a hospital, but I doubt she spent a single moment unattended by at least one of them.) Finally, in the old days, there was less divorce, and fewer people who were single for a lifetime, so networks of friends caring for friends (a growing solution but extremely challenging to organize), were all but unheard of and might still be, were it not for the AIDS epidemic, which opened a curtain on the existence and devotion of "families of choice" versus "families of origin."

All of these social upheavals, which make elder care so much more challenging, can be mitigated, in part, by workplace policies that recognize and accommodate the role of the nonprofessional caregiver (estimates range from 16 million to 20 million employees) who tends to the aged and infirm, not as a paid job but during "spare" time. The vast majority of workplaces have no such policies. This failure, besides making caregiving almost an undercover activity for some, has cost corporate America billions of dollars in absenteeism, lost productivity, premature retirement, workday distraction, leaves of absence, reduction from full-time to part-time work, stress-related health problems, and other consequences of employees attending to the unpredictable crises that are the hallmark of elder care.

These costs have been calculated in many studies, notably *Caregiving in the U.S.,* by the MetLife Foundation, AARP, and the National Alliance for Caregiving. This study, first published in 1997, has been updated several times. In 1997, overall costs to employers ranged from $11.5 billion to $29 billion a year, using a method of calculation that factored in how many hours a week of hands-on care employees were providing, the so-called level-of-burden index. By 2006, the numbers had jumped by more than $4 billion a year, and costs to employers ranged from $17.1 billion to $33.6 billion. The safe assumption, based on population figures of both the aged and the affected employees, is that those numbers will continue to rise.

Here are some specific examples of ways that employers are affected:

- The cost of replacing experienced employees who quit was $6.6 billion in 2006, up from $4.9 billion in 1997. (Employees who quit, retire early, switch from full-time to part-time work, or refuse promotions incur a dollar cost at their end, too, not only in salary but also in pensions and other benefits that accrue with tenure and status.)

- The cost of workday interruptions was $6.3 billion in 2006, up from $3.7 billion in 1997. (Arguably, an individual's workday interruptions ripple across a workplace, as one distracted or temporarily unavailable employee makes it impossible for several others to complete a task.)

- The cost of absenteeism was $5 billion in 2006, up from $85 million in 1997. That is a whopping 550 percent increase. Again depending on the workplace culture, the attitude of a given supervisor, and the enforcement of certain employment laws, being absent from work can result in an employee's dismissal.

Since the late 1960s, when working women made child care a key part of the feminist agenda, companies have routinely provided maternity leaves, job sharing, and pre-tax savings accounts to pay for child care. In companies that make accommodations for elder care, these benefits tend to be the model. But the so-called mommy track and daughter track are more dissimilar than similar, and the child care paradigm, say both academic experts and those in the business of caregiving, does not transfer well from one life stage to another.

"These benefits fall under the same umbrella but are fundamentally different," Chris Gatti, a provider of both child care and elder care, told me a few years back. "Child care programs are relatively straightforward and easy to administer compared to elder care, which is a maze with lots of sharp corners and dark, secluded places."

In those dark, secluded places, employees get lost, both emotionally and in the amount of time they must be there, during the workday and in their supposed off-hours. Prudential Financial, in Newark, New Jersey, has long been a very forward-looking company in its elder care benefits. But even there, according to Maureen Corcoran, a vice president in charge of this area, "it's a new and very confusing skill set. You don't just give people a list; you have to lead them there. Otherwise they spend hours upon hours figuring it out themselves."

The most obvious difference between child care and elder care is that nondisabled children's schedules (discounting surprises like the flu or a broken arm) are predictable: a school holiday is coming up next Monday, summer vacation falls in July and August. By contrast, elderly parents' needs are crisis-driven: a trip to the emergency room or a sudden turn for the worse during what had seemed a routine hospitalization; getting lost while driving in the neighborhood or taking a dangerous fall, thus requiring immediate home supervision. A portion of it can be planned for in advance, but only with much foresight.

Moreover, parents raise children at home, under the same roof, but an adult child's elderly relative often lives far away, and supervision requires either lots of travel (much of it unexpected and thus very expensive because of having to pay full fares) or someone to function as the on-the-scene eyes and ears (say, a geriatric care manager), and often both. Guiding the decisions that an elderly parent makes, moreover, requires understanding the delicate psychology involving issues of control and a family's hierarchical roles. "Because I said so" might work with a child, but it doesn't work with a parent, and it would be disrespectful besides. Except for disabled children, routine child care does not involve the arcane legal, financial, and medical matters that come up regularly with elder care. I have never heard of a package of elder care benefits that includes easy, affordable access, and rarely even referrals, to medical, legal, or financial professionals.

The elder care benefit most commonly offered is referral information: lists of service providers throughout the country. Since they are generally not screened for quality, that leaves a time-pressed adult child to call, vet, and arrange all the services. Similar information is available on the Internet, through various "locators" that permit you to punch in a zip code and get a list of local providers (often with ads for the very same providers stacked down the right-hand side of the search page). A few employers have a single for-profit company under contract, akin to a geriatric care management agency, available to employees 24/7 via an 800 number. The fees they would pay as individuals are adjusted according to economies of scale. That service may reduce a dozen phone calls to one, but the adult child still must find a way to pay for the service, beyond an original consultation, which sometimes is free; rarely there is also a small, ongoing employer subsidy. In these best-case situations, an employee needing help does not get to comparison-shop beyond the one all-purpose provider that the company has under contract. That, in some ways, can be viewed as an advantage, as having too many options throws you back into the exhausting loop of phone calls. I, for one, would have happily forgone choices in favor of simplicity.

To better understand the practical implications of using the same model for both child care and elder care benefits, consider leaves of absence. Most pregnant workers know when they will take maternity leave and for how long. Someone responsible for an aged parent, however, faces an unpredictable series of emergencies. When the unexpected happens, the caregiver must use some of the *unpaid* time off granted under the federal Family and Medical Leave Act and under a few similar state laws (only California and New Jersey offer paid leave), depend on the goodwill of a supervisor, or take vacation or personal days. Your federally mandated leave time is a guaranteed twelve weeks, but because it is unpaid, it is unaffordable for many who would otherwise use it. A benevolent employer might offer six months or even a year, with a guaranteed return to a comparable job. A new mother would know when to use that leave time, probably at the tail end of her pregnancy and then just after the baby is born. An adult daughter or son, by contrast, must guess whether to use it during a current situation or to hang on to it, lest a parent linger or undergo future, more serious crises. It's an utter crapshoot. Unlike, say, for a child going off to college, there is not even a chronological marker for when day-to-day responsibility will mostly cease.

Similarly helpful to parents of young children, but not to adult children of elderly parents, are flexible spending accounts, which permit you to use pre-tax dollars off the top of your paycheck for dependent care. These payroll accounts are designed and governed by the IRS, which defines dependents as those who receive at least half their financial support from and live under the same roof as the employee. That is generally the case with children but rarely with elderly parents. One accountant–financial planner, Evan Gilder, in White Plains, New York, who does a lot of work with the elderly and their children, told me that employers, more likely lazy than venal, have been slow to recognize that the IRS had only one group in mind with these accounts, the dual-income family with children needing to cover the expense of a nanny or day care. Yet those of us caring for parents are encouraged by human resources departments to consider this "our benefit," too, often with no apparent understanding of its limitations. Not having access to these benefits leads to what my brother and I (not begrudging my mother what she needed) called the "ka-ching, ka-ching" that gradually becomes part of adult children's lives and in some cases throws them into deep debt.

My mother, for instance, never lived in my house or my brother's, nor did we ever cover half her financial support. But over the years we spent thousands upon thousands of dollars supplementing her expenses in assisted living, buying her both essentials (groceries, clothes, furniture) and luxuries (books, restaurant meals, a VCR), hiring private-duty home health aides when she was in the nursing home and staffing was poor on holiday weekends, and getting her a motorized wheelchair and a certain assisted speaking device when strokes robbed her of the ability to walk and talk. None of this was covered by Medicare, by Medicaid, or by her long-term care insurance policy; none of it was considered a tax deduction for either of us on our tax returns or via a dependent care account. What we did not know then is that my mother could have paid for some of it out of her dwindling bank account, hastening her Medicaid spend-down, despite her Depression-era parsimony and determination not to game the system, however legally, by giving her assets to us outright while she was still alive.

The unmet needs, and sometimes dismissal, of employees caring either for children or for their elderly family members is a growing area for employment-related litigation, according to data collected by the Center for WorkLife Law in San Francisco, which handles such cases and has coined the term "family responsibility discrimination" to cover this broad arena. The center tries these cases using a legal arsenal that includes federal sex discrimination law (Title VII of the 1964 Civil Rights Act), the federal Family and Medical Leave Act of 1993, and state laws that mimic or expand upon both. In its litigation update for 2010, the first to include cases involving elder care, the center reports that "family discrimination cases" have increased by more than 400 percent in the last decade, to 2,100. Of those, 181 involve elder care, an almost eightfold increase in that time period. The vast majority of cases (67 percent) remain related to pregnancy and maternity, but a distant second is elder care (9.7 percent). The center reports that what differentiates the elder care cases from the far more routine ones involving pregnancy and maternity is that the percentage of male plaintiffs is far higher (42 percent as opposed to 12 percent) and that the employee wins less often, whether at trial, in summary judgment, or in settlement (37 percent of the time as opposed to 50 percent).

The report doesn't speculate about the disproportionate number of male plaintiffs, compared to the broader, majority female, pool of family caregivers. My guess would be that fewer men leave work entirely when faced with this "second shift," or that they are more confrontational when employers obstruct their efforts to be attentive caregivers. Neither does the report speculate about the lower success rate on the part of the plaintiffs in elder care cases. One possibility, lawyers at the center say, is that in the elder care cases, the only legal ground is violation of the Family and Medical Leave Act, not sex discrimination, and that the issue is newer, for demographic reasons, and thus less familiar to judges, juries, and executives, who might otherwise be more understanding and thus settle. Given the sharp spike in these cases in the last decade, lawyers say, it is fair to assume that the gender of the plaintiffs and the outcome of the cases may be a trailing indicator and look very different a decade from now.

My first call about my mother's imminent discharge was, of course, to my brother. My second was to my childhood friend on the board of directors of the Hebrew Home—one of those favors you ask only in a true emergency. He must have intervened immediately, rather like the "fixer" in a Middle Eastern bazaar or Soviet Russia, because within moments, while I was letting an appropriate interval pass before directly calling the home's director, Dan Reingold, he called me. Dan had heard what was happening with Mom, he said. That's what he called her, from that first you-are-my-savior conversation through what has since become a long friendship. Even before he told me everything would be all right, which he did, in the next sentence, I knew by the simple fact of the call, and its speed, that it would be. A resident at the home whose name I would never know had died just hours earlier, a pretty regular occurrence there. My mother would get her bed, solving part one of our problem.

Michael took the baton for part two: how to get my mother to the Hebrew Home and in whose charge. As we had already done so many times, and would do so many more, we fell into the roles that fit our skill sets and temperaments without ever discussing a division of labor. Not that we glided through this entire experience as loving siblings holding hands and skipping down the path; our blowups were ugly, and our silences were long. Our judgments of each other, spoken or not, were harsh and unforgiving. Certain patches were worse than others, and some seemed beyond repair. But meeting fast-moving, what-the-hell-do-we-do-now kind of challenges—more task-oriented than emotional—was easiest, whether the results were unnecessarily hurried, selfishly motivated, and thus imperfectly executed, or models of efficiency, good judgment, and luck. September 12, 2001, fell into the latter category, one of our finest collaborations, where our respective abilities seemed to mesh perfectly.

We shared some skills: we both respected deadlines and thus were quick out of the starting block; we knew how to find out what we needed to know, by the most direct route if possible and circuitously if not; and we understood who held power and how best to align their interests and ours to get what we needed from them. We weren't shrinking violets. We were articulate enough to make our case specifically and forcefully. We took notes and saved them for future reference. We asked people for their names and phone numbers. We thanked those who came to our aid and cultivated them for the next go-around. The list goes on.

But some of our skills, thankfully, were different. Michael goes after information like a dog after a bone. If the people who have it say no a dozen times, he will wear them down with his persistence. If someone doesn't like him as a result, he doesn't care; indeed, he thrives on conflict. He wastes no time, asking crisp questions, getting answers, and moving on. I, on the other hand, have more of a give-and-take discursive style, opening myself up to people so they will open themselves up to me. Both work, especially in tandem.

I saw the vast difference in our techniques in a new light when I asked Michael for help with this book. When neither of us could recall the circumstances leading to my mother's belated decision to have the surgery, which he saw as a crucial missing link in the chain of facts, he spent hours going through his old computer disks of e-mails between the two of us and between him and the professionals. When he could not find the disks we needed, he guided me through the formal process of getting her records and shared my sense of accomplishment when I wore down the recalcitrant bureaucrats.

By contrast, when I interviewed Michael for this book, he found my rambling style annoying. We'd set aside a certain time interval; when the time was up, I wasn't even halfway through my list of questions, partly because I wasn't sticking to it and partly because I was attempting to squeeze more than monosyllables out of him by telling him my recollections of certain events, priming the pump so he might elaborate on his own. I wanted to know how he "felt." He seemed determined to tell me the facts, efficiently. I asked him, for example, what he recalled about being in the surgical waiting room at Sloan-Kettering during my mother's three-plus hours of surgery. He had been a basket case, I remembered, jumping out of his skin. Yet here is how he remembered that day: "A bright room? Big windows?" (I confirmed his memory as accurate if rather limited.)

Mitigating elder care costs, which can be considerable and are different for everyone, would require even enlightened companies to rethink many of the options they offer to employees. One benefit with real utility for caregivers is backup care, usually provided by an outside company under contract with an employer, one of the proliferating elder care cottage industries. Anytime an employee has a temporary need for child care or elder care—say, a sick babysitter or an absent home health aide—he or she can get a temporary replacement, by the next morning, by making one phone call. Alas, that benefit is offered, at last count, by only 3 percent of the companies that are members of the Society for Human Resource Management. One percent of those subsidize the service to some extent.

The 200,000-plus human resources professionals who are members of the society were last surveyed in 2003, and 39 percent said that elder care benefits were "too costly to be feasible," a concern more likely in the current economic climate than back then. Clearly they were either unaware of or unimpressed by the downstream costs when valuable workers quit, spend half their working hours dealing with family issues, or simply can't concentrate. Of those who offered any elder care benefits at all, 76 percent said they helped employees on an informal case-by-case basis, leaving lots of room for favoritism or simply doing nothing at all. Just 6 percent had written policies. The most common benefit was a referral service, most helpful for a long-distance caregiver who lives in one place while an elderly parent lives halfway across the country. But the referral service consists of little more than offering a list of providers, such as you might find yourself with a Google search. Screening the available providers, and then arranging for and supervising their service, takes many hours a week, sometimes many hours a day, absent a care manager to do it for you.

It is hard to keep track of the nation's ever-changing and merging providers of backup care—companies with names like Visiting Angels, Home Alone, and Comfort Keepers; some are franchises, and others are centrally managed. One of the leaders was the Work Options Group, based in Superior, Colorado, whose clients included Microsoft, Verizon Wireless, Princeton University, and Prudential Financial. In 2008, Work Options served 600,000 employees, a 30 percent increase in just two years. The following year, Work Options was purchased by Bright Horizons, much as Fine Newcombe & Winsby, the boutique geriatric care management company that we used, was gobbled up by the nationwide SeniorBridge operation. Only time will tell what these formerly mom-and-pop operations gain or lose in the process.

Before the merger, Work Options CEO Cindy Carrillo said 90 percent of the employees using the service were mothers (and some fathers) rather than daughters (and some sons). I asked her why this was so, given the number of employees nationwide with responsibility for aging parents. One explanation, she said, is the average age of employees who used Work Options: thirty-five to thirty-seven years old at high-tech or telecommunications concerns, and forty-five to forty-seven years old in more old-line businesses. In either case, she said, they were more likely to have young children than dependent parents.

But numbers tell only a small part of the story. Employees with young children, Carrillo explained, are far more comfortable seeking help from their human resources departments and far more likely to press for what they need if they're not getting it. Few companies want to be seen as politically incorrect regarding child care. By contrast, she said, when talk turns to incontinence or dementia, some bosses and colleagues avert their eyes or change the subject, and thus those caring for parents (as she was) tend to hold their situations together with "rubber bands and bubble gum" and keep their problems to themselves. I know that at the end of my mother's life I felt isolated in my plight, especially compared to colleagues being feted with showers and welcomed back to work with oohs and aahs at new baby pictures. I was tempted, out of pure small-mindedness, to put on my desk a photo of my mother, slumped in her wheelchair. Empathy was what I needed, and it was in short supply back then.

Carrillo noted, too, that few of us plan in advance for the time and money we may have to spend on extended elder care, arguably because we don't want to think about it and are hoping it will never be necessary. By contrast, the arrival of a new baby is preceded by elaborate and lengthy preparation; child care arrangements and college savings accounts are set up in advance. Denial, she was saying, affects everything, including how workers use elder care benefits even when they are offered and whether they advocate for them if they are not offered. "We close one eye, look the other way, handle one hurdle at a time, and don't realize how much trouble we're in until it accelerates," Carrillo said. "Nobody wants to think about it beforehand. When you're in the throes of it, you don't have time. And when you're done, you don't want to go back there again."

This mind-set may account for the absence of activism among today's caregivers of the elderly, who have not made their voices heard as working mothers did decades ago. Experts disagree about whether women, as more have the elder care experience, will push employers for help with their parents, as many of the same women did thirty years ago when child care was their pressing issue. Ellen Galinsky, president of the Family and Work Institute, led the charge for a day care center at Bank Street College when she was a researcher there in 1969. After "huge resistance," the center opened in 1974. Galinsky predicted a similar awakening to elder care issues, because "demographics are destiny" and "everyone I know is dealing with this," but her prophecy has yet to be fulfilled.

Todd Groves is the founder of LTC Financial Partners in Seattle, primarily an agent for long-term care insurance policies. Having advised human resource managers on long-term care, he is not convinced that activist women like Ellen Galinsky will have the same galvanizing effect this time around, regardless of their numbers or their passion. "Back then you still had a paternal business culture," Groves said. "Now people feel out on their own. They are fearful about their careers and don't feel they can ask for help."

When Michael takes on a task, there is nobody better at accomplishing it. Even in those disorienting post-9/11 days, he took command of logistics to which I hadn't given a moment's thought. My mother was at Sloan in Manhattan; the Hebrew Home was in the Bronx, on the far side of a small bridge that spans the Hudson River. On September 12, the day of her move, Manhattan remained cordoned off for security reasons; traffic could leave but not enter the borough. So if I took my mother to the nursing home, Michael had already figured out, I wouldn't be able to return to work; if he took her, he wouldn't be able to return home. Almost immediately, he made a sensible mental calculation that would have been beyond me: however our mother got from point A to point B, she was going to be a very unhappy camper that day, and probably would be for days to come. There was nothing to be gained by either of us taking her to Riverdale and winding up stranded there.

The solution was to locate an ambulette (no easy task under the circumstances), and to find and hire the private-duty aide, Hyacinth, who had taken care of my mother at the Meadowview when I was on vacation. Mom had liked Hyacinth, Michael told me. I should focus on doing my job. He would call the discharge planner at Sloan and tell her we were on the case; ditto the nursing home. Then he would call every ambulette company he could find; put Hyacinth on the clock for as long as we needed her, at a higher-than-usual rate, so she'd be willing to cancel or turn down other jobs; have her supervise my mother's discharge and her delivery to the nursing home; and see to it that Hyacinth got home afterward. So labor-intensive were these tasks, I could not have performed them while working. Michael did them all, without complaint or rebuke. I'd gotten her the bed, which he considered the hard part. This, to him, was simply a wise and fair division of labor.

I have no idea how he found an available ambulette during the continuing, hopeful wait for wounded from the World Trade Center. Or how he located Hyacinth, no doubt in the middle of another case. Or how he orchestrated the many other moving parts of this operation. My admiration was matched by my gratitude. I also felt some guilt for playing a minimal role, and for leaving my mother in the hands of strangers at a time like this. But Dan Reingold, the director of the home, assured me that even under less chaotic circumstances, it would have been wise to stay away for a few days and let the professionals settle my mother in. He compared it to sending a child off to sleepaway camp for the first time. The well-run camps (at least in the old days before the advent of helicopter parents) permitted no calls to or from home for a long enough interval to keep the frightened child from begging to leave and the pushover mother from coming to get her. Dan's advice armed me with the resolve to let Michael carry out his plan to get us through one more day. I knew I wouldn't be capable of staying away much longer than that (which is true of virtually all adult children, I learned later).

But how did I handle myself in front of my colleagues? Did I act as out of control as I felt? This is not only a prideful question. *Take care of yourself,* everyone says. *You can't take care of someone else if you don't take care of yourself first.* They cite the airplane rule about putting on your own oxygen mask before putting on your child's. The most obvious ways of taking care of yourself are eating well, sleeping, exercising, and scheduling time off for pure fun. But another way of taking care of yourself is doing your day job well—making work a place where you feel capable, useful, satisfied, and engrossed—at a time when feelings of incompetence and futility dominate the other half of your life.

My colleague Janny, as outwardly imperturbable a woman as I know, confirmed that by focusing heart and soul on my job, I was indeed taking care of myself. "You mentioned it very briefly," she said. "That you were moving your mother, but in a 'by the way' way, alongside all the other bizarre stuff. It didn't intrude. You were thoroughly engaged in what you were doing." (Michael, fairly and wisely, noted that "you, too, are capable of turning off emotions"—compartmentalizing—"to get something that you feel needs to be done, done." *Touché.*)

CHAPTER 7

September Twelfth

Like the day before, September 12 didn't end until the wee small hours of the following day. I knew via periodic updates from the Sloan-Kettering discharge folks, calls from Michael (who was in touch with the ambulette company and with Hyacinth), and bulletins from the people at the Hebrew Home that my mother had arrived safely and was tucked in for the night. After her extraordinary discharge from Sloan, any vacant room would have been a welcome temporary lodging until one opened up on the floor appropriate to her medical needs. Had she not had the surgery, which is what the Hebrew Home expected when we formally made our application, she would have needed only limited skilled nursing attention and routine physical therapy, not intense post-operative rehabilitation. So she was slated to live on the second floor of the Resnick Pavilion, the lower floor being a badge of relatively good health and fitness. Her disability, given the sudden surgery, was greater, so she would need to live on a higher floor.

It took someone else's death and that family's bereavement to smooth our way directly to the floor where my mother now belonged. Her new home would be room 606, a rare single room at the southeast corner of the building. Its one window faced a staff parking lot and loading dock for food and equipment deliveries. But right outside the door was a small terrace overlooking the Hudson River, upstream from the George Washington Bridge. You could go out on the terrace or sit on a sofa just inside, against the plate-glass window, and watch the tide and the New Jersey Palisades beyond. I would later hear stories from residents who had seen the World Trade Center towers crash and burn from that sixth-floor overlook. They were watching at around the time the household staff was preparing room 606, packing up the belongings of the dead and setting things up for the living in the routine manner of nursing homes, not heartless in their hurry so much as naturally circadian.

My mother's exit from Sloan was in the hands of professionals, but I worried anyway, since hospital discharges can be a rushed and sloppy process. It pained me, given where she was headed, that she had gone through it without either of her children present. So out of a combination of heartsickness and scrupulousness, I spontaneously decided to stop at Sloan when I headed home from the office. My mother's old room had been stripped bare, but like an experienced traveler checking out of a hotel, I opened all the night-table drawers to be sure nothing had been left behind. There I found her eyeglasses and her dentures. Grateful they'd not been pitched into the garbage and too tired to be angry they'd been left behind, I stole a hospital washcloth, to cushion either from breaking, put them in my purse, and left. (Later, several experts on aging told me you can judge the quality of geriatric care from hospital to hospital by "how they manage dentures." Are they removed often enough and cleaned properly? Is the patient asked if she is used to sleeping with them or not? Are complimentary denture tablets offered, like complimentary toothpaste? I would add to the list of questions, Are patients discharged toothless? Apparently, nobody even noticed that my mother was not "wearing" her teeth.)

We were spared most of the other normal glitches in the discharge process that Medicare defines as a "smooth move from one level of care to another" at a set point in time determined by diagnosis and recovery. That we knew where my mother was headed, had done all the research and paperwork, and were only waiting for a bed meant that we weren't starting from square one, scrambling to decide where she was to go next within the following twenty-four hours. That's the window that Medicare requires of a hospital before it pushes a patient out the door, sicker and quicker than in years past, in order to turn over the bed and maximize reimbursement. The government says these discharges, however hasty, must be "safe and adequate," without defining what those terms mean. There are no universal protocols for how to do a discharge, although several advocacy organizations, led by the United Hospital Fund of New York's Family Caregiver Project, are trying to establish them.

Messy and potentially dangerous discharges are the rule, not the exception, which creates far more serious problems for family caregivers than eyeglasses or dentures left behind. A patient going home may need wound care, a feeding tube, a catheter, complex medications, help transferring from bed to chair or toilet, and an array of other kinds of assistance that would be daunting even to a nurse in training, let alone a totally unprepared wife, son, friend, or other amateur suddenly responsible for all this. The patient may be eligible to receive professional services at home—from a visiting nurse, physical or occupational therapy—but the family caregiver may be ignorant about how to set that up and whether Medicare or private insurance will pay for some or all of it. The medications a patient took before hospitalization may have changed—new ones added, old ones subtracted, doses altered—and the family needs adequate explanation of what the home regime is supposed to be. A patient may be discharged without the right prescriptions, or at night or on a weekend, when certain prescriptions, like opiates, can't be easily filled. What about so-called durable medical equipment—a hospital bed, a wheelchair, or a commode? Locating a vendor and arranging delivery takes time and effort.

All of this should be arranged prior to discharge, by someone assigned the duty at the hospital, and explained in understandable words and in the right language to the caregiver. The person responsible at home should have a phone number to call for help 24/7, a follow-up appointment that is already scheduled, and contact information for all the outside agencies and vendors involved in providing services. Insist on all this, along with a comprehensive list of medications that reflects what the patient is supposed to be taking once he gets home. Make sure the discharge instructions are written legibly, both for your own use and for the physicians who will be following the case in the future. The caregiver should not only be told about medications, diet, and other home care instructions but asked to repeat everything back to whoever is coordinating the discharge so it's clear the person now in charge really understands and isn't just nodding compliance while in a confused stupor.

The caregiver should also have a comfortable opportunity, without explicit or implicit judgment, to discuss her own capabilities and limitations, in terms of the tasks she is being asked to perform, her willingness and availability to perform them, and the competing demands on her time, including those of work and other family members. If the primary caregiver (male or female; I am using the pronouns interchangeably) lives elsewhere and has come to help in an emergency, the availability to remain away from home and for how long must be taken into account.

If you think all of this seems obvious, think again. I have been at continuing medical education courses for geriatric physicians where during role-playing exercises the "doctor" or "social worker" doesn't even ask the out-of-town caregiver when she is going home. Since this stunning omission came at a class taught by the Department of Geriatrics and Palliative Medicine at Mount Sinai Medical Center in New York City, the nation's first such department and one of its best, I would guess that most discharges do not even come close to the properly executed one I've described above, which should have been in the planning stages from the moment of admission. As it is, 40 percent of Medicare patients leaving the hospital experience medication errors after discharge, and 20 percent are readmitted within thirty days. Medication errors and readmissions are costly to the patient, the hospital, and the insurer; both have inspired efforts, at some hospitals, to do better. There has also been a marked increase of high-quality instructional material available on the Internet, primarily from the United Hospital Fund. (In addition, by 2014, the Obama health care reform package is expected to withhold Medicare reimbursement for avoidable discharge errors that cause costly readmissions and is funding pilot projects that investigate ways to avoid such errors.)

A discharge to a rehabilitation facility or a nursing home requires finding a place for the patient to go. Meanwhile, the hospital's financial incentive is to empty the bed as soon as Medicare stops paying, which depends on the length of stay the government program permits based on codes pegged to the severity of diagnosis. That means that your interest (a nice place) and their interest (a fast exit) may diverge, and unless the family submits its preferences, the hospital can discharge the patient to any licensed facility. Thus, doing your homework, visiting facilities, and giving the discharge planner a list, in order of preference, is essential to a good outcome.

Following past scandals involving heinous nursing home care, the Medicare website rates nursing homes numerically, based on various indices. These ratings are worth looking at, and I'd surely avoid any place with bad numbers across the board. But all too often the ratings are skewed by relatively foolish licensing requirements, which are weighted equally with crucial matters like staffing ratios, incidence of bedsores, and whether residents are restrained or tranquilized. Also, most of the indicators used on the "Nursing Home Compare" page are self-reported and thus easily manipulated by the home.

More useful, on the government website, is the "Nursing Home Checklist," which itemizes questions to ask and things to look for during scouting visits. Go eyeball and sniff the place—it should smell neither of urine nor of heavy disinfectant. Try to go at mealtimes, when you can chat with residents, or on weekends, when you can talk to family members. Be suspicious of a nursing home that won't let you come at those times or that won't let you wander around without a tour guide glued to your side.

Some states, New York among them, require the discharge planner to seek a bed at one of five choices made by the patient or family before looking elsewhere. It is easy to see why it would be simpler, and faster, to find beds at the worst places, so don't be passive or lazy. One geriatric care manager (and discharge is an especially useful time to hire one, or some other kind of independent advocate, since they work for *you,* not the hospital) told me she advises clients to list places that they know definitely won't have beds, simply to slow the discharge if they think it's moving too quickly. An accountant who specializes in geriatric cases, when faced with his mother's imminent discharge to a rehab facility after a double knee replacement, listed only one choice on the form, repeating it in each of the five spaces, and hoped for the best. That he had connections at the place of his choice didn't hurt, and he was not shy about letting the discharge planner know that he did.

This is look-after-yourself time. Don't settle for a plan you have doubts about. Try to get what you want with a combination of sweet persuasiveness, knowledge of the local facilities as the result of doing your homework, and delicate mention of the important people in your corner, if you are fortunate enough to have them. Make clear that you know that when all the jawboning is over, you have the legal right to appeal. Avoid that if possible, since if you lose, and the process is time-consuming, you will be personally responsible for every penny spent in that hospital bed after Medicare said your parent's time was up.

·   ·   ·

I had already imagined my mother waking in a strange place, and a nursing home at that. Yes, she had chosen it, agreed that it was where she belonged, and knew she was going to live out the rest of her days there. But it was a nursing home nonetheless, with all its layers of meaning, none more obvious than that this was life's final stop. Facing that fact, and the loss of privacy and autonomy, was all but unbearable to contemplate. But to be taken there by strangers and then wake without teeth or glasses would be shocking. My mother, however reasonable and unemotional, was vain about the first and all but blind without the second.

So I had one more stop to make before dawn broke, an almost-welcome detour, as spending time alone in the car was tranquilizing, and seeing her, presumably asleep, might make me feel better. I called ahead to the sixth floor. The nurse, Eileen Dunnion, or the social worker, Hannah Curry, or someone else must have been diligent and kind enough to give me that number earlier, because I'd written it down on that day's page in my daily calendar and again in my address book, on the inside back cover. It would be the first entry on the new iteration of the "Mom List." This one would include in-house extensions for the various professionals we would interact with at the nursing home, as well as cell numbers (and even a few home numbers) for some of the people we became closest to during my mother's time there. I also confess that Michael and I copied some from caller ID when we got return calls from an off-premises phone, often cell or home.

That night I called ahead because I had no idea about security procedures for entry to the nursing home campus, and my mother's individual building—always tight, but surely heightened in the wake of the terrorist attacks, since the Hebrew Home was a well-known largely Jewish facility. Eventually I would have a photo ID and parking pass. But with my mother a new resident and me a total stranger, I wasn't simply going to breeze in at three a.m., proving my bona fides by showing them her teeth and glasses.

They were careful, in a gentle way, about my middle-of-the-night arrival. When I got to the guard's gate, someone had already given him my name. He welcomed me to pull into the circular drive in front of Resnick Pavilion (forever after forbidden to all but ambulances) and permitted me to leave the car there for as long as I wanted and go upstairs. If the kindly guard had been hired from central casting to make me feel like everything might actually turn out all right, there couldn't have been a better choice. I parked at the main entrance to Resnick. A woman who turned out to be the night nurse on my mother's floor was waiting at the curb. Clearly she was an old hand at this and had seen many first-night daughters, weak-kneed because they'd done the unthinkable in putting their mother in "one of those places." She escorted me upstairs.

At the end of a long corridor, in a corner as private as you could get in an old-style nursing home (which the Hebrew Home was then) where there's no such thing as privacy, was a room almost identical in size and decor to the one I had lived in as a college student. In the daytime, when the television lounge was at peak capacity, the residents mostly in wheelchairs and mostly in some stage of dementia, a certain kind of bedlam prevailed: old women crying out for their own mothers, long dead; the TV volume loud enough for those nearly deaf; the clatter of Hoyer lifts moving down the hallway and then cranking people from bed to wheelchair.

At this hour, it was quiet, dim, and institutional in an innocuous way. I wasn't worrying about God punishing me for putting my mother in a hellish place as I walked to her room. Rather, I was counting on the fact she'd be asleep, peaceful as a child. I would tiptoe in and put her glasses on the night table next to her bed and her teeth in their regular overnight fizz-them-clean denture container. And then I'd creep away, comforted by the sight of her and by having done the right thing of seeing her safely at rest. Had my brother or one of my women friends been with me, they'd have reminded me that nothing had ever been that simple between me and my mother and wasn't likely to be now.

My mother's eyes snapped open when I walked into the room. Her bed had risers at the side and a tray on squeaky wheels that rolled over it as in a hospital. I had expected, despite our earlier visit, more the ambience of chintz. She stared at me, furious, and then spoke: "I wish those planes had hit this building." My mother, the newshound, knew exactly what had been going on in the world for the last two days. I was impressed. In fact, she wasn't confused even in the minor details of time and place. The day before, when I had been immersed in my job, ignoring her and callous of my brother's distress, he had made the difficult trek from Greenwich Village to Sloan, on the Upper East Side, to see her. She had said exactly the same thing to him, in the exact sullen tone, and then banished him. I had been forewarned about this all-encompassing blanket of misery. The home's director, Dan Reingold, had told me that no amount of participation in the nursing home decision, no amount of mental preparation, would ease this transition, and that her anger and despair would fall hardest on her children. For many days, these are the only words she spoke to either me or my brother: "How come those planes didn't hit this building?" Each time, they were a dagger to our hearts. Yet how could we stay away?

Eventually that one line—*How come those planes didn't hit this building?*—became a running joke between me and Michael, a reminder of what I now think of as the turning point in our family ordeal. We would not actually round the corner for about a month, but both of us were feeling the beginnings of relief, knowing we wouldn't have to be at her side constantly or startle every time the phone rang, knowing other people were in charge of her physical well-being. That knowledge took the edge off the awful first few weeks, when she was sometimes nasty and sometimes inconsolable, sometimes overwrought and sometimes catatonic, and so were we, passing through yet another part of this voyage for which no warning adequately prepares you.

My mother was now in the round-the-clock care of people who knew what they were doing. Here were nurses and social workers who wanted her comfortable and content, not doctors who wanted to fix the unfixable. These professionals cared about us as a family unit—neuroses, nastiness, unresolved issues, and all. Those early weeks were as Dan had predicted: my mother hostile, while we hovered helplessly. Nothing we said or did could have made any difference, but that was clear only in hindsight. In my experience with the parents of friends, even those who fight mightily against a move to a facility, be it assisted living or a nursing home, the vast majority eventually appreciate feeling safer and less lonely, and are grateful not to be a burden to their children or in their charge. For me, even as early as that awful first morning, greeted by the employees with such kindness at the break of dawn, it was clear that the roller-coaster ride had smoothed considerably. On this point all three of us would eventually agree. We had ended up in the right place. Or at least the right place for us.

We weren't at a typical nursing home. Rather, it was one of the very best of a sorry lot, some all but criminal in their neglect and mistreatment of the frailest people among us, some merely dreadful, smelly, understaffed, unloving places where old people get warehoused when they have no families, when their families don't know what else to do with them, or when their families live someplace where the choices are all bad. News reports, lawsuits, and reports by advocacy groups have painted an ugly picture, which, despite regulation and oversight, has gotten worse in some ways in recent years as worker shortages and turnover have gone up and Medicare and Medicaid reimbursements have gone down. Nursing homes commonly, to my naive astonishment, physically or chemically restrain patients, generally those with Alzheimer's disease, because behavioral methods of managing them are so much more labor-intensive. The use of antipsychotic drugs, such as Risperdal and Seroquel (lately the focus of much media attention because of their potential overuse, with no prior testing, in children), goes unremarked upon in nursing homes, despite studies that show they hasten death in the cognitively impaired. Other symptoms of neglect and abuse of nursing home patients that seem common (none of which I've seen firsthand) are bedsores allowed to fester; malnutrition and dehydration; patient smoking areas, used by those tethered to oxygen tanks, with neither smoke detectors nor fire extinguishers; rapes perpetrated by staff members or other residents; failure to immunize patients for influenza or pneumonia; rampant undiagnosed and untreated urinary tract infections; using catheters rather than taking residents to the toilet or using diapers, because of staff shortages; falsified death records when a staff member may have been to blame; and encouraging the elderly or their families to sign away their right to sue, and commit to arbitration instead, by burying key documents in the stacks they must sign at admission.

In its 2010 report on nursing homes, *U.S. News & World Report* said that of the 17,000 skilled nursing facilities in the United States, home to 1.5 million extremely vulnerable people, 1,855 received the government's highest rating, five stars, and another 3,661 a four-star rating. But the magazine and, more tellingly, the Medicare website warn that these ratings are partial, haphazard, and easily manipulated because of the degree of self-reporting involved. The Medicare website, in the "Nursing Home Compare" tool for consumers, lists three broad categories: Health Inspections, Staffing, and Quality Measures. The first is derived from on-site monitoring every twelve to fifteen months by state inspectors, who then report to the federal government, as well as an examination of the prior three years of resident and family complaints. The second category, Staffing, does not distinguish between time spent on administrative tasks and time with patients, and is self-reported by the home, based on payroll records for the two weeks prior to the state visit. The third category, Quality Measures (including severe pain, extreme weight loss, and use of restraints), is also self-reported, an honor system that includes no audits. In 2010, there were 131 homes on the "special focus" watch list. (If they fall short again, Medicare and Medicaid will drop them.) Imagine if anyone were actually watching all the things that matter. The list would top 131.

Apart from brute treatment and dangerous neglect is quality of life. In that arena, a movement for "culture change" in nursing homes is growing, which advocates, among other things, organizing the floors as neighborhoods, not as long hospital corridors; giving patients the choice of when to get up and eat and do other things that have historically been rigidly scheduled; consistently assigning the same nurses and aides to patients so they will be more familiar with their problems and develop more meaningful relationships; and encouraging humane touches like pets. Yet between 2000 and 2005, when "culture change" ideas were taking hold, the Kaiser Family Foundation found a significant increase in nursing home deficiencies reported by the government and by resident complaints. And researchers at the University of California at San Francisco reported that registered nurses spent thirty-six minutes a day with residents in 2008, down from forty-eight minutes a day ten years earlier (forty-three minutes is generally recognized as the "safe" amount of time, more for the sickest patients). According to the most recent data from the Centers for Medicare and Medicaid Services (CMS), nursing home residents average, in addition, forty-eight minutes of one-on-one care a day from LPNs and two hours and twenty-four minutes a day from CNAs (certified nursing assistants, or aides), who experts say provide 90 percent of a resident's care. Many homes, by the way, have neither RNs nor LPNs working the overnight shift, when the staffing of aides is also thinner and Alzheimer's patients are most likely to wander or be belligerent. Many also don't have staff physicians, social workers, activities coordinators, dietitians, or clergy.

The Hebrew Home, back then and now, has a five-star government rating but is still weak in its staffing (the ratings include only nurses and aides) and weakest of all in the quality, consistency, and turnover among CNAs. My family had an overwhelmingly good experience there, but even so, to provide my mother with the attention she needed, and thus give me relief from her increasingly desperate calls that this or that wasn't being taken care of, I had to supplement her extravagantly expensive accommodation with private-duty help, hired (by choice) from one of the home's subsidiaries. Both the aides and the agency's service were exemplary, but it galled me to feel that I was paying the same organization twice for the same service.

The Hebrew Home's overall physical amenities have improved, more consistent with the precepts of "culture change," but back then it was no spa, except in the public areas (the riverfront café, the outdoor sculpture garden, and the Judaica museum, which rivals the world's finest collections). The home had just broken ground for a beautiful new building (now fully occupied and organized by "neighborhood") that has only private rooms, an Olympic-size swimming pool, massage alcoves, Internet access, and other amenities meant to appeal to the headed-this-way-sooner-than-we'd-like-to-think baby boomers. Later, Resnick Pavilion would be renovated along homier lines. But at the time my mother was there, her floor had scuffed linoleum, a central nurses' station, a windowless dining room rather than intimate tables looking out on the river from wheelchair height, and a depressing lounge, the television turned to hearing-aid volume, where residents nodded off in front of *Jeopardy!* in rows of wheelchairs pressed hubcap to hubcap.

Dan finds it an affront to his efforts to do better when I describe my mother's floor, as I often did on the *New Old Age* blog—the "feeders" spooning mush into the mouths of vacant-eyed residents who could no longer do it themselves; the braying and silverware-banging of the cognitively impaired, who I mistakenly assumed would live in the Alzheimer's wing, although 80 percent of the home's population is, to some extent, cognitively impaired; the stalled traffic jam of wheelchairs at the elevator as aides pushed people, one at a time, to activities elsewhere in the building. All of that is real, and awful. What he missed in those less-than-idealized word pictures was that ultimately the aesthetics didn't matter. My mother, my brother, and I knew how blessed we were. Here, in a well-run, safe place, we could enjoy one another's company without worrying about attending to my mother's hands-on physical needs, participate or not in the larger community, and forge relationships with the staff (which for me have lasted long past my mother's death). It wasn't beautiful, but it didn't matter, because everyone (or almost everyone) cared so much and tried so hard to help us find shards of pleasure at a time of such loss and sadness. We attended a piano concerto, and my mother insisted on a seat up front so she could watch the elegant finger play. We took bumpy wheelchair rides in the spring breeze on cobblestone paths that led to the riverbank. Nurses a fraction of my mother's age enjoyed hearing her stories of an RN's life before and during World War II. No Q-tips was the favorite.

•   •   •

While my mother was still muttering about the planes she wished had hit her building, not persuaded yet that there were good times still to come, she added another sentence to her repertoire: "Throw it out." Each day we would bring her a few of her treasured possessions, which had dwindled to almost nothing after the moves from the house on Long Island to the one-bedroom apartment in Florida to the studio in Westchester and now to this dormitory-size room in Riverdale. Family photos: "Throw it out." Her children's bronzed baby shoes: "Throw it out." The tall stack of books my brother had written: "Throw it out." A collection of porcelain, silver, and glass boxes from trips she had taken with my father, and others we had bought for her on our travels: "Throw it out." The first few times I tried to cajole her: *We could make this room your own.* I was way too sunny, way too soon. Eventually I tried matching her gloom with my own. "Okay, Mom," I'd reply to each "Throw it out," and march the treasures, none valuable but all precious, out of the room. I didn't throw anything out, though. I didn't even bring things home and put them in my basement. All of them went into the hatchback of my car, where they stayed, for several weeks, until her mood lifted. Then, with no mention that I was bringing them for the second time, I filled the bookshelves, countertops, and bureau with what little was left of home.

My paternal grandmother had once sat on a stoop in Brooklyn bragging about her son Milton, the famous sports columnist for the *New York Post;* now my mother, with Michael's books on her shelves, could show off his accomplishments as an author. To this day, the staff knows which book of his was published during my mother's time there and which one he was then writing. She shared pictures of my garden in Berkeley (where I lived during a long California assignment), which was featured in *Sunset* magazine, and front-page stories I was then writing. Since her once-avid interest in current events was gradually fading, and she could not have managed the physical challenge of reading a broadsheet anyway, she refused my offer of a newspaper subscription. But I brought, and she enjoyed, tearsheets of my bylined stories. Dominating that little room was a poster-size sepia-and-white picture of my father, then nearly thirty years dead, which had hung in the press room of the old Madison Square Garden, on West Fiftieth Street in Manhattan. He was a solemn man—my mother said he fell in love with her because she made him laugh. In the fifteen-by-twenty-two-inch photo, he wears a broad grin that makes him almost unrecognizable. It's the last picture of my father I'd have chosen as emblematic, and it hangs in my house now only because it reminds me of my mother, who must at one time have been capable of bringing out that smile in him. I suspect nobody else ever saw or inspired it.

A week after my mother's arrival at the nursing home, Michael e-mailed her social worker. It was one of those rare occasions when he was as worried as I was, or worried enough to express it out loud and at great length. Adjustment to a nursing home, even for someone without my mother's history of depression, does not happen quickly, but we were being our usual impatient selves. Later, in the elevator or the parking lot, I would see other sons and daughters, their shoulders slumped in defeat and their faces stained with tears, whose parents had recently arrived. Some would recognize me as one of them, by my age and lack of a uniform, and confide that their mother or father was either berating them or turning away, refusing to speak at all. *There's nothing to do but wait it out,* I'd say. Don't take anything he or she says seriously for three weeks, maybe more. Deflect somehow the wounding accusations or condemning silence. More than likely, it will pass.

How easy it is to sound wise after the fact. I had at first reacted just as they were, taking everything to heart, believing I was to blame both for where my mother had wound up and for my inability to instantly make her feel better about being there. No wonder Dan begged me and Michael to stay away during those early weeks.

Michael's note to Hannah, the social worker, took account of Dan's "multiple warnings that the face she presents to [us] right now is not necessarily the same one she is presenting to you"; that "a transition to a nursing home, especially after surgery, is not a pretty sight and that it will take some time for the professionals to sort out what is going on, how much of it is transitory and what to do about it." Michael told Hannah that he found it easier to follow the guidance that we stay for only five minutes when she was "furious and demanding"; but it was "all but impossible" for him to just turn on his heels and leave when she was "pathetic." For me, fierce Mom and pitiful Mom were equally trying. No matter how she behaved, or how long my visit, halfway to the elevator I'd find an excuse to return to her

room, often multiple times. I'd forgotten to tell her something. I'd accidentally left my container of coffee behind. I'd neglected to loosen the caps on
the bottles of Snapple I put in her refrigerator. Even when things got better
for her, I was never able to make a clean break at the end of a visit. I couldn't
simply walk away and leave her there. What did change, as she regained
equilibrium, was that she started to make fun of me ("I thought you were
gone already!") each time I circled back.

Listing his concerns to Hannah, Michael cited my mother's total loss
of appetite. Usually she'd clean her own plate and everyone else's besides,
creating a weight problem that plagued her until nearly the end of her days.
He cited "slurred speech and lower cognitive function than we have seen
before," as well as "difficulty following simple conversation and no interest
in anything going on in the world." Despite the fact that she had walked a
few steps in the hospital after surgery, and that the surgeon believed she
would walk even more after intensive rehabilitation, she was refusing physical therapy, or balking at its frequency, setting herself up for never again
leaving the wheelchair. Michael also mentioned "much conversation about
wanting to die and a lot of crying, which is a rarity." (I can count on one
hand the number of times I saw my mother cry, all of them in the last two
years of her life.) Finally, he described my mother's numerous "unfounded
complaints about not being cared for properly—left in uncomfortable
positions, not getting a response to the call button." This, he thought, was
"an old tape," the residue of her time at the Meadowview and at Sloan-
Kettering. He was careful to say, not for effect but because we both truly
believed it, that she was being well attended to now, which we could see on
our visits. But he described "a spooky edge of paranoia to it: the doctor is
lying, Dan Reingold is lying, all in nasty tones."

Our first family meeting, which included all the staff members involved
in my mother's care, was scheduled for mid-October, giving her time to
settle in. Meanwhile, a psychiatric consultation was ordered, less because
of her behavior (which Eileen, head nurse on her floor, would later tell
me was typical) than because of her history. In fact, Eileen said, during
those early weeks, when a newcomer is in the slow process of building
trust with the regular professionals on the floor, almost anything she says
is best ignored. A premature consultation with a white-coated stranger,
Eileen said, can be read as a betrayal by the day-to-day floor staff, like
you've ratted a newcomer out to "the authorities," when the emotions she
expressed were entirely appropriate to her circumstances. The strategy

wasn't to ignore distress but to keep it in the family, so to speak, Eileen said: get to know the resident slowly and give her a chance to get to know you. In retrospect, I can see Eileen and Hannah's skill in this regard. From the very first, both of them recognized my mother's preference that others keep their distance rather than invade her privacy or try to win her over with what she considered premature, insincere, or unwelcome intimacy. Making friends with her, as both of them eventually did in a way I'd never seen before, was a whole lot more like making friends with a wary cat than like making friends with a dog, who wants to be your pal for life the first time you fill the food dish.

But rules were rules, and rules dictated an urgent psych consult, since my mother's case was special: a lifelong history of depression, several psychiatric hospitalizations, and on-again, off-again treatment with various antidepressants. A geriatric psychiatrist was summoned for several consultations. The first time he came (my mother never spoke to us of these visits; I later saw the psychiatrist's notes in the Hebrew Home's records) she was blunt and self-aware in a way that would have both impressed and terrified me. She told him she'd had episodes of depression, treated and untreated, her whole life. She defined herself as "a control-freak personality" and said "living like this"—dependent on other people for the rest of her life—was "intolerable." She told him she had cried in front of Michael and me, which we'd never before seen, and talked about killing herself but without any specific plans. (Mental health professionals say "suicidal ideation"—an actual plan—distinguishes those who really intend to do themselves harm from those who are simply signaling great distress that needs attention.) "I'm as bad as I can be," she told the psychiatrist, according to his notes, which I take to be verbatim because he placed them in quotation marks to distinguish them from his own observations. He made some medication changes, said he'd return in a few days, indicated he wasn't alarmed, and did not mark subsequent visits as "urgent."

The nurses shortly reported to the psychiatrist that my mother had perked up a bit and that her appetite was returning. Her next account to him confirmed that. She told him she continued to feel sad a lot of the time and to sometimes wish she was dead but not to the extent of imagining how she might accomplish it. Absent a plan on her part, he remained unalarmed, continued tinkering with the medication, and said he'd visit again soon. In the next two weeks, the nurses' notes reveal a woman having good days and bad. Sometimes she was cooperative and pleasant, other times demanding and morose. In the space of an afternoon, she'd go from "anxious" to "adjusting slowly." She was obstinate about the physical and occupational therapy and alternately refused one or the other.

She had arrived from the hospital with a catheter still in place and wound up with a urinary tract infection; oddly, the elderly are more likely to manifest infection with cognitive symptoms (sometimes to the point of delirium) rather than physical discomfort or fever, as in a younger person. It would take a month for the infection to clear, after which she became (but for some lesser episodes) her old self: antisocial, but a lively conversationalist with the few people she deigned to talk to. She was sharp as a tack, to the point where her piercing words sometimes wounded. She was also more able than most to tolerate the physical limits of old age and the confines of nursing home existence, because in many ways it resembled the life she had always lived, sedentary and solitary but for the company of books, television, and a deck of cards for solitaire.

The nurses, social workers, and rehabilitation staff rolled with the punches. Her case was clearly routine to them. With direction from the geriatric psychiatrist, they found the right mix of psychiatric drugs, adding and subtracting, changing the dosage. No one had ever worked so hard to get the cocktail right, and for the first time she complied. In the past she'd taken these meds at will, like aspirin, starting and stopping when a symptom went away. Now the pills came several times a day in a little white cup. Someone handed it to her, and she swallowed what was in it. She was finally taking antidepressants the way you'd take medication for any chronic disease—say, diabetes or high blood pressure. By taking her meds regularly, I see now, my mother was "happier" (a peculiar word under the circumstances) than she'd ever been. I wonder if this could have happened in any environment but a nursing home.

While her mental health history was far from typical, there is a broad lesson here, maybe several. However depressing old age can be, and for most people it is, geriatric psychiatrists can manage the symptoms well and should be an essential part of the care team. Also, in my parents' generation, therapy was rare and often considered shameful; psychopharmacology wasn't ubiquitous and sophisticated, as it is today, and emotional problems were often kept secret. Don't assume that your parents were happy-go-lucky in middle age and suddenly have fallen down a black hole. They may have hidden emotional problems their whole lives because of ignorance, social opprobrium, lack of options, and a generational gestalt that could not be more different from our own. Their mental health was none of your business before, but it is now. Attend to it as you would to their physical health, without judgment or differentiation from any other common, chronic, and treatable disease. Outside an institution this may be harder, surely less automatic, but perhaps even more important, since living at home with no company all day but an aide can be very isolating. A professional should be on guard for depression and prepared to judiciously medicate.

The day before the family meeting, the psychiatrist described my mother as "clinically very different from previous evaluations." Her intense sadness had passed, she told him. She didn't want to die and may never have really wanted to. "It was all talk," she said. She was trying to "develop a new attitude" and "have more patience." She recalled the circumstances of her arrival—directly from the hospital after surgery, amid the destruction of the World Trade Center, "which made everyone crazy." Yes, her lifetime pattern had been to minimize distress, to do the stiff-upper-lip thing to excess. But at the family meeting with ten professionals—nurses, social workers, physical and occupational therapists, dietitians, a doctor, my mother, my brother, and me—she was as forthright about her own concerns as I'd ever heard her. She was also totally engaged in the conversation, joking about a welcome loss of weight over the course of the past months, discussing her food preferences, and making suggestions about a physical and occupational therapy schedule that she thought she could manage. Here we were in the dreary dining room of a nursing home, and I felt like I had my mother back. No, I felt like I had my mother for the first time, with the rough edges smoothed from the depression and anxiety she had carried around all these years, like an armload of heavy stones. On the sign-in sheet for the meeting, her handwriting was wobbly, as it had been for months. But her voice was firm, her observations incisive and unsentimental. I saw that day the lineaments of an indomitable woman who for the next twenty-one months I would learn from and love.

CHAPTER 8

The Biology, Sociology, and Psychology of Aging

Here are some of the things we never understood about my mother's health problems in old age. A geriatrician, had we known such a specialty existed and had we been able to find one, given the mismatch between supply and demand, would have told us the following:

- My mother could not rise from a chair without pushing off with her hands. That inability is one of the primary predictors that an elderly person is approaching the point of dependency on others. It is a far more accurate barometer of how they are likely to progress in the coming years than any standard medical test.

- Her vertigo has been labeled Ménière's disease by some doctors while others doubted the diagnosis. It could have been caused by overmedication. Subtracting drugs one at a time and monitoring her progress might have solved that problem and others besides.

- Up to a point, my mother's incontinence was "functional," not "real"; it was the result of her inability to get from chair to bathroom in time, given the last-second signals that an old person's bladder sends. Carefully scheduled trips to the toilet—say, using an egg timer—would have gotten her there without the rushing that led to falls, trips to the emergency room, and the ultimate practical decision that soiling herself was preferable to injury.

- In emergency rooms or when hospitalized, she verbally abused her children and medical professionals, and her agitation sometimes reached the level of paranoia. This behavior was probably not idiosyncratic to my mother's disposition. Doctors now officially refer to these classic symptoms as delirium, and it is very common in the elderly in these environments.

- While some portion of her increasing hearing loss could be attributed to the natural aging process, some was likely due to the hardening of earwax, which occurs often among the elderly. Dissolving or removing the wax more often might have helped.

- Similarly, her bouts of potentially deadly cellulitis is also common in this age group because the skin thins, becomes less elastic, is more easily torn, and the immune system is weaker.

- Her chronic constipation, rarely cured by even heavy-duty laxatives and sometimes requiring very unpleasant enemas, might have been helped by simply drinking sugar water.

- Many of the tests she was given, sometimes more than once because the different doctors who saw her didn't communicate with one another, were ordered to diagnose ailments that my mother would have had no interest in treating even if they had been discovered. Sometimes she was good at saying no, a rare spunkiness in the face of medical authority figures. But she was never asked if she wanted the tests or told the pros and cons.

- Some, although not all, of her medical appointments took place without a family member in the room to help ask questions, take notes, or otherwise absorb information when she was in a compromised state. She had not requested this privacy. She simply did not know that her adult children were welcome to accompany her, and no one suggested to her—or to us—that having an advocate was an advantage.

- Until she reached the nursing home, no doctor or other medical professional ever asked her for her goals of care. Did she want to live as long as possible? Or was day-to-day quality of life, independence, and level of functioning more important than longevity? In the same vein, no medical professional ever suggested or assembled a family meeting on this subject, even though Michael and I would surely have a role in how she met those goals.

- Again, until she was in a nursing home, she was never referred to a geriatric psychiatrist. Depression is a different beast in the elderly than in the middle-aged. It manifests itself and responds to medication in age-specific ways.

I knew nothing about geriatrics while my mother was still alive. Geriatricians are doctors trained in family or internal medicine, with the additional requirement of a year's fellowship in the specific needs of the elderly. They are like pediatricians at the other end of the age spectrum. Pediatricians came into their own at the turn of the last century by making the case that children were not simply miniature adults. Nowadays virtually everyone with children uses a pediatrician. Similarly, everyone who is eighty-five or older, and anyone past the age of sixty-five with multiple chronic conditions (20 percent in that age group have five or more), should be in the care of a geriatrician.

As long as the Medicare system is based on paying fees for procedures and treatments, the less-is-more, treat-the-patient-not-the-disease kind of doctoring isn't going to proliferate or even hold its own. This, more than anything else, is the hallmark of geriatrics and the reason why this relatively young specialty is hemorrhaging doctors. It is all but impossible to examine an elderly person in fifteen minutes (a common increment for an office visit these days), especially one who suffers from dementia, has limited mobility, can't hear or see well, and arrives with a retinue of family members or a home health aide, who may or may not speak English. For the elderly and their caregivers, a conversation about the risks and benefits of a certain procedure often leads to a decision *not* to do something. Doctors get paid for *doing*, not for talking, so geriatricians earn, on average, only $160,000 annually. Of the nation's physicians, about 1 percent, or 7,590, specialize in geriatrics. This is down more than 20 percent in the last decade and is half the number needed, according to various expert estimates. While geriatricians consistently rank at the top of the list in job satisfaction when surveyed by medical journals, it is easy to see why few make that choice to begin with.

Only one in forty-five residents in internal medicine choose to specialize in geriatrics, and those who do are often looked down upon for choosing such an unglamorous and poorly paid specialty. I learned this several years ago when I made the acquaintance of a medical resident, Amit Shah, at the Johns Hopkins School of Medicine. At the top of his class and without the burden of debt, he decided to follow his heart into a geriatrics fellowship. He was attracted by the complex and multidisciplinary task of managing so many different diseases, medications, professionals, and venues of care, as well as being involved with entire families and having the opportunity to make huge changes in the quality of life of the frailest among us. To Dr. Shah, this was a calling for the best and brightest. Yet each time he'd pass a certain noted pulmonologist in the hallway, the esteemed older doctor would shake his head and mutter, "Waste of a mind."

Dr. Marie A. Bernard, now the deputy director of the National Institute of Aging, once ran the geriatrics department at the University of Oklahoma City College of Medicine, a top program. The field's image problem, she said, like its income problem, had to do with technology. Doctors in training "want to do laser-guided this and endoscopic that," she said. Many geriatricians joke that all their problems would be solved by the invention of a "geriascope" that would turn theirs into a procedure-driven specialty like radiology or gastroenterology.

Instead, almost half the geriatric fellowships in American medical schools go unfilled, and fewer than half of existing geriatricians choose to get recertified, as they must be, every ten years. As I write, only 9 of the nation's 145 medical schools have full departments of geriatrics, and many geriatricians never see the inside of a nursing home or a senior center until their fellowship year of training. Nobody anticipates future success in recruiting students to geriatrics. So the default doctors of choice for the elderly patients, who consume the lion's share of America's health care dollars, are internists and family doctors. Most are not properly qualified for the task, and their numbers, too, are dwindling. Few medical schools require geriatric rotations of even a few weeks for other kinds of doctors, and a resident in another specialty, including internal or family medicine, receives as little as six hours of dedicated instruction in areas as complex as incontinence, end-of-life conversations, cognitive impairment, bedsores, depression, and elder abuse.

Because of the geriatrician shortage, experts in aging are looking at other solutions. Most involve leveraging the geriatric expertise that is already available unless (or until) the pay-for-performance system is overhauled. The most frequently discussed method for leveraging expertise is teaching the core principles of geriatric medicine to all health care professionals who interact with the elderly, including surgeons, discharge planners, pharmacists, nurses, social workers, dietitians, dentists, home health aides, and the like. Another method is to make the most of the existing trained geriatricians by using them as consultants, called in by other doctors or family members to assess a patient and design a plan of care but not to provide ongoing treatment. Still another option is to use existing geriatricians as instructors in continuing medical education programs, like the ones doctors attend during the recertification process, with a focus on nongeriatricians. Other suggestions are to limit existing geriatric practices to patients eighty-five and older or those between sixty-five and eighty-five with complex needs; to make better use of existing geriatric nurse-practitioners and geriatric RNs, and create training programs to swell their ranks; and to start a government service corps for medical professionals who dedicate themselves to the elderly.

Interestingly, the common explanation for the dearth of geriatric training (both dedicated departments and curriculum requirements) is that hospitals are full of old people, and so medical students, internists, and residents see and treat them all the time. The late Dr. Robert N. Butler, a pioneer in the field as the first dean of a geriatrics department, in 1982 at Mount Sinai Medical School, and later the head of the International Longevity Center, scoffed at that notion. "All patients have hearts," he frequently said. "That doesn't make all doctors cardiologists." But even if every member of a hospital's house staff, and every doctor in private practice, understood the physiology of aging, they still would not be prepared for three other crucial elements of geriatric practice.

One is the essential collaboration with other health care providers, both professionals and paraprofessionals, including case managers, social work-ers, psychiatrists, physical therapists, occupational therapists, speech ther-apists, visiting nurses, lawyers, financial planners, unskilled home health aides, family caregivers, clergy, and law enforcement officials in instances of suspected elder abuse, both physical and financial.

The second is the array of venues in which the elderly receive care, often toggling back and forth from one to another: their own homes, their chil-dren's homes, acute care hospitals, rehabilitation centers, assisted living facilities, nursing homes, senior centers, Alzheimer's units, adult day care centers, and hospices.

And the third is the way in which their care is paid for (or not). It is far more complicated than ordinary health insurance, including Medi-care (Parts A, B, C, and D), Medigap policies, long-term care insurance, and Medicaid (in all its state-by-state iterations). As the system is cur-rently constructed, the cornerstone services of a good geriatric practice are not reimbursed: lengthy assessments, telephone consultations with fam-ily and paid caregivers, and medication management. Smart doctors know how to play with the billing codes and thus get paid, but they are still eating a lot of the cost. In specialties, even internal medicine, that involve differ-ent age groups, the assumption is that costs will average out; some patients will be cheap to treat and some expensive. But in a practice dominated by geriatric patients, the averaging doesn't work. The fee schedule set by Medi-care and Medicaid acknowledges none of this (unlike, say, in Great Britain, where physician reimbursement is indexed by the age of the patient).

Medically, what most distinguishes the elderly are their overlapping chronic and acute conditions (among them heart disease, diabetes, osteo-porosis, depression, pulmonary diseases, frailty, cognitive impairment, hearing and vision loss, malnutrition, incontinence, and even ill-fitting dentures); the way certain diseases present themselves (for example, a heart attack with no pain or shortness of breath but rather mild confusion, or a urinary tract infection with no physical symptoms or fever but eventual delirium that is either ignored or misdiagnosed as Alzheimer's disease); and the routine prescription of a dozen or more medications (which may interact dangerously, are metabolized differently because of poor liver or kidney function, and often cause otherwise avoidable falls, mental dete-rioration, and other complications). Adverse drug reactions occur, for example, in more than one-third of those sixty-five and over, and nearly 20 percent of them are hospitalized at an annual cost of $20 billion.

The granddaddy of all geriatric practices is the one at Mount Sinai Medical Center, where the quality of care has always been exceptional. This was true long before a donation from Martha Stewart turned a dowdy clinic for the elderly at the edge of East Harlem into a sleek "medical home" in precisely the same Latin street-bazaar setting. Its staff and longtime clients still refer to it as the Coffey geriatrics practice, not the Martha Stewart Center for Living, despite such Martha-esque touches as stark black-and-white photographs of exotic flowers, textured wall fabrics, sleek stainless-steel fittings, and classes for patients and caregivers in tai chi, meditation, nutrition, and fall prevention (as well as wreath-making and other holiday arts and crafts). All but the arts and crafts are oversubscribed, as stress reduction, health promotion, and prevention have been part of the zeitgeist there from the start. The signs are bilingual, and all the public restrooms contain pull cords for help. Widely posted signs advertise reasonably priced car services, and everyone on the staff speaks at least a little Spanish.

The class on fall prevention (similar to what is offered at the best, and only the best, senior centers) is a combination of education and sociability. The day I was there, the attendees saw a PowerPoint presentation explaining that one-third of older adults take a fall every year (more than suffer strokes), and between 20 and 30 percent result in a serious injury like a broken bone or head trauma. (Famous fallers in recent years include Nancy Reagan, the Queen of England, Billy Graham, Hillary Clinton, and the late Kurt Vonnegut.) Prevention techniques include getting proper hydration, using the fewest medications possible, exercising for strength and balance, making one's home safe and clutter-free (tape down or remove throw rugs, put power cords out of the way), having regular vision checkups, being sure eyeglasses are always clean, and not walking around in reading glasses. Shoes should be sturdy, with flat and thin soles, low heels, and coverage of the entire foot. Bedroom slippers should be avoided, even at home. Since many falls are the result of blood pressure dropping when going from bed to chair to standing up, the instructor, a Mount Sinai geriatrician, recommends changing position slowly and clenching one's fists or flexing one's ankles to get the blood flowing. She also suggests a hydration regime. Drink either water alone or water mixed with juice; consume it a half cup at a time every half hour for the first eight hours of the day, but not after dinner, to limit nighttime trips to the bathroom. Physical therapists at the clinic are available to demonstrate the right technique for using canes and walkers, which should be checked for proper height. The PTs will also explain how to get off the floor if one falls—absent serious injury—when at home alone. Grab bars should be in place in the shower (a doctor can write a prescription), and a mat or nonslip strips should be secured in the tub. Staircases should have handrails on both sides, and there should be nightlights on staircases, in the bedroom, and in the bathroom. Pendants to summon help are advised.

Dr. Patricia Bloom, one of Mount Sinai's staff geriatricians, invited me to shadow her at this clinic for a full day, seeing every patient she saw (with the caveat that none be identified). That way I could get a random cross-section, a wide-angle view, and thus be able to generalize about the average patient, rather than see only a close-up of a self-selected individual and family who may or may not be typical. It also gave me the opportunity to see how this unusually labor-intensive kind of doctoring gets done, as Dr. Bloom saw eight complex cases in the space of a day. This was not the fifteen-minute-long, in-and-out visit that so many of us are sadly getting used to at our own medical appointments; here each patient got Dr. Bloom's undivided attention for an hour on average.

Before I recount my visit, I want to make some broad observations. I saw multiple conditions and medications, the hallmark of geriatrics. Only one of the eight patients was sufficiently independent to come to her appointment alone; the rest were accompanied by relatives, paid aides, or both. Five of the eight patients had Alzheimer's disease or some other form of dementia, and two more were borderline. Most of those with dementia took expensive drugs for Alzheimer's, which Dr. Bloom and most others in the field, here and elsewhere, believe to be all but useless, prescribed for the comfort they provide relatives who want to think "something is being done." Most also took antipsychotic drugs to control paranoia, violence, or other behavioral issues related to middle- or late-stage dementia. All the family caregivers accompanying parents were daughters; some had serious financial or health problems of their own, but none begrudged this added burden. Most of the elderly were steadily losing weight—what would be called in infants "a failure to thrive." Geriatricians consider it a concern when a patient loses 5 percent of body weight in six months. So prescribing snacks was as important as prescribing medicine or diagnostic tests, since physical frailty leads to broken bones and a certain amount of extra body fat helps one weather a medical setback. Last, many would have benefited from therapies, pieces of equipment, or vaccinations that were not usually covered by Medicare: a certain kind of walker, protection against shingles, properly fitting dentures, swallowing therapy, and other relatively small things that would have improved their quality of life. But they did without.

Now on to the eight patients.

The first was a spry eighty-three-year-old, still able to garden and go on camping trips with her family in the Adirondack Mountains. She complained of pain in her right groin after a heavy day of weeding, and of being so tired that she needed an afternoon nap, when not so long ago she was still working full-time. Anemia had been a problem in recent visits, and Dr. Bloom worried about how thin she looked. "Can you try and eat more?" the doctor begged. "Work on the snacks." Also, one weak vocal cord was making it increasingly difficult for her to talk on the telephone without taking frequent deep breaths. Dr. Bloom thought voice therapy would help, but it cost $200 a session and was not covered by either Medicare or the patient's Medigap policy. "Maybe one class with an expert and then practice at home," Dr. Bloom suggested. "I know it's very expensive, and I wish I could explain to you why Medicare doesn't cover what it doesn't cover." When the old woman left for the lab, where blood tests would be done on-site with no need for another appointment, Dr. Bloom personally called several patients due later in the day to be sure their home health aide remembered and had transportation. One patient, coming with her daughter, was already late, and the doctor phoned them, too. There was no answer, so probably they were on the way. She would shuffle the schedule.

The second patient, with advanced dementia, arrived with both her daughter, who is a nurse, and an aide. Her ongoing medical situation was awful: blood clots in her lungs, very high blood pressure, a series of small strokes, and multiple myeloma that had left her anemic. But far more pressing was the agitation and violence she was exhibiting as a result of her Alzheimer's, which made it nearly impossible to keep home health aides from quitting. The current one, a placid West Indian woman, was in her second week, and the old woman had already hit, scratched, and threatened her, brandishing a cane. Dr. Bloom had given the daughter, because of her profession, wide latitude to tweak her mother's antipsychotic medications so the aides wouldn't quit and she could avoid a nursing home. Her medication list, besides multiple dementia drugs and antipsychotics, included numerous blood thinners (already at the maximum possible dose), a stool softener, and vitamins D, B$_{12}$, and iron. The daughter asked what stage (there is an official ranking from 1 to 7) of Alzheimer's her mother had now reached. Dr. Bloom hadn't tested her for a year and a half because there wasn't much value in knowing; the timing of death is unpredictable even at stage 7, the most severe. The woman was still able to speak, but barely, and her daughter understood the gravity of that. She also understood the pointlessness of the dementia medications, but they consoled her brother and sister. Both doctor and daughter suspected the patient had recently had another small stroke, as she now listed sideways in her wheelchair, a new development but one for which there is no remedy. "Being a nurse . . . ," the daughter said, "sometimes it helps, sometimes it doesn't, 'cause I know." Dr. Bloom nodded sympathetically. On the prevention side, Dr. Bloom suggested a shingles vaccine, as the disease is common in the elderly and often excruciatingly painful. It cost $200 and wasn't covered by Medicare. They postponed the decision until the next visit.

The third patient was accompanied by her daughter, whose car had gotten a flat tire somewhere between her workplace at City Hall, the home she shares with her mother in the Bronx, and Dr. Bloom's office on Ninety-ninth Street and Amsterdam Avenue. She had to buy two new tires on the spot and surely was ripped off. That combination of events would have sunk many of us, but she just laughed it off, blessed with the perfect disposition to be caretaker for an old woman with dementia related to Parkinson's. The daughter herself, at fifty-two, for reasons unclear to me, was tethered to an oxygen tank and had to use an often unreliable public van service to get to work because she couldn't manage the subway stairs or afford daily parking. An aide was with her mother twelve hours a day, and friends helped out when she was late coming home from work, which happened often. Her mother, who was from Puerto Rico and spoke no English, had low blood pressure and swollen ankles unless her legs were elevated. One stent had already been put in, and she would not likely survive surgery to insert another. She had trouble swallowing, stomach problems, and no interest in food, except maybe a few grapes or a mini-muffin. Dr. Bloom made no changes in her medical regime but suggested the daughter tape down the scatter rugs so her mother didn't fall, since she refused to use a cane or a walker and the daughter couldn't afford to buy wall-to-wall carpeting. The daughter was profuse in her thanks that Dr. Bloom had rearranged her schedule for their lateness.

The fourth patient, also Spanish-speaking, had taken a bad fall on the way to the bathroom recently. Luckily, she broke no bones, but her blood pressure was very high and her pulse alarmingly low. Dr. Bloom called her cardiologist, had a whispered conversation, and returned to the patient and her aide with suggestions about how to get out of bed to avoid dizziness—by sitting on the edge and counting to ten before getting up, then standing and counting to ten before walking. The patient had recently had a colonoscopy, at the age of ninety-three, because scarring from another medical issue had blocked her intestines. She had had several bad drug reactions while hospitalized. She also had advanced kidney disease. Her appetite was nonexistent, and her weight was plummeting. The aide couldn't answer all of Dr. Bloom's questions, so she left a message for the woman's daughter, who usually came along but had had an emergency at work. Dr. Bloom sent the aide home with only one prescription: "Her assignment is to eat." The woman, in Spanish, told the doctor that she hoped to live to be one hundred.

The fifth patient, once an esteemed academic scientist, had had a cascade of medical emergencies that left him greatly diminished at the age of eighty-five. He had been shocked back to life during a cardiac episode and suffered a stroke as a result, a common side effect of defibrillation among the elderly. Now his left arm was completely useless, and the right one had a tremor. He had both vascular dementia and early Alzheimer's. He had once played the flute but no longer could. He needed help tucking in his shirt. He took a complicated cocktail of antidepressants, blood pressure and heart medications, a cholesterol drug, and something for gout. He was unsteady on his feet and fell often. He was losing weight at a rapid clip. His aide was a gem. She suggested a different cream for the patient's psoriasis. Dr. Bloom agreed. His wife was also in the examining room, thumbing through a magazine and looking oddly disengaged. She, too, Dr. Bloom and the aide would tell me later, had early Alzheimer's but still tried to rule the roost at home. Keeping her out of harm's way, despite her angry resistance, was more work for the aide than taking care of the old man. "The situation," Dr. Bloom said in quiet understatement, "is not good." And these, in a way, were the lucky people. Money was no object.

The sixth patient, by contrast, was about to move out of one assisted living facility and into another because she and her daughter could no longer afford the nicer place. The ninety-year-old woman, mildly demented and

almost deaf, was mostly oblivious to the impending move and the fact that
her daughter had a complicated kind of cancer. Rather, she was cheerful
in a silly-looking straw boater. She took antipsychotic drugs to quiet the
voices in her head at night. She had had her left knee replaced a while
back, so the pain there from Paget's disease was gone. She repeatedly com-
plimented me on my blouse and shoes. Dr. Bloom moved her chair close
to the old woman's so their knees were touching. The doctor urged her to
be patient with the change of location, and to understand there would be
a period of adjustment. The old woman said, as if repeating something her
daughter had told her many times, that she knew "it's not as lush as where I
am now," but she would still be able to read and watch television. Then she
told me again how pretty my shoes were.

The seventh patient was a ninety-two-year-old man, his wife by his side,
whom Dr. Bloom hadn't seen in more than four years; they had lived half
of each year in Florida. Now back to New York full-time, the couple had
pushed for a quick appointment, as if it were an emergency; the doctor
had preferred a longer time slot a few weeks hence, so she could do more
than "just get the lay of the land." This visit might as well have been their
first, since the man's chart had been purged when Mount Sinai went to
electronic records. He had had a pacemaker for a long time for arterial
fibrillation, high blood pressure, bowel problems, and chronic insomnia.
His wife said he now barely slept at all, "running to the bathroom all night
long, every hour on the hour." When he got up, he was dizzy, so each trip
to the bathroom meant turning on the light and making sure he didn't fall.
Two urologists had told him there was no prostate problem. Dr. Bloom
was dubious. In addition, his legs were swollen and black and blue. He
tired during his regular walks. A vascular specialist had said he had no
circulation issues; again, Dr. Bloom was dubious. She suggested compression hose until they could figure out exactly what was going on. Dr. Bloom
questioned him about whether he was having any cognitive issues, and he
immediately asked if he had Alzheimer's. He often couldn't retrieve certain
words when he searched for them, he admitted, but he could remember
them later. No, he hadn't gotten lost, he told her. No, he hadn't left the stove
on accidentally. Dr. Bloom asked if the memory issues were worse or the
same as they had been. He said the same, but his wife's face said otherwise.
Dr. Bloom needed a longer appointment with him. She needed test results.
She wanted another urologist's opinion. The patient mentioned that his

wife had terrible vertigo and that she, too, needed a local doctor and a full physical. "We'll work on you first," Dr. Bloom told him.

The eighth patient was an African-American woman, eighty-five, with high blood pressure, high cholesterol, and diabetes, all risk factors for dementia. After a recent hospitalization, when her blood sugar had plummeted dangerously, she had suffered a fairly typical hospital-related delirium, which never cleared. Dr. Bloom said she had probably already been in the early stages of dementia, which became florid after the hospital episode. The patient insisted otherwise, because she could recite her Social Security and ATM card numbers. She also insisted that the niece who had taken her into her home because of her deteriorating condition was stealing her jewelry, reading her mail, and using her food stamps to buy what she wanted at the grocery store instead of what she was supposed to buy. Amid the harangue, Dr. Bloom tried to remind her that her niece had put the jewelry away so it would be safe and had stepped up to the plate when she was alone with nobody else to help her. But the doctor, not denting her paranoia with these facts, also commiserated about the loss of independence after a lifetime living alone. She suggested the old woman do her own grocery shopping, accompanied by her aide, as she was more than capable of the walk, which would do her good, in terms of exercise, fresh air, and getting the items she wanted. To prove the point, Dr. Bloom took her out into the hallway and had her do long laps. The aide, who had accompanied the old woman to the visit, told Dr. Bloom that she tried to get the patient to go out, but that she responded angrily to any pressure. "That's what I'm worried about," Dr. Bloom said.

Both to recertify existing geriatricians and to expose other doctors to the principles of geriatrics, the physicians from Mount Sinai, with guest faculty from other departments across the country, conduct periodic four-day continuing medical education courses in New York City. I have attended twice, in 2006 and 2009. These are breakneck events, one hour-long class after another, with brief bathroom stops in between, plenary sessions at the start and end of the day, and lectures followed by Q&A sessions during the lunch hour. Just as I could get a glimpse of a typical geriatric patient by spending a day with Dr. Bloom, the days of classes I attended helped me understand some of what a geriatrician needs to know to take better care of your mother or father than a nongeriatrician, and what nongeriatricians who attended might want to learn, since most of their patients are old and getting older.

"SCREENING FOR DEMENTIA"
Presented by Audrey K. Chun, assistant professor at Mount Sinai and medical director of the geriatric clinic

Dr. Chun's classroom mission was to offer alternatives to the gold standard of dementia screening tests, known as Mini-Mental State Exam (MMSE). "In 2040, there will be close to nineteen million people with dementia," she told the class. "That is not a small thing." But the MMSE takes ten to twelve minutes to administer, and often a patient doesn't even mention his "senior moments" until he is on his way out the door and the next patient is already in the waiting room, she said. In addition, the test works best with middle-class, high-school-educated, English-speaking patients, and it is more effective with Alzheimer's than with other forms of dementia. The test is copyrighted, so technically a doctor needs permission to use it and must pay. The copyright and payment issue has not loomed large until now, Dr. Chun said, because few people get caught using it, but that will change as electronic medical records become the rule. But mostly, in a busy practice setting, sad to say, the MMSE just takes too long. So *The Journal of the American Medical Association* analyzed all the available tests, and from those Dr. Chun culled four that are "as good, take less time, and aren't proprietary."

The tests, in different combinations, involve remembering words, with a distraction between hearing them and repeating them; setting the hands on a clock to a prescribed hour; and recalling words without or with cues (for instance, *checkers* as the word and *game* the cue). Being able to recall a word without a cue is a better sign of cognitive health, but using the cue at least means that the word is encoded "in the filing cabinet" of the brain, and thus with the progression of dementia the patient who can use cues will be more likely to compensate for lost skills. Sometimes the patient is distracted between hearing a word and recalling it by being asked for a list of animals. Those with Alzheimer's can generally name a few and then stall. Some patients group them in categories—farm animals, wild animals, ocean animals. This ability to categorize will be helpful in the event of dementia, as it facilitates various compensatory behaviors that make it easier to get through the day in the disease's early stages. Some of the tests are harder for doctors to score than others; some have rules that are harder to remember.

All of this matters, as it adds to the doctor's time but not necessarily to the compensation from Medicare. Dr. Chun advised physicians who use the tests to bill with the code for memory loss, not dementia, because the first is considered diagnostic and pays more; the second is considered a psychiatric disorder and is reimbursed at a lesser rate. Any of these tests, she said, could be done by a well-trained nurse practitioner. At Mount Sinai, she said, medical students were used. Both alternatives save physicians' time and thus money for the practice.

She also discussed her objections to Aricept and other costly Alzheimer's drugs, which "are not that efficacious." But nothing better is available, and sometimes, if a patient or family can afford it, prescribing a drug makes everyone feel less helpless. A tight financial situation is probably reason enough not to use them. She suggested that a patient who is on a drug could go off for a while; maybe the family would see that it made no difference and quit. During the question-and-answer period, someone asked about screening people with no symptoms. Were families asking for the tests because they'd been sold a bill of goods by the drug companies? Dr. Chun said that whether they were or not, testing was probably reasonable because the risk goes way up with age. Families, she said, benefit from early diagnosis in terms of adjustment, planning for the future, and thinking about living arrangements. Dr. Chun was asked about phone calls from worried relatives. A true diagnosis cannot be made by phone, she said, but you could ask about unpaid bills, stoves left on, and car accidents—all suggest trouble.

"PROGNOSTICATION OF CHRONIC DISEASE"
Presented by Eugenia Litvirus, assistant professor at Mount Sinai

Dr. Litvirus would like to see an end to overly optimistic diagnoses, despite scientific evidence to the contrary. Intentionally or not, doctors who make them encourage overtreatment and leave families ill prepared for the future. Studies find that 85 percent of patients want accurate information, good or bad, she said. Other studies show doctors being wrongly optimistic by a factor of three. She used as examples the available data for predicting the arc of heart failure, chronic obstructive pulmonary disease, end-stage liver disease, and dementia. Some are harder prognostic challenges than others, but even diseases with highly predictable trajectories and timelines are rarely discussed in those terms by physicians. "There is an attitude of avoidance," she said. "The patient is waiting [for the doctor to say something]. The doctor is waiting [for the patient to ask]. There's a huge elephant in the room. . . . We have limited training [in such discussions] and are naturally avoidant. We also lack the tools to communicate. . . . But we can improve, with practice . . . and it is our job to give the patient and family a framework for decision-making."

"FAMILY MEETINGS"
Presented by Dr. Gabrielle Goldberg, assistant professor and education director of Mount Sinai's Palliative Care Institute, and Sue McHugh-Salera, a nurse practitioner

Dr. Goldberg and McHugh-Salera described the very communication tools that Dr. Litvirus believes most doctors don't possess, in the context of a family meeting. The setting should be quiet, with cell phones and pagers turned off. Be sure there's a box of tissues at hand. Avoid medical jargon. As you begin discussing prognosis, assess how much the family wants to know, and be very tuned in to their emotional reactions. Ask them about their goals. Does the family want the patient to hang on long enough for an important milestone? To maintain the highest possible level of functioning? To avoid pain? To go home? Make suggestions as to how those goals can be translated into a plan. Depending on the family's emotional reactions, talk about stopping or continuing specific interventions. Make sure end-of-life documents are in order. Discuss hospice as an alternative. Afterward, the professionals should assess how the meeting went, so the lessons learned can inform such encounters in the future.

The professor and nurse practitioner suggested the students commit to memory two acronyms for communicating bad news, one cognitive and one emotional, to guide them formulaically through a process that doesn't come naturally. The first is SPIKE. There's *Setting,* in which a doctor makes sure the environment is conducive to sharing tough news. *Perception* is figuring out what the patient and family generally understand of the situation.

Information is the further details and who should deliver them. *Knowledge* is the meaty stuff the patient and family need to know, presented not in the language of medical school but rather in plain English. Last, there is *Emotion/Empathy*.

The second acronym, NURSE, stands for *Naming* ("It sounds like _____ is upsetting to you"), *Understanding* ("I'm hearing you say _____"), *Respecting* ("I'm impressed you are able to say _____"), *Supporting* ("I'm available to you to help with _____"), and *Exploring* ("Tell me about your mom," or "It would help me to know what your dad would say").

Dr. Goldberg and McHugh-Salera organized a role-playing exercise, using a Mount Sinai staffer (and former actress) and a nervous volunteer doctor from among the students. They set the stage: A ninety-three-year-old woman with advanced dementia has been rushed from a nursing home to the ER without her carefully prepared advanced directive in hand. The ER tried to reach her adult daughter, but she was in the theater with her cell phone turned off. The old woman was intubated and given antibiotics, both life-saving measures that neither she nor her daughter would have wanted, which had been clearly laid out in her living will. Finally, the daughter arrives at the hospital; she is pacing and venting. She refuses to sit down and discuss the situation and possible ways to reverse course with the physician so her mother can die as she had wished. The doctor's task is to ride out the emotional storm, not be argumentative or defensive, and bring the daughter to a place of calm so that her mother's wishes, even after the unfortunate series of events, can now be honored.

"We're part of the system they're angry at," Dr. Goldberg said. "And we have the opportunity to give them back some control in an uncontrollable situation."

"DISCHARGE PLANNING"
Presented by Dr. Jeff Farber, assistant professor and hospitalist at Mount Sinai; Dr. Ancea Dinescu, assistant professor and hospitalist; and Catherine Thompson, geriatric nurse practitioner

This class also used role-playing, focusing on medication management instead of on the broader array of issues that arise around a transfer home from the hospital. Still, the case demonstrated many things that can, and often do, go wrong in this key baton-pass.

The "patient," after spinal surgery, was sent home late on a Friday night with her adult daughter. She was given a referral to the Visiting Nurse Service, a prescription for new postsurgical pain medications, and a list of regular medications that excluded some of those she had taken before hospitalization and included some that she was unfamiliar with. This left both patient and daughter utterly confused. The family was not given an emergency contact for the weekend. The visiting nurse wasn't due until Monday. The daughter wasn't warned that her mother would likely be unable to do for herself many of the things she had done prior to surgery. The entire discharge conversation, which did not include a social worker, physical therapist, pharmacist, or any of the nonmedical members of the care team, took place only an hour before mother and daughter left the hospital, when it should have started at admission. And while the brief conversation was going on, the patient was distracted (looking for her dentures) and the daughter was on the telephone (making travel plans to return to California, her home).

What a mess this sloppy exit caused! The daughter had no idea that her mother would need help getting in and out of bed and using the toilet. No meal was waiting for them at home, so she called out for Chinese food. The local pharmacy, on a weekend, didn't carry the pain medication that had been ordered and couldn't get it until Monday. Since the new medication list didn't match the old one, both mother and daughter were afraid to take the wrong pills, so they decided to wait for the visiting nurse on Monday. The daughter reached out to her mother's regular primary care doctor, who had received no instructions from the hospitalist. The regular doctor knew as little as the daughter and had no one to contact to find out more. The visiting nurse failed to appear on schedule, and again the daughter had no one to contact. By Tuesday, her mother was short of breath and her lower extremities were swollen, likely from all the missed medication. The daughter called 911, and her mother was readmitted to the hospital, which was costly and would have been unnecessary absent all the crossed signals.

Dr. Farber and his colleagues explained the missteps to the class, then outlined how to do the discharge better. They stressed starting the discussion sooner, avoiding medical jargon, and having the patient and the caregiver repeat what they'd been told to test their understanding. They talked about the importance of "medication reconciliation," jargon for making sure the pre- and post-hospital regime is clearly explained, since doses may change, branded drugs may be swapped for generics, new ones added, and old ones subtracted. They also talked about how important it is to provide the family with a contact person from the hospital team, to make a follow-up call to the family the next day, to send a discharge summary to the primary care physician within twenty-four hours, and to schedule a visit with the hospitalist within two weeks.

Dr. Farber noted that hospitals, partly because of health care reform legislation, were giving new attention to the wasteful costs of readmission, and to medication errors related to poor discharge instructions—an incentive to thorough discharge planning. Many students, during the Q&A period at the end of the class, noted how medical the presentation had been, giving little attention, for instance, to the role of social workers. Striking to me, at no point in the discussion or during the role-playing exercise did anyone ask how long the daughter would be able to stay in New York, three thousand miles from her job, her family, or both, or what provisions would be made for care after her departure. The unspoken assumption seemed to be that she was staying indefinitely. Maybe she was, but probably she wasn't.

One of the distinguishing characteristics of geriatrics is that it sees the caregiver, whether paid or unpaid, as a member of the team, not as an afterthought or an impediment. The paid caregiver is generally a poorly compensated aide who earns perhaps $15 an hour and often requires food stamps to get by. The unpaid caregiver is generally a family member, often but not always a grown daughter, with or without a job, children of her own, and siblings to carry some of the load. The geriatrician, like a pediatrician in this respect, is taking care of a patient who is being taken care of by others. Doing that properly means considering the caregiver an essential collaborator. Yes, that slows everything down. No, that time mostly isn't reimbursed. Some doctors find it a disqualifying annoyance and financial drain; it is one of the reasons they shun geriatrics. Others see it as the joy of their profession, because they know they are improving the day-to-day life of an entire family. Geriatricians often facilitate reconciliations among parents and adult children and among siblings, both of which are easier when there is a paid caregiver involved to do the dirty work, thus leaving the family more time to take care of the interpersonal matters that make redemptive change possible.

I have said much here about the role of adult children, including what they can do to make it easier and more satisfying for doctors and other professionals to do their difficult jobs. We must try to do this well, because it's the right and respectful thing to do. Also, selfishly, it provides our parents with better care and ourselves with a smoother ride through this bumpy period in our own lives.

Less has been said about the aides, especially those who work in the home, not in institutions. Home aides are solely responsible on a moment-by-moment basis for our parents. Some are agency employees, who operate under stringent rules and varying degrees of supervision; some are so-called gray market aides, hired by word of mouth and supervised and paid directly by the family. Both kinds of aides tend to be female, poor, nonwhite immigrants (legal or illegal, English-speaking or not). They are asked to do a job that includes both mundane household tasks and highly sophisticated ones, often requiring the judgment of a graduate-level social worker.

Dr. Chun, the medical director of Mount Sinai's geriatric clinic, said that these aides, above all others, have "the job of ultimate importance in the health and quality of life of our parents." Sometimes, she said, doctors can make referrals to aides with whom they have worked on prior cases and found to be particularly good. But mostly the doctors, like the patient and family, are stumbling around in the dark in terms of hiring quality people or even knowing whether to use an agency (with additional costs and often arbitrary regulations) or taking the risk and bearing the responsibility of managing such crucial employees alone. The obvious advantage of the agency employee, Dr. Chun and other experts have noted, is that they are trained, supervised by a nurse or social worker, bonded, go through criminal checks, and are automatically replaced for the day or longer if they are unable to work. They are also paid less, and the employer pays more, since a part of their fee goes to the agency. Only the classiest agencies provide the aides with health insurance, although their paychecks are subject to withholding for Social Security, disability, and other employee protections that the law requires. Often they must moonlight to make ends meet.

The advantages of informal hiring, Dr. Chun and many other experts said, are the huge cost savings and the loyalty engendered in an employee who works for the family directly, makes more money, and has the ability to use her judgment. Agency employees are bound by regulations that allow them to supervise but not, for example, administer medication, for liability reasons. However, Dr. Chun said, many "cross the legal boundary because they care about their patients," who because of dementia or mobility issues may not be able to take their own pills. Most agencies also prohibit aides from using a client's credit cards (which complicates shopping) or from driving a client's car (making transport to medical appointments a hassle, with unreliable van services, public transit, or expensive taxis). I have been struck that most medical professionals, even some with executive positions at home health care agencies, themselves use aides that they have found by word of mouth. One reason, they say, is financial and bureaucratic. Another is preference on a relative's part—say, for an aide of a certain ethnicity. Remember, though, that these professionals have the expertise and connections to make good hiring choices. They can also provide training themselves and supervise, in an educated way, what is going on in the house, as many of us could not.

I asked Dr. Chun, among others, to itemize the many skills that a home health aide needs that one would not expect to find in a paraprofessional of limited formal education. (A few, to the good fortune of the families who employ them, are overqualified for the job; some were even physicians in their home countries but are in the United States illegally and thus unable to practice their profession. But they are the exceptions, not the rule, and looking for that needle in a haystack would be a waste of time.) Dr. Chun pointed out, first and foremost, that we as adult children expect aides "to be as devoted as a daughter or son," which is a lot to ask for such a paltry wage. In the more nuts-and-bolts arena, Dr. Chun said, the typical aide is responsible for helping with day-to-day activities like shopping, preparing meals, and light housekeeping, as well as intimate ones like bathing, toileting, dressing, and eating, depending on the patient. That is the easy part. In addition, whether they supervise or administer medications, they must *manage* them—a sophisticated task when a patient takes a dozen a day, at different times, in varying dosages, some on a regular schedule, some as needed; the list potentially changes with every doctor's visit, hospitalization, or other change in health status.

An aide, as we saw by following Dr. Bloom through her day, often accompanies the patient to the doctor and is thus the second pair of eyes and ears as instructions are given; often she is the only reliable person in the room for follow-up if the patient is cognitively impaired, deaf, or blind. The aide may schedule the appointment, arrange the transportation, follow up on test results, and be in charge of ordering or at least taking delivery of equipment required in the home. If the patient has dementia with certain common behavior problems, the aide bears the brunt of either verbal or physical abuse. She must cajole a recalcitrant patient to follow the doctors' instructions, be the intermediary between sometimes warring family members, and worry about her own family at the same time. Aides who live in see their own loved ones only on weekends. Those who work eight- or twelve-hour shifts often travel long distances. In some instances, their travel time is not compensated, which is why hiring help for less than eight hours is so difficult.

One medical professional who hired a nonagency aide for her own parents is Dr. Diane Meier, head of the Palliative Care Institute at Mount Sinai and a recent winner of a MacArthur genius grant. The aide formerly worked for one of Dr. Meier's patients who had died, so she saw the woman's talent up close. The choice has turned out to be inspired, given the complex medical and cognitive issues involved with Meier's parents, a schedule that takes her out of town frequently, and two sisters who live at a distance. The aide has the intelligence and self-possession to make instant decisions even when she can't reach Dr. Meier or her siblings, like summoning a trusted friend and fellow aide to fill in if she is ill. For her part, Dr. Meier has been scrupulous about filing all the legal paperwork for the aide, seeing to it that she is enrolled in Social Security and protected in the event of a disabling injury. This payroll work, which is onerous to handle on your own, is done by an accountant who specializes in elder care cases and who encourages all his clients who can afford it to assign this task to a professional. The payroll work he does is yet another of the many cottage industries that have sprung up to assist overwhelmed families blessed with the funds to afford it.

Dr. Meier says elements of the aide's job both overlap with and diverge from child care. The main similarity is that the person being cared for is vulnerable and dependent, whether a frail or demented parent or an infant; as in child care, in elder care the daughter might feel ambivalence, guilt, even envy in farming out this responsibility to a hired hand. While my sample is too small to be scientific, Dr. Meier and Ellen Galinsky, like virtually every other woman I have asked, say that the daughter track is, by a wide margin, harder than the mommy track, emotionally and practically, because it has no happy ending and such an erratic and unpredictable course. Dr. Meier, the mother of two teenage children, notes that pregnancies are usually planned and there is time to interview many possible babysitters before the blessed event, while an elder care emergency forces an instant hire and thus creates much greater room for error.

Also more complicated than child care is that in elder care the elderly person is the employer, whether officially or circumstantially, unless he is so impaired that he has no say in what goes on in the household. "So what do you do," Dr. Meier asked hypothetically, speaking of her own family situation, with two frail parents, "if they say, 'I don't want dinner till ten p.m.,' but you [the aide] know if they eat then, they won't sleep till the wee hours of the morning, and it will throw off their schedule and their well-being? Do you insist? Do you cajole, jolly, influence them through the force of your personality, the relationship, the intimacy, the warmth? This requires enormous emotional intelligence. It is not a purely professional relationship with the clarity of boundaries of, say, a lawyer. Given the relational complexity . . . it's about finding the match."

Dr. Meier was fulsome in acknowledging that an aide's job is "unbelievably complicated, underpaid, underregarded." The work is mostly invisible, except to those in the thick of the experience, and includes tasks as lowly as cleaning up messes to those as sophisticated as family mediation. "All I can say," Dr. Meier concluded, "is that the souls who take this on are heroic."

CHAPTER 9

A Nursing Home Thanksgiving

Thanksgiving was the only holiday that mattered in my childhood, the one my brother and I still miss and have never quite managed to re-create as adults. The house always smelled delicious. My mother would be flushed from cooking and justifiably proud of her giblet gravy, which has never been duplicated since to our satisfaction. My father, who traveled a lot and missed most family celebrations, was always home for this one and made a well-meaning if awkward attempt at carving the turkey. Without belaboring life's complexities, let's just say it was the one night of the year when we passed for a normal family.

So in 2002, I set out to stage the perfect holiday, for just me and my mother, in her nursing home room, a contradiction in terms if I ever heard one. First, she'd always mocked, accurately, my uselessness in the kitchen and was thus skeptical that I was capable of feeding and feting her properly. Second, there was no ignoring the un-festive environment. In her cramped room, the only place to lay out the good china and the cross-stitched linen tablecloth and napkins was on the hospital table that swiveled across the bed, and it never occurred to me to ask if there was a more suitable envi-ronment for our holiday à deux. From the lounge down the hall, where the television blared, my mother and I could hear the Thanksgiving Day parade and later a serenade by a roving musician. Two doors down from our ad hoc Thanksgiving, a woman named Helen howled for a nurse's attention and banged cutlery on her dinner tray. Ted, once a famous radio personality and shameless flirt, sat in his usual spot by the elevators, where, freed of inhibitions by Alzheimer's, he could ogle or grope women visitors. Doris, here since she was diagnosed with multiple sclerosis in her forties and now a justifiably sour woman of seventy-something, waited for a holiday visit from her sister, who might or might not show up.

My point is that even the Cadillac of nursing homes is a sorrowful place, especially on holidays. So what if the late Beverly Sills's mother lived downstairs or Joe Lieberman's mother-in-law was in an adjacent building? My mother enjoyed hearing Sills's arias, which drifted up the stairwell when she staged extemporaneous concerts during visits. And every Sunday, when Senator Lieberman accompanied his wife, Hadassah, for a weekly visit, my mother found the Secret Service bustle and the door-to-door campaigning, even in a nonelection year, a welcome distraction. But they were rare entertainments, not the bread and butter of daily nursing home life.

My brother, out of town that Thanksgiving weekend, worried that I was setting myself up for disappointment, even humiliation, by going overboard to please my mother, something that generally ended in failure. "Remember the vacation to Sint Maarten after Daddy died?" I did. She couldn't stand the heat and humidity (or the powdered-sugar beaches and exotic Indonesian rice table) and complained constantly. "And what about the drive up the California coast?" Michael reminded me, recalling her one visit west during the decade I lived there, when my every exclamation about the redwoods or the vineyards had prompted a sneering "Since when have you become Nature Girl?" She was totally mobile then, the beneficiary of two successful knee replacements that had left her pain-free, but she refused to even get out of the car at Muir Woods or Point Reyes. Michael was right, of course. All I had to do was think back to my "welcome home" dinner when she moved from Florida to New York two autumns before. Staging a Norman Rockwell Thanksgiving, no question about it, was a high-risk endeavor.

But in recent weeks I felt that I was finally making her happy. Was she reaching out to me at the end of her life, as I was to her? Or was she just too diminished and dependent to be mean to me? With time running out, was I simply lowering my expectations, or had I maybe grown a thicker skin? I believe it was all that, and more, and that one of the astonishing things about this time in a parent's life might be that redemption is possible. The it-isn't-over-till-it's-over thing. Considering this possibility, working toward harmony, is a constructive way to get though a hard time. There is no guarantee it will happen. But be open to the chance, which could transform the rest of your life.

Given my deficiencies as a cook, I'd enlisted friends to help. We had a big fat turkey leg, because my mother thought white meat was for sissies and much preferred something she could gnaw on. We had stuffing and gravy, inferior to her own but the best I could muster; green beans, crisp to the bite, with slivered almonds; biscuits and strawberry butter; sparkling cider; and for dessert, marzipan, one of the few sweets my mother enjoyed. (I'd made the marzipan with a neighbor over the course of several weekends. First we bought the almond paste at exactly the right store; then we prepared the dough; and finally—the fun part, and my only real contribution—the ultimate arts-and-crafts project of coloring the almond paste and sculpting it into orange pumpkins with curly green stems, blazing autumn leaves punched out with a cookie cutter, and turkeys with fanned tail feathers and droopy wattles. If I do say so myself, it was gorgeous. So gorgeous that Eileen, the head nurse, took Polaroid pictures, which hung on the bulletin board long after my mother died.)

My mother was pretty confident about the main meal, because she knew which friends had done the cooking, seasoned hostesses all. But bragging that I'd helped make the marzipan was a tactical error: it would have been so easy (but less vain) for me to pretend it was someone else's handicraft. Without mercy, she warned off the other residents and staff members eager for a taste. "I wouldn't if I were you," she said. "My daughter, and she'll be the first to admit this, can't boil water." I didn't flinch, but neither have I forgotten nearly ten years later. I guess the unqualified notion that I was making her happy was closer to wishful thinking than the truth. It is never that black-and-white. I might have been making her *happier,* or happy more often, but her way of expressing it (or mine of hearing it) sometimes reverted to form. For sure, my mother wounded me less than she once had, although she never lost the ability to hit her mark with a stinging dart, and I never lost the impulse to try harder for an outright "Attagirl!" or at least a warm glance that said I'd done her proud.

· · ·

On balance, Thanksgiving was a success, surely better than the alternatives. The year before, I'd joined her in the dining room. As jolly as they'd tried to make the midday meal, I had left under a black cloud, which I then let spoil a friend's festivities by describing it with what I foolishly thought was humor. If you can't pass for normal at times like this, which means shut up or talk of other things, hide out at home or go to a movie. Nobody wants to hear about your nursing home holiday, no matter how sprightly the telling. No gift of gab is sufficient to turn one of life's black moments into a cocktail party story. Old-people-in-nursing-home tales are never amusing to other people, unless they're having the experience themselves, and then only sometimes.

Some of my friends are responsible for spending holidays with more than one elderly relative, so they traipse between their own family, their parents, and their in-laws: turkey and brussels sprouts at eleven a.m. at the nursing home, then more turkey and brussels sprouts again (maybe here they will offer string beans) at one p.m. at the assisted living facility. Or perhaps, given early-bird meal schedules, by then it will be time for pumpkin pie and Reddi-wip. The elderly hate that you have to visit them in these surroundings on a holiday, so act like you're having a decent time even if you're not. Make it seem okay, but don't go overboard—that would insult their intelligence.

For me, that almost-good-enough Thanksgiving at the Hebrew Home is a precious memory, and more than once, after my mother was gone, I decided to visit the home on that very day. I'd call Eileen to make sure she'd be there, working the eight-to-three shift before her own family's feast, as she used to do. Eileen takes holidays seriously and has nursing smocks patterned with the Stars and Stripes for the Fourth of July and with gobbling turkeys for Thanksgiving. Patronizing? I thought so at first. The residents aren't kindergarteners, after all. It's like bingo: Why do we assume people in their eighties and nineties want to play bingo when they wouldn't have dreamed of such a thing at forty or fifty? But everyone loves Eileen's silly holiday fashion statements because they love Eileen.

I bring my dog, Henry, a standard poodle, with me on these sentimental journeys. My mother never knew him, but she would have approved. Nothing made her sparkle during her last few years like my brother's Westie, Calpurnia. Oh, she was always glad to see me or Michael. But only Calpurnia sent her into gales of laughter. Tears would roll down her face as the little pooch slobbered her with kisses, a messy and demonstrative kind of affection that she'd have found intolerable, and rejected, from a human being. Only after my mother died did I learn from my brother that she had had an Airedale as a child. He knew this about her, and I didn't. I don't know what to make of that except that such discrepancies are not uncommon when siblings later in life match memories and knowledge of their parents. I loved the new things I learned about her, often from him, during these bittersweet years.

During this sentimental visit, Henry and I visited Blossom, one of two people left on the floor from when my mother was alive. Blossom's walls were covered with pictures of animals, so it was a safe bet that Henry would make her day, as Calpurnia had made my mother's. Blossom said Thanksgiving dinner had been excellent, the best in the ten or so years she'd lived at the home (an amount of time I couldn't fathom, but that seemed but a blink of the eye to Blossom, confirming what experts, counterintuitively, have told me about time flying for the very old). Blossom was singing Eileen's praises. Wasn't it wonderful, she said, that Eileen always worked the holiday, even though she had the seniority not to?

Before heading home, Henry and I paused to listen to the roving accordionist performing "I'll Be Loving You Always" and then "God Bless America." I used to hate this sort of forced gaiety when my mother was alive, as she did. Now I found it sweet, even consoling, in part because the two of us had made fun of it together. Outside, Henry and I wandered down the sloping back lawn to the edge of the Hudson River. It was just past three p.m., and the sky, in a portent of winter's claustrophobic early darkness, was already pink above the George Washington Bridge.

Out front, the shift change was in full swing. Muscle cars pulled up, spilling Caribbean music, and young Latina aides piled in. Older African-American women trudged up to the bus stop on Riverdale Avenue, headed home to Washington Heights or to Harlem. Eileen lived just five minutes away with her husband and two sons; her widowed mother lived in another apartment in the same building. Eileen would be there in plenty of time for Thanksgiving dinner, the first without her father, who had died in 2007 at the age of seventy-six.

I didn't know it when Eileen was caring for my mother, but during those years she was working the ultimate double shift (or the ultimate triple shift, if you count her own children): days at the Hebrew Home moving other people's parents from bed to Hoyer lift to wheelchair, and then nights doing the same thing for her father, who suffered from a neurological disorder that is a cousin to multiple sclerosis. Something similar was going on with Hannah, my mother's social worker. *Her* mother was barely managing in her own home back then and, as I write, is a resident at the Hebrew Home, as is Hannah's aunt, so her workdays are interrupted with routine visits to them or sudden interventions in their crises, real and imagined. She also has teenagers at home. Nobody warned us that middle age was going to be this hard.

Lily Ford is the private-duty aide whom Michael and I hired in the nursing home to give my mother a little extra attention. She would be there for a few hours in the morning to make sure my mother was cleaned up, dressed, transferred from bed to wheelchair, and served a hot cup of coffee without having to wait her turn. Lily would return later, during the afternoon shift change, between four and five p.m., when the handoff of paperwork meant my mother's requests went unheeded. I'd picked these early morning and late afternoon hours once I realized they were when my mother was most miserable. One-on-one attention then could make or break her day—and mine, since it prevented her phone calls of complaint. Lily used her vacation time each year to go down south and care for her own mother, who died at the age of ninety-one in 2007. She was also responsible for an older brother with prostate cancer, who lived in a nursing home, as well as a younger brother, who had had a stroke, plus one adult son still at home. Hers was a job of heavy lifting. It finally became too much. Lily's knees were arthritic. The subway stairs were steep. The bus trip between Harlem and Riverdale took forever. She retired at sixty-six and missed her job terribly. (Studies show that aides are getting older, that the next generation of aides is smaller than this one—as is the coming cohort of adult children—and that the workforce, paid and unpaid, taking care of *us* in old age will be both way too small and too old for the task.)

Does it bear repeating how many of us are going through this experience paddling leaky boats? So consumed can we be by our own situations that we are oblivious that our parents' professional caregivers are experiencing it, too, usually without our financial resources and other advantages. If we realized this common bond, commiserated, and displayed concern for their relatives as they did for ours, how much richer these otherwise lopsided relationships might be.

●　　●　　●

That Michael was out of the country during my nursing home Thanksgiving dinner was no surprise and also no problem. He and his wife were in Europe for the same holiday during my mother's move to New York a few years earlier without causing even a minor glitch in our exacting schedule. They are devoted, hardy travelers with a schedule honed over two decades of marriage: London or Paris at Thanksgiving or Christmas, St. Barts in late January, the beach resorts of Italy or France in July, a friend's Northern California ranch in August, and long weekends at other friends' country houses scattered throughout the year.

As time passed, Michael and I both became increasingly frayed, with the situation in general and with the unfamiliar experience of being yoked to each other. It was then that his travel schedule became my major bone of contention with him and the jumping-off point for our nastiest fights. I recall no serious disagreements about my mother's medical care, residential choices, money, end-of-life decisions, or other common hot-button issues. He insists to this day that the travel thing was not *our* issue but *my* issue, and I can't entirely disagree, since I was the only one bothered by it and vocal about my displeasure. Does that mean we otherwise would have collaborated in perfect harmony? It seems unlikely, given that every study I have seen on the subject of adult children as caregivers finds the greatest source of stress, by far, to be not the ailing parent but sibling disagreements. This surely matches my experience and that of everyone I know, and also of the readers of my blog.

On the subject of vacations, Michael was determined that life would go on, in a way as close to normal as possible, and in retrospect and for the most part I see the wisdom in that, especially since he never once tried to stand in the way of my doing the same. Except I wouldn't; I couldn't. Sometimes that's because I was replaying old tapes, fighting old battles. *Mommy liked you better, so now I'll be the perfect daughter and teach you both a lesson.*

It sounds completely neurotic, but believe me, you'll have some of these feelings; it goes with the territory. Sometimes my objections to his plans were rational, like my conviction that one of us always should be close by, within sprinting distance, in the event of an emergency and available to keep watch on daily conditions at the Hebrew Home. Weekends there meant bare-bones staffing, mostly by so-called floaters or casuals (employees with the least seniority who cycled from floor to floor and didn't even know the residents' names) or, even worse, freelancers hired by the day who didn't know much of anything.

During a long July 4 or Labor Day weekend, I would call the nurses' station to check up on my mother, introduce myself as "Mrs. Gross's daughter," and be asked, "Who's Mrs. Gross?" Maybe I was spoiled by the unusually high standards at the Hebrew Home, or maybe I was hearing my mother's voice in my head saying, *Imagine the worst thing that can possibly happen,* but I found this downright scary. So did my mother, who by then felt safe, comfortable, and mostly happy when the familiar staff was around but edgy, out-of-sorts, and needy when they weren't, even if nothing actually went wrong. The easy solution was that Michael and I took turns going away, as we did for big planned trips. But if Michael decided to take an impromptu three-day jaunt and I was already scheduled to be out of town, he was perfectly comfortable with both of us being gone simultaneously. To avoid conflict, I'd change my plans and stay home, but I made certain he knew my feelings. My self-righteous behavior was surely not helping the situation but rather hardening the old stereotypes of goody-goody sister and screw-up brother, which had been tamped down until this situation kicked up all the old dust.

I asked him, much later, which were the best and worst qualities that each of us had brought to this experience. His best quality, Michael said, was his ability to put on "blinders" (what I would call compartmentalizing). His worst was "being selfish," feeling "put upon" and "victimized." In the quiet of his own mind, Michael said, he was always asking, *Oh, Lord, why are you doing this to me?* As for me, my best quality, which Michael said he appreciated only much later, was my "incredibly annoying ability to plan ahead, which proved to have significant value." And my worst? "You make everyone around you feel guilty for failing you." Tough stuff on both counts, but true.

If mine was a relatively fair sibling collaboration, what must an unfair one feel like? How is a sister to make sense of her inequitable role (she deals with the diapers, he deals with the checkbook) and her inequitable reaction to that role, even her passive-aggressive participation in the inequity? She won't let her brother near a messy job because he won't do it right; then she gets mad because he took her at her word and didn't even try. I was guilty of this; I was my own worst enemy in getting what I needed from my brother. I set him up to fail, then fumed when he did.

I mention this in the hope that men reading this might learn something about how your sisters' minds work (or don't) when it comes to their mothers or their brothers, two of the most fraught relationships. I also hope some other sisters figure out how and why this happens to us, even to those of us who came of age at a time when feminism wasn't something to apologize for. How is it that we find ourselves, as caregivers, dealing with our elderly parents, and our male siblings, as if it were still the 1950s? This gender divide, and the raw anger it creates, was apparent to me from a blog post I wrote, "Dividing the Caregiving Duties, It's Daughters vs. Sons," which produced 282 comments. Reading them, then and now, is painful. Men and women going through this caregiving experience bray at each other, from ends of a great divide, like anchors on FOX and MSNBC.

I'd rather read a novel than a journal article, so initially I went to fiction looking for a story of this upending time in our lives. That our parents grow old and frail, in our middle age, should come as no surprise, nor that we will have a role in it, either by choosing to help or choosing to flee. Yet it knocks some of us over. I could find no contemporary fiction on the subject. That forced me to Google Scholar, where a haphazard search turned up the article "Making Sense of Sibling Responsibility for Family Caregiving," from the journal *Qualitative Health Research* (December 2008).

The piece presumes that middle-age daughters are overwhelmingly the primary caregivers, consistent with all available data; that it is a stressful experience for them; that they don't get the help they need from siblings; and that some resent that and others don't, while most fall somewhere in between. By analyzing narratives, not data, the article's four authors set out to determine what was going on: how the siblings negotiated the division of responsibility, and how they interpreted or justified the uneven distribution of labor.

Turning our lives into stories, the psychological literature tells us, is how we make sense of chaos. Out of a vast array of details, we pick what we remember and consider important and arrange it in an orderly way. Memory and selection make any account of the same event different from any other. Every "story" is a snowflake. But the one we create is the one that spools through our minds, over and over, and also the one we share with the world. With each telling of the story, the authors say, the "sense-making device" hardens the experience. In this case, the caregivers seek a rationale for their behavior and the behavior of their siblings.

In their twenty-five interviews for the article, lasting between 45 and 120 minutes, the researchers spoke to twenty-three women and two men, ranging in age from their early forties to their mid-sixties. The parents they were caring for lived in all permutations: independently, at the home of the caregiving adult, in an assisted living facility, or in a nursing home. While the location would presumably affect the workload, the resentment, and the satisfaction, all in the study lived close to their parents and reported assuming extensive responsibility and commitment of time. Also, all had been in caregiving roles for at least two years, making them veterans, not rookies, to use the authors' words. (I can surely attest to the fact that caring for a parent close by, even in assisted living or a nursing home, is a heavy burden and that two years can seem like forever, partly because you have no idea when the need for caregiving will end.)

Pencil in hand as I read the article, by two Ph.D.s and two doctoral candidates in the Department of Communications at Texas A&M University, I underlined with the indiscriminate frenzy of an undergraduate. Everything seemed true, wise, and essential to share with my fellow caregivers, both the sisters and the brothers—a helpful way of thinking about how and why we assume the roles we do. If we understood it better, would we feel less buffeted by circumstance, less put upon by others, and more the authors of our own narratives? Would reading this years ago have changed anything in the dynamic between me and Michael? I don't think so. But maybe I'd have understood my own behavior better, and his, and been easier on myself, easier on him, and easier inside my own skin at a time when nothing felt easy.

The study's first finding about the sibling division of labor was that, as in so many aspects of the caregiving experience, very little consideration was given ahead of time to how it would work. Candace, one of the caregivers quoted, was typical in her mistaken belief that this situation would never arise. "We all got blindsided by this," she said. "I don't think we even gave it any thought because our parents were just so self-sufficient, and so competent, and so not needy." The authors point to the reluctance in the family to initiate conversations about elder care and express hope that this will change as today's adult children understand firsthand that denial makes everything worse.

The second finding is that the primary caregiver falls into one of two categories. In one scenario, she considers the role to be a "highly individualistic endeavor" suited to her beliefs, personality, worldview, and skills. The absent sibling was always hardwired differently, and his or her nonparticipation is consistent with that. This kind of caregiver would automatically take on "the lion's share." It is who she is, who she has been in other circumstances, and likely who she will continue to be as life unspools. This sister has *chosen* her role; it isn't a matter of getting stuck with it by default. Even though caregiving was never discussed, it would have worked out this way anyway.

In the second scenario, the primary caregiver sees the "concept of filial responsibility" as an essential part of family life. That makes the nonparticipating sibling either an outlier or someone she must make excuses for. Here, the authors say, the stress comes from reconciling "two competing narratives." One way to do that is to identify the absent brother (or sister) as a black sheep, a deadbeat. Another way is to say that he (or she) would help if asked, but the primary caregiver already knows the drill, so it's easier for her just to continue to do it. Yet resentment that there are no affirmative offers of help seeps through the cracks of this explanation. The authors call this form of making sense of the experience "verbal backtracking" and consider it the most problematic of the sibling situations.

My family fit squarely in the first scenario. We were never a close-knit unit, as I've said; we never spent time together or watched one another's backs. Even at home, mostly we kept to ourselves: my mother in the kitchen, my father in his basement office, my brother in the den, me in my bedroom. Whatever relatives we had were peripheral to our lives. My mother was effectively estranged from her own brothers. She kept up with my father's widowed sister and her daughter while all of them lived in Florida, but neither came to visit during her final years up north, nor to her funeral.

Once I asked Michael if he ever felt isolated, just the two of us, in the task of caring for my mother—whether the absence of relatives made him sad or resentful, as it did me. "I wasn't raised to expect a family to be helpful," he said. The reply was somber, without his characteristic sass or irony.

Studies show that sons are increasingly involved in elder care—33 percent in 2009, according to *Caregiving in the U.S.*, the latest study by the National Alliance for Caregiving, AARP, and the MetLife Foundation, compared to 27 percent in 1997. That isn't a huge change in a dozen years, although the media made much of it. Drill down farther, as the studies do, and it's evident that women—why would this surprise anyone?—carry a disproportionate burden. This sequence of studies, the only ones I'm aware of to track this landscape at regular intervals, measured somewhat different things each time around, so item-by-item comparisons aren't possible. But it is safe to say that women devote more hours per week; take most of the responsibility for intimate, hands-on tasks like bathing, toileting, and dressing; are more likely to make accommodations at work that hurt their careers and their own retirement savings and benefits; and suffer more physical and emotional health issues. They also are the likely candidates (I could find no data on this) for taking their parents into their own homes, or moving into theirs, even if that means abandoning their own lives and relocating halfway across the country. And they talk about caregiving among themselves, as men hardly do; are more likely to attend support groups (which rarely draw more than a handful of people anyway, since who has time?); and complain more to whoever will listen.

Except for one trip to Martha's Vineyard, when my mother was within weeks of relocating to a nursing home, I don't believe I went out of town once during the last four years of her life and actually relaxed and had a good time. When I wasn't worrying, I was calling. When I wasn't calling, I was worrying. Whether I was doing one or the other, or willing myself to do neither, I was a nervous wreck and also furious because I was supposed to be having fun and wasn't. Actually, regularly checking up on her, however disruptive to a holiday, was the least bad of the bad alternatives. Once I made the call, I bought myself a few hours of guilt-free time. Round and round I'd go in this agitated, irrational loop, knowing I had nobody to blame but myself.

My mother never called and bothered me when I was out of town; nor did she behave, before or after, as if she expected me to be more attentive. She had never been that kind of mother and didn't change now. My brother, who truly believed we both needed and were entitled to time off, was just as comfortable and generous as she with my absences. Of the three of us, only I felt the phone—such a reassuring tether when at home, especially the commiserative calls between me and Michael—turn into a noose on vacation. The Martha's Vineyard cabin, until those years my favorite retreat, didn't have a telephone. To make a phone call, except from one of the few spots with a decent cell signal, I'd have to drive down a rutted road to the general store, which had the closest pay phone. When it was out of order—and it often was—I drove to pay phone number two, this one miles away. Often there was a line of people waiting. If I got my brother's voicemail, I couldn't very well stand by the phone until he called back if there was someone waiting behind me. In those instances I'd move to the end of the line, wait my turn again, call Michael back, and hope to catch him. "Is everything okay?" became my afternoon activity.

One of my first thoughts after my mother's death—is this too selfish to admit?—was that now I could go on vacation and not call my brother. I didn't have to be available all the time even when I was at home. I could turn off my cell phone while working, at a movie, in the car. I didn't have to take it with me when I went out if I didn't want to. It was also safe to let the home phone go unanswered when I didn't feel like talking to anyone. Never again would the number on caller ID be that of the nurses' station on my mother's floor. If it was Michael's number glowing on the screen, I was free to ignore the call. I felt lighter, liberated. Before my mother's final years, Michael and I had spoken by phone only rarely. For a while after her death, we returned to that customary communication pattern. He clearly found the silence a relief, too. But as time passed, we resumed what had started as a necessary chore and become a pleasant habit. We are now more haphazard about it, for sure, and mostly talk a few times a week, rarely several times a day. But when one or the other of us is traveling by plane, a vestige of those days remains inviolate: once on the tarmac, we contact each other with the message "The eagle has landed." That meant then, and still means, "I'm back. You're not alone."

Feeling I had to call him while I was on vacation was, of course, my invention, not his expectation or my mother's: part worry, part guilt that I'd left her side even if nobody but me seemed to think there was anything wrong with that. I also was convinced he wouldn't look after her the way I did. In fact, he didn't. I still don't *really* believe he could have been in and out of that dreadful assisted living apartment without smelling the early signs of her incontinence, although if anyone was capable of hiding it from him, it was my mother, and she surely wouldn't have announced it to him as she did to me. I still don't *really* believe he visited often enough or for a long enough time when she was in the nursing home, and I think he spent far too much time while there tap-tap-tapping on his BlackBerry. I still don't *really* believe he bothered to loosen the caps of her Snapple bottles, or even saw the point, or paid attention to her dwindling supply of coffee candies, or took home articles of her clothing that needed dry cleaning or otherwise shouldn't be sent to the nursing home laundry. That said, my mother seemed perfectly content with his level of devotion and vigilance, perhaps even preferred it to my hovering and eagerness to please. What I have come to see is that my standards weren't the only standards, maybe not even the best standards, and that measuring him against them was unfair to him, a waste of energy for me, and not necessarily in my mother's best interests. There is a lesson for you in that.

In our case, as in most, I, as the daughter, was the primary caregiver. But Michael was a better-than-average brother, especially with legal, financial, and logistical tasks. I once mentioned to a friend that I'd never even been inside the finance office at the Hebrew Home, where Michael went regularly to pay the bills, or seen a Medicaid application, since that was also one of his jobs. Only while hearing myself say this did I realize the extent of his effort and the value of his expertise. Would an hourly breakdown of actual work done (not worry or heartache, which is a matter of temperament, psychology, or even neurosis) show a 50/50 split? Probably not. But neither was it 80/20, or 100/0, as some of the female readers of my blog described. My gut tells me even their situations were not as inequitable as their accounts would have you believe. I'm not accusing them of lying but rather of being tired, overwhelmed, angry, and choosing, perhaps wisely, to direct all that negative feeling at a sibling rather than at the helpless parent. Deadbeat siblings do exist, but they are probably fewer in number than conventional wisdom would have it and more than there need to be if we looked for practical and realistic ways to divide the labor. Whoever said "Don't let the perfect drive out the good" could have been an adult female child with an elderly parent and a male sibling who she wished would do something more, or something different, or would do it her way. Appreciate whatever it is your male siblings *are* doing. Better yet, stop your constant micromanagement and shrill resentment of sex-role generalizations, and they're likely to do more.

Like it or not, the tasks of elder care are largely divided along traditional gender lines. When I wrote about that in *The New Old Age*, I suggested that it didn't matter all that much, as long as both sisters and brothers were pulling their weight. My suggestion to sisters who didn't feel they were getting the help they needed was to delegate tasks that their brothers were comfortable with and good at—boy stuff—rather than fight and refight the gender wars over who did what in the midst of an already debilitating family drama. Get through it without all that added angst. Organize as fair a division of labor as you can. Don't wish your male siblings were the same as you, since there's an obvious efficiency when partners in any enterprise have different, rather than duplicative, skills.

The result of that blog post was that I was set upon by female and male readers alike, virtually none agreeing with what I thought to be such hard-won, practical advice. It seemed so obvious and uncontroversial, both to me and to the expert I quoted, Marsha Foley, a semiretired geriatric care manager who had previously run a website and support groups for aggrieved female caretakers called Dutiful Daughters and Saintly Sons, a memorable name that was perhaps more responsible for the firestorm than either my observations or Foley's.

In my post, I referred to a common daughterly grievance, to wit: There I would be in the nursing home, switching my mother's winter and summer clothes in the closet, cleaning the dentures she could no longer clean herself, and feeling utterly taken for granted. Then Michael would breeze through for a short visit—handsome, charming, and often bearing gifts—and would be anointed "Mrs. Gross's wonderful son" by all the other old ladies, without a peep about devoted Jane.

"So what else is new?" I asked. Every nursing home employee can vouch for its accuracy.

Yes, there are daughters who ignore or abandon their aged parents and more and more sons who prove to be devoted caregivers. But they are not the norm. And as I've tried to make clear, the kinds of chores that fall to daughters and sons tend to be different. I have nothing but admiration and gratitude for my brother's labors on my mother's Medicaid application and in choosing the perfect motorized wheelchair. But I did all the unpleasant stuff. I'm not angry anymore, but I sure was while it was going on.

In the years since, I've urged female friends and colleagues, and later blog readers, not to waste energy this way. It is what it is. Take what you can get from your brother. To be self-righteous, as I was, is counterproductive and won't make you feel very good about yourself anyway. I asked Foley if, as the readers mostly wanted, her seminars taught dutiful daughters how to push back against saintly sons. "The experience is bad enough in its own right, without all that resentment," she said. "You really must give up expecting people to feel and behave as you do. Expectations are what create stress. Having no expectations, if you can get to that point, as a female, is the key to good sibling interactions."

Foley added that "part of why women get so mad" at their brothers is that "they're not suffering enough." Men "compartmentalize better, do what needs to be done, and then get on with their day. . . . And if they can delegate or pay for what Mom or Dad needs, they're satisfied that [they] took care of it," and often rightly so.

"They're not as obsessed," Foley continued. "Women think if they don't do it themselves, it doesn't count. But degrees of dedication are all subjective. There's no great doctrine that says this is enough and that isn't enough. Those are internally generated rules. And men aren't so quick to take on guilt or worry about what other people think of them."

The women saw me (and Foley, too) as traitors to the cause. Ours was a "patronizing lecture," female blog readers said, that "harkens back to . . . the Victorian era." It was "appallingly offensive," "dumb sexism," and "about the stupidest thing I ever heard." Three of my favorite comments—tart but not unduly shrill—bear repeating in full.

This may be the way things are, but I abhor anyone telling me to just accept it and shut up, especially another woman. Women have come too far to slip back. Racism is abhorrent in this country, but sexism is still okay.

Lowered expectations . . . great advice! You know things would also be a lot smoother if women didn't expect to be paid the same amount for the same work as men.

Cut the nonsense, lady! You're making the problem worse!! Men do this crap because we let them get away with it.

I wondered if these women were all so much younger than I that they really believed men and women were the same. I wondered what Germaine Greer or Gloria Steinem would have said if either had had the experience of sharing responsibility for an aged parent with a brother, especially one like mine, who was conscientious, competent, only once failed me, and even in that instance looks better in hindsight than he did at the moment. I wondered, to quote my mother, who had told them that life was fair.

The men who commented were, for the most part, enraged at the commenters' reverse sexism. "Would you like some cheese with that whine?" one asked. "Equality = My Brother Will Do Everything Exactly the Way I Want or I Will Stomp My Foot and Lecture Him on How He Is Doing It Wrong," said another. One, bless his heart, took my position that it was far more practical to make the gender differences work than rail against them:

You know that we men are good at some things and hopeless at others. Make us pay a disproportionate share of care expenses. Make us fight the system. We will grumble, sure, but we'll do it. If you make us change our elderly parents' diapers, we'll do it with a disgusted expression on our face that our parents would interpret as proof that they are a burden to their children. This isn't about equality, this is about recognizing that men have weaknesses they can't overcome, no matter how pure their hearts. Just forgive us and make us buy Mom a new wheelchair instead.

CHAPTER 10

The Make-A-Wish Foundation

My mother was never a joiner, and old age wasn't going to turn a loner into somebody who worked and played well with others. In the two assisted living facilities, and later the nursing home, my brother and I gently, and sometimes not so gently, warned a legion of kindly professionals who were eager to get her more socially involved that they would be wise to leave her alone or face a tongue-lashing. She snarled disdain at attempts to lure her from her room for sing-alongs. She had nothing but scorn for activities directors. Even when the rabbi came calling, she saw no need to be polite. She was a cultural Jew (translation: she read serious books and watched public television), she told him, not an observant one (translation: she didn't go to temple and ate shellfish). He was wasting his time making pastoral calls.

She went to one exercise class that I'm aware of—in her early and more active years in Florida—but only because I dragged her, having yet to learn the lesson of letting her be. There, a twentysomething aerobics instructor bounced around on the stage in a sequined leotard. The students, well into their seventies and beyond, worked on strength and balance from the safety of chairs, wearing underwire bras and sensible shoes. Even I found the chirpiness unbearable. It suggested that my mother, by dint of age, was pathetic, but she was never that, even at her most diminished, not in her own eyes or in the eyes of anyone who knew her. Surely there must have been a fit sixty-five-year-old to teach chair exercises to the likes of my mother, rather than the limber beauties leading yoga or Pilates classes in Santa Monica or on the Upper West Side. And if they couldn't find somebody age-appropriate, good for my mother for wanting to stay away.

Then there was bingo. My mother and I were of one mind on this subject. Eventually she joined the games, but only because she realized that as one of the very few people on her floor with her mind intact, she'd win every single time. It wasn't about bingo or, God forbid, being one of the girls. It was about getting something for nothing and gaming the system. The chits she won could be used at the nursing home store to "buy" snacks or dental floss. She liked it best when the time-stamped prizes had expired and Michael or I managed, at her instruction, to fool the cashier and "spend" them anyway, pretending not to notice the date. Until the bitter end, my mother remained frugal, contrarian, clever, and antisocial.

Then one day she got a flyer about a class at the nursing home taught by the assistant director of the MFA program in creative writing at Sarah Lawrence College, that mecca for fiction, memoir, and poetry that had produced Alice Walker, Allan Gurganus, Ann Patchett, Tina Howe, and A. M. Homes, to name a few of its esteemed undergraduate writing students. The start date for the class was unclear, since grant money was required to pay the faculty stipend. But my mother's enthusiasm was instant and unmistakable. Here was an activity she actually wanted to do, the first since bridge had become more painful than pleasurable because of her crippled hands. She'd always insisted she wasn't interested in "the family business" of writing, but the gleam in her eye and the constant inquiries about when the class would start told me otherwise.

Late in 2002, a date was set for the seven-week class. But by then the little strokes that were diminishing my mother bit by bit—death by a thousand cuts—had aggregated into more global disability. It wasn't just that check number 115 to "White Plains Radiology" was legible and check number 116 to "Cash" was written in a wobbly hand. It wasn't just that her voice was hoarse and she choked sometimes when food went down the wrong pipe. My mother could no longer hold a pencil. Her speech had gone from gravelly to very hard to understand for all but the few of us who spent a lot of time with her. The course description was unambiguous and required the abilities to write and to engage in class discussion. "We will read some wonderful writers and talk about what we, as writers, can learn from them. Then we will do some writing ourselves—inspired by the readings and our conversations and reminiscences, anecdotes and stories. . . . Don't worry if you've never written before. We will all have fun learning."

That buoyant "we will all have fun" couldn't possibly include my mother, not when "talk" and "conversation" and "do some writing ourselves" were central to the enterprise. She was the first to note, with quiet resignation, that she had missed the moment and wouldn't qualify for the class. My role by now, as I saw it, was sort of like the director of the Make-A-Wish Foundation for kids with cancer. Had she wanted to go to Disney World, I'd have booked a plane, a hotel, and a wheelchair, and off we'd have gone. I was there to solve all problems that came our way and make it look easy. So I needed to muster an optimistic counterargument about the writing class. "Of course you can take it, Ma," I'd say. "All we have to do is _____." Except I couldn't figure out how to fill in the blank.

My mother, scarred by a mean-stepmother childhood, had always been a glass-half-empty type, and I had learned that from her. "What's the worst thing that can possibly happen?" she would ask me as a youngster burdened by worry. Then she'd pause long enough for me to fathom something truly awful. "Well, plan for that, and then you'll be fine," she would conclude. It would have been practical advice in the right circumstances, had I been an adult, but it was pitiless to a teenager.

In advanced old age there can be great wisdom in this mind-set. Not that optimism and cheerfulness aren't wonderful qualities, regardless of age, and many studies show they extend both the quality and quantity of life for the elderly. But foolishly high expectations can be a setup for disappointment, and my mother could see the realistic obstacles to her taking the class. This clear-eyed view of her current situation was nothing like the clinical depression that had plagued her for most of her life. Depression is a distorted state, when mood and circumstance are completely out of sync. At this point, well medicated and more cheerful about her situation than most of her peers I met in the nursing home, my mother's glass was truly half empty—no, three-quarters empty—and was growing emptier by the day. Age and illness had already snatched from her such vitally important things as independence, mobility, and privacy. Now they were claiming smaller things, too, like the ability to write or read aloud. Anyone in his right mind could see this. I, however, was intent on moving heaven and earth, like one of those women who manages to bench-press an automobile off a trapped child. I wanted to make everything right for my mother, if I could. Being that kind of advocate meant summoning, by turns, creativity, persistence, cool reason, and theatrical tears or lacerating rage, whichever worked best in any given situation.

For the adult children of frail elderly parents, there is so much we cannot do. We can't make them young and healthy again, their lives spread out before them. We can't restore their dignity or deny their fear. What we can do, up to a point, is get their needs met and their wishes fulfilled. The needs part is obvious. Of course it was my responsibility, and Michael's, to be sure my mother was housed, fed, and clothed. It was our responsibility to be sure she wasn't left for hours in a dirty diaper; to be sure she was not in unnecessary pain or medicated into a stupor; to be sure the nurses came when she needed them and that the aides didn't toss her around like a sack of rice; to keep track of her finances and her dry cleaning; to make it clear we were on the case, ready to jump in and demand better if the professionals weren't doing their jobs.

It was also our responsibility to improve the quality of her life in whatever small ways we could. I could go to her preferred shop for the hard candy she liked, even though the neighborhood supermarket had something similar. I could search out the brand of dental adhesive she liked best. I could replace the wire hangers at the nursing home with plastic ones. I could hire a private-duty aide for the hours of the day when she felt most neglected. I could "sneak" her favorite foods into the nursing home for her birthday, even lobster Cantonese, which the kosher rules forbade. I put the Chinese food in an ice chest and wrapped the ice chest in woolen blankets so nobody would smell it. When it still reeked of forbidden pleasures, I added a layer of plastic sheeting. My mother ate with gusto and also got to tweak the pious, a happy twofer.

By the late fall of 2002, I had already had many such small occasions for advocacy. I would have many more. But with the Sarah Lawrence semester upon us, my job was clear: to get my mother into this writing class.

The vitally important role of adult children as advocates for their frail, elderly parents cannot be overstated, especially once they're in an institutional setting, whether it's a hospital, an assisted living community, a nursing home, or anyplace else where a myriad of authority figures a fraction of their age control what happens to them. For the adult child living a long distance away, this is an abiding problem, as nothing substitutes for your physical presence. It is one of the main reasons, according to Howard S. Krooks, an elder care attorney who practices in Florida and New York, why the reverse migration of snowbirds is both increasingly common and generally wise. A local geriatric care manager is the next-best solution, Krooks and others say, but nobody advocates for the elderly better than their own children when a gentle, or not-so-gentle, push is needed. (Hence the fear of many childless people, me among them, who wonder who will do for us what we did for our parents.)

"Management" is what my mother called the people who ran the show and thus controlled her day-to-day circumstances and, to some extent, her long-term fate. She totally understood their power and, as she grew ever more helpless, came to fear them. Indeed, this uncharacteristic cowering, though I knew it was common among the institutionalized elderly, was a key marker of her accelerating decline and of the growing role Michael and I would have to play as her protectors. You will have to play this role, too— by building meaningful relationships or, failing that, by currying favor. See to it that the management types like you. (In a perfect world, they'd like your parent, too.) And make sure they're on your side. Your role now, as one geriatrician, Dr. Woodson, told me, is like that of parents in a school community, interacting one-on-one with teachers and bringing their talents to bear in the collective enterprises of the classroom and PTA. Whatever you did to kiss up to your kids' teachers, find an age-appropriate way to do it now with your parent's professional caretakers.

In elder care environments, however, the squeaky-wheel approach isn't always effective. If you say nothing when you're unhappy about a parent's care, then nothing will change. But if you say too much, or say the wrong thing at the wrong time—as I did at the Meadowview—you're likely to be labeled a "problem child." You'll be ignored, at best, and may make a bad situation worse or create problems where they don't already exist. Do not berate the staff, constantly complain, or micromanage unless your parents are in a truly awful place—and then your energy and enterprise would better be used getting them to someplace better. The nurses on my mother's floor couldn't bear the devoted son of the woman in the room next door. A retired civil servant in his late fifties, he arrived before breakfast and left only when his mother was asleep. She was demented, had had many strokes, barely knew he was there, and didn't even need his help at mealtime, as she was tube-fed. He had little to do all day but bother the nurses. So that's what he did. The best that can be said is he was always polite, yet he did more harm than good with his hovering.

Ulterior motives don't necessarily conflict with effective advocacy, but they certainly can, and it is worth asking yourself, *Who am I doing this for?* When I tried to nudge my mother into making friends, handpicked by me, most were either inappropriate or unwanted, or they reflected my interests, not hers. My job would have been easier if she were a social creature, busy with the other ladies and thus less dependent on me for companionship. My efforts to find friends for her were selfish, and pointless, except to show the staff what an engaged and engaging daughter I was. Only in retrospect do I see how often being the "perfect" daughter means doing the wrong things for the wrong reasons.

Similarly, when I cajoled my mother into picnics on the banks of the river, it had more to do with my desire to escape her claustrophobic room and the institutional sights and sounds in favor of the sun on my face, the smell of flowers, and the feel of fresh air in my hair. She, for sure, preferred a hot dog from the local deli to the standard lunch offering but would have been happier eating it indoors, especially when I dragged her onto the lawn not just on the fine days of spring but on the muggy summer afternoons she detested. This wasn't helpful. The food Michael brought and shared with her in her room, dreary location notwithstanding, pleased her far more than my forced excursions into the great outdoors.

By the time my mother landed in the nursing home, both Michael and I had mostly mastered effective advocacy, the result of accumulated wisdom, a new facility that had an entirely different attitude toward both residents and families, the realization that we had to conserve our energy and pick our spots, and the serendipitous differences in our temperaments. At the Hebrew Home, Michael's easy charm was an instant asset. He figured out that my mother's primary nurse shared his birthday, July 16. He flirted shamelessly with the pretty young aides but never crossed the line from flattery to creepiness. He brought his dog to every visit, the ultimate social emulsifier. He knew whose children played football and whose were professional dancers. He brought the staff autographed copies of his books, which many treasure to this day.

When it was necessary, Michael and I played good cop–bad cop, keeping our interlocutors off balance by alternating roles, rather than the attentive daughter–neglectful son scenario, which is surely what they were used to, so they never knew which of us was going to charm and which of us snarl. But usually we got what we needed without resorting to such tactics, because the staff liked our mother and liked us, and we came to them with problems we hoped to solve in partnership, not harsh criticism or high-handed orders about what we expected them to do for us. Generally, once we'd arrived at a solution, I took over, put my micromanaging skills to useful purpose, and got us to the end zone. The creative writing class was one example of advocacy where everything went right: no voices were raised, no threats made, and what had seemed the longest of long shots resolved itself in a way that was easy and satisfying for everyone involved. Indeed, while my mother was the first person so impaired ever to take the Sarah Lawrence class (taught then by Alexandra Soiseth), recent classes have included Hebrew Home residents who needed much the same kind of help we did, provided in much the same way. I know that because I've helped Alexandra teach the classes, taking dictation for a blind woman and for a man who could no longer hold a pen.

Back in the fall of 2002, the social worker on my mother's floor had just been assigned an intern from a graduate school of social work and was casting about for a project that would engage her. I knew nothing about this when I went to see Hannah to discuss my mother's longing to take the writing class and what seemed the insurmountable obstacles to that happening, but she was ready with a solution. Before the class started, she would assign the intern to spend time with my mother, who enjoyed the company of a bright young graduate student given how few of her fellow residents were cognitively intact. Hannah didn't make explicit to my mother that her goal was to see if Christine, the intern, would be able, with lots of exposure, to understand her speech. But if she could, she would then serve as Edgar Bergen to my mother's Charlie McCarthy in the writing class.

The experiment worked. Like the rest of us who spent a lot of time with my mother, Christine eventually understood most of what she was saying. In the classroom Alex would explain the building blocks of good writing and the exercise for that day. Then Christine and my mother, in her wheelchair, would retire to the hallway so the dictation process wouldn't disturb the others. When they had finished, they'd return to the classroom, where Christine would read aloud for my mother when it was her turn to present her work. As the term progressed, other students came to understand my mother's speech well enough that she could participate, in a limited way, in class discussion. Sometimes Alex brought a teaching assistant from Sarah Lawrence who shared the dictation task with Christine. Sometimes Alex herself wound up as the transcriptionist. Sometimes I came, too. What had seemed an impossible problem became instead, for all of us, truly pleasurable.

The class, back then, met in a cramped basement room, redolent with the smells of canned vegetables and overcooked meat from the vast institutional kitchen and the sizzle and steaminess of the nursing home laundry. The six elderly students barely fit around the table, what with their walkers and wheelchairs. Only one was ambulatory. Only my mother had a snazzy motorized wheelchair, English racing green, chosen for her by my brother as if it were his very own sports car, once she could no longer push herself around in the nonmotorized variety. Everyone in the class was clear of mind, which led to friendships among residents who might otherwise never have met since they lived scattered in many buildings. All were hard of hearing, one pretty close to deaf, so Alex used a portable microphone. Except for that remediation, she taught in an entirely unpatronizing way, not that differently from how she taught at Sarah Lawrence.

Cultural programs for the elderly conducted by accomplished professionals like Alexandra have obvious benefits. These were documented for the first time only recently in a three-year study called *Creativity and Aging,* sponsored by the National Endowment for the Arts and conducted by the late Dr. Gene Cohen, founder and director of the Center on Aging, Health, and the Humanities at George Washington University and a pioneer in the field of elder care. Dr. Cohen and his fellow investigators compared subjects, whose average age was eighty, who participated in artistic pursuits—such as painting, dance, music, pottery, poetry, or oral histories—with those in a control group whose activities were more catch-as-catch-can. They didn't quite put it this way, but the distinction was between rigorous artistic endeavors and amateurish (some might say infantilizing) pursuits like making potholders or Valentines. Those engaged in artistic pursuits showed improvements in overall health, less frequent doctor visits, fewer medications taken, fewer falls, and improved morale—an impressive inventory of change that was not evident in the control group.

The Sarah Lawrence class at the nursing home was not among Dr. Cohen's three demonstration sites, but it cut its students no slack. It was built on the same pedagogic principles that Alex and most creative writing teachers use with workshop students: free writing and the timed exercise. The point of free writing is to just let it rip, write without stopping, however mechanically, regardless of topic, quality, or logic. It doesn't matter if you produce good writing or garbage, if you stick to the subject or follow stream of consciousness. The goal is process, not product. The timed exercise is a variant, intended to keep your hand moving without crossing out or worrying about spelling, grammar, or staying within the margins. The idea is to lose yourself in the subject, not get self-conscious and stuck. The increment may be ten minutes or an hour. The only requirement is that you commit yourself to writing for the full period of time.

The only difference with the elderly, Alex told me later, is that for this age group the past looms larger and larger and the present recedes. They write about their childhood homes and playmates, long-ago family holidays, the deprivations of the Depression and World War II, streets lit by gas lamps, and woolen stockings darned long past their prime. This rewinding backward is a well-known characteristic of Alzheimer's disease, where memories and skills are lost in the reverse order they were acquired (so hauntingly captured in the movie *The Curious Case of Benjamin Button,* which was far more than a Hollywood trope). Hadassah Lieberman's late mother was cared for by the same private-duty aide who later tended to my mother, and Lily once told us that the European-born old woman first forgot how to speak English, then Hebrew, and later Yiddish, the reverse order in which she had learned the languages. An elderly friend of mine, literally losing his fine mind to this epidemic disease, cannot remember what he had for breakfast or what I do for a living, but he can still tell me in detail about commanding a unit of Japanese-American soldiers in World War II or taking his first parachute jump.

Even those of us blessed with parents who are not losing their short-term memory to a neurological disease should not dismiss how much more important the past becomes than the present. Take the time to listen to your parents' stories, however tedious they may sometimes seem when told over and over. And take no offense at their waning interest in *your* stories.

During the heyday of New York City journalism, my mother had devoured newspapers, several a day. She was devoted to radio and TV public affairs talk shows, especially the Sunday morning lineup. When Adlai Stevenson was humbled by Dwight Eisenhower, she wept at the kitchen table, and in the hours after John Kennedy's assassination, glued to the TV, she burned a pot roast, a nearly impossible event. Unlike my father, whose early and brave support of civil rights and other liberal causes gave way to befuddlement and a lean toward the right during the 1960s and 1970s, my mother moved ever leftward during the Vietnam War, Watergate, and beyond. During the years when we shared little else conversationally, we always had that. Until we didn't. Until the world stopped mattering to her—or so it seemed to me.

Little by little she lost interest in current events, newspapers, and the talk shows that had been such essential fixtures in her week that she would interrupt phone calls with her children to watch them. She also lost interest in our work and our friends, and stopped asking the usual questions about the professional and social details of Michael's and my lives. When I told her about a home repair project or the seasonal ebbs and flows of my garden, she mostly looked bored and sometimes even said aloud that she didn't really want to hear about it. She never stopped caring about us, per se, only in our babble about a world she no longer lived in.

The past was another matter. We talked about the weeping willow in the front yard of my childhood home on Long Island that had come crashing down in a thunderstorm, about the violets planted by a babysitter that had run wild, taking over the backyard. We talked about the years I skipped two months of elementary school, to be tutored on the beach in Florida, along with all the other spring-training brats, when my father covered the New York Yankees. We talked about how my mother had filled the basement with canned goods during the Cuban missile crisis and then regularly raided the larder until nothing was left to feed us through a nuclear winter other than ketchup. We talked about my maternal grandfather, long past retirement as a store owner, working in a subway newsstand near New York University, to the embarrassment of most of the family, because he liked talking politics with the college students. We talked about her nursing career during World War II—before the invention of Q-tips, she never failed to say—when she ran the premature nursery at Lenox Hill Hospital, relishing her new authority because most of the doctors were off to war.

In his wise and readable book *My Mother, Your Mother: Embracing "Slow Medicine," the Compassionate Approach to Caring for Your Aging Loved Ones* (New York: Harper, 2008), Dr. Dennis McCullough, from the Dartmouth Medical School, describes this "gradual separation" as part of what he calls the Station of Decline, the fifth in eight steps of caring for an aging loved one. "The river widens and the busy world on the banks recedes," he writes.

> Along with Mother's failing hearing and eyesight comes less penetrating interest and understanding. Recent events, politics, what is happening in the community, down the street, or next door are simply of less interest. . . . "What the weather's like today," "what I had for lunch," and "how I slept" are central topics for conversation. Life is greatly simplified. . . . What your mother reports on doesn't change much day by day, and what you report on from your world seems to interest her less and less. She doesn't seem to want the details. Just some reassurance that everything is OK.

Our physical presence mattered, our love and attention, and so she would let us go on and on about things she really didn't care about anymore. But she was happier when we asked questions about the past, and happiest of all when it was clear we were listening, enjoying learning things about her that we hadn't known before, and just glad she was there to tell us.

Speech was a monumental loss for my mother in a family where talking was what we did. We *always* talked. We interrupted one another, cacophonously and to the great discomfort of outsiders, as if conversation were a contact sport. All of us had the verbal dexterity and stubbornness to elbow our way into a conversation, and we would rather talk over someone else than be talked over. We actually read the dictionary at the dinner table, to freshen and enlarge our vocabularies. My father, who initiated the activity, hurried down the columns of words, not stopping unless we signaled we didn't know what one meant. When he came upon a word that stumped us, he read the definitions, in all their iterations, along with the word's derivation and its various uses in context. Then we competed to see who could use the new word first in conversation, because only then was it considered part of our working vocabulary. My mother was no slouch in the language department. Ours was a household where words mattered.

Toward the end of her life, my mother's speech failed her completely, probably as a result of a succession of small strokes that would also affect her swallowing, two functions controlled by the same area of the brain. She worked hard at therapy but with minimal results. Michael and I, among the last to be able to understand what she was saying, saw what was coming. My mother, trapped in a nursing home bed, would be unable to move or call out for help if she needed it. She would not be able to convey the simplest request to an aide or a nurse, like asking for a glass of water or that the shades be closed.

Loss of speech would mean she could no longer lash out caustically, either at the aides she considered indifferent or at us. It would mean she could no longer call and interrupt me at work with petty issues, which I'm ashamed to admit I welcomed. I could check up on her morning and night by calling the desk rather than speaking to her directly, but she wouldn't be able to phone me when she had a complaint serious enough to warrant instant attention: a diaper unchanged for a full shift or an aide handling her so roughly as to break the paper-thin skin on her legs.

So Michael and I, after much head-scratching, decided to get her a talking board, a device I had first seen used by autistic children who had no speech. Many autistic youngsters have the ability to type, so they can use a computer and voice synthesizer, but others are too impaired physically to turn letters into words and words into sentences. One boy I had met on an assignment had a contraption strapped around his waist, like the coin collectors that bus drivers once wore. The device had a number of buttons, each programmed with a comment or request. It enabled rudimentary conversation with classmates and communication with adults without having to tug at sleeves or gesture.

It seemed to me that something like this would work for my mother. So I gave Michael the name of the school where I'd seen the devices used and the task of tracking down the manufacturer and finding out the technical details. He went a step further and persuaded the sales rep to come to the nursing home so we could see which model was easiest for my mother to use, given the limited movement she had in her hands. Here was an example of children effectively advocating for their parent by identifying a problem, sometimes ahead of the professionals, and then collaborating in an effective way to solve it, each using his or her particular competencies.

The rep came with a bunch of devices. My mother and Michael tried them and chose one with great big buttons, thirty-two in all. Then the three of us convened to make a list of all the things my mother might need to say: *I'm cold. I'm hot. I'd like a cup of coffee. Close the curtains, please. Could someone call my children?* Michael suggested we keep the list at thirty. Then we recorded all the messages in his voice, which entertained everyone on my mother's floor until the day she died. She'd press a button, and he'd "speak." In an environment with so little to amuse, the joke never got old.

The last decision we made that day was what to do with the unused buttons. Michael had cleverly saved two and encouraged my mother to "say" whatever pissy thing she chose. She thrilled to the task and thought up two messages. One was directed mostly at aides who lacked a certain je ne sais quoi, the ones my mother concluded were either stupid or sadists or both: *You'll be old someday, too, you know.* Michael recorded it with the perfect mixture of disdain and prophetic threat.

The other message, and the button I'm told my mother wore out from overuse, was the ultimate plaintive cry of a woman who treasured her privacy above all else. The nursing home had an open-door policy: anyone could march right into her room, strike up a conversation whether or not my mother wanted to talk, and try to jolly her into going to some activity in the kind of chirpy voice she detested.

On this last button Michael recorded *Get the fuck out of my room.*

She had not intended humor, although the male voice made that unavoidable. At my mother's funeral, the rabbi recounted a visit when she had sent him packing with one fierce stab at the obscene button, then seemed ever so slightly contrite at having cursed at a member of the clergy. "I'd say it to people all the time if I thought I could get away with it," the rabbi had told her, being kind and also, I think, telling the truth. From that day forward, he and my mother were friends.

The weather was fair, my mother was in her wheelchair, and, whether she liked it or not, we were headed outdoors for lunch on the patio. She understood better than I in the spring of 2003 that the losses were piling one upon another. That day, as we made our way to the elevator, she recalled how balky she had been back when she still lived in Florida and a cane first became necessary, followed by a walker. By the time she needed a wheelchair, it was more a relief than a defeat. Then, for a brief period, she was one of the privileged few allowed to use a motorized chair, because she passed the geriatric equivalent of a "road test." With the light touch of a joystick, my mother was able to come and go as she pleased without waiting on line for a "pusher," a nursing home job title not quite as jarring as "feeder" but right up there. One geriatric psychologist, who regularly commented on the *New Old Age* blog, said that no single piece of technology improved quality of life in nursing homes more than motorized chairs, which are rarely reimbursed and thus are available only to those, like us, who could afford to pay several thousand dollars, even for a used one. Alas, just as my mother's ruined shoulders and loss of arm strength first made a manual chair impossible for her to operate herself, within months, her hands now clawed, even the joystick was beyond her.

When Michael or I were there, we did the pushing. That's what I was doing that day when she said something that silenced my idle chatter with a surge of emotion. My mother was staring at the grab bars that lined the hallways so ambulatory residents could steady themselves as they walked. *What I wouldn't do,* she told me, *to stand on my own two feet one more time. Upright, holding those bars, even for just a minute.* For me, it was another of those Make-A-Wish Foundation moments, like the writing class. If only I could make it happen! As I left after that day's visit, I stopped in the physical therapy area. I often came there for a cup of coffee and a moment of repose before heading home or to work. As always, the therapists welcomed me, and I told them of my mother's heartrending comment.

Some months into her stay at the home, my mother had been removed from the roster of physical therapy patients—"taken off program," in the jargon of Medicare. She was making no further improvement, and at that point the government stops paying the bill. That seemed perfectly reasonable to me in the zero-sum game of long-term care financing. Why should limited tax dollars, whether Medicare or Medicaid, be spent pretending that a paralyzed woman would walk again? Later, enlightened geriatric professionals told me that physical therapy had benefits, even absent improvement, and that the reimbursement rules were penny wise and pound foolish. Even later, I would learn that these "rules" were not even part of the law or the written regulations but stemmed from misunderstanding calcified into decree. Still, rightly or wrongly, without physical therapy to maintain even limited mobility, people wound up bedridden, with the attendant risks of pressure sores, pneumonia, and other potentially deadly maladies. And what of the psychological aspect for someone trapped in a body that doesn't work, isolated in a small room (perhaps with an unpleasant roommate), and with nothing to do all day and hardly anyone to talk to? The physical therapist was not merely a person who might get my mother out of the wheelchair and walking again. She had become a friend.

Being "taken off program" ended my mother's regular social contact with the physical therapists, whom she missed terribly. Until my visit to tell them what she had said, it had never occurred to me that they missed her, too. In a nursing home the cognitively intact elderly and the staff don't have many people to have real conversations with—one reason many of the people who worked there became so attached to my mother. Among the residents on my mother's floor, there was Nellie, who soon relocated downstairs because of roommate issues; Doris, a generation too young to be there and rightfully angry most of the time; Bertha, who talked only of her son the rabbi in Jerusalem, which my mother found more tedious than the repetitive questions of the demented; and Lenke, who at 105 had her wits about her but was stone-deaf, which can be as socially isolating as dementia.

My mother had briefly made one friend, Ann, who was lively, bright, and always perfectly turned out in expensive clothes, jewelry, and makeup, but, unknown to us, already hiding symptoms of dementia. One day, after a visit with my mother and me, Ann couldn't remember where she was or how to get back to her room, which was just a straight shot down the corridor. Nor, for the first time, could she fake it, as she so deftly did in conversation. My mother and I pretended we wanted to take a "walk," she in the chair and me pushing, and we unobtrusively led Ann back to her room. In a matter of months this beautiful and vibrant woman turned the corner to oblivion. After that, my mother withdrew from what passed for the social life on her floor, except for her relationships with Eileen, the nurse; Hannah, the social worker; Diana, the physical therapist; and later, when she decided he was more regular guy than clergyman, the rabbi, Simon Hirschhorn.

On the day I showed up in the basement physical therapy area, it was Diana who responded to my mother's yearning to stand again, as Hannah had to the impossible dream of taking that writing class. As I drank my coffee, Diana was mentally chewing on how she could justify bringing my mother back to the PT unit. "You have to be creative," she told me later, herself not understanding what was law and what was custom. "Write it up in a way that seems reasonable. Go through the proper channels." People at the Hebrew Home, she said, were more willing to think out of the box than at most of the other places. Sometimes that was for the benefit of family members who were not ready to accept that a parent's walking days were over. "We'd let the family down gently," Diana said, "keep someone on program until we could convince them to let her be; that she didn't need to walk anymore, didn't even want to."

My mother's situation was the opposite. I have no idea how Diana wrote the orders, or how much money Medicare paid to fulfill an old lady's wish, something that I suspect happens more often at five-star nursing homes than at hellholes. For the nation as a whole, including my generation, this sort of thinking "out of the box" is, arguably, dubious public policy, given Medicare's shrinking trust fund. But I was thinking like a daughter, not like a health policy wonk. From that day forward, Diana wheeled my mother downstairs once a week and stood her at the parallel bars with someone in front of her and someone behind. My mother knew she wasn't really standing up, but that was beside the point. The activity was a diversion for her—the ride down and back, then spending time with someone she enjoyed talking to—and apparently it was for Diana, too. "Your mother was always unassuming and understanding about what we could do and what we couldn't," she told me. "She was also a successful professional, an intelligent woman, someone you could have a conversation with. She didn't just miss me. I missed her, too."

CHAPTER 11

Follow the Money

On December 1, 2002, my mother, in her own eyes, officially became a welfare queen. She had used up her money and thus was "spent down" to Medicaid status, which extends its benefits *only* to the poor. For her, a solidly middle-class, upstanding citizen who had never taken a dime from anyone in her life, this was a source of shame that would last until her death. That it shouldn't have been shameful is beside the point. She had reached this juncture without gaming the system, not even in the legal ways, like giving money to her children. What makes her humiliation even more disturbing to me is the discovery, years after the fact, of how little Medicaid actually wound up spending on her, compared with how much she spent on herself, without help from anyone. These discoveries were also an eye-opener, a lesson in how this most muddled of government programs works, and a testimony to the thrift and grit of a woman typical of her generation.

Medicaid is a confusing and potentially boring subject, depending on how you feel about numbers and abstruse government policy, but it's essential for you to understand. So I've attempted to lighten the load by using my mother's story as an anecdotal example of exactly how illogical, incomprehensible, unfair, and also unkind our current system of long-term care really is. Her story illustrates some of the myths about Granny scamming the government, an idea debunked by both academic and independent government research, yet so persistent in certain circles that it was the driving force, in 2005, behind enormous legislative changes in how the system works, some draconian and others reasonable, given the current fiscal climate. That said, even the reasonable ones are only minor darning of a huge unraveling garment.

Very few people except professionals even understand the difference for the elderly between Medicare and Medicaid; people use the terms interchangeably or call them both "Medic-whatever." So first, a primer. Medicare, a pillar of Lyndon Johnson's Great Society and a social insurance program financed by all working people and their employers, was created in 1965 as a result of a messy political compromise. It was an incremental and imperfect solution to the huge problem of providing health care for the elderly, as Social Security, a generation before, had replaced some of their lost wages with a small but guaranteed monthly income. How imperfect Medicare was was not clear to its framers at the time, since they never contemplated that men and women, benefiting from advances in medical science, would survive for years past the age of eighty-five in a state of increasing dependency, potentially outliving their resources and overwhelming their families economically, physically, and emotionally. The oldest of the old, who are likely to be chronically ill and helpless in the most basic ways, would get nothing from Medicare except for what is known as acute care—doctors' bills, hospital stays, surgery, a certain amount of rehabilitation afterward, and, in a later addition, prescription medication.

Chronic care is not covered by Medicare. Often referred to, unflatteringly, as custodial care, it involves home companions, transportation when driving is no longer safe, assistance with everyday nonmedical tasks like shopping or bathing, and residential care, whether assisted living or a nursing home. The cost is enormous—unless the elderly person is impoverished, or so depleted of money, to meet the means-testing criteria of Medicaid, a separate government program. Medicaid was passed into law at the same time as Medicare but was intended for a different group: the poor of all ages, not the elderly in particular (least of all was Medicaid intended for the once-middle-class elderly who have become dependent on it as longevity has devoured their lifetime assets). Medicaid also differs from Medicare in its structure: it is a welfare program, not a "social insurance" program, in the lingo of social science. That means, essentially, that it is "charity" from the government, rather than a benefit paid for in advance by its ultimate users, as Social Security and Medicare are, through payroll taxes. Intended for "those" people, Medicaid is thus inherently unpopular with many citizens and politicians who don't need it and assume they never will or simply have no sympathy for poor people. It is that implicit, and all too often explicit, judgment that Medicaid beneficiaries are inferior that leads to needless humiliation for people like my mother.

Theodore R. Marmor, in *The Politics of Medicare,* notes that Medicare was a political compromise, passed only after Lyndon Johnson's landslide presidential victory and with a key assist from Wilbur Mills, chairman of the House Ways and Means Committee. It was intended to be a first step in an incremental expansion of benefits. Congressman Mills's contribution was to split Medicare and Medicaid, making it possible to get passage of health coverage for the elderly by, in Marmor's words, "differentiating it from the demeaning world of public assistance," which "in American parlance implies stigma." Marmor does not condone this stigmatizing arrangement. In fact, he observes that the results of this "accommodationist posture" were "largely unforeseen" and are "easy to criticize with the full benefit of hindsight." More than four decades after Medicare's passage, with explosive growth of the eighty-five-and-over group and the huge boomer cohort right behind it, America faces a crisis in which Medicare benefits do not match the most distinctive medical circumstances—the need for chronic care—of the group it set out to serve.

Larry Minnix, president of LeadingAge, formerly the American Association of Homes and Services for the Aging, has called elderly Medicaid recipients the "middle-class poor, which is what most of us will become if we live long enough." Those sixty-five and older who need chronic rather than acute care, Minnix says, face two "punishing" alternatives: they can truly exhaust their life savings because Medicare doesn't cover what they most need, or they can shelter those assets or give them away ahead of time, which currently is legal, for the sole purpose of making themselves eligible for Medicaid. Neither choice, Minnix says, is "psychologically healthy" for the elderly or their families.

One anecdotal measure of how essential Medicaid has become to formerly middle- and upper-middle-class Americans is a lengthy memorandum, "A Summary of the Medicaid Program for Our Clients," recently distributed by Peter Strauss. In his eighties, Strauss is the dean of elder care lawyers in New York City, at the firm of Epstein Becker & Green. Strauss's clients are the crème de la crème, on average far wealthier than my family, and not the sort of people who expect to wind up needing to know anything about Medicaid. But Strauss writes that these days "the cost of long-term care can quickly impoverish [our] clients." A poverty program that was intended to be a "payor of last resort" has by default become "a major source of financing long-term care for middle-income Americans." In his speeches, Strauss is more colloquial. More than four decades ago, he says, President Johnson promised that seniors would no longer be bankrupt and stranded by the cost of medical care. But the ex-president, he says, was "a lousy prophet." Those "lucky enough to have cancer will have their bills paid," Strauss notes, while most of those past the age of eighty-five will "be unable to wipe their rear end" and get no help paying someone to do it for them. Shame on us.

So let's take a look at my mother's situation, the one I know best and can itemize for you. It started when she became unable to safely take care of herself without a certain amount of assistance, and thus was a perfect candidate for assisted living. It ended when she was completely dependent on others, living in a nursing home. All told, the period lasted for nine years, and it likely would have gone on much longer had she been afflicted with Alzheimer's disease. During that span, my mother's long-term care cost was $609,123, or more than $67,000 a year. This figure does not include doctors' bills, hospital stays, surgery, or any of the medical care categorized as "acute," which, as I said, is paid for by Medicare and, in my mother's case, a supplementary Medigap policy, which many of those sixty-five and over purchase to pick up some of Medicare's deductibles and copayments.

Of my mother's $609,123 expenditure on long-term care, she paid $470,818 out of her own pocket, with very modest help from her grown children. Only through ingenuity, frugality, and smart investing of a small inheritance from my father, three decades earlier, had my mother wound up with almost half a million dollars, many times more than she and my father had when he was alive. I cannot reconstruct how she did it, since for most of that time she reasonably considered her financial business her own affair, and I have bank statements and other records of her assets beginning only in 2001. My admiration for what she accumulated, through thrift and cautious investing, is enormous. I do know that long before she needed assisted living, her solution to worn furniture at home was to cover the frayed spots with towels; that she canceled the perpetual maintenance service at my father's grave since we were not a cemetery-visiting family; that she permitted herself no luxuries and few modest creature comforts; and that she invested in Fannie Mae and Freddie Mac when that was a smart thing to do. When she sold her Long Island home (purchased for less than $20,000 on a veteran's mortgage, long since paid off) for $180,000, she assured me and my brother that she had crunched the numbers, with help from accountants and lawyers, and that continued conservative investing and careful penny-pinching would leave her in good shape for the rest of her life. We all believed that because we wanted to.

Her seven years in Florida were spent in a $2,000-a-month apartment that included many kinds of support for the elderly, including van transportation to shop, handicap features in her own quarters and elsewhere on the grounds, two meals a day in a congregate dining room, social activities, and help from an able concierge twenty-four hours a day. Ring those years up on the Estelle Gross long-term care cash register at $160,432. A few unhappy months at the Meadowview in suburban New York, at about $3,000 a month, added a total of $27,900. She had a long-term care insurance policy, purchased in 1993 when she was seventy-eight, for almost $7,000 a month, a most unusual expenditure for someone in her age group, that wound up costing a total of $53,600. The Medigap policy addded $56,000. I no doubt have left many things out of this bare-bones calculation, so figure it's more than I've estimated.

Now, as an adult child, ask yourself: Does either of your parents have a half-million dollars on hand to provide for himself or herself in old age? Their care may be way more expensive while both are alive, depending on their respective conditions, but they will more likely be making decisions together, or for each other, than depending solely on you. The responsibility and worry will shift when only one is left behind. The surviving parent is likely, by a huge margin, to be a widowed mother. Women not only live longer than men but wind up with more meager assets, especially in the generation when they had no jobs, benefits, or pensions of their own. So figure, for the sake of argument, since no two situations are the same, that Mom alone needs half a million. I would guess that most of your parents don't have it, and even if they do, it may not be enough. Instead, they will need the government's help, yours—and more likely, both.

Once my mother's condition made nursing home care all but unavoidable, life really got expensive for her. She lived in a single room, unquestionably a luxury, that cost between $449 and $471 a day, including room and board, all of her medical and pharmaceutical needs, social work, activities, 24/7 nursing care, shared home health aides around the clock, and loving attention that extended to me and my brother. (Think of it as a prix fixe resort where nobody wants to go.) That day rate computes to about $14,000 a month, or more than $160,000 a year—in a major metropolitan area, not an outlandish price. (Few people believe that. The first time I used the $14,000-a-month figure on my blog, so many readers asked if I meant $4,000 that I had to post a blanket reply to all of them to the contrary.) Take a look on one of the many nursing home locator websites, and you will see that the cost of even a second-rate home is eye-popping. But had my mother lived in her own apartment, paying rent, with round-the-clock aides, and perhaps geriatric care management to keep a fragile at-home system working, it would have been just as expensive, perhaps more.

My blog readers' shock, long after my own had subsided, that a nursing home bed cost $14,000 a month led me to ask Dan Reingold, the director of the Hebrew Home, a nonprofit institution and the only kind I would advise you to consider (for obvious reasons), why that was. He told me straightforwardly that the monthly fees for self-paying residents are purposely inflated to make possible equal care for the Medicaid residents, who make up about 85 percent of the home's census, given the wide gap between the real cost and Medicaid reimbursement. In other words, as long as my mother had money, she would pay more than her care was actually worth in order to amortize the cost of the vast majority of residents who were virtually penniless.

Maybe that $14,000 a month also helped pay the stipend for creative writing teachers from Sarah Lawrence College, lawn furniture, or the outpatient Alzheimer's center that is open all night, so exhausted families can sleep while their loved ones, who grow more agitated when the sun goes down, are entertained, supervised, and sent home in the morning bathed, dressed in fresh clothes, and already fed breakfast. Somebody has to pay for both the basics and the frills, since the government doesn't. I'm proud that, in a small way, it was us.

If I believed, all evidence to the contrary, that the people whose care my mother—and thus me and Michael—were subsidizing were the Medicaid millionaires of myth, I would of course feel differently. Are there people who give away their money, ahead of time, usually to their children, so they can qualify for Medicaid at the earliest possible moment? Yes. But precious few, if any, are millionaires, because really rich people care more about protecting their estates than about having a free ride in a nursing home, and the two kinds of financial planning are incompatible. Rich people can age and die at home, tended by servants, surrounded by family and friends, as all of us wish we could. Are there exceptions to the rule? I'm sure there are. But that's not where our focus should be.

My mother's total stay at the Hebrew Home cost about $315,000. Over those twenty-three months she spent $172,886 of her own money. I had always thought that Medicaid paid the difference. How wrong I was.

It turns out, to my shock, that Medicaid's total contribution, in her eight months of eligibility, was a whopping $7,590. That belies the myth that people like my mother are bankrupting the nation and the states with their Medicaid shenanigans, which induced Congress, in the Deficit Reduction Act of 2005, to build in all kinds of roadblocks to eligibility for others in her circumstances, most of them honestly broke. At the time, the Congressional Budget Office (and several academic studies) scoffed at the notion that little old ladies in nursing homes were fleecing the rest of us and were therefore responsible for the fiscal woes of the nation, states, and counties. According to Douglas Holtz-Eakin, then head of the CBO, "It is unlikely that imposing these additional restrictions [will] have more than a modest impact on Medicaid's expenses for long-term care."

So who paid for my mother's care from September 12, 2001, when she entered the nursing home, until her death on July 23, 2003? She paid the lion's share, $172,886, as I've said. Medicare, in what is known as subacute care, kicked in the next biggest portion, $71,083, about half of that for the hundred days after her arrival from Sloan-Kettering and the other half for one hundred days after a later hospitalization for several days of diagnostic tests at another Manhattan hospital. Whenever someone is discharged from an acute care hospital after spending at least three days there, not counting the day of discharge, Medicare is required to pay for anywhere between twenty and one hundred days in a skilled nursing home or a rehabilitative center. This care is not considered to be long-term or chronic; the rationale for the brief Medicare coverage is to move people out of acute care hospitals and into less expensive settings as quickly as possible. The three-night rule is important to know about because some hospitals, sad to say, will discharge patients so quickly that they lose this option and thus are on their own, not well enough to go home but with no way to afford anyplace else.

But more often the rehabilitation coverage is a fair and cost-effective way of moving someone who has had, say, a hip replacement or other surgery that requires intensive physical therapy and a modicum of skilled nursing into a more economical setting than a full-service hospital, which must amortize the cost of an ICU, operating room, departments of cardiology and oncology, and other heavy expenses. In bygone days, these patients would have spent weeks in the hospital until they were well. Now, as the saying goes, they leave sicker and quicker. But because of subacute facilities, most patients (although not always the frail elderly) will soon head home, up and about far more effectively and in less time than if they had skipped this step in the process and had, instead, only an hour a day or a few hours a week from a visiting physical or occupational therapist, without a nurse on hand all the time for post-operative procedures like changing dressings.

After my mother's spinal surgery at Memorial Sloan-Kettering, this was her situation, and subacute care was unquestionably necessary, so one would expect Medicare to pay for her first hundred days, the maximum, at the Hebrew Home. But why did a few days of diagnostic tests in the spring of 2002 qualify her for another full hundred days rather than, say, fifty or even the bare minimum of twenty? Regulations are murky, and thus allow for considerable wiggle room. There is no manual that says a hospital stay for diagnosis X or diagnosis Y entitles a patient to a set number of days, only that each diagnosis must be different from the previous one, or Medicare will not pay at all, and that a certain amount of time must have elapsed between hospital episodes. So, following the letter of the law, my mother's second diagnosis (figuring out whether anything that was wrong with her could be ameliorated if not fixed) was not the same, and came long after, the first (a spinal tumor).

Who decides how many days Medicare will finance, and what difference does it make? For a patient already on Medicaid, there is no practical impact; one government program or the other foots the bill (although the bureaucrats at the federal, state, and local level surely care which one it is). But for a private-pay resident of a nursing home, as my mother was after both hospitalizations, each day that Medicare paid for saved her more than $400. To use the two extreme examples, one hundred days of Medicare would save her $40,000, while twenty days would save her $8,000, a significant increment. I haven't a clue who ruled that those tests in May 2002 entitled her to the Medicare maximum, nor does anyone I've asked. Peter Flores, then the medical coordinator in the finance office at the Hebrew Home, said my mother was "lucky."

I suspect luck is only a small part of it and that a nursing home of this caliber has relationships and connections that advantage their residents, or themselves, when some local Medicare bureaucrat is deciding how many days to dole out. Had my mother been on Medicaid already, finding a clever way to push the full cost off to Medicare would have benefited the home, since she was in a $471-a-day room that Medicaid would have reimbursed only to the tune of $216, or less than half, leaving the nonprofit facility to make up the difference. In our case, what seemed to me excessive Medicare reimbursement directly benefited my mother. Either way, the loser, in terms of the program's solvency, was Medicare, with its trust fund dangerously depleted just as the baby boomers are turning eligible for benefits.

Once my mother's hundred days ran out, on December 1, 2002, the nursing home itself absorbed a goodly portion of the cost of her remaining stay. When she was a Medicaid patient, which she was for eight months, they could have moved her from a private room (as other high-quality nursing homes do when a resident is no longer paying his or her own way). They did not, according to long-standing policy. So in her waning time there, 234 days in a private room that otherwise would have yielded more than $100,000 from a private-pay resident, the nonprofit home spent about $60,000 on my mother, not exactly small change. And the remaining $40,000-plus? That came from my mother's so-called monthly budget—in other words, *her* money—without which Medicaid would have spent $50,582, rather than $7,590. When she was a private-pay resident, money moved electronically from her bank account directly to the Hebrew Home each month, as Michael had arranged at the time of admission, and we didn't have to worry about it. Once she was in the hands of Medicaid, money of hers that none of the three of us had ever thought about, but that had been part of that payment to the home all along—my mother's Social Security ($721 a month), my father's veteran's benefit that had gone to her since his death ($90.46), and her long-term care insurance benefit ($5,373.96)—passed invisibly to the federal, state, and local governments, divided percentagewise at 50/40/10. Once that money was factored into the equation, Medicaid's contribution was less than $1,000 a month. My mother had felt like a welfare queen. It turns out she wasn't.

When your mother cries to you, as mine did, that she never intended to be a charity case, that she had worked and saved her whole life so as not to be a burden to either her children or the government, you can probably tell her that she isn't and won't be, at least not to the extent she may think. Tell her that now, not after it's too late to comfort her. Go to the finance office of the nursing home, assuming that it's large enough to have one, and ask to see her files. You are entitled to do that under HIPAA, the government act that protects the confidentiality of health records, unless your parent has explicitly put you on a list of people *not* allowed to see them. In other words, the patient must *exclude,* not explicitly *include,* family—or anyone else, for that matter (say, a friend in a position of responsibility). But medical people, especially those in low-level jobs, can be overly cautious in interpreting the law. Saying no to you is safer than saying yes if they have not been properly trained, are afraid of getting in trouble, or simply don't want to be bothered with pulling the records.

This is another of those instances, as time goes on and you become more and more run down, when it would be so much easier not to argue. Far too many people around you who control your loved one's care and its cost are depending on you to be too depleted to fight back. Your request for Medicaid spend-down records may not be as important as getting reimbursement for medical equipment or reporting an aide who leaves your parent in a dirty diaper for twelve hours. In our case, reassuring my mother that she needn't be ashamed of taking charity would have been wonderful and worth the effort. In your case, you might find examples of sloppy bookkeeping, or want to ask questions about how Medicare benefits fit into the financial picture. Plus, those records are educational in terms of how chaotic the long-term care payment system actually is. For instance, I thought being on Medicaid meant *being* on Medicaid. That isn't necessarily so.

A Medicaid application, in and of itself, thrusts middle-class people into an unfamiliar world and should make them acutely aware of how hard it is to be poor, not merely in terms of putting food on the table but in terms of coping with a bureaucracy that seems to willfully flummox those among us who are already the most overwhelmed and in some cases the least capable. Medicaid is a joint federal and state program but is administered at the county level, and that is where the application emanates from. In New York, for example, by way of the county department of social services, it is sixteen pages long, a dizzying sea of green and white blocks, some to be filled out by the applicant and some by the processor of the application. The same form is used to apply for food stamps, foster care, and other forms of public assistance, and I dare you to figure out which sections are meant to be filled out for your elderly mother and which for a pregnant teenager. It asks questions about domestic violence, alimony, college tuition, pregnancy, eviction, child support, noncustodial parents, drug rehabilitation, liens on automobiles, and all manner of things that have nothing to do with your situation. In tackling this application, you have officially entered the world of the underclass, even if you grew up in suburban comfort, with college-educated parents, multiple cars, and summers at sleepaway camp. Experts note that the application experience is actually less daunting for the disadvantaged than for those of us accustomed to privileged lives, since they navigate this world on a regular basis, sitting in plastic chairs in the welfare office day after day, only to have it close at four p.m., before their case is called.

Thankfully, my mother's Medicaid application was done, free of charge, in the finance office at the Hebrew Home. Elder care lawyers often handle them for clients who can afford their services, with rates varying by region; in New York, at the high end of the scale, the range is between $7,000 and $10,000. Peter Strauss, at Epstein Becker & Green, has a full-time paralegal who does nothing else, for a flat fee of $8,500. While lawyers generally charge for their service by the hour, the cost of a Medicaid application—which legally counts toward a Medicaid spend-down—is fixed regardless of the difficulty and the time spent finding the myriad supporting documents that must accompany the application. In many states, only photocopies are accepted. Send in the originals, and the application will be returned and the clock start anew on what could be a yearlong process under the best of circumstances. Among the photocopied documents there must be a Social Security card; a Medicare card; a private insurance policy, if there is one; a Social Security award letter and/or a pension award letter (each showing both gross and net amounts); proof of citizenship; proof of age; a marriage certificate, a spouse's death certificate, or divorce papers (if any of the three are applicable); a current utility bill; a current phone bill; proof of residence for the last three years (a lease and rent receipts for tenants or a deed and statement from the Realtor of the current value of a home for owners); bank statements (including deposit slips or canceled checks for any transactions over $1,000); a life insurance policy (if the applicant has one) and a statement that it is paid up-to-date from the insurance company; any stock or bond certificates; discharge papers for a veteran (if applicable); and a burial trust (if one has been purchased). I'm uncertain if this list is complete, but you get my drift. Assembling this packet—and maybe more—is no fun.

My brother had already gathered some of this documentation in preparation for my mother's move from Florida to New York, because it was required for admission to the assisted living facility here, and again for her admission to the nursing home, including her back tax returns, bank statements, and long-term care policy. In our unspoken division of labor, the Medicaid application was his job. I once mentioned to a friend who was asking me something about preparing one that it was on Michael's to-do list. In effect, her reply was: If your brother has taken responsibility for the Medicaid application, you should kiss the ground he walks on and never complain again. Her point was well taken. Michael also took care of the "assignment of benefits" form required when my mother arrived at the nursing home, so that her long-term care insurance payments and my father's pension and veterans benefits went directly there, and later to Medicaid. It was Michael who organized moving my mother's money into a brokerage account, with his financial adviser, so he could monitor its management and pay her monthly nursing home bills with electronic transfers from that account. He paid the private-duty aide once we had one, for a few hours a day. He was also in charge, on a monthly basis, of accounting for any money we spent on my mother from her bank accounts, to which we had access because of our powers of attorney, all of which counted toward her Medicaid spend-down. The two lawyers who helped us at various junctures, Gregg Weiss and Peter Strauss, both have files full of Michael's meticulous accounting of every dime spent. With their help and an obscure provision known as the "rule of halves," two $30,000 Treasury bills that my mother owned, with interest unheard of today, were legally transferred to us.

What follows are excerpts from several of Michael's spend-down memos to Weiss and Strauss. (I have taken the liberty of combining items from different months, using the category breakdown that he consistently followed, so you can see the range of expenses we were required to document, lest her Medicaid application be rejected even after her money was gone.)

Out of Pocket by Jane (with receipts)
Move from Florida $3,589.78

MRI (portion not covered) $505
Groceries $35.73
Fruit basket for Dr. Bilsky $72.53
Meadowview phone bill $39.26

Out of Pocket by Jane (with no receipts)
Knee Brace $20
Toilet seat riser $30
Adult diapers $27
Assorted tolls, gas, mileage, garage and taxi for medical appts. ?????

Out of Pocket by Michael (with receipts)
Meals in Florida during medical crisis $94.77, $85.67, $21.63, $32.19
Cabinet for room $75.72
VCR $97.41
Gasoline $16.49, $28.66, $15.50, $25.17
Xeroxes $12, $6.50
Sundries $7.59, $4.89
Hardware (for move in) $69.25, $10.81, $32.48
Groceries $49.52, $10.17, $16.39

Out of Pocket by Michael (no receipts or need to find)
FedEx to Peter Flores, MRI to Dr. Bilsky, medical records to Dr. Saltzman   ?????
Tips $41, $209

Additional Expenses
Fine & Newcombe, from Morgan Stanley account $1,803.42
Gardner and Weiss, from Morgan Stanley account $1,268.50
Move from the Meadowview to Hebrew Home (cash, with invoice) $240
John Hancock long-term care insurance quarterly premium from Morgan
    Stanley account $1,677.18
Prescription drug (emergency, thus no insurance-covered delivery) $60.29
Fee to replace missing Florida bank records $180
Home health aide at Meadowview, 8/11–8/31 $3,679.50

A postscript: In addition to Michael's memos, still in the lawyers' files, we both have kept receipts (from the Food Emporium, Duane Reade, Verizon, Hunan Village, and Visa, to name a few) and ATM withdrawal slips from this period, lest Medicaid come after us. (We were not clear then, and remain ignorant, on how long they have to challenge our claim. And even knowing how little we'd owe them if they came after us, I'm loath to throw away these little slips of paper. No doubt they'd charge us interest, too.)

I recently asked Gregg Weiss, aware of his obvious bias, about the pros and cons of letting the nursing home do my mother's Medicaid application, as we did, as opposed to paying a lawyer's fee, a decision we made out of convenience, not thrift. The nursing home was where we already were. Its administrators had her records. They knew how to fill out the application. Leaving it to the finance office there meant no work for us. Also, I assumed she would outlive her money, Medicaid would kick in at some point, and there would be no inheritance after her death; thus any expertise a private lawyer would bring to the process was beside the point. While in our case that proved to be correct, my logic was flawed. Had she died while still paying her own way, rather than having already spent down to Medicaid eligibility, with even just a few months of private funds left, Michael and I would have gotten the "crumbs": the $14,000 per month she was paying the home from her own resources, divided in half, or the $28,000 if she had died with two months' worth of money left, and so on.

Weiss believes that the nursing home finance departments and private lawyers sometimes have different techniques and timing strategies on Medicaid applications and that in some situations paying a legal fee of $8,000 might leave adult children with an inheritance, however small. But this means looking at how much money someone has left as the end of life nears and then gambling on the timing of death. In our case, given my mother's already limited resources, Weiss thinks we made the wise choice.

Weiss, Strauss, and other elder care lawyers now function in a world of dramatically restricted Medicaid regulations, largely aimed at curtailing abuse by the elderly and their adult children, which were passed by Congress in the 2005 Deficit Reduction Act and have been gradually phased in since. The laws and regulations that we operated under in 2002 were confusing. What replaced them is all but incomprehensible to a layperson and even to many lawyers. The Strauss memorandum to his clients talks of its many ambiguous provisions, and the various clarifications and policy statements from the state that, in his view, do little to resolve the confusion. Using italics to drive home the point that the document is intended to be useful but not the last word, Strauss writes, *"No planning should be undertaken without consulting counsel with respect to individual situation."* Bottom line: hire someone if you can. If you can't, various websites help a bit. In broad strokes, let me tell you what I know.

The most significant, and widely felt, change is that gifts of money to children and others that once had to be made three years before applying for Medicaid now must be made five years ahead of time, known in the trade as the "look-back period." Some elderly people begin giving away their money early, often to help grown children build a nest egg to buy a home, save for college tuition, or make other things possible that might otherwise not be in a world that is much more expensive than the one they grew up in. They do this out of love, as well as careful and wise financial planning, and often as the result of legal advice. My mother was urged to do this as far back as 1993, by the lawyer updating her will, power of attorney, and health care proxy. She declined. The lawyer, Michael, and I did not push her because she was competent to make her own decisions, and holding on to her own money was a point of pride and a way of feeling in control at a time when control was slipping away. That said, any money that she had given to us then, before the look-back period, would have hastened her Medicaid eligibility. Essentially, she would have been seeing to it that we got our inheritance up front. As her attorney put it, "The perfect scenario is three years [now five] and one day after you give away all your money, you go into a nursing home. That's a home run. But it doesn't often happen that way."

If money is given away after the five-year window of opportunity, that does not disqualify someone for Medicaid, but they are ineligible during what is known as the "penalty period." To compute the penalty period, divide the value of the gift by the average monthly cost of a nursing home in your area (determined in most cases at the state level, and in New York by the counties). Most experts agree that the figures cited by those agencies are far less than what the average cost actually is. In 2007, for instance, the divisor in New Jersey was $6,655, in Connecticut $9,096, in New York City $9,074, and on Long Island $10,123. I can tell you with certainty that in New York City $9,000-a-month nursing homes would be mediocre places or worse—understaffed (often without a full-time physician), smelling of urine, residents vulnerable to bedsores and urinary tract infections, those with behavioral issues medicated for the convenience of the small staff, and activities limited to low-budget items like bingo. If the home is for-profit, the conditions will likely be terrible at that monthly rate, since a nursing home owner makes money only by scrimping on costs. Once you do the calculation on the penalty period, you will know how long it will take before your parent will be Medicaid-eligible if he or she has given away money too late. The idea in lengthening the look-back period is to make it harder for people to game the system, even in legal ways. With a longer look-back period, the elderly must be brutally honest about the realities that may await them, rather than be rewarded, in effect, for denial. Under the old rules, they could hang on to their assets longer, assume they would live independently and die suddenly, with no need for long-term care, and then give everything away in a bigger hurry if it became clear they were in for years of custodial care that they couldn't afford. Under the new rules, the government assumes, they will still harbor that hope of never needing help, hang on to their money as they did before, and then find themselves ineligible for Medicaid for a longer time because of the penalty formula. In other words, the longer look-back period is designed to save the government money and shift more of the burden to the family.

Lawyers say, and my experience bears out, as do the studies on the subject, that few in this generation of elderly actually set out to hasten their Medicaid eligibility this way, out of pride in their self-sufficiency and an ethic that said charity was for the hard-core poor, not for people using legal loopholes to impoverish themselves on purpose. I know that's how my mother felt, as did her Depression-era peers in the nursing home. In the rare instances when men and women of this era agree to a calculated spend-down, lawyers say, it is usually under pressure from adult children, who make clear that they expect that their parents' money will pass to them, either while Mom and Dad are still alive or after their deaths, and that hanging on to it now risks seeing it all spent on the custodial care that Medicare doesn't cover.

Among the elder care attorneys who told me that the idea of inheritance protection usually comes from "the kids, not the parents" is Vincent Russo, a longtime leader of the National Academy of Elder Law Attorneys. "Do I have Mary saying 'I want to game the system and get on Medicaid?'" he said. "No. All Mary wants is control and to stay in the community. If I say to her, 'You have $100,000, so give $50,000 to your daughter today because you might wind up in a nursing home,' she'll say, 'Over my dead body.' And that's the last time I'll see her in my office." Bringing the conversation even closer to home is Steven A. Schurkman, an elder care attorney in Westchester County. He advised his mother-in-law, a widow and former bookkeeper with $200,000 in assets, most tied up in a Florida condominium, to transfer ownership of the condo to her two daughters in 2005, when she was eighty-one. She refused, despite understanding the consequences: the possibility of winding up in a nursing home, running out of cash, landing on Medicaid, losing her condo to the state after death, and her daughters inheriting nothing. Schurkman, despite his professional expertise, demurred after laying out the legal and financial consequences, and this widow's daughters put no pressure on their mother. All respected her choice to remain in control rather than utilize wise, legal Medicaid-planning techniques.

More has changed since 2005 than the look-back period. Before the new law, the clock started ticking for the purpose of Medicaid eligibility on the first of the month following a gift of money. Now someone not yet approved for Medicaid must be admitted to a nursing home *first,* and only then does the calculation of the look-back period begin. In practical terms, that means the nursing home accepts someone with no money to start living there immediately in the expectation that many months hence the resident will be declared eligible, and only then will the home get paid. If the application is denied, the home receives no money but cannot evict the resident and thus must absorb the cost of his or her stay, however long it lasts. According to Rosemary Pignone, the assistant controller for resident accounts at the Hebrew Home, this makes them very picky at admission time, with closer scrutiny of applications, looking for any hint of illegal gifts, to avoid getting stuck with residents who are denied Medicaid and have no way to pay their bills. It has always been easier to gain admission to a top-notch nursing home as a self-pay client than one who is "Medicaid pending," since it can take a year for the application to go through. Now there are far more "Medicaid pending" applicants, far more who wind up rejected by the state, and far more who never get in the door of good nursing homes in the first place, because nursing homes, quite reasonably, are protecting themselves from this unintended consequence of the 2005 legislation.

These are but the simplest of the changes wrought by the 2005 Deficit Reduction Act. Some are so convoluted—like the elimination of the aforementioned "rule of halves"—that I've never been able to make sense of them. Others, like the maximum value of exempt real estate, vary so widely and are applied so differently in each state or county that there is nothing universal to say about them, other than that you should be sure to ask the right questions in the state where your parent lives. A few involve complicated financial instruments like supplemental needs trusts, historically used for disabled children and now sometimes available to those past sixty-five, or annuities for the spouse who lives in the family home when the other is in an institution. It is rough sledding, I know; a thicket of regulations and a tangle of emotions will hit you in the face all at the same time. That is why I recommend getting professional help if you can afford it or taking the time and trouble, which can be considerable, to find it for free or on a sliding scale at a local agency for the aged.

CHAPTER 12

Therapeutic Fibs

I was pushing a shopping cart through the grocery store at ten p.m., the only free time I had for such chores, between my "Mom job" and my "real job," when exhaustion got the better of me. This weariness had amplified with the passage of time. It was totally different from what I'd experienced earlier, during my mother's frantic migration north and all that soon followed it. Yet even with her successful transition to the nursing home and the relief that came with it, my cumulative fatigue was such that I could barely lift my feet off the ground, haul myself out of bed in the morning, or stay awake at night long enough to read even the simplest paragraph without nodding off.

The cause, I knew, was more emotional than physical, as I wasn't doing the hard, hands-on work of caring for a parent at home. (God bless all of you who are.) Mine was in a relatively cushy nursing home (a piece of unusual good fortune, as I cannot reiterate enough times), where others lifted and turned her, dressed and bathed her, prepared and served her meals, and even did her laundry and put it back in her bureau, if not exactly as she'd have liked. But when I was with her (and also when I wasn't), I was sad, trying to pretend cheerfulness, guilty that I wasn't doing more, angry that I had to do this much. When I was at the nursing home, I was worried that I should be at work but was determined not to look at my watch or otherwise flag competing responsibilities. When I was at work, by contrast, I was distracted and unproductive, afraid my bosses would notice my state of mind and either coddle or punish me (each unappealing in its own way), and equally afraid they wouldn't notice (thus signaling my insignificance or their inattention).

Wherever I was, I wasn't where I was supposed to be, and I wasn't doing what I was supposed to be doing. I had no idea how much longer this was going to last and saw no silver lining at the end of the process, as I assume I would have if I'd been raising a child, not caring for a parent. I doubted my endurance and was disgusted by my own impatience and the implied wish that my mother would die. And unlike my brother's, all my efforts to leaven my misery with fun—travel, parties, nights on the town—failed. I had neither the social grace nor the energy for much more than dinner at home (takeout or microwaved), a glass of wine (or other soothing potion), and bad television at day's end.

Some days it hit harder than others, and this particular grocery-store meltdown came at the end of one of those days. So, amid the depressing fluorescence of an almost-empty suburban market, its nighttime denizens all a little off-kilter, too, I indulged in the luxury of falling apart without much notice. It wasn't quite as private and comfortable a crying spot as the car, but it would do. I was running on empty, needy enough to go looking for help in a most uncharacteristic way.

Long ago, one of my mother's physical therapists had given me her home phone number and said to feel free to use it at any hour, day or night. How very generous, I thought at the time, and how unlikely—no, impossible— that I'd impose in such a way. My need for someone to lean on right now, however, was similar to the brief period, pre–nursing home, when we first had a geriatric care manager and I was racking up take-out-a-mortgage- size phone bills while throwing myself on Barbara Clark's mercy. But the physical therapist, Diana Lubarski, wasn't a care manager who would get paid for her time and trouble. The meter wouldn't be running on this phone call, if I made it. She had surely been sincere in her offer; she was that kind of woman. I liked and trusted her, and vice versa. Yet I'd never been tempted, even at a decent hour, let alone so late at night, to call. On that grocery line, sure I didn't have another day of acting like a grown-up left in me, and oblivious to good manners, I dialed her number.

Diana let me vent for a while, then turned the conversation to possible solutions. What was I doing to look after myself? A lot of weekend yoga and retail therapy, but always right before or right after a nursing home visit and thus in its dark shadow. Clearly it wasn't working, she said. I needed to carve out some real time for myself, a long, uninterrupted stretch to get the kind of relief I needed. What were my options for doing that? she asked. One possibility, I realized, if I could broker such a deal, was a four-day workweek. I'd lose one-fifth of my salary, pension rights, and vacation time, but that was manageable, no matter how long this went on. (Yes, this was another blessing, limited to those of us not struggling to put food on the table.)

What I didn't know was whether my employer would agree to the plan. So, once home, I marshaled an argument that seemed to me compelling. For as long as I could remember, the *Times* had allowed new (and not-so-new) mothers to work four-day weeks. I knew the executive in charge of such decisions well enough to know that he'd see the basic fairness of applying the same rules to someone like me in an elder care situation. I suspected, based on the silence on this subject at work, that I'd be the first to make such a request (as indeed I was), and thus the executive might be inhibited not by lack of sympathy but lack of precedent. The request did take him by surprise, but the answer was an immediate, unqualified yes.

So I had my four-day week, and every intention to make my "freedom Fridays" a pure personal indulgence, from the end of the workday Thursday to the start of the normal weekend, when I'd return to my regular nursing home visiting schedule. My employer likely assumed I'd be at my mother's side, but since they weren't paying me, it was really none of their business. Somehow I'd resist the temptation to do bits and pieces of work from home, thereby making my four-day workweek into a compressed five-day week. My plan, and I kept to it, was to spend the day catching up on errands, like grocery shopping; working in my garden; swimming laps at the village pool; and enjoying my yoga classes and trips to the nail salon and local boutique without then having to rush to the nursing home. Just organizing and imagining this pleasurable one-day holiday from real life improved my mood.

When I shared news of my plan for a free day with the nursing home professionals—Eileen, my mother's nurse, and Hannah, the social worker, who needed to know how to reach me—they embellished it with advice that was a postscript to Diana's. They suggested I tell two white lies (geriatric professionals call them "therapeutic fibs") to further guarantee that the day really wound up belonging to me. Such lies of omission or commission, but lies nonetheless, become ever more common between adult children and aging parents as their role reversal accelerates. The elderly person wants less and less information of a certain kind, and the adult child wants to protect a mother or father whenever possible, while doing what needs to be done for both of them.

Hannah suggested that I not tell my mother, who, she predicted, would be upset about my loss of income and other benefits. Worse, she would have to face up to how beleaguered I felt, on her account. No mother, Hannah reminded me, wants to be a burden to her children, not even the demanding whiners. My proud, self-sufficient mother was never a whiner, even at her most diminished. In her own inimitable way, with wit, not pathos, she had long ago made clear that she was still running this show, even from a nursing home bed. Once, during a particularly difficult time for her at the home, I suggested that she come live with me. She refused, delivering her explanation with the crisp timing of a Borscht Belt comedienne. "I'd rather you feel guilty about my being *here* then me feel guilty for moving in *there* and ruining your life," she'd said with bracing honesty.

Then Eileen, the nurse, begged me not to tell my brother, either. She assigned no meanness or selfishness to Michael, but she said he would be practical, in the way men are practical. If he knew I was working part-time, he could off-load extra responsibility on me. It would make sense for him to think, about anything that came up on a Friday, *Jane can do it.* Eileen's goal was both to protect me from that and to protect both of us from unnecessary squabbling, which she knew upset my mother, her primary charge, and all the rest of us besides.

Caregiving in the U.S., a trio of studies funded by the MetLife Foundation, the National Alliance for Caregiving, and AARP, devised a five-tier "level of burden" index regarding caregivers. First in 1997 and again in 2004 and 2009, the advocacy and research groups studied the characteristics of caregivers, care recipients, and the emotional, physical, financial, and professional costs of the experience. Given my exhaustion and stress, I felt like I ranked at least a 3 and maybe a 4, more because of my temperament than my actual circumstances. The data can be dry reading but are also reassuring in their message that you are far from alone, that your personal experiences are more typical than not, and that you are not the first person to find this an arduous time in life.

All three reports, based on a combined 4,236 caregiving respondents, are considered the gold standard in comprehensiveness and methodology, and explored certain core areas:

- the prevalence of caregivers in the United States
- the demographic characteristics of both caregivers and care recipients
- the nature of caregiving tasks—which ones, how many, and the number of hours per week—which in combination create the five-tier "level of burden" index
- the health and living situation of the person receiving care
- the availability of unpaid and paid help, in addition to the primary family caregiver
- the effect on the caregiver's work, home life, and health
- the sources of information caregivers are most likely to use and their unmet informational needs

The 2009 report adds a few new subjects, including:

- the extent and areas of Internet use by caregivers
- public policy changes that family caregivers would most welcome

The research data (and I am looking only at findings that apply to caring for older adults, not for special-needs children) are a bloodless way of thinking about the typical caregiver. But you know who you are: a middle-aged woman looking after a widowed mother who needs help with everyday tasks or medical issues. You probably have a full-time job, a husband with his own needs, and maybe children of your own still at home. You spend nights and weekends neglecting your own family, and yourself, while doing your mother's errands and visiting her because she rarely gets out anymore. When she has a doctor's appointment, or must go to the emergency room, you skip work or time with family and friends to take her. If your mother has paid help at home, you hire and supervise the aides or ride herd on the agency that does. Your mother calls to complain about the aides, and they call to complain about her. You try to listen patiently and broker solutions. If your mother has moved to assisted living or a nursing home, you're still in charge, in countless ways, and your frequent presence and advocacy are essential to her well-being, plus you feel guilty that you're not doing it yourself. If Mom lives with you, you've won best-in-show among daughters, but you're always on call—always!—and you'd better have a saintly husband. Are your siblings helping? Or is that a whole other story? You and those like you provide 80 percent of the long-term care in this country. AARP calls you the backbone of the nation's long-term care system. You *are* that system.

A total of 65.7 million Americans, or 28.5 percent of the current population, serve as unpaid family caregivers; of these, 43.5 million, or 19 percent, are responsible for an older adult (defined in the report as fifty or older). Close to nine in ten of these caregivers assist a relative, 36 percent of the time their mother and 14 percent their father. The average caregiver, more than two-thirds of them women, is fifty years old, up from forty-eight in 2004. On average, she provides nineteen hours of care in a typical week, or the equivalent of a half-time job. The "job" usually lasts four years. More than 40 percent feel they had no choice but to take on this role. Fifty-five percent of them are employed, and 59 percent are married. One-third are also responsible for children or grandchildren. To make this juggling act work, 64 percent are cutting corners on the job by going in late, leaving early, or taking time off during the day. Other work accommodations include taking leaves (17 percent) and reducing hours (9 percent).

The people they are caring for are also mostly women (68 percent), averaging seventy-seven years of age (two years older than their 2004 counterparts), with 33 percent between seventy-five and eighty-four, 18 percent between eighty-five and eighty-nine (up from 13 percent in 2004), and 13 percent ninety and older. Asked the main reason that help is needed, 15 percent of caregivers say old age, and another 15 percent say Alzheimer's disease or some other form of dementia, a dramatic increase from 8 percent in the previous report. Almost 60 percent of these elderly people in need of assistance still live in their own home, and another 20 percent live with their caregiver, usually a daughter, who provides an average of forty-three hours of care a week, more than a full-time job.

How do these caregivers spend their time?

All help with at least one activity of daily living: providing transportation (84 percent), going grocery shopping (75 percent), changing diapers (20 percent), spoon-feeding someone who can't eat without help (19 percent). Nearly 100 percent of the care recipients are on multiple medications, and nearly half need help organizing or taking them. A bit more than half require advocacy with medical professionals or government agencies of one sort or another. The more personal the task, such as dressing or bathing, the more likely it is to be done by a daughter rather than a son. And in all categories, those caring for someone with Alzheimer's do more work, both in number of hours and number of tasks, than any other subgroup, and experience the most physical and emotional stress.

Seven in ten family caregivers say theirs is a shared responsibility, up from 65 percent in 2004. But rarely is the responsibility shared equally, or even close to equally; the other involved relatives do less than 10 percent of the work. And while unpaid assistance has increased since 2004, when the last report was compiled, the opposite is true of paid help, like aides or housekeepers, who were part of the care team 46 percent of the time five years ago but 41 percent today. This change, researchers say, is related to the economy. (The finding that 57 percent of today's caregivers report no financial hardship, as opposed to 77 percent in 1997 and 68 percent in 2004, flies in the face of current economic realities. The report does not address the possible reasons why. The only one I can think of is that with unemployment high, women who would otherwise be working and paying for surrogates to care for parents are doing it themselves and figure they'd be jobless anyway, so this is not a hardship but a blessing in disguise.)

Even in situations where there are paid employees, which directly correlates with income, family and other volunteer helpers provide 60 percent of the care. It is the primary caregiver who is most likely to say she had no choice but to assume the role, and is also most likely to report a high level of burden (42 percent as compared with 22 percent for their less-involved siblings and other relatives). The caregiver's absence of choice; the number of hours put in and the tasks performed; gender, age, and income; the parent's level of cognitive impairment; and whether caregiver and care recipient live together all affect the caregiver's health status, leading to a predictable increase in both physical and emotional problems. More than half of all caregivers say they have less time for friends and family; one-third feel they need more time for themselves and more help with their caregiving duties.

The finding that caregivers feel isolated and in need of more help is oddly dissonant with what researchers learned about how they use—or more to the point, don't use—the Internet. Almost half of caregivers surveyed have never gone to a website as a source of information, and just 12 percent say they consult the Internet often. Those who actually use the Internet for caregiving-related purposes were asked what they looked for there. Topping the list, at 77 percent, was information about health conditions and treatments for their loved ones, just as many of us now use the Web for health information for ourselves. Caregivers also used the Internet to search for community services and information about assisted living facilities and nursing homes. Just 9 percent turned to the Internet for personal support. (No comparisons can be made here, because these questions were asked in the latest report for the first time.)

In both the most recent and the earlier studies, respondents said their primary resource for information was other people, both professionals and amateurs. In the last five years, more said they turned to friends, family, and word of mouth for information and fewer to doctors, although other medical professionals, such as nurses or physical therapists, remained popular resources. Support groups, which I found to be poorly attended when I visited them in recent years, were considered valuable by 1 percent of respondents, the same as in the last report. (I assume, although the researchers draw no conclusions, that caregivers don't have the spare time for such groups and that if they did, they would rather spend it in more diverting ways.)

For the first time, respondents were asked about public policy changes that would be of help to them. Most popular, at 53 percent, was a caregiver tax credit of $3,000. Next came respite service—someone to take care of the frail elderly, or a safe place to take them, while the caregiver takes a break (29 percent). Other popular forms of assistance were a voucher program that would pay family caregivers minimum wage for at least some of the hours they now put in for free (27 percent); and reliable transportation services to get the elderly person to appointments and activities (25 percent), sparing the caregiver that time-consuming and sometimes logistically challenging responsibility.

The subject engendering far and away the most denial and contention among aging parents and their adult children is driving, which generally becomes a perilous activity for the elderly long before they are willing to part with their car keys—a powerful symbol of independence, just as they are for teenagers. This is a huge issue in most families, and I've heard endless stories of adult children unwilling or unable to take action even when their parents' driving is a severe danger to themselves and others. Various websites (like those of AARP, organizations dedicated to family caregiving, and the American Medical Association) answer questions on how to handle this situation, run frequent essays of advice by geriatric experts, and produce an array of informational brochures.

Some of the stories recounted in news reports, by friends and colleagues, and on my own blog and others are chilling. An eighty-six-year-old man at the farmers' market in Santa Monica confused the brake with the accelerator and mowed down seventy-three people, killing ten of them, including a three-year-old. A woman with early-stage dementia at an assisted living facility near Clearwater, Florida, on her regular drive to the nearby grocery store, mistook a boat ramp for the continuation of the roadway and drove into the Intracoastal Waterway, drowning in her car. After a fall, a woman drove herself to the doctor, who said not a word about her method of getting there; on the way home she had a collision at a gas station, injuring several people and avoiding an explosion at the pumps only because of the fast intervention of the station's attendants. A man with Alzheimer's, still driving short distances in daylight, thought he was driving himself to the hospital amid chest pains but wound up at a laboratory instead. His daughter, a geriatric nurse practitioner, knew he was no longer fit to drive but felt powerless to stop him. An old man driving the wrong way on the interstate caused a three-car accident that killed a much younger man headed to work, a mother and three children, and himself. Another old man abruptly cut in front of a truck in a blinding rain, causing the truck to swerve. The four-vehicle accident left one couple dead and a child in a vegetative state.

A poll a few years back by a website called Caregiving.com, along with the National Safety Council, highlighted the reluctance of adult children to stop their parents from driving, which might add to their responsibilities when the elderly can no longer transport themselves. The poll found that adult children considered this the hardest topic of all to broach with their parents, with 36 percent saying this was the conversation they most wanted to avoid. (Twenty-nine percent said the hardest was the discussion of funeral plans, and 18 percent said it was suggesting a parent move from a family home to a more supported environment.)

The same poll found that seven in ten adult children favored mandatory retesting before the renewal of driver's licenses for those over seventy. But only 17 percent were in favor of mandatory age limits, certainly because of the varying abilities of people at different ages and perhaps because the adult children would have to take up the slack. Fifty-five percent of the adult children queried said there was no public transportation where their parents lived. The 14 percent who said there was deemed it inadequate, and 58 percent said their parents wouldn't use it even if it were available and appropriate.

In comments on the Caring.com website, in AARP chatrooms, and on my blog, adult children reported that they had asked the Department of Motor Vehicles to pull a license from an elderly person, but the DMV refused, saying it would do so only if a physician intervened. The adult children then asked for help from doctors, who demurred. In the *Physician's Guide to Assessing and Counseling Older Drivers,* a new guidebook and collection of online handouts, checklists, and referrals (American Medical Association, 2010), Cecil B. Wilson, the incoming AMA president, explicitly (if belatedly) instructs physicians "to make driver safety a routine part of office visits for the senior patients"; they should, he says, identify drivers at risk, counsel them and their families, and "ease the transition to driver retirement."

The warning signs that an elderly person shouldn't be driving and advice for adult children on handling it are all but identical on various websites and in guidebooks. The warning signs include repeated fender-benders, however minor; near misses; getting lost close to home or in familiar territory; friends' or relatives' expressions of worry or reluctance to ride with the person; other drivers on the road honking more frequently than normal; a driver unable to turn and look over his or her shoulder; complaints of glare at night; and driving either too cautiously or too aggressively. An adult child should begin raising the issue before a dangerous event occurs. Explain your concerns using specific examples; expect to be ignored or get a defensive reaction on the first and probably several subsequent conversations; bring the subject up again; take seriously a parent's concerns about being stranded, isolated, or dependent on others; and present a parent with a detailed and concrete plan for getting around that does not require asking for help from family and thus feeling like a burden. Such a transportation plan might include a list of names and telephone numbers of willing drivers with available days and times; an actual calendar that assigns certain days or certain trips to various family members or others; a list of available public transportation options to all the places the parent regularly goes; an offer of your companionship on the first foray on a bus or van; information about local shuttle services for the elderly or volunteer driver programs sponsored by senior centers, houses of worship, or local agencies; and suggestions of things appropriate for home delivery (groceries, medications, merchandise from catalogs). In other words, don't tell your parents to stop driving and then leave them to their own devices. That is not fair, kind, or healthy, since it could lead to poor nourishment, no social activities, and other unnecessary diminishments in quality of life.

In my family, the problem solved itself with no intervention from me or Michael. The one accident my mother had that I know of—she was in her seventies at the time—failed to raise the red flags it should have for us. She pulled away from a curb, oblivious to a moving car that had the right of way, because arthritis had made turning her head to use the side-view mirror or to look over her shoulder too painful. Not long afterward, she gave up the car keys of her own accord. The accident wasn't the sole consideration. She had had it with the Northeast's snowy winters and was ready to move to Florida, where she wouldn't need to drive.

My anecdotal observation is that men are more stubborn about driving than women, just as women are more stubborn about leaving their own homes. So in this particularly difficult moment of role reversal, frequently the first of many, adult children are often facing down their father.

When the adult child can't persuade a parent to stop driving, or is afraid to even bring up the subject, a common tactic, a version of the "therapeutic fib," is to disable the battery, say the car is broken, have it towed to a mechanic, and hope the subject never comes up again. This, obviously, would work for only a few days, unless the parent is cognitively impaired and losing short-term memory. Some adult children with powers of attorney cancel a parent's car insurance. Some succeed in getting the Department of Motor Vehicles to intervene. One "hid" the car at a sibling's; as a result, his father threatened him with both legal action and disinheritance. Another persuaded a parent to give the car to a grandchild, claiming it was necessary to get a desired job. Surely, none of these decisions was easy, comfortable, or respectful on the part of the adult children. Their parents must have pushed back hard. Dr. Audrey Chun, the Mount Sinai geriatrician, once told me that "my biggest problem is taking away driver's licenses," which she cannot do literally but can facilitate with a call to the DMV. Whenever she has done so, or sometimes even merely broached the subject, Dr. Chun said, "I lose patients and get calls from lawyers."

Adult children and doctors who prefer to look the other way, as well as the understandably recalcitrant elderly, seem the biggest offenders in this situation. But the government also has a role, which it is playing unevenly, from state to state. In certain places, teenagers, as they grow into the driving experience, can obtain restricted or graduated licenses. That would be a promising approach for the elderly. Some states already require more frequent renewal for older drivers, at varied intervals, and others require that after a certain age (again, variable) drivers renew in person rather than by mail or online. A few states require repeat road tests after a certain age or vision tests, performed and submitted by opticians or eye doctors. Some, however, require no special provisions for the elderly. In British Columbia, where there are daylight-only and maximum speed limits for older people, researchers recently reported in *Gerontologist* that there was an 87 percent reduction in accidents among those sixty-six and older between 1999 and 2006.

With the exploding incidence of Alzheimer's and other dementing conditions, and no formal means to keep such drivers off the road, several states, beginning with Colorado in 2006, have added so-called Silver Alert programs to existing Amber Alert ones, for missing and abducted children. They use radio, television, weather service bulletins, and illuminated highway signs to ask the public for help in locating missing old people. Because these alert systems can piggyback on existing technologies, they are not expensive, and in the vast majority of cases they lead to safe rescues. In addition, police officers could be better educated about cognitive impairments, so that if an elderly person who is lost asks them for help, they might see them home rather than simply point the way.

Therapeutic lies are not limited to the car-key dilemma and are more often ad-libbed than found on websites or in guidebooks. As in so many aspects of elder care, we are often flying by the seat of our pants, making it up as we go along, in what can feel like a constant state of improvisation. In the moment, there are no set rules about how and when to shade the truth, omit unnecessary information, or out-and-out lie. My examples are anecdotal and idiosyncratic, and they may never apply to your situation. But all are informed by certain general principles: that our parents want to be in control of their own lives, stay in their homes, drive their cars, not be a burden to their children, and also not be dependent on paid help to do the things they have always been able to do unassisted; and that little by little, and not necessarily in a linear way, their safety and well-being will require more of the very kind of supervision (and financial help) they most resist, which we, too, will resist when our time comes.

Helping our parents transition from total independence to partial or total dependence is a delicate balancing act that is impossible to do perfectly. Empathy, I would argue, is our best guide. While it may be impossible to escape the complicated feelings engendered by being thrust into a quasi-parental role toward one's parent, you can try to leaven those thoughts by considering how *they* feel about the same role reversal. The work, and ultimately the grief, is ours, but the accretion of losses is theirs. They are giving up their independence, their physical or mental capacities, their pride, their role as head of the family, their spouses, and their friends. Their reward for longevity is often a wheelchair and diapers and being ordered around by their children. On the days when I wished I could run away from my responsibilities, I'd practice this mind game: *If I can't bear one more day as my mother's mother, imagine how she feels.* The lies couldn't totally disguise the role reversal for either of us, but they could sometimes take the edge off it, blurring this harsh and unavoidable reality.

A common theme among the evolving lies I told my mother had to do with money. Like so many of her generation, she was frugal. Because she was widowed so young and knew she would be living on limited means for many decades, routine Depression-era thrift became outright self-deprivation. I watched, over two decades, as a once well-furnished home became shabbier and shabbier. When the upholstery wore out on a favorite footstool, she covered the frayed fabric with a towel. When she needed a side table next to her favorite chair, she dug out of the recesses of the basement that folding plastic model I described earlier rather than buy something larger and sturdier. When she could no longer open the garage door herself, because of shoulder pain, she left the car under mounds of snow on the driveway instead of buying an electronic opener she could activate with one push of a button from inside the car. Sometimes, as with the garage door opener, she would accept what Michael and I thought she needed as a gift. But we weren't doing her routine shopping, or making big lifestyle or financial decisions on her behalf, until very late in the game. Until four years before her death, we considered subterfuge, or even seriously manipulative behavior to get her to look after herself better, as disrespectful, inappropriate, and just not how our family went about things.

That changed in Florida, when our visits always included going to the supermarket for her. She had moved from Long Island, in part, because she didn't want to drive anymore, but in Florida she was at the mercy of the Horizon Club van and its scheduled trips, intended for small purchases that she could carry. She used the grocery cart as an ad hoc walker and couldn't reach the high shelves or carry more than a few items back home and put them away. So on each visit one of my top priorities was to make a circuit of local stores to stock up on staples and other heavy or cumbersome items for months to come. Sometimes she'd give me a list, and off I'd go. When I returned with dozens of grocery bags and she asked me what she owed me, I'd ad-lib a dollar figure that was well below the actual cost. She surely knew I wasn't telling the truth—how could she not?—but she didn't argue. Other times she'd hand me a twenty- or fifty-dollar bill before I left the apartment, eyeball what I'd bought on my return, halfheartedly ask if I was sure she'd given me enough money, and then drop the subject when I said yes. The time for pretense (and pride) had begun.

I've heard many versions of this story, kind lies about expenses that adult children assume for aging parents. Michael and I vaguely noticed the "ka-ching, ka-ching" phenomenon when it seemed like every time we turned around we were paying for something, be it plants for her patio; a bench for the end of her bed, where she could sit to put on her socks; a restaurant meal; a newspaper subscription; or plane fares for our visits. We didn't begrudge her anything, or want for anything ourselves as a result. We never tallied what we were spending until lawyers asked us to for purposes of her Medicaid spend-down, and by then we'd shelled out plenty. That said, we were aware. Spending money to save a parent's pride is hardly uncommon.

An accountant I know specializes in managing families' elder care payrolls, the fees and taxes we pay if we're following the law for our parents' home health aides, assuming they are not agency employees but informal hires. Anyway, in his personal life, this accountant was having his own "ka-ching, ka-ching" experience. His eighty-six-year-old grandmother needed trifocals. Medicare doesn't cover eyeglasses. She could afford them but was too stingy. So her grandson got the optometrist to lie and say the trifocals cost $100, her psychological limit. He paid the difference.

He sometimes helps his clients do similar things. For example, an elderly woman saw no reason she should hire him to handle the payroll taxes for her home health aide. (The paperwork dissuades a lot of people from following the law in this regard.) He advised the adult daughter to change the address on the bank statement so it went to her own house, instead of to her mother's, who never missed it. The mother didn't know the daughter was paying for the service, but the service was getting done. You can't "reprogram their brain of a Depression mentality," the accountant said.

Nobody I ever spoke to about this subject, or who commented on it on my blog, objected to spending money on a parent, after it became a wink-and-a-nod enterprise. "There's a myth out there that families abandon their frail elders," Dr. Robert L. Kane, a geriatrician at the University of Minnesota, told me. "Instead, across the income spectrum, children are sacrificing to care for their parents to the limit of their means and sometimes beyond." They pay for eyedrops, new windows, manicures, heating oil, and groceries ordered on their own FreshDirect accounts. They pay for these things even if they know their parents have plenty of money. They pay because they love their parents and empathize with their penny-pinching. "I'll put it on your tab," one middle-aged son would joke with his father, who owned a condo in Florida and a house in Westchester and had enough money for round-the-clock aides but wouldn't buy himself a new coat. His son bought the coat. The father was glad for the gift. "What most of us do isn't sound financial planning," said Steven Schurkman, an elder care lawyer in White Plains, New York, "but it's good for the family dynamic."

Given the Medicaid spend-down, this way of going about things is not fiscally sound if the parent is likely to outlive his money. Had Michael and I understood this point, we might have insisted that my mother spend her own money on everything, or else we would have used another subterfuge—checks or debit or credit cards from the bank accounts we already held jointly with her under our powers of attorney. Then she would have been Medicaid-eligible much sooner. We could (legally) have used her money, rather than our own, to buy groceries, the garage door opener—*everything* we bought her. But we didn't yet understand the intricacies of the Medicaid spend-down or why that would have been smart financial planning. What we did understand was my mother's need to maintain control as she felt it slipping away. We believed in respecting that and not infantilizing her. Still, not knowing what you're doing and then figuring it out later makes you feel dumb, as we did when we finally learned the rules. It is so much better to know your options while you can still exercise them to the fullest.

Not all adult children agree on whether and when this kind of behavior is appropriate. Martin Petroff, an elder care attorney formerly with the New York City Department on Aging, defines it as a "social, not a legal" question. For sure, Petroff said, there is nothing illegal about using money from a joint checking account for a parent's needs and wants. But he swore it was not something he would advise a client to do or something he would do himself. "Aren't you taking over too much?" he asked. "Overreaching?" Petroff had thought his own father-in-law, sound of mind but very frugal, should have a medic-alert pendant or some system in his apartment to summon help in an emergency. The old man insisted that he didn't need it. Then he dropped dead at home and went unfound for five days. Despite that baleful and unnecessary end, Petroff feels the pendant still should have been his father-in-law's choice. Besides, he said, "If I'd have bought it, he'd never have used it." (You or I might find that a borderline irresponsible decision on his part. We all decide for ourselves the right balance between risk and autonomy, within the context of our families. Others' experience, though, can give us food for thought.)

Once my mother got to the Hebrew Home, where her monthly room, board, medical care, pharmaceuticals, laundry, activities, and many other things were all included, first as a private-pay resident and later as a Medicaid recipient, deceptions about money became a very small subset of the greater therapeutic fibbing. Sure, we still paid for extras for her room: Michael got her a better answering machine and told her it was a spare he had at home and wasn't using. We paid for "real" food rather than the bland offerings in the dining room, books when she was still interested in reading, simple clothing that I ordered for her by catalog (like elastic-waist pants and bathrobes that closed with Velcro, not a zipper), certain brands of denture grip or hand cream that she preferred to the standard offerings, and cheer-up-Mom luxuries like a cashmere throw for her bed. They were either gifts or incidentals, and we had long ago stopped even discussing who was paying for them.

But her private-duty aide, Lily Ford, was another matter. My mother needed more one-on-one attention than even an excellent nursing home could provide. I needed her to have enough help so my days weren't spent listening to her complain about tasks done poorly, slowly, or not at all. Lily therefore improved the day-to-day quality of life for both my mother and me.

Lily's role was not essential, but since Michael and I could afford it, and it made such a significant difference, why not? The obstacle, he and I knew when we hired her, would be my mother's refusal, out of thriftiness or self-sufficiency, if she knew we were paying for it. Lily's hourly rate back then, as an employee of an agency owned by the Hebrew Home (which thus got a cut), was $15. Hiring someone over the back fence would have been cheaper, but since all Lily's jobs were at the home, she was there all the time, knew her way around, and was treated like staff by the nurses, social workers, and everyone else. So that's what we pretended she was: part of the package deal, not an extra expense. I recall no conversation with my mother about this issue; I have no idea if I outright lied or if I just acted as if that were the case and avoided the discussion. Michael paid the bills monthly, from a pot of money we had jointly set aside for that purpose.

When we first hired Lily, she worked for us for only two hours each morning. Later, we added two hours in the late afternoon. For the last few days of my mother's life, I hired overnight private-duty help until Lily came home from a vacation spent with her own mother and was again with me the last day. I have no idea how much it cost, since that arrangement was Michael's job and he never kept a running total. Nor do I know what we would have done had my mother outlived the money we had put aside. I imagine we would have paid for Lily as long as we could without compromising our own retirement security and then, as countless people less fortunate do, got along with the staff-to-resident ratio in the nursing home and counted ourselves lucky that we were in a good one. All nursing homes, even the best, are deficient in this area, so families who can pay extra for it usually bring in private-duty help.

Many caregivers don't pay attention to what they're spending. Only one study has been done of the phenomenon: "Family Caregivers—What They Spend, What They Sacrifice" (Evercare and National Alliance for Caregiving, November 2007). Its one thousand phone interviews showed that caregivers spent an average of $5,531 each year, or one-tenth the average American's salary. Long-distance caregivers spent the most, $8,728, while adult children who had taken a parent into their home or vice versa spent $5,585, and those who lived nearby, as I did, spent $4,570. The study asked some caregivers to keep detailed diaries of their expenses; it found that the forty-one who did so spent much more ($12,348) than the phone interviewees. Gail Gibson Hunt, the head of the National Alliance for Caregiving, guesses the diarists were more accurate. Either way, many members of a generation that is approaching or already in its retirement years is using its nest egg to care for parents. This is not a happy prospect for the future, especially if our needs trickle down to our children, a much smaller generation with less savings than our own.

One geriatric care manager told me of the many therapeutic fibs that she has told over the years to get professional help into the home of a frail elderly person who needed it desperately but was flatly refusing. If the old person is so resistant that he won't accept even a social work evaluation, she will send a caseworker into the home under the guise of being "just a friend" of the adult child, someone tagging along on a visit. Or she might say, "This is so-and-so's daughter, who is doing a research project, and I thought you wouldn't mind talking to her." Often, the geriatric care manager said, a client will accept a driver but not a home health aide; once he gets used to the driver, he will be open to more help. In my experience, introducing the first helper is the sticking point; after that, your parent may find he or she likes having someone around, or may take greater enjoyment in pleasurable activities now that simply getting dressed or putting away groceries doesn't consume every bit of energy.

I have friends who first brought help into the house by offering free room and board to a college or graduate student, perhaps in a related field like nursing or social work, as an on-site pair of eyes and ears. The accommodations in your parent's way-too-big house may be vastly superior to the dormitory, so everybody wins. Or you could hire a responsible local high school student to drive your parent around. Close mentoring relationships can evolve out of what begins as a part-time job. *Help* has a different meaning when it's provided informally and seems a mutually convenient arrangement, not a professional "you're old and helpless and I'm being paid to take care of you" job. Some older people are more comfortable when their helpers are of the same race or social class; others just the opposite.

Similar therapeutic fibs are used by senior move managers, who specialize in relocating the elderly from a big house to something smaller, or from home to a supervised facility, or from one part of the country to another.

One move manager told me of a client who steadfastly refused to get rid of decades' worth of *National Geographic* magazines. (By the way, an extreme iteration of such hoarding would be considered pathological. When elderly people live amid so much clutter that they might be trapped in the event of a fire or at risk of being crushed under collapsing pyramids of junk, that behavior should be dealt with by a psychologist.) The client was unwilling to throw away the magazines, and the manager unwilling, out of respect, to do it behind the client's back. So she suggested donating the magazines to a local school that would use them for art projects. Her ruse worked. In another case, when a client was shocked at the cost of moving her furniture, the manager claimed that she had found a mover to do it at half the usual cost, and the adult children secretly paid the difference. Once, when a client downsizing from an unmanageably large home balked at paying the rent for an apartment she could easily afford, the manager had the daughter arrange for a "dummy" lease with a rent the old woman accepted and a separate—and again secret—side arrangement in which family members paid the difference.

Home health aides can also effectively keep their clients out of harm's way by telling a carefully constructed white lie. One aide I know tends to an elderly couple: the husband is an easygoing man with multiple physical problems, including heart arrhythmia and the aftereffects of a stroke that left one arm useless; the wife is a more high-strung sort, with early-stage dementia that she doesn't acknowledge. She resents any suggestion that she is no longer as capable as she once was and finds help in the house threatening to her domain. They are a cultured and worldly pair, without financial worries, who are still able, under the right conditions, to attend concerts and other cultural events. But the wife sees no reason why they can't ride the bus to get there, which could be dangerous to them both, especially if she were to get confused and lost, as she has. So their aide will go downstairs to pick up a loaf of bread that she doesn't really need just as they're leaving the house and then sweet-talk them into a cab, or will fabricate a bus ride she is about to take to a friend's apartment in order to accompany them to their destination.

Sara Myers, who has thirty years of experience in the field of aging, has on and off written a blog called *Good Enough Daughter,* a name that says it all. When Myers was in her late fifties, her mother's cognitive function and physical health were in steep decline, so she moved the old woman, then past ninety, into her own home on Bainbridge Island, Washington.

Only then did she learn that, try as she might, she would never get everything right; hence the blog's title. In one post, "Aunt Babe Died: What Do I Tell My Mother?" Myers writes of deciding on the truth. Her mother, already quite demented, was briefly upset about her sister's death, then quickly forgot there had ever been a conversation about it. Another option would have been to pretend that Aunt Babe was still alive and hope it didn't come up again. This is not the kind of dilemma that has a right answer or a wrong answer. You do the best you can, often with little time to ponder and no guide other than your heart. A loving decision is rarely wrong.

CHAPTER 13

Cruel Sorting

There is a hierarchy of disability among old people that leads to what I have come to call "cruel sorting." Adults who once went out of their way to be kind to those less fortunate now, as elderly people, shun anyone in their age group who is worse off than themselves. I saw it first with my mother when she still lived at the assisted living facility in Florida.

Except for the smell of institutional disinfectant, the facility was a pleasant place. The staff greeted everyone by name, even the adult children who showed up from distant precincts only every few months. It had lushly landscaped courtyards and a swimming pool, and the well-appointed apartments opened onto a breezeway, typical of local motels and apartment complexes. Almost everyone used a cane or a walker. Few drove anymore; instead, they rode the facility's van to the mall or the movies. The elevator doors opened and closed so slowly that residents could amble out at their own pace. But I saw no wheelchairs, no aides, nobody in the dining room who needed help eating, and nobody with serious memory or behavioral issues.

"*Those*" people—and my mother and her friends referred to them exactly that way, with audible quotation marks, or with frank insults masked as jokes, like referring to them as "the droolers"—lived elsewhere on the campus. Their one-story building was hidden from view by gigantic birds-of-paradise. Only if you knew exactly where to look was it even visible. Tiny, gnarled women lay under lap robes even in the hot Florida sun, dozing on the veranda in their wheelchairs, many with private aides in alert attendance. They were so out of sight, it was easy to forget they were there—or to pretend they weren't.

I was curious about this other building, mentally exploring our future what-ifs. "Let's go see what it's like, Ma," I said during one visit, as casually as suggesting we check out a nearby Palm Beach mall. She steadfastly refused, and I didn't push it. Months, maybe years, later, I tried another tack to get her to take a look. I suggested that maybe she'd like to volunteer to read to the people who lived there, those who had lost their eyesight to macular degeneration or could no longer hold a book or turn pages. She liked the reading part of my idea and began recording books for the blind, for the Horizon Club library, but in the privacy of her own apartment. As a voracious reader, she found her good deed was so satisfying that she'd keep at it until she was hoarse. But in seven years she never ventured across the way. My mother's behavior was not exceptional. The etiquette of these communities did not include friendly visits to "those" people.

Independent or assisted living facilities remind me of high school in so many of its most unattractive ways. This ostracizing and name-calling seemed like the behavior of "mean girls" or the comparable cruelty directed at nerdy teenage boys. As one reader of the *New Old Age* blog put it, "It's an old adage that the elderly grow more childlike. We can hardly be surprised that the social tolerance on display . . . more resembles the playground than what the grownups expect or wish."

The high school dynamics were most evident in the dining room. Without assigned tables, there was a proprietary understanding about who sat where, and it could get downright nasty if protocol was breached. Should you perch for even a minute in someone else's customary chair, you risked an immediate rebuke and the threat of tattling to someone in charge. To avoid this sort of pettiness, and the forced camaraderie of tables for six, my mother often ate alone. That made her like honey to bees for the rare men in residence, in whom she had no interest. "I'm not picking up any more socks or being anyone's nurse ever again," she would say tartly, having made only one halfhearted stab at dating after being widowed decades earlier. The fellow had had several heart attacks but had not told her about them right away. When she found out, she withdrew from the fray once and for all.

It was at her Florida home—the Horizon Club—that my mother for the first time showed herself to me as a skilled raconteur. She told side-splittingly funny stories about the tiny cohort of men in residence; among them, the handful who still drove were the equivalent of the most popular boys in high school. Even loftier in the social pecking order, sort of like the captain of the football team, was the rarest of the rare: a man who could drive at night. To the competing women in Love That Red nail polish and sequined poolside cover-ups, a man's intellect, worldly success, looks, charm, and health status were beside the point compared to car keys and night vision. I remember one woman in particular. Each time I visited, she had a different gentleman friend. My mother would brief me on the one who had recently died and tell me the name of the new one. I never quite figured out whether I was supposed to say I was sorry for her loss. Another woman in the complex, with a Texas twang, hennaed hair, a sharp tongue, and a refusal to play by the rules, moved from facility to facility once she'd worked her way through the available men at any one locale. I begged my mother to write down these stories; she did so enthusiastically, years later, in the Sarah Lawrence creative writing class.

At the Hebrew Home, to my dismay, sorting by disability was even harsher than it had been at the Horizon Club, even though it was otherwise a gentler environment. Here cognitive function was the dividing line; despite being paralyzed from the waist down and incontinent, my mother was at or near the top of the heap. Her most obvious peers were Nellie, who was tethered to an oxygen tank, and Doris, in a wheelchair because of advancing multiple sclerosis, because both of them were all there mentally. From day one I decided they were my mother's likeliest friends. But trying to pick my mother's friends at this stage in life was a mistake. She must have been as annoyed and embarrassed as I had been when she and my father tried to do that to me at college. The role reversal of becoming your mother's mother is fraught territory every step of the way, perhaps because you never are—quite. Saying to a parent new to a congregate facility, in a voice more suitable for freshman orientation, "Oh, Mom, she looks like someone you could be friends with," is disrespectful, and also counterproductive.

I was surprised, upon our arrival at the Hebrew Home, by the rarity of residents who didn't have some form of dementia; I'd assumed all such people would be in the Alzheimer's wing, not on the regular skilled nursing floors. Be prepared for a similar shock in any nursing home: only the tiny percentage of dementia patients with end-stage disease wind up in the special wings. By then they are quiet, no longer able to speak, and mostly bedridden. In a way it would be easier for people like my mother if the end-stagers were on the regular floors, since they are long past the incessantly repeated questions, jarring rantings, wanderings, sexual disinhibition, and other inappropriate behaviors that swirl around you all the time. I can't say I ever got used to it, but it did move from foreground to background; from something that made me recoil and want to run out of the place to something I simply lived with, as my mother did, keeping mostly to herself or enjoying the company of the staff and her children. I tell friends to try not to overreact to the bedlam as I did at first. In time it becomes white noise.

Living with it is something that my mother did with little complaint, consistent with her stoic nature. Unlike Michael and me, she actually found humor in the demented lady next door who climbed into bed with her from time to time. We couldn't stop it, no matter how loudly we objected, because the fire code prohibited closing my mother's door at night, lest she be trapped in a blaze. Tolerating what she couldn't avoid, however, wasn't the same thing as avoiding the avoidable. So my mother purposefully didn't mix with people who were physically or mentally worse off than she was, just as she hadn't in Florida. She didn't want to see what easily could be her own future, what *would* be her future sooner rather than later. Here "those" people weren't hidden behind birds-of-paradise half a campus away. In the early or middle stages of the disease, and thus not entirely oblivious to their surroundings, they were mostly in the TV lounge, far from their own rooms and either uneasy solitude or annoying roommates, as well as close to the nurses' station and eyeball-to-eyeball supervision. When my mother went from her room to the elevator, she avoided them by taking a circuitous course. I pushed the chair as instructed, on this elaborately devised back route, all the while lecturing her for being unkind. Far more gently, the nurses and social workers told me the unkindness was mine; at this stage of life she had a right—indeed, a need—to protect herself however she chose. Some forms of denial are healthy, they told me, and this was one of them.

•   •   •

The congregate living setting for the elderly where one would least expect "cruel sorting" is the continuing care retirement community, or CCRC, which is marketed as the ideal way to "age in place." A CCRC offers, if only to the wealthy, a true continuum of care. It has apartments suitable for active, healthy retirees, who can then transition, as their needs change, to more supervised settings on the same campus without uprooting themselves over and over. Relocation trauma, a term bandied about by gerontologists, packs a wallop, seen most dramatically in the aftermath of Hurricane Katrina. While the circumstances of hurricane relocations are unique, the deleterious effects of moving old people are well known. Every time Michael and I relocated my mother, she suffered a steep decline in her ability to function, physically and emotionally. We, too, experienced wear and tear from orchestrating and carrying out the move. For this reason, I advise friends whose parents need a period of skilled nursing after a hospitalization to choose a place that would satisfy them were the short-term placement to turn into permanent nursing home care. The shock of never being able to go home again, when you expected to, would itself be traumatic. An extra move from a rehabilitation center to a skilled nursing facility would be an added blow when someone is most fragile.

In this regard and others, there is much good to be said of the CCRC model, but an easy mix between the fit and the not-so-fit turns out not to be one of them, according to Tetyana Pylypiv Shippee, in "'But I Am Not Moving': Residents' Perspectives on Transitions Within a Continuing Care Retirement Community," published in *The Gerontologist* 49 (2009). A research associate at the Center on Aging and Life Course at Purdue University in Indiana, Shippee, at age twenty-one, lived full-time for twenty-three months at Pickwick Village, an upper-middle-class, moderately upscale CCRC in a midwestern college town. She shared the lives of the residents, observed the culture of the place, and conducted thirty-five face-to-face, in-depth interviews with men and women between the ages of seventy-six and ninety-nine at all three levels of care: independent living, assisted living, and skilled nursing. Her primary research goal was to examine how residents transitioned from independent living to higher levels of care, easily or painfully.

In the process, she found marked "social boundaries and stigmas" between the higher-functioning elderly and the more disabled, largely because the first group chose to keep its distance from the second, even in what is intended to be a cohesive, one-for-all-and-all-for-one community.

Some of this distancing, Shippee concluded, was the result of the busier lives of the independent living residents, and some she attributed to their separate dining and other gathering places. More significant, the healthier residents perceived, correctly, the depressing ambience at higher levels of care and were reluctant to confront their own mortality by being there.

Becoming marginalized was the norm as one moved along the continuum, according to what Shippee saw and heard at Pickwick Village. Those in independent living apartments reported happiness in their choice to move there because of the level of social engagement they had found, while those in the other two levels balked when their declining health forced them to move, and they often felt stigmatized and abandoned by their former social network, despite being just a short walk away. Interestingly, they noted this new isolation more with resignation and understanding than with surprise or anger. They didn't blame their more independent friends or expect them to behave differently. The reminder that they were that much closer to the end, because of the move, led to comments like "It's time to say goodbye" or "My life is over as far as I'm concerned," Shippee recounted.

Unless you are visited by a wife or close relatives, you are alone, said a man identified as Evan, a nursing home resident: "I don't know how you change that. It's just the way it works out."

The independent living residents acknowledged their responsibility for creating precisely the isolation that they feared for themselves. "It may exhibit a bias, even bigotry on our part," a man named Jim told Shippee, adding that "a lot of us don't want to be reminded that we may be only a few years from that ourselves." A man named Ken agreed: "You don't want to admit that you are [going to be] the same way, so you stay away from them."

Continuing care retirement communities, in large measure because of the attraction of aging in place, are the fastest-growing segment of the long-term care residential market. According to the American Association of Homes and Services for the Aging (AAHSA), 1.4 million people lived in nursing homes in 2007, a shrinking portion of the pie, as public policy has made other options affordable to the poor, like Medicaid reimbursement for services in the community, so they are not forced into skilled nursing facilities they otherwise would not need simply because they had run out of money. In the same year, 2007, AAHSA's most recent data showed that 900,000 people lived in assisted living facilities and 745,000 in CCRCs, more than double the population in such communities a decade before.

CCRCs have a complicated financial model that you must study carefully before making a substantial up-front payment, as some fail, leaving residents to fend for themselves. For the most part, they sign up residents only at the stage when they are suitable for independent living and are seeking security for themselves and for their adult children, the peace of mind of knowing that their parents are settled in, that in a crisis they can move from one level of care to the next without disruptive relocations. It is an especially attractive arrangement, financially and otherwise, for couples who will likely decline on different trajectories, because they can live in separate parts of the same facility, without additional cost, while in close proximity to each other. As a rule, there is no additional cost, or very little, for the second accommodation. Whatever the couple pays per month for their original apartment, on top of the entry fee, will also cover the vastly more expensive housing and professional services for the frailer spouse, in skilled nursing or dementia care, so it winds up a far better deal than simply two for the price of one. Plus, having no transportation issues, the couple can be together throughout the day. The healthier spouse, for instance, can go from her apartment to the nursing facility for meals or to watch television with her husband (as couples at the Hebrew Home did, though they lived on different floors or in different buildings). For the couples, it seemed fun, like having a date. But friends and neighbors, even in CCRCs that pride themselves on a family ethos, rarely venture from their independent living quarters to the other levels of care for a meal or a visit, according to Shippee's research.

In the *New Old Age* blog, the writer Paula Span observed:

> In Ms. Shippee's facility, where introductory tours often bypassed the assisted living/nursing wing altogether, the health and vigor required for independent living had become an important source of status. To leave an independent living apartment meant not only losing one's home and social network, but also a part of one's identity. Friendships often did not survive the move; visits became more like duties or favors than part of reciprocal relationships. Small wonder, then, that Shippee observed anger, stress and a keen sense of loss when residents were faced with moving.

> Span asked Shippee whether CCRCs could improve the situation by promoting more interaction, and by reducing the physical and social barriers,

say, by consolidating the different dining rooms. Shippee doubted it would help much, although I have seen at least two CCRCs where physical design, among other factors, trumped the apparently natural sorting by level of disability. "Independent living residents don't like that," Shippee told Span, speaking of shared common spaces such as dining rooms. "They want to feel like they're in a nice restaurant, conversing with friends; they don't want to be faced with those in declining health." Overall, "they view themselves as healthy and active," she said. "If you try to integrate them with people in wheelchairs who have problems, they will object." (The mother of a friend of mine was in an assisted living facility with two dinner seatings. Once the old woman was no longer ambulatory and needed a walker or wheelchair, she was forced to switch to the seating dedicated to the more handicapped and was deprived of the company of longtime friends.)

On *The New Old Age,* a professional, commenting on the post, agreed that residents had the right to be shielded from physical decline and mental incapacity. This consultant to nursing homes, assisted living facilities, and CCRCs said that "the issue of prejudice of the able-bodied toward the ill and infirm is thorny." When a facility administrator at a CCRC asked the consultant to "speak to the independent residents about being more accepting of the disabled residents," she reluctantly declined. The facility, she said, was the "person's home" and thus a place where "as adults they had a right to choose with whom to socialize."

I visited only one congregate living environment for the elderly where I saw *no* stigma or social isolation whatsoever among the more infirm, and that was the mother house—essentially a CCRC for aging nuns—at the Sisters of St. Joseph's convent in suburban Rochester, New York. The ratio of independent living, assisted living, skilled nursing, and dementia beds is like that of a typical, secular CCRC, but the physical configuration intentionally unites, rather than isolates, the sisters of different levels of physical and cognitive disability. Some of the sisters reside in the west wing's independent living apartments, with raised toilets, grab bars, and the like; others, who are quite infirm, occupy assisted living studios, under much closer medical and nursing supervision; and still others are in the nursing home or dementia unit, in the east wing. But the two wings are an easy distance from each other and, at the central intersection, share a chapel, dining rooms, and a library, for all who can get there, whether ambulatory or in wheelchairs.

While the physical configuration and the shared common spaces surely encourage mixing rather than sorting, what most distinguishes the sisters from others living in age-segregated communities, or institutions for the frail elderly, besides their religious faith, is that they have been friends and colleagues ever since they took their vows as adolescents. The situation of nuns might seem to have no applicability to you or me, or to our mothers or fathers. Yet it highlights what makes most congregate living arrangements such unnatural and often unwelcome places for the elderly to wind up in and why they overwhelmingly say, when polled or in informal discussions, that more than anything they want to age and die in their own homes.

Unlike Sister Dorothy Quinn, who was eighty-seven years old at the time I met her, living in the skilled nursing wing at the Sisters of St. Joseph's mother house, tethered to an oxygen tank, and wheelchair-bound because of congestive heart failure, my mother did not live out her last years among friends of a lifetime. Rather, she wound up at the Horizon Club, the Meadowview, and the Hebrew Home for no other reason than age, disability, and needs that could not be met elsewhere. (More recently, a growing number of enclaves in the United States have adopted the so-called village concept: Beacon Hill Village in Boston, and its clones in the Capitol Hill neighborhood in Washington, D.C.; Alexandria, Virginia; New Canaan, Connecticut; and Bronxville, New York, among others. Here elderly neighbors band together and hire the equivalent of a concierge to find, vet, and organize an array of services that allow them to remain in their own homes. But such places are true "villages" only for those who have lived there for a long time, not for newcomers.) Few elderly have any option but to settle among strangers, once they need the services that congregate living affords.

Sister Dorothy's room was often filled with other old women, in various states of decline, who felt such ease with her, and such devotion, that they overcame their own fears to be by her side. By contrast, my mother's neighbors in various congregate facilities—a tiny number who became casual friends—were not people who had known her for nearly seven decades, back to high school or college, and had shared life experiences along the way. When my women friends and I envision our own last years, whether we have children or not, we fantasize about all living together, communally, in a big old house with rocking chairs on the porch, reminiscing. Rather than being a burden to our children or dependent on the kindness of strangers, we imagine helping one another, hiring others to help us when that is no longer sufficient, and replicating what those nuns have—or what we ourselves had in summer camp cabins or college dormitories.

To a lesser extent, I also saw the elderly resist the natural impulse to shun those worse off at a CCRC in Hanover, New Hampshire. There, while it was far from universal, I saw kindness, attentiveness, and continuing contact among the eighty-year-olds who were still playing tennis and their former independent living neighbors now consigned to the skilled nursing or dementia unit. Kendal at Hanover is part of a highly regarded Quaker-run chain of CCRCs, many attached to college campuses, that are attractive to a liberal, intellectual clientele. They are very monochromatic racially and socioeconomically and are inclined toward the Quaker ethos of community in the true, not the marketing, sense of the word. In that way, they are like the Sisters of St. Joseph's mother house.

At Kendal, the assisted living units, a skilled nursing facility, and a dementia unit are all located in one wing of the main building; independent quarters are in the other wing. The two hundred or so independent living residents do an unusual amount of volunteering. About eighty of them choose to push wheelchairs, play music, read aloud, and otherwise spend time with the other residents and are trained in specific skills for dealing with the conversational and behavioral aspects of dementia. As at the Sisters of St. Joseph's mother house, Kendal at Hanover made a conscious decision to locate the outpatient medical facility (with geriatricians, nurse practitioners, and other professionals) in the same area as the frailest residents, both for their own proximity and to ensure contact, even if only in passing, with residents who needed no more than a flu shot.

But not all of the Kendal facilities are equal; some I've visited are no better in this regard than the CCRC that was grist for Shippee's study. One differentiating characteristic at Hanover is that its original medical director, Dr. Dennis McCullough, author of *My Mother, Your Mother,* brought to the facility a distinct approach to end-of-life care that used mindful decision-making and a less-is-more approach to high-tech medical care for the elderly. At Kendal residents have lengthy and evolving conversations about end-of-life planning. Should a resident have a hip replacement if she has advanced dementia and will never walk again, since she will be unable to do the necessary physical therapy? Should another resident be resuscitated in the event of cardiac arrest, even though the results in this age group, among the survivors, usually include serious brain damage? Some might consider Dr. McCullough's approach to be age-based rationing of health care. However, no one is denied aggressive care if they choose it after informed discussion. Some may consider the conversations to be "death panels," the phrase used by critics in their overheated reaction to the Obama administration's original health care proposal. But regardless of outside opinion, all but a handful of the residents at Kendal at Hanover have embraced "slow medicine" and unite around that pioneering cause.

Many of Kendal's residents are academics, including several college presidents and other top administrators who had long known one another as both friends and colleagues in various professional incarnations; a good number of them moved in the day the doors opened in 1991. Like young families who populate a neighborhood en masse when their children are toddlers, and are still close friends in retirement, the Kendal residents started a new adventure together. They put their professional talents to work, building a community from scratch, and many are still together two decades later, effectively for a full generation of their lives. They thus have far more in common than simply old age and infirmity. When a spouse living independently goes for a meal in the dementia unit, for instance, her friends often join her. Their long, shared history eases conversation with those in the middle stages of Alzheimer's disease, who can generally participate easily in conversations that are intentionally focused on the past. Only when talk turns to the present do they become confused, having lost short-term memory, and drop out of the conversation—and they may become either unresponsive or agitated.

Would these men and women have tended the garden of friendship had they met in their late eighties? I doubt it. So does Carol Armstrong, ninety as I write, and one of the original residents, along with her husband, Jim, ninety-two, a college president several times over. "It takes somebody rather special," Carol said, "to meet someone out of the blue [at that age] and take the responsibility any friendship requires." Edie Gieg, eighty-six, the Armstrongs' friend and another original resident, agreed. "Most people don't make close friends at this stage in life," she said. "There's a latent feeling we'll all lose each other pretty soon and thus a hesitancy to get too close."

My mother had made friends in Florida when she was in her seventies but was unwilling to do it all over again when she arrived back in New

York in her mid-eighties. The Kendal residents came together at an age when they still had the time, energy, and motivation for the hard work that friendship requires. They were building new lives for themselves, not readying themselves to die, which may be the hardest work of all and also the most solitary.

As my mother would learn, the able-bodied, relatively speaking, often become the ill and infirm and then find themselves on the wrong side of the divide. In the last few months of her life, it was her turn to be shunned by fellow residents of the nursing home, because to spend time with her was to see where they were likely headed. I was slow to see this coming because it played itself out primarily in the dining room, a locus of mean-spiritedness. (I rarely visited my mother at mealtimes, in order to spread out her social opportunities, since she mostly kept to herself in her room the rest of the day.) There were maybe six women she regularly dined with. They had little in common but advanced age and, to use my mother's words, "all their marbles." She was a popular member of the group, a lively conversationalist when she left her hermitic cocoon, and she seemed to enjoy these women, in small doses. But when she lost her ability to speak, even after Michael and I bought her the contraption that employed his voice, she lost her social utility as a dining companion. At about the same time, the imperceptible strokes—never definitively diagnosed because she refused brain scans as pointless and a waste of Medicare dollars—were making her hands increasingly useless, and eating was becoming a problem. She refused any adjustment to her diet (in other words, the introduction of pureed food) other than having the regular meal cut into tiny morsels. She even more vehemently refused a "feeder," an actual job title that grates on me to this day. My mother had become, to put it gently, a sloppy eater; her food wound up almost anyplace except her mouth. The other ladies, not entirely unfairly, therefore found her an unappealing dining companion and asked that she be fed where they didn't have to watch.

This, Michael and I later learned at a family meeting, prompted an unpleasant and unusual disagreement among the staff. Should they allow my mother's table mates to exile her to eat with others who were more impaired? Should they assign her a "feeder," out in the hall, and give her pureed food whether she wanted it or not? Should they ask her to take her meals in her room, thus depriving her of the little social contact she had?

Or should they take a stand on behalf of a dignified woman who had never lost her ability to follow a complex conversation and even found a way to participate minimally once she got that assisted-communication device? To solve the messy-eating problem, Michael and I could have suggested finger food, had we been more clever, as she was still nimble enough for that, long after utensils were beyond her command. I'm confident that had we suggested it, it would have been provided.

My mother's lone defender on the staff prevailed, and a decision was made that she would still eat in the dining room. I applauded that woman's courage and also the fact that the majority backed down after thoughtful discussion. We all assumed my mother was unaware that her mealtime companions had tried to have her banished. Now they would be put on notice not to treat her as a pariah, and we hoped that would make them fall into line. Alas, my mother had been keenly aware of the entire brouhaha. From that day forward she took her meals in her room. It was the beginning of the end for her.

CHAPTER 14

As Complicated as a Rubik's Cube

When my mother made the common reverse migration from Florida back to New York, her health care proxy, meticulously prepared far in advance of any emergency, listed me and my brother as equal partners in decision-making. This was a bad plan on its face. The whole idea of having an agent to make health care decisions (not merely a living will that sets out one's general wishes about end-of-life care) is to ensure that there is *one* person in charge, aware and respectful of your wishes and cool-headed enough to carry them out, regardless of interference or disagreement from others. But total equality between my brother and I was, in all formal ways, my mother's habit, and there was no dissuading her that a proxy, unlike a last will and testament, need not split everything down the middle. Her lawyer explained the risk—I might see something one way, Michael another, and her preference could get lost in a contentious mess between us—but she had her mind made up, and that was that.

As long as she was in Florida, the joint proxy, however unwise, was at least legal. What my mother, Michael, and I didn't know, nor did we check at the time of her move, is that this kind of proxy is not recognized in New York. There, two agents may be named, but one must be designated in the primary role, while the other is called upon only if the first can't be found in a timely fashion. (The Florida version is known as a "joint proxy"; the New York version is a "serial proxy.") This turned out not to matter, as my mother never lost the ability to make her own health care decisions and also because the nursing home, knowing that her existing proxy would not be binding in the state, had her fill out another immediately upon admission. Absent this step, which most nursing homes would neglect, due to having few or no social workers, we could have been in big trouble at the most inopportune time. If my mother had become unconscious or cognitively impaired, and if my brother and I had argued about what to do, she might have suffered unduly. The medical establishment has a natural propensity to sustain rather than to end life if there's a scintilla of doubt. My mother likely would have wound up in some hellish legal and medical limbo while the case was turned over to a guardianship proceeding, a court process in which someone is designated the legal decision-maker, which is both time-consuming and very expensive.

We avoided that as a result of good luck, not proper planning, because we didn't have a clue that innumerable laws, practices, and regulations differ when crossing state lines. Medicaid eligibility, benefits, and reimbursement are set by the states, as long as they meet or exceed minimum federal guidelines; assisted living and CCRC regulations vary, as does the availability of home care services; estate taxes differ. Elder care already requires a steep learning curve about complex bureaucracies, but switch states and you are all but starting from scratch. Even Medicare, a federal program that conventional wisdom says is uniform across the country, and the regulation of nursing homes, presumably governed by federal standards since the scandals of the 1960s and 1970s, are not one-size-fits-all.

The Medigap policies that supplement basic Medicare are offered by different carriers in different states and must often be replaced following a move. Also, in practical if not in statutory terms, Medicare is run according to local standards, overseen by local bureaucrats, and implemented by local vendors. Possible complications and roadblocks to coverage vary greatly from jurisdiction to jurisdiction, and the need to figure it out could not come at a more stressful time. Thus, as with almost everything else, the more you know beforehand, the better.

Howard S. Krooks, a lawyer in Boca Raton, Florida, saw this state-by-state problem early on. He built his practice around so-called snowbirds, former New Yorkers who came to southeastern Florida in what would turn out to be their first old age. But a seventy-year-old and an eighty-five-year-old can be worlds apart in independence and mobility. The seventy-year-old is most likely enjoying year-round summer, with golf, tennis, and water aerobics. The eighty-five-year-old, even in balmy climes, doesn't venture out much anymore, because a fall could be fatal; at that age a parent is not as mobile, as healthy, or as cognitively intact as she once was. Often this signals a move back to where her children live, because that's where she will get the help that family generally provides, like getting to doctors' appointments, going to the store, and advocating on her behalf in the hospital or any other medical setting. Those are places where terrible things can happen to someone who is alone, especially the elderly, who may have poor vision or hearing, or dementia, on top of garden-variety timidity or fear. The advocacy of nearby children can also protect them from scam artists. Old people, out of loneliness, or helplessness, can be too quick to "adopt" a handyman/grifter offering assistance around the house. They may fall for duplicitous telephone solicitations for products and services like bogus insurance or medical alert systems. In many ways, they are easy prey.

Krooks, a member of the bar in both states, is based in Florida and also serves as "of counsel" at a Westchester County law firm, shuttling back and forth to meet New York– and Florida-based clients' needs. A few years ago his client base was mostly newly retired men and women relocating to Florida. Now a similar group of clients is returning home. Census data on people moving from one state to another doesn't tell us why they moved, so it isn't of much use in determining the volume or route of these reverse migrations. But it's a safe bet that the busiest corridor is between the New York metropolitan region and the southeastern part of Florida—Miami, Deerfield Beach (where my mom lived), Fort Lauderdale, Palm Beach, and Boca. Krooks calls this "the big daddy" of migration pathways. Midwesterners, by contrast, have clustered on Florida's Gulf Coast, many in Sarasota. People from Washington State wind up in Arizona. Military retirees from all over head for San Diego. For the less well-off, the busiest corridor is between Puerto Rico and New York. Krooks said he hears from lawyers in all these places who are considering doing what he did: becoming expert in the laws of the states at both ends of a popular corridor. His business is not telling people to stay or go, although he leans toward elderly parents making a second move once they become frail and dependent, largely so children can advocate for them regarding medical care and fraud. The second-best alternative, he says, is for the children to hire a geriatric care manager in an elderly parent's Florida community, to keep a close eye on matters, communicate information regularly, and advise you to jump on a plane when the situation warrants, since parents can be either too needy ("Come!") or too proud ("I'm fine!") to accurately assess when their children's presence is appropriate.

Since every jurisdiction is different, you need to do your homework in many subject areas regarding where your parent is now and where he or she is headed, to hire an adviser with technical expertise, or both. Since it's impossible to offer a list of discrepancies between every combination of states, and in some cases counties, I've chosen to give you a sense of the complexity by focusing on New York and Florida, both because of the high traffic back and forth and because of my own familiarity with what differentiates them.

The most obvious difference between them is Medicaid, the only government program that pays for custodial care for the aged, provided they fall below certain income and asset limits. It is more generous and easier to get in New York than in Florida (or just about anyplace else), although that could change at any time due to New York's fiscal woes. As you know by now, Medicaid is for poor people, but you become a poor person very quickly once you're paying assisted living, nursing home, or home care expenses in old age. My mother's room at the Hebrew Home, as I've said, cost $14,000 a month, a high-end price for a high-end facility in a high-end region, but it was not as over-the-top as it may seem. A live-in home health aide in these parts would have cost us maybe $5,000 a month, more if we hired through an agency (which would take a cut off the top but also offer all sorts of protections and supervision), and less if we chose, paid, and supervised the aide without an intermediary. And managing her care at home would have required other costly help, too—as well as rent or mortgage and taxes, food, and other household expenses.

When my mother arrived in New York, she still had $175,000. Even without giving Michael and me her money within the legal time frame, she was still going to be "on the dole" (her phrase) in no time flat. Currently (and this has increased dramatically since my mother's death and could change again, in either direction, at any time), to qualify for New York's Medicaid program, you can have $13,800 in assets, not counting a home that you (or a spouse or disabled child) live in or intend to return to, plus a car, a burial fund, and a few lesser items. In most states, Florida among them, your assets are limited to $2,000, the baseline that is set by the federal government, which then lets the states adjust upward in sixty-odd categories (*way* upward, as New York did, phasing in the new ceiling, and other new regulations, between 2005 and 2011).

All states, on sliding scales based on local conditions, reimburse nursing home care for those who are eligible, again a federal requirement. But New York is one of the few states that also cover home care for Medicaid recipients: not just for eight to ten hours a week, as in Florida (even that is "very hard to come by," Krooks said), but for round-the-clock assistance if you need it and meet certain criteria (which I'll detail shortly). If your parent is past eighty-five, he or she is probably going to need this kind of care for several years and likely will wind up on Medicaid. If that's the case, New York is where he or she will fare best. One can argue that certain states have overly generous Medicaid benefits and others are miserly. Such variability would not exist in a better-designed system. I believe that our elders deserve beneficence, which they had in earlier generations and continue to get elsewhere in the world, but New York's benefits do seem to me unrealistically generous in such pinched times.

Before returning to the jurisdictional idiosyncrasies of Medicaid, which vary not only state by state but county by county, let's take a look, guided by Howard Krooks, at what else the elderly and their adult children should know about Florida versus New York law. Though the Medicaid reimbursement rates, benefits, and eligibility standards make New York the obvious winner in most categories, depending on one's individual circumstances, Florida has other advantages, arcane though they might seem. The complexity argues for legal help. To drive that point home, Peter Strauss, dean of the New York City elder care bar, says that he regularly sees lawyers from other specialties who would not even try to navigate this maze without help. And many of the elder care lawyers I've interviewed (Strauss among them) often did not know the answer to one technical question or another and referred me to yet another elder care lawyer with more expertise in that corner of the field.

So, Florida versus New York:

- In Florida, assisted living facilities that are not part of the major corporate chains like Classic Residence by Hyatt or Atria are called "stand-alone" facilities. They participate in a statewide "diversion program" that is Florida's limited answer to so-called community

Medicaid in New York. Under this program, Medicaid money can be spent on "cost of care" but not room and board. Medicaid covers only six hundred or so assisted living beds in New York, as part of a small pilot project. That's a tiny number, especially per capita, compared to the approximately seven thousand in Florida. (The nationwide chains decline all Medicaid funding, thus freeing themselves to cherry-pick only clients who can pay their own way.) Krooks said there were "loads of nice" stand-alone assisted living facilities in his area. However, in all surveys, the vast majority of the elderly say they want to live out their lives in their own homes if possible. To state the obvious, assisted living may be *homelike*, but it isn't *home*. In New York a Medicaid recipient need not move from home to an assisted living facility to get round-the-clock Medicaid assistance with daily tasks.

- Nursing homes in Florida run the gamut in quality, as they do everywhere, but all retirement havens (including Arizona and Southern California) have a disproportionate number of "unattended" residents, far from family. Since their "kids tend not to be around," Krooks said, "there is a greater chance that a loved one will receive less than adequate care," perhaps 50 percent, by his estimate, in institutions in such locations, meaning they may be ignored or mistreated. A top-notch geriatric care manager can mitigate the absence of nearby children but can never fully replace their level of attention or advocacy.

- Elderly married couples face special challenges, none more daunting than the fact that expensive long-term care for one could leave the other impoverished for the remainder of his or her own years, if funds and other assets are tallied jointly. There are many complex ways of protecting sufficient money and the family home for the so-called community-dwelling spouse (the one who isn't in a nursing home or other congregate facility), but they all require the assistance of one of the nation's approximately four hundred certified elder law attorneys.

  One of the most common, and controversial, is "spousal refusal," in which a husband or wife signs a document effectively abdicating financial responsibility for the other. This seemingly uncomplicated

option is an emotionally wrenching choice, but it's not as awful as
the other alternative an elder care lawyer might suggest: divorce.
For a couple wed half a century or more, divorce as a means of
economic protection is fraught with grief and trauma. But spousal
refusal carries risks, after death, that divorce doesn't. In a spousal
refusal situation, in both states, Medicaid enforcement officials are
permitted to pursue the survivor for repayment of government
funds. While federal law governs the process, Florida rarely if ever
exercises its right to do so, Krooks said. New York, by contrast, "has
a much richer history of pursuing the refusing spouse," in other
words, knocking on the door after the death of a husband or wife
and saying, in effect, "Give us back all the money we spent for that
nursing home."

Certain New York counties are "very aggressive" about this
practice, while others are "asleep at the wheel," Krooks and others
said, but a refusing spouse in New York should be emotionally
and financially prepared both for the unpleasantness and for
the payback. (Counties handle this differently, more or less in
accordance with how they handle overall Medicaid eligibility,
benefits, and enforcement policy, which are governed by federal
and state law but implemented locally.)

- In recent years the federal government has tightened the law in
  many ways regarding parents' "gifting" of money to their children,
  making it much harder for them to deplete their assets this way in
  order to qualify for Medicaid. Studies show that "gifting" is much
  rarer than most people think, presumably because the World War II
  generation tends to be too proud to do it, even if it is lawful. The
  exaggerated beliefs about inappropriate Medicaid gifts in the current
  generation have been documented most thoroughly by George
  Washington University and the Congressional Budget Office. The
  richest among them employ sophisticated estate planning, which
  has a conflicting strategy to Medicaid planning and generally
  wins out.

  The vast majority of old people currently in their eighties and
  above, like my mother, worked hard all their lives, put their children
  through college, now don't have much money left, hang on to what
  they have for dear life, and are appalled at the prospect they might

wind up on welfare, which is what they consider Medicaid. (Only time will tell whether this attitude will change among baby boomers, who arguably are more practical and less high-minded about such matters than their parents.) Nonetheless, in 2005, the laws were dramatically rewritten to make gifting much more difficult. As an alternative, Krooks and others say, families took note of the fact that many relatives were providing care on an unpaid basis. Guided by elder care attorneys, they drew up "personal care contracts," which permit parents to formally pay children and other relatives a lump sum of money for taking care of them. That lump sum isn't a gift (assuming the care is actually delivered), but it is subtracted from the parent's assets for the purpose of calculating Medicaid eligibility.

These contracts are legal under federal law, but states have wide discretion in determining whether to allow the basic version or to add bells and whistles. New York, in an exception to the state's usually more liberal Medicaid policies, permits personal care contracts only for the purpose of eligibility for "community Medicaid," essentially care in the home. The assumption is that adult children are either living at the parent's home, spending lots of time assisting paid aides, or both. New York argues that if your mother or father is in a nursing home, professionals are providing the care and your involvement is minimal and social, like weekend visits. Florida honors personal care contracts for nursing home patients, on the grounds that the children are still spending lots of time, energy, and money. (I can attest that this is true, but in these tight economic times, with Medicaid expenditures bleeding New York's treasury, I'm not sure I should have been paid for time spent looking after my institutionalized mother, no matter what it cost me physically, emotionally, or financially.)

- Legal documents in the two states are different in many ways (not only in health care proxies). A power of attorney is the document that permits someone to manage financial affairs for another person. New York considers a Florida power of attorney "foreign" and may not honor it. This is a matter of practice, not law, since states overwhelmingly accept legal documents from other jurisdictions, POAs among them. Howard Krooks said that when he tells his clients that they should draw up two, many of them balk because of the extra cost. "Those who say, 'It *has* to be honored,' God bless them," he said. "While they're having the fight, the desired results"—paying bills, moving money from one account to another, getting information from a health care provider who is being hyperdiligent about the patient confidentiality provisions—"are not achieved." Krooks also notes that many snowbirds divide their time between the two states, and their adult children will face all kinds of aggravation with only one POA that cannot be seamlessly utilized in both locations.

Wills from other states generally do not present jurisdictional problems, he said; they get tangled up in the courts only when there are issues of competency on the part of the signer or questions regarding undue influence, as in the notorious Brooke Astor case. But the executor of a will in Florida, unlike in New York, must be either a family member or a resident of the state. Assigning the duties of executor to someone who is not legally qualified would deliver the family either into the mire of probate court or into litigation, with all the attendant costs and miseries.

- Floridians have the annual opportunity to fill out an application that designates any residence in the state as a "homestead." A homestead designation has advantages and disadvantages that people must weigh and that are different for those whose only home is in Florida and those with multiple homes in different states. Both Florida's state constitution and its laws provide certain protections for a homestead. A house or apartment so designated, for instance, has substantially lower property taxes than an identical property that is not considered a homestead.

  In addition, the state does not count the value of a person's homestead property when determining the owner's Medicaid eligibility. A homestead property is also protected from creditors—say, in a bankruptcy proceeding—and after the owner's death, the state cannot put a lien on it, which would prevent the children from inheriting it. Further, when it comes to Medicaid eligibility (which can include real estate unless a spouse or disabled child lives in the home), its value is capped in Florida at $500,000 versus $700,000 in New York.

  One reason someone may choose not to register a residence

for homestead status involves marriages between elderly men and second wives, often younger women. Suppose the husband's name is on the deed of a homestead property. The current wife has a "life estate" in the property, meaning she can live there for the remainder of her days, thereby disappointing his children, who may have assumed that they would inherit the real estate. She is the only one who can relinquish that right, unless it has already been formalized in a pre- or post-nuptial agreement. According to Krooks, ignorance of the homestead provision can cut two ways. A home owner can register for it, unaware that it gives his wife full rights to the residence and his children none. Or he can not register for it, thus stranding his wife without a place to live in favor of his children.

I have an acquaintance in New York State whose elderly mother, going downhill both physically and cognitively, lives by herself in an apartment in Yonkers, the southernmost community in Westchester County. Her mother has resided there her whole adult life and very much wants to stay, but she likely would end her days more comfortably just a few blocks south, across the county line in Riverdale, the northernmost neighborhood in New York City.

How could this be?

I had always thought Medicaid was a joint federal and state entitlement program in which the federal government sets broad guidelines and a minimum set of benefits, while the states determine eligibility rules, reimbursement rates, and any add-on services. Hence the vast discrepancies from state to state regarding such things as how much a nursing home is paid per day by the government for a room or how much money an elderly person is allowed to keep for incidental expenses like a soda or a haircut. Would that it were so simple. The federal-state configuration is accurate as far as it goes, but the counties do the on-the-ground administration. Thus, what happens to an applicant or beneficiary can vary widely from county to county. The local social service agencies monitor eligibility, oversee individual services, and are responsible for enforcement. In New York, the state's fifty-eight local government entities (fifty-seven counties and the City of New York) have practical decision-making power. They determine eligibility for Medicaid-reimbursed home care; the extent of those in-home services; whether to pursue recovery of government funds from a surviving husband or wife who exercised their right to spousal refusal; and whether to pursue a lien on a house. As I write, my acquaintance (with the help of a geriatric care manager) is doing the arduous paperwork to qualify her mother, who has only a few thousand dollars to her name, for Medicaid. It all plays out differently in Yonkers than in Riverdale, since New York City is the most generous regarding benefits and the upstate counties the most limiting. They are also more aggressive in terms of enforcement.

Political scientists and health policy experts of varying political hues have written many a scholarly tome on the legislative history of Medicare and Medicaid, why they were designed as they were, and how they intersect for the elderly. In 1935, with the passage of the Social Security Act, and then in 1965, with Medicare, the American government deemed that its elderly citizens deserved the guaranteed dignity and safety of a small income and medical care at the end of their lives. Most of us in the middle class know a little bit about those two programs, see their cost deducted from our paychecks, and plan our futures in expectation of their benefits. We know almost nothing about Medicaid, which we assume (incorrectly) has nothing to do with people like "us."

But people like "us," through no chicanery, failure of character, or inept financial planning, wind up on Medicaid. This included my mother and may include yours. Women of that generation often outlive their money, which is generally survivor's benefits like Social Security and a pension, accrued by their working husbands while the women were stay-at-home wives and mothers. My mother, for instance, had a monthly income of $721 from Social Security and $90.46 from my father's pension, plus the surprisingly large nest egg she had built up by being a more attentive and smarter investor than he ever was, with the small sum of money he left to her in his will. That money would last her until the final eight months of her life, when Medicaid kicked in and paid a portion of her nursing home bills until her death. On average, eight in ten residents of America's nursing homes are on Medicaid. Some of those homes market to private-pay clients by putting them on special, better-appointed floors and giving them other special attention. It makes sense economically, since Medicaid does not come close to matching the actual cost of decent institutional care, so the private-pay clients are essentially subsidizing the Medicaid clients. High-end accommodations may attract wealthy people who expect to live out their days paying their own way and don't want to live among the riffraff. But imagine the shock and humiliation when someone like my mother, hardworking and self-sufficient all her life, finds herself out of money and, as a result, wheeled from the first-class section of the plane (this is how one administrator defended the practice to me) to the economy class, to sit in a middle seat in a row adjacent to the overused bathroom?

I had no clue, and neither did my brother or my mother, that New York was one of the rare states that paid for home care for Medicaid beneficiaries. By the time she returned from Florida, of course, my mother had no home in the traditional sense of the word. But once she moved back to New York, we could have rented her an apartment, paid for it as we paid for assisted living (with her remaining money), and then arranged for round-the-clock help under the state's community Medicaid program. She might not have qualified, because of her deteriorated physical condition—she eventually required two aides to get her in and out of the Hoyer lift—and it might have been too isolating a life for her and too labor-intensive for me. But we never got to make a purposeful decision, because of our own ignorance and because nobody told us it was possible—not the doctors, not the assisted living providers, not the geriatric care manager, and not the social workers and lawyers we interacted with, and paid, during her transition from Florida to New York.

Should we have done better research? You bet. But I'm not sure that lets off the hook all the paid "experts" who considered it either someone else's job to tell us or our responsibility to know. I had the opportunity to query Claudia Fine of SeniorBridge (the successor agency to Fine Newcombe & Winsby) on this point. Her explanation satisfied me: that my mother was probably already too physically compromised to qualify and that confusing me with too much information, particularly information unlikely to be pertinent to our case, would have burdened more than helped me.

Community Medicaid, even in the generous areas of the state, requires an applicant to meet certain requirements in terms of his physical condition, the configuration of his home, and the capacity of his family to augment a Medicaid nurse or home health aide. The client has to be stable enough medically, Fine said, to manage without the full-time, on-site attention of the many medical professionals in a nursing home. Someone with congestive heart failure, say, or complicated diabetes would be a poor candidate for home care. The client also must have a certain degree of mobility, so that even if he needs a cane, a walker, or a wheelchair, he has to able to transfer from bed to chair, or from bed to commode, with the assistance of only one aide, since Medicaid does not pay for two.

As for his home, it has to be configured in a way he can navigate or have retrofitted for this purpose. Someone who lives in a rented apartment in a brownstone, for instance, would likely not have the freedom from a landlord to replace the steps, either leading from the street to the front door or from floor to floor inside, with wheelchair ramps; nor would it be permitted, in many rentals, to widen too-narrow doorways or to replace a bathtub (for some, impossible to climb into) with a shower stall, grab bars, and a bench. The size of the apartment matters, too, Fine said. For various reasons, getting a twenty-four-hour live-in aide is easier, cheaper, and more effective than having several share the job in eight- or twelve-hour shifts. That means the apartment must have space for the aide to sleep and have some privacy, to avoid overcrowding and the attendant tensions for both employee and employer. Finally, aides from licensed agencies (which Medicaid requires) are limited by law from performing many medical activities, including actually dispensing rather than merely laying out medication, or changing catheters. Thus home care works best when there are adult children nearby—if not in the same dwelling—available to do what the paid aide can't and also providing additional companionship for the parent.

"If you have a certain kind of job, a stressed marriage, a disabled child, if your shoulders aren't strong enough," Fine said, "then you probably can't handle this." My mother was already close to paralyzed when I first met with Fine's agency; she would soon need more than one aide to transfer her in and out of bed, and both Michael and I had jobs that would make supervising a home care setup all but impossible. Claudia said that she and her colleagues figured out immediately that we were unlikely to be eligible, or suitable, for home care and, given my already confused and depleted condition, chose not to overload me with information that was, in our case, beside the point.

Aides, whether in New York, in California, or in other areas in the country, are easier to hire in dense urban communities that have public transportation and large immigrant communities. Even at a time of high unemployment, theirs is an occupation in which supply does not meet demand, allowing the aides to be choosy. They may refuse a job that they cannot get to easily or that requires short shifts and long bus rides, as they are often paid only for the hours they work and not for the time they travel. Immigrants from certain poor countries leave their own families behind when they come to America. A live-in job provides them with room and board while they accumulate money from their wages to send home or eventually to bring their families to this country.

Medicare, the federal monolith, is supposed to be the simple part of all this. It isn't. In practice, what you get, what the man next door gets, and what Aunt Sally gets depends on a hidden substructure of intermediaries. These intermediaries are fiscal organizations (essentially insurance companies) that the Center for Medicare and Medicaid Services (CMS) contracts with in each state, presumably because they know the local lay of the land.

"You can read *Medicare and You, 2010* and never see any recognition of this substructure," said Carol Levine, the director of the Families and Health Care Project at the United Hospital Fund in New York, who navigated this maze for seventeen years with a paralyzed and brain-injured husband. "There is more variability in what's covered than anyone recognizes. It may seem more consistent [than Medicaid], but that's not how in practice things work out for people."

Few people know more about family caregiving, personally and professionally, than Levine. She is the creator of the United Hospital Fund's Next Step in Care website, in my view the single most useful and coherent source of Internet information on the subject. She managed her husband's care at home while also working and raising a family, and for part of that time she was her mother's long-distance caregiver as well. She mastered a system that few of us can even dream of mastering. There are few questions Levine doesn't know the answer to, and no episode of self-pity that she hasn't stared down herself and can't help you stare down.

Levine is the one who opened my eyes to the hidden decentralization of responsibility within the Medicare system and thus the hurdles it places before consumers, arguably more difficult to surmount than Medicaid's because they come at you without warning. She describes the Medicare bureaucracy as an "interlocking directorate," as impenetrable and obdurate as any old-style Eastern Bloc nation. All the rules are set nationally, but don't assume that CMS, which ostensibly runs the show, actually handles your case. The claims are processed by those local fiscal organizations, which may well know the norms on what individual goods and services cost in any given state but can be capricious in their rulings.

Then there are the local providers of multiple services like home care agencies and the subproviders of specialty care (companions, nurses, and physical or occupational therapists) under contract to those agencies. There are vendors who sell medical equipment and other vendors who repair it. Since Medicare, unlike Medicaid, has no official state presence, there is no official to talk to, or at least try to talk to, in the event of a problem. CMS is located in Washington. When you are wondering why the "nurse from Medicare" didn't show up, it has to do with the local agency, not with Medicare per se. The journey from eligibility for a certain kind of wheelchair to actually getting one can be many telephone calls long, requiring information, stamina, and emotional wherewithal, all in short supply. And there is no guarantee of success: a claim can be improperly denied, for arbitrary reasons, because of incompetence, or due to a lack of clear guidelines as to what is covered and what isn't.

When my mother could no longer crank and push her manual wheelchair, her doctor authorized her need for a motorized one. My brother and I made a calculation. How much money is our time worth? We didn't even submit a Medicare claim for the motorized chair; rather, we bought it ourselves and later donated it to the home for someone who couldn't afford one or didn't have children to help. The staff at the nursing home, who had nothing to gain either way, told us that the application process would have been daunting and that my mother would be unable to move around without someone to push her in the meantime. The personnel at the home also suspected, based on past situations, that we'd lose in the end anyway, first the original claim and then any subsequent appeals. I trusted their judgment and was doubly assured that we'd made the right decision once it was obvious how brief the time would be when she'd be able to operate the joystick on the fancy chair. Had we gone the Medicare route, we would still have been fighting with the local fiscal organization after my mother's death.

It sure would have been nice to take that chair, and many other things we paid for, as a tax deduction, but the IRS doesn't permit children to do that for costs incurred on a parent's behalf. The IRS allows parents a deduction if they have enough income to file a return and if they spent more than 7.5 percent of their adjusted gross income on medical expenses. So, for Michael and me, buying my mother the motorized chair fell into the "ka-ching, ka-ching" category. This serves to support the argument for setting up a joint checking account as part of a power of attorney and paying your parents' bills, or your expenses on their behalf, out of that account. It has the multiple benefit of hastening a Medicaid spend-down, giving a parent a larger tax deduction, and allowing you to hang on to more of your own retirement savings.

Carol Levine thought she had wrestled Medicare to the ground when she obtained for her incapacitated husband, Howard, a motorized hospital bed with a certain kind of frame that allowed her and the one home health aide there twelve hours a day to move and turn him without injury to either patient or caregiver. Then the bed broke. First the motor sputtered out, a major problem all by itself. Soon the frame was on the verge of coming apart. Only the Sumo wrestler types among the shifting cast of aides dared move Howard under these circumstances, since it could have led to a disabling injury for one of them. Unattended in bed, with the unsafe, rickety frame, he could have fallen out while alone in the room, or the bed could have collapsed with him in it. So Levine got on the telephone. The agency that had supplied the bed for which Howard was indisputably eligible referred her to the supplier. The supplier referred her to the repair division. The repair division referred her to the maintenance office. Each needed authorization from whichever entity was one notch higher in the chain of command.

Did I mention that Levine was working full-time during these years? Then she was coming home to be her husband's sole caretaker through the night. She not only found the time but, hardly a novice, took detailed notes on every phone call: who she spoke to, the date and time, the outcome of the call, and the next step to be taken. How many of us would even know who to call? How many would give up after the third failed attempt, or the fifth? "That's what they're counting on," Levine said. She was resolute but knew she was looking at "several days of absolutely unsafe" conditions, at best, for Howard and the rest of the household. At that moment, as at countless others, she faced the fact that some of these jurisdictional squabbles simply cannot be solved, or solved quickly enough. "You wind up paying yourself," Levine said. "The only way you can fix it is by buying your way out."

CHAPTER 15

The Time for Talking

Michael worried that my behavior at family meetings at the nursing home would eventually land me in prison.

At those meetings my mother set the agenda, and from the start she and I looked for every opportunity to discuss her end-of-life philosophy: that quality counted, not quantity; that old age wasn't a disease with a cure; and that she wanted an escape hatch if she needed one. Nearer to the end, she hoped she'd still be calling the shots; if not, while she could, she would tell the crowd of nurses, social workers, occupational and speech therapists, nutritionists, and doctors who gathered regularly in the dreary dining room on the sixth floor of the Resnick Pavilion what her wishes were. She would discuss what she wanted—the more times the better—before the largest possible audience. She wanted no misunderstanding. She was, in effect, preparing her witness list, with my help, so that we could wrest a good death for her when the right time came.

My mother and I knew that, most likely, she'd missed the moment for a quick and easy passing. No clapping "Come on, Tink," as Michael later described his own wishful thinking; no attenuated heroics. The reward for living this long, she often said, and studies support it, is that you get "to rot to death" rather than die. This is not a remembered remark but rather her exact words, blunt but true, repeated so often that there was no forgetting them. It was, she thought, the perfect trope for what happened to anyone who had the misfortune to need a nursing home or to have to pay someone to live with them at home, babysitter style, because they were too compromised to be alone.

For someone of her nature, that long, slow, humiliating decline—mentally or physically—was unacceptable. And ignoring the inevitable wouldn't help. My mother was one of those rare birds who wanted the topic on the table, right from the start. And I agreed with her. Talking about it candidly and often, in front of the nursing home personnel, was valuable, her best chance for getting what she wanted. She would do anything to avoid what one of my blog readers described as "watching my mother un-live."

We also discussed at family meetings the more mundane elements of her "care plan," as it's known in medical and social work circles. We talked about the course of her physical and occupational therapy, and how both would have to be discontinued once she stopped making progress, under the conventions of Medicare and Medicaid, even if further sessions would prevent backsliding. When speech became an issue, another therapist was added to the team. Eventually there was also a swallowing specialist. None of it worked for very long, despite my mother's diligence; since her original depression had lifted, she had become a straight-A student, giving each therapy her best effort.

It was first at these meetings, and later in conversations that we would have just between the two of us, that I saw my mother at her very best. She was an unsentimental woman, about herself as much as about others. She didn't whine about her own situation, just as she didn't want you whining about yours. She was without self-pity and had no tolerance for it in others. She was not in denial, which experts have told me is widespread and the biggest impediment to opening end-of-life discussions like the ones we had. No matter how bad things got, she never lost her sense of humor, always a bit black for some people's taste but uniformly appreciated by the nursing home staff (if not by all the other "inmates"). You could see the respect in their faces as this old woman ran these meetings like a CEO, which is what she was, the chief executive officer of her own life, never more so than in this hard season of loss. I easily took on the role of her trusty second-in-command. We never spoke of it in direct terms until the very end, but she knew which of her children would cover her back now.

Michael was way more fun but also way more attached to her. He would have a terrible time letting go.

These conversations made him really nervous. Still, Michael knew my mother well enough to know how she felt about such things, and he wanted her wishes honored. He knew that conversations like these, conducted honestly, were a good thing: here's what could happen; here's what you'd consider doing for me, and I don't want any part of it. Or, here's what could happen, and I want you to fight like hell to keep me alive. Or, here's what could happen, I haven't a clue what I'd want, so let me adjust my thinking to the moving target of circumstance. He just didn't want to participate in them, or so it seemed to me from observing his behavior. "You're entitled to your opinion" was all he said when we revisited my observations later.

At these meetings (as at others I've observed involving families not my own), we talked about the various situations she might face, and the medical interventions that made sense and those that didn't, in her view and in the view of the professionals. Over the course of almost two years at the Hebrew Home, the contingencies, the potential remedies, and my mother's attitudes about them evolved. Michael's fear was that I was too forcefully expressing my position. Should something untoward happen to my mother—if against all odds, say, she died in her sleep—I'd be suspected of having intervened independently or of being in league with her. My mother and I found his fears ridiculous. So did the nursing home staffers, who were vocally grateful for how proactive the two of us were on this subject. They were used to trying to force unwilling parents and their children to think—and talk—about the unthinkable. And here we were, bringing it up ourselves. Our openness made their jobs easier and promised a better result in the long run, even if in the short run it bothered Michael greatly.

Whatever Michael's discomfort, he always came to the meetings, never claiming to have too much work or an appointment he couldn't cancel. Sometimes over those years I felt he let me down, but he never let my mother down. The staff tried to accommodate our schedules, but with so many staffers expected to be present, theirs were harder to mesh, and we cooperated and appeared when summoned. Michael, as in a hospital waiting room or sometimes during a visit, was too jumpy for these social-worky conversations. All this talk about feelings! Sometimes he'd answer e-mail. Sometimes he'd be up and down from his chair, pacing the room, fumbling through his shoulder bag, going into the kitchen next door for a soda. Sometimes he shot me a "shut up" look if I made one of my "princess of death" remarks. Sometimes he left the meeting early, fleeing what made him nervous or sad, I thought. We were talking about my mother's death—hypothetical and eventual but no longer just an abstraction.

It was at one of these meetings, early on, that the team decided my mother was a good candidate for a motorized wheelchair and arranged the equivalent of a road test, which she passed more easily than the one in her thirties. It was at one of these meetings that we came up with the idea for how she might take the writing class. It was also at one of these meetings that my mother decided she was not willing to go to the hospital ever again for any kind of medical treatment. Much later, she announced that she had no intention of drinking the thickened liquids that the staff recommended because of her swallowing difficulties. Here my mother was a bit cagey. At first she said she didn't want them because they tasted disgusting. Who wouldn't prefer apple juice to Ensure? Eventually she owned up to the fact that aspiration pneumonia—less likely with the thickened liquids, however counterintuitive—wasn't, in her mind, such a terrible thing. And if she got pneumonia, she wanted no antibiotics. Each of these changes in her wishes, once she elected to be a "comfort care" patient, was noted on her chart. That meant she got to say yes or no to pretty much everything and to change the rules at will. She stopped getting weighed, by choice, because of the unpleasantness of being carried down the hall to the scale in a canvas hoist, in full view of all the nosy-bodies. What difference did it make how much she weighed? She also stopped having her vital signs checked. The one thing she wanted until the very end was for the wax to be cleaned from her ears, so she wouldn't miss what was going on around her.

My mother's unscientific theory of death by rotting has been confirmed by scores upon scores of studies in scholarly journals. Many of them were written by Joanne Lynn, a private consultant and scholar who in previous incarnations was a medical officer at the federal Center for Medicare and Medicaid Services, a scientist at the Rand Corporation think tank, a professor of medicine at Dartmouth College and George Washington University, and a fellow at the Hastings Center. Such research can be dry, but put Dr. Lynn on a podium and her audience is riveted.

Dr. Lynn, a geriatrician who pulls no punches in her critique of America's sorry system of end-of-life care for the elderly, calls herself an "old person in training," one of many warm-up-the-crowd lines that she has mastered over years of such appearances. She has spent her entire working life battling the denial, even among experts, about what the last few years look like for nearly half of America's elderly, whose numbers are inexorably on the rise, due to the advent of Medicare, advances in medical technology, and improved public health.

Not long ago, she looked out from the dais of a Washington ballroom at a sea of middle-aged faces, an in-the-know audience. These men and women were attending a legislative briefing, awards ceremony, and power breakfast sponsored by the Hastings Center—in other words, the very people who spent their days immersed in the same data as she did. Dr. Lynn, a jolly-looking woman with a Dutch boy haircut, pounced with her very first question.

"How many of you expect to die?" she asked. The audience went silent, laughed nervously, and only then slowly raised their hands, one at a time, until all had finally conceded the inevitable. What took them so long?

"Would you prefer to be old when it happens?" This time the response was swift and sure, given the alternative. All hands flew up in unison.

Then Dr. Lynn offered them three options. Who would choose cancer as the way to go? Just a few. "What about chronic heart failure or emphysema?" A few more.

"So all the rest of you are up for frailty and dementia?" she asked slyly. She had the audience's full attention.

Dr. Lynn clicked to a PowerPoint demonstration derived from one of her 250-plus scholarly articles, this one a 2005 Hastings Center report, "Living Long in Fragile Health: The New Demographics Shape End of Life Care." The highlight of the show was a trio of graphs showing the three most common ways that old people die and the trajectory and duration of each scenario.

With each graph on the screen, Dr. Lynn narrated. Cancer deaths, which peak at age sixty-five, she said, come after many years of good health, despite an underlying fatal illness, followed by a few weeks or months of steep decline. The 20 percent of Americans who die this way, she said, need excellent (and aggressive) medical care during the long period of high functioning, then hospice support for both patient and family during the eventual rush to death.

Death from organ failure, generally heart or lung disease, peaks about a decade later, at seventy-five, and takes the lives of about one in four Americans after a far bumpier course. These patients' lives are punctuated by bouts of severe illness, emergency hospitalizations, and episodes that appear to be terminal but turn out not to be. In between, the patients hold their own, without much change in their day-to-day conditions. Then, at some point, rescue attempts fail and death is sudden. What these patients and families need, Dr. Lynn said, is consistent disease management to reduce the likelihood of crises and to sustain all possible function (appropriate medication to control symptoms, diet and exercise, regular monitoring), and then bold intervention at the first hint of trouble. From the time of diagnosis, with all involved parties at the table, there should be advance planning for how to handle the final, overwhelming emergency.

The third option is many people's nightmare, surely my mother's and also my own: a drawn-out and humiliating series of losses for the patient and an exhausting and potentially bankrupting ordeal for the family. Approximately 40 percent of Americans, generally past the age of eighty-five, follow this course, and the percentage will grow with improvements in prevention and treatment of cancer, heart disease, and pulmonary disease and the aging of the 77 million baby boomers into this age cohort.

These are the elderly who for years on end will be dependent on the care of loved ones, usually adult daughters, or the kindness of strangers, in skilled nursing facilities or from home health aides. This was my mother's fate and that of her peers at the nursing home. Those suffering from physical frailty, as she was, lose the ability to walk, to dress themselves, and to move from bed to wheelchair without a Hoyer lift and the strong backs of aides who earn so little that many qualify for food stamps. They require diapers, feeding, and frequent repositioning in bed to avoid bedsores. Often, after years of dwindling functional and personal care, death comes as a result of a "physiological challenge that would have been a minor annoyance earlier in life—influenza, urinary infection, pneumonia, a broken bone."

Those with dementia, most often relentlessly progressing Alzheimer's disease (although there are other kinds), lose short-term memory, can no longer judge the passage of time, repeat themselves, pace incessantly, fail to recognize loved ones, wander off and get lost without constant supervision, ignore or refuse help with basic hygiene, are agitated, restless, or sometimes violent (especially at night, hence the term *sun-downing*), and can no longer learn anything new. Along the way, they lose distant as well as more recent memory, judgment, and cognitive function. Eventually, they can't speak, chew and swallow, or use the bathroom—not because those parts of their bodies no longer work but because they can't remember how. The disease is invariably fatal and can last for decades.

In her Hastings Center special report, Dr. Lynn began with the simple observation that "not long ago, people generally 'got sick and died'—all in one sentence and all in a few days or weeks." She cites a geriatric patient who once told her, "No one in the Bible died like this." People lacked "ancient texts for comfort and advice," the patient said, on how to go about "inching toward oblivion."

They often also lacked preparation and adequate conversation with professionals and family, usually more than once, about what this kind of extended disability would mean. "When you're never again going to live independently, you need to reorganize your thinking," Dr. Lynn told me. And people need the kind of data in her three graphs to impress upon them that this protracted dying is the rule, not the exception, and needs to be approached with a plan. "Really good care," she said, "is coherent and built around thoughtful decision-making. It has to be built around our real demographics, the huge number of people who only have one available 'illness' to die from anymore, a serious decline over a long period of time. This is not uniquely bad luck; it's now a generalizable phenomenon."

Her mission, Dr. Lynn told her Washington audience, was to get the powers-that-be to catch up to this reality. "We're doing this so badly because we've never been here before," she said. "But the care system we've got didn't come down from the mountain. We made it up, and we can make up a better system."

A post about Dr. Lynn's research on my blog drew 268 impassioned comments. Many were from the elderly themselves, rather than from the usual gang of adult daughters and interested professionals. Over and over, and with near unanimity, those in their eighties and nineties talked of assisted suicide, of Dr. Kevorkian, of veterinarians gently putting down animals while doctors tortured old people by keeping them alive beyond reason. They made dark jokes about joining the Hemlock Society or reading Derek Humphry's *Final Exit*. (*Final Exit* describes—and its author gave public demonstrations of—a technique for killing yourself with pills and a jerry-rigged plastic bag that smothers you if you fall asleep before taking all the narcotics. It doesn't always work on the first try, so others may have to get involved in helping to finish what you started.) Two blog readers said their "health reform plan" was a gun. Another reader was more Victorian than melodramatic: "I am old enough to have been taught in early adulthood to always leave a party while you are still a welcome guest. Nowhere is this more important than in life itself."

In Oregon, where assisted suicide has been legal for many years, and more recently in Washington State, experience has shown that the terminally ill don't so much want to die as to know they have a legal and dignified way to do so if they choose. Far fewer people than anyone expected actually exercised that legal right once they had it.

My mother often mulled the pointless but compulsively compelling question of whether mental decline would be better than physical decline. Wouldn't being round-the-bend demented be an easier way to go than being paralyzed, losing the ability to talk, becoming incontinent, and being totally aware of every second of it? Her point of view was that the oblivion of Alzheimer's disease would be preferable. For a caregiving adult child, it's more complex. Alzheimer's, I imagined then and know now, would be so much worse for me; I'd have to expend all that energy doing the right thing for someone who didn't even know who I was.

A dear friend of mine whose mother had Alzheimer's for more than a dozen years before her recent death visited her in a nursing home, five hours away from home, every few weeks for years. Her mother was curled in a ball, in bed except when it was time to eat. My friend scheduled her visits for mealtime and felt like she'd had a successful encounter if she got a few spoonfuls of ice cream into her mother. Only rarely—and even then she is only guessing—did her mother look at her with what passed for recognition. My friend was distant and edgy before these visits. Afterward, she often got a migraine. I don't know how she did it. I often wondered why she didn't just leave her mother with people she knew treated her well, and disappear. Her mother wouldn't know the difference. But my friend would, and couldn't live with herself. I wonder what I'd have done.

At this point in my mother's life, every conversation we had—and we were both now greedy for them—involved her struggling, gutturally, to get out an audible sentence. Once, when I was on the way to celebrate a holiday with another friend, dressed for the occasion, I stopped in to say hello first. We talked of everyday things until I was about to leave. That's when she croaked out these words one at a time, with long pauses in between to gather her strength:

"You . . . look . . . pretty."

When she spoke, I had already turned the corner to leave her room and was out of her line of sight. I had no memory of her ever saying that before, after all those years when we'd mostly said the wrong thing to each other or, worse yet, said nothing at all. "Leave it to you, Ma, to wait till I'm past fifty to tell me that," I said, knowing she'd prefer a tart to a treacly reply. She laughed in recognition.

How interesting, and how fitting, that my mother's full-throated laugh would come so easily long after her speech was gone. Soon the only way we had to "talk" was the alphabet board, a handmade replacement we used when even the device with the buttons was more than she could manage. I'd ask her some long-winded question, and she'd tap out an answer, one letter at a time. Her half of the conversation was economical, her replies like haiku. The effort alone made every exchange important.

So when she posed the question, painstakingly, about which would be better, her condition or Alzheimer's, I felt she deserved a totally honest answer. I was quiet for a long while, considering what to say that would be true, kind, and worthy of the moment. Finally, I said that for her, right now, Alzheimer's surely seemed better. She wouldn't have a clue. But getting to that place of oblivion would have meant living through the long, frightening muddle that comes before. So, on balance, I wasn't sure. For me, this way was unambiguously easier. Her gratitude motivated me to continue. Without it, I told her, I'm not sure I could go on. I also told her that if she weren't still here, in the true sense of *here,* present and paying attention, we wouldn't be having these conversations, better late than never. I never articulated what I was searching for, nor did she ask. Yet unspoken between us, simply part of the ether, was the notion that we were headed somewhere, trying to set things right. It was a rich and interesting time.

This kind of conversation came easily to me and my mother, but for many parents and adult children it doesn't, and they tend to disagree, predictably, about who stands in the way. The parents say the children avoid it, and the children say the opposite. I have yet to see research that parses out who the real culprit is, although I'm not sure it matters or that it isn't a combination of both. One study on the subject, conducted by Home Instead Senior Care, a home care business with more than eight hundred franchises nationwide, surveyed one thousand American adult children in a caretaking role a few years back to find out what inhibited them from discussing these issues with their parents and what subjects they found most difficult to bring up.

The biggest obstacle to dialogue, those surveyed said, was being stuck in the old parent-child roles (31 percent), the refusal of their parents to engage (16 percent), lack of preparation on their part (10 percent), distance (8 percent), and fear (5 percent). The most difficult topics to discuss were the need for a parent to leave home for a more supportive environment (42 percent), the loss of driving privileges (30 percent), finances (11 percent), and health (11 percent). Of those who participated in the telephone survey, between the ages of forty-five and sixty-five, 35 percent communicated with their parents on a daily basis about "everyday things" and 26 percent every couple of days. As a solution for breaking the ice, 71 percent thought involving a sibling or other family member, and doing it together, would be helpful; half suggested seeking the help of a professional, like a social worker or a member of the clergy. One in ten said they had already enlisted surrogates—family members or friends—to have the conversation in their place. And women were more comfortable talking to their parents about needing help at home than men, by a margin of 57 percent to 41 percent.

Following the survey, Home Instead Senior Care, on its website and at its local franchises, made available companion guides for adult children and their aging parents, based on what they call the 40–70 (or 70–40) rule, that "if you are 40 and your parents are 70," or vice versa, "it's time to start talking." I don't find the suggestions in the guides—such as "get started" and "forget the baby talk" for adult children, and "be assertive, not aggressive" and "pick your battles" for the elderly—particularly edifying. But the impulse, and more sophisticated guidance from other sources, surely can't hurt. To my great good fortune, once my mother got past her historically secretive and dishonest behavior, and her poorly treated depression, she realized this was a new phase of family life and was an exemplar of clarity, openness, and wisdom, at least with me.

More advice on opening the lines of communication comes from AARP, both on its website and in a clearheaded book, *Caring for Your Parents: The Complete Family Guide,* by Hugh Delehanty and Elinor Ginzler (New York: Sterling, 2008), a straightforward how-to guide. In the foreword, Mary Pipher, psychologist and author of the best-selling *Another Country:*

Navigating the Emotional Terrain of Our Elders (New York: Penguin, 1999), makes some thought-provoking observations about the inherent generational obstacles between boomers and their parents, who came of age at a time when " 'consumption' referred to tuberculosis and Depression was not a mental health problem but an era of economic disaster." Our parents, Dr. Pipher continued, are not "psychologically minded." They don't "analyze family relationships or openly discuss pain and anxiety." They rarely "let it all hang out," or "emote and take [their] psychological temperature. Think Queen Elizabeth vs. Princess Diana." These differences, she wrote, aren't "pathological, characterological, or personal but rather generational." Both age groups are "trying to do the right thing, but we have been educated differently about what the right thing is. Our folks try to buck up and look on the bright side. We consider that denial. But when we share our feelings or 'process our experience,' they call it whining."

Ginzler and Delehanty, writing of the unnerving role reversal, compare this late-in-life moment—the Big Talk—to our "squirming through the conversation about s-e-x" as adolescents, when our parents were worried about our health and safety and we wanted nothing so much as to establish our independence. Now the tables have turned, the stakes are high, and the moment, to say the least, is awkward, as history, decades-old family baggage, and ghosts we thought we had put to rest "bubble to the surface again."

AARP's advice on not letting the voices of ghosts drown out the conversation with your parents is sensible if unsurprising. Assess the relationship over time and take all that into account before broaching the subject. Ask for help from a "neutral third party" if you think you will need it. Note whether your parent's attitude to your first overture is "resistant," "reluctant," or "ready." If it's resistant, prepare for the fact that it may take several tries. If it's reluctant, proceed gently, look for openings, and encourage any expression of willingness to review current and changing circumstances. If it's ready, let your parent guide the conversation because it means he's already been thinking about it and has just been waiting for you to give him this chance.

AARP also recommends dividing the conversation into at least two stages, "breaking the ice" and "nuts and bolts," with time for a "deep breath" in between. Talk early and often, Ginzler and Delehanty urge. "Don't get frozen waiting for the perfect opportunity. An emergency might beat you to it." Listen, don't lecture. Ask questions rather than making commanding statements. Avoid saying "you should." Look for conversation-starters in routine chatter, like your dad saying his eyes are bothering him. Approach the subject indirectly—say, by mentioning a friend whose car was in the shop longer than expected and was discovering the joys of public transportation. Ask for your parent's help with something you are doing, like early estate planning. Offer to help with a specific and onerous task, like figuring out which Medicare drug plan might work best for him. If all else fails, write him a letter even if you live down the block.

More good advice appears on Caring.com, an elder care website with a cast of experts who answer readers' questions, often blandly but sometimes with flickers of wisdom and originality. In "How to Make Difficult Conversations Less Stressful," Paula Spencer, one of the site's senior editors, divides her answer into reasons why these discussions are so hard and how to start one. They're hard, she says, because it's not our "place" to "call our elders on certain topics"; because most of us, "let alone a parent," prefer privacy about certain matters, like money and personal hygiene; because we don't know as much as we'd like about matters like powers of attorney or hospice care, and it's "a challenge to talk turkey when you don't really feel comfortable with the material"; because the relationship in the past had a "closed-lip history"; because of "squeamishness" about topics we'd "rather not think about ever," like adult diapers; and because of denial, when we "kindasorta know there's a big problem but it's easier to ignore or avoid it."

How to start? Remember that "the consequences of not speaking up are usually worse than the talk itself." Bear in mind that your parent may have "similar concerns" and an equal discomfort in raising them, thus creating a "conspiracy of silence." Acknowledge that this moment is a benchmark in the process of loss but also an opportunity to make some small improvement in your parent's comfort and well-being. Do your homework first so you sound "knowledgeable," "trustworthy," and "confident." Pick the right moment for your parent, a time of day when he is generally most alert or in the best mood, and then "bracket the discussion with pleasant activities," like an outing of some sort. And be candid about your own discomfort and fear: "This is really hard for me to talk about, and it's also probably really hard for you to hear, but I've been really worried about . . ."

I could find no studies that queried the elderly on whether they encouraged or blocked these conversations and why, and far less advice directed at them on having them. But anecdotal evidence suggests that they are more open than their adult children, more realistic about what's going on and about the fact that its course, while variable in length and trajectory, is irreversible. I saw this in comments to the blog, in conversations with contemporaries and their parents, and among those I interviewed and then stayed in touch with long enough to have more intimate and open-ended conversations. One male friend, whose attachment to his mother runs deep, has had all the appropriate sit-downs with her, although she told me that they came mostly at her instigation. She sometimes found him unrealistically upbeat as she moved into her mid-nineties, still living on her own but more limited in what she could do without help and more frightened of what lay ahead.

Another friend's parents recently careened into what seemed to him a sudden crisis but what an outsider could see had been many years in the making. My friend claimed that until everything fell apart his mother and father would not entertain discussion of the future. But his wife, out of his hearing, said that the denial was her husband's, not her in-laws', that they'd spoken to her often of their fears and demonstrated to her an early willingness to explore alternatives while they were still able.

Then there was a woman nearing ninety who, with her late husband, had had the foresight to move to a continuing care retirement community in their seventies, mostly to relieve their children of future burdens. Still, she had things to discuss—last wishes, if you will. The one way she could get her children to sit still and hear her out on various hard subjects, she said, was to organize a family car trip. Only when her children, in late middle age and with children of their own, were literally trapped in a vehicle could she get through her list of concerns without one or more of them fleeing. Despite careful and clever planning, she recalled with a chuckle, the drive was as squirmy as any she could remember since they outgrew car seats.

My mother's deterioration accelerated.

Her right arm, the essentially useless one, and her right butt cheek were causing her so much pain that she would beg to be put back to bed after just a few hours in the wheelchair. This was a signal event for a woman who was never a hypochondriac and had never sought attention by whining, someone who had endured decades of severe arthritis with occasional crankiness but rarely complaint. The motorized chair quickly outlived its usefulness, once the joystick was beyond her abilities. Nothing was wrong with her eyes, but reading, the one activity that still gave her pleasure, had become impossible because she couldn't hold a book, and she refused all suggestions that a rack or some other tool for the handicapped might solve that problem. She had always resisted new ways of doing things, like giving up a rotary phone for a touch-tone model, or getting an answering machine. Even the motorized chair, the answer to every nursing home resident's prayer to get around without a "pusher," was all but outside her comfort zone for gadgets. She nearly gave up on it after the battery didn't recharge one night (someone had knocked the power cord out of the socket) and again when she backed into a wall on her first attempt in reverse.

When spending a full day out of bed became all but impossible for my mother, her caregivers agreed that she should have a thorough geriatric and neurological workup to try and find out, one last time, if there was a unifying diagnosis to explain the apparently unrelated ailments that were ruining what little quality of life she had left. We would also explore whether a reshuffling of medications might help. She was taking at least a dozen, not uncommon in someone her age. Which were working and which might be making things worse? My mother had already complained about Neurontin, which had been approved by the FDA as an antiseizure medication but was frequently used to alleviate pain. It wasn't doing any good, she said, and was making her feel lousy in other ways. When I discussed it with the doctor assigned to my mother's floor, she was balky about eliminating it. (On her desk was a ceramic cup filled with purple ballpoint pens emblazoned with Neurontin's logo.) Anyway, given how draining days of multiple tests would be for my mother, we all agreed it would be easier in the hospital. The tests could have been done at the home, one at a time, over the course of days, in the basement medical unit, which would have allowed her to be in her own room, eat familiar food, and sleep in her own bed. But it would also discombobulate her, perhaps enough to cause a Ménière's attack. A short hospitalization might be more efficient and less taxing.

Plus, as much as we loved the nursing and social work staff at the Hebrew Home, we didn't have much faith in its doctors and hoped for a more skillful diagnosis in the hospital. Under ordinary circumstances, the nursing home hierarchy, with nurses and social workers at the top of the pecking order, was to my mother's liking. She hated doctors, dating back to her working days, when RNs were treated more like stewardesses or maids than fellow professionals. She loved nurses, knew the difference between good and bad ones, and wouldn't trade Eileen for a thousand doctors. The idea of social work was, at first, a little touchy-feely for my mother's taste. Hannah was highly competent and, to my taste, chilly, but she was perfect for my mother, who liked chilly. Now Eileen and Hannah were suggesting that we try one last, and likely pointless (although none of us said that out loud), hospitalization. Was there a whisper between me and Michael that we wanted "the best doctor money can buy"? (Those doctors don't work in nursing homes.) I honestly don't think so. All of us knew that the purpose wasn't to "fix" my mother but to smooth the rough edges from her increasingly dreadful days. (Instead, the diagnostic workup found no overarching diagnosis and nothing but ad hoc remedies for all the things that now ailed her.)

Until the weeks leading up to her hospitalization at Weill Cornell Medical Center (my mother had relented on never wanting another hospitalization), we'd had several months of relative tranquillity. Now settled in at the nursing home, she grew accustomed to its routines and found comfort and companionship in the staff, whom she liked and trusted and vice versa. Michael and I had each taken winter vacations that year with little Sturm und Drang, and we were deep into making summer plans. I'd attended my book group without last-minute emergencies getting in the way, as well as many festivities. I'd bought a new car, taken up biking, and improved my yoga practice. At the movies, I turned off my cell phone for a few hours at a stretch. I didn't socialize much. I had dinner maybe once a week at the home of a childhood friend, who fed me delicious, healthy meals and enjoyed reminiscing about my mother's days as a camp nurse. Maybe twice a week I'd stop at the nursing home for a short visit on the way to work, and I'd spend one weekend day there. I wouldn't say it was my old life, but it was certainly manageable.

Until it wasn't. Until my workdays were again disrupted by my mother's frantic summonses, and life again was all Mom, all the time.

I found this note scribbled in my date book from this period: *Was bringing her up from Florida a mistake? Should we have let her have the surgery? How much damage did I do at the Meadowview?* It was grandiose, I see in retrospect, to think I had this much control. But members of my generation think there is nothing we can't fix. We can do a full lotus pose, or a century bike race, in our sixties. We can rise to the top of our professions, own real estate, and helicopter-parent our children. But we can't protect our mothers and fathers from Joanne Lynn's third trajectory. That's the one my mother was on, and there was no longer any pretending, even for an hour or two, that it was otherwise. Oh, we tried codeine and Oxycontin and a fentanyl patch for my mother's hand and buttock pain. But she didn't get enough relief to justify being constipated all the time. Michael began looking for a private-duty aide—this would wind up being Lily—who could work for us a few hours every morning and a few more every afternoon. That way my mother wouldn't start the day waiting her turn for a clean diaper, and she wouldn't be unattended during the three p.m. shift change, crying out to be put back in bed. I wanted to be there every day to do it, but I couldn't. To use Claudia Fine's phrase, my shoulders weren't strong enough.

Finding an aide for a couple of hours here and there was harder than we expected since, as I've said, aides would rather have a full-time job than be chasing from place to place, unpaid for the time between clients. We'd have loved to hire somebody full-time but were afraid of running out of money. My mother's long-term care insurance—what I had thought was my $7,000-a-year security blanket—went to the nursing home when she was a private-pay patient and to the government after she was on Medicaid. That was another of those things I didn't know, and didn't know I didn't know, when I was insisting upon the policy.

I have my own policy now. Getting one was a rock-and-a-hard-place decision, a gamble on an unknowable set of circumstances. But long-term care insurance isn't the solution to every problem, contrary to what my blog readers overwhelmingly believed. For the lucky people who could afford the expensive insurance, everything would be all right, they'd write. Well, we were among those lucky people. We could pay for the insurance. Then we had to pay for Lily, too, and got no direct benefit as a family from the years of paying premiums. That isn't my definition of "everything would be all right." Long-term care insurance is a big crapshoot, and once all of the boomers buying it now start collecting, it could become even less dependable, as the insurers themselves are starting to recognize by refusing new customers or raising premiums by increments as much as 40 percent. Experts express widespread concern that this product either will fail because it can't pay out or will be obsolete by the time the boomers need it.

While Michael was seeking an aide, I made a many-times-postponed trip to the cemetery where my father and maternal grandfather are buried to pay for my mother's eventual funeral. It's a standard part of a Medicaid spend-down and, as close as we were, the legal step that would get us to the point of poverty that we needed to achieve eligibility. We already had a family plot on Long Island, bought in the era when grave sites were the first real estate many families owned. I had not been there for twenty-eight years, since the unveiling of my father's tombstone a year after his death, so it was a safe bet that it was an overgrown mess. My economical mother had long ago canceled the contract for "perpetual maintenance." I'd deal with that, too.

The gentleman from the funeral home who met me there, Zach, had a business card that read PRE-NEED CONSULTANT. I arranged for a thorough cleanup, to trim all that runaway pachysandra back from the neighboring grave. I asked Zach idly about selling the fourth and soon-to-be last plot, since I intended to be cremated and didn't need it. He told me single plots were hard to sell. Why not buy a limestone bench for that spot? he suggested. I could use it as a contemplative spot for visits. My mother would have had a smart-mouth response to that, if she had been with me, and she would have enjoyed a surreal, laugh-out-loud moment to see me arranging her funeral while she was still alive. I'd always assumed my paternal grandmother was buried in the same plot, but she wasn't there. I called my brother. "Any idea where Grandma is?" I asked him. He put me on hold and called my father's sister in Florida. "Grandma's in *their* plot in Brooklyn," he returned to tell me. We laughed ourselves silly. Zach seemed not to get the joke.

From that spring to the next, nothing much happened except a slow but steady decline, and the addition of Lily to our little circle. She was close to my age but matronly in that southern African-American way. Unlike the West Indian aides, she never called my mother "Mommy" but "Mrs. Gross." She told me later that no other appellation was appropriate in her culture and that she addressed all her patients that way. But Lily also understood instantly that formality felt right to my mother, creating a needed distance in this most intimate of relationships. My mother always asked that I be sent from the room and the door be closed when Lily changed her. I'd sit on the couch by the window, wondering what kind of daughter pays someone to diaper her mother. I figured out eventually that my mother preferred it this way and that it was better for all of us. Lily worked for her. I was her daughter.

•　　•　　•

When the light finally left my mother's eyes, it happened in the space of a month.

I have a series of Eileen's Polaroids, several taken on June 3, 2003, and the others on July 4 of the same year. The first was my mother's birthday, and Michael, his wife, and their dog were joining in the celebration. We arrived to find my mother with oxygen tubes in her nose—a first. It was more than a little disconcerting. (She was excited by all the attention, Eileen said later.) But her hair had been done at the home's beauty parlor, her color was good, and she looked festive, even if bedridden, in a pretty pink nightgown. Before long, her normally hearty appetite would overtake whatever necessitated the oxygen tubes, and she asked Michael for food. He fed her shrimp in lobster sauce, her generation's Chinese delicacy, a slow process, as her ability to swallow was mighty close to gone. Even hooked up to the tubes, she devoured it, slapping back Michael's hand a few times when he tried to take his share. When Eileen came in with the camera, my mother looked happy, as Michael, the dog, and I hammed it up around the bed.

A month later (and I know it was July 4 because of Eileen's red-white-and-blue smock in the photo), my mother was a slack-jawed, tilted-off-to-one-side broken puppet in a wheelchair. What a job it must have been to encourage her to get up, dress her, settle her in the chair, and take her on a spin around the floor. She's wearing her talking board, but her hands are so clawed, it's hard to imagine her using it. Her eyes are vacant, her skin grayish, her mouth half open, and she looks like she weighs half what she did a few weeks before. Her clothes are all but falling off her and carelessly chosen. Her hair is plastered to her head, unkempt. It wasn't that she was ill cared for, but rather not quite there, compliant about the picture-taking for our sake but eager to be returned to bed and just be left alone. In one of the photos, with me beside her, cheek to cheek, I'm smiling so hard it's like my face is going to break in two, as if all I had to do was pretend we were having fun and we would be.

CHAPTER 16

N-O-W

On an otherwise ordinary July day in 2003, my mother decided she had had enough.

She had been telling me for weeks, one letter at a time on the cardboard alphabet chart I'd made, that she was ready to die. But her options grew more limited with each passing day. Pneumonia, my mother knew from her nursing days, would have been a blessing, as it has been for generations of elderly. Her original plan—refusing thickened liquids to increase the odds of contracting aspiration pneumonia—had worked. Her next plan—refusing antibiotics and letting nature take its course—did not. Three bouts of untreated pneumonia hadn't, in fact, killed her. One tough cookie, my mother. She was strong enough, Eileen said, that she could easily live a half-dozen more years. I resisted the urge to ask whether that was the good news or the bad news.

My mother and I had already discussed the possibility of stopping food and hydration, and now this alternative dominated our conversation. I even read to her from books, at her request, that described this manner of dying, which didn't sound awful. She could be sedated if necessary, I explained. I would stay with her the whole time.

She had worried that in a nursing home she would be forced to eat and drink. I assured her, many times over, that that wouldn't be the case, without ever asking anyone there if I was right. Essentially, I was telling her it was both legal and doable in a state-licensed institution, without knowing if either was true. But as best as I could figure, this *was* her legal right, the equivalent of refusing treatment, and nobody had balked when she declined antibiotics. Plus, the only way to make her eat and drink, if she was determined not to, was with a feeding tube and intravenous hydration. Surely that would be considered a form of assault if done against a patient's wishes. Most important, by then I knew the cast of characters at this nursing home, not just their names and titles but their hearts and souls. Unless it was outright illegal, they wouldn't stop us, and I trusted they would do all they could to guide us through the process. What better proof than their suggestion, months earlier, that my mother switch to "comfort care" and tell them what she did and didn't want in the way of treatment? In addition, the Hebrew Home had recently contracted with a hospice at a New York City hospital whose wide net of professionals came there to tend to the dying, just as they would in their own homes. This has become fairly common in nursing homes in recent years, but it was cutting-edge at the time.

I knew my mother was turning the idea over in her mind, revisiting it, frequently, with new questions, requests that I reread something or bring yet another book. Meanwhile, in the space of a month, the pace of her decline had accelerated like time-lapse photography. I look at those last pictures now, the ones Eileen took on June 3 and July 4. In the second set, her eyes are wide as if with fear, but there is no light behind them. She is already gone in all the ways that matter. Exactly a week after the Independence Day photos, on a blisteringly hot morning, I stopped by to say a quick hello before heading to work. She wasted no time with pleasantries. Instead, she grabbed the alphabet board with a vigor I hadn't seen in ages and spelled out her intentions:

N-O-W.

This neither scared nor surprised me. Indeed, I'd expected her to reach the point of no return much sooner than she had. I vaguely thought she might ask for help dying when diapers became necessary, way back when she was still living at the Meadowview. Or during the early weeks in the nursing home, when she talked openly of suicide. Or when the Hoyer lift, that medieval-looking contraption, came clanking down the hallway for the first time, with a burly attendant who from that day forward would be needed to hoist her from bed. Or when she could no longer hold a book.

Or when Michael and I could no longer understand her speech, and conversation, our best and last family pastime, became impossible. Or when the other ladies tried to pitch her from the dining room for making a mess with her food, and she declined to have it pureed and wouldn't let anyone, including me or Lily, feed her.

But each time I thought she'd crossed the line and arrived at the place where life was no longer worth living, the line moved. And moved again. Not that we discussed it in those terms. I never asked why she still hung on, how she tolerated each new diminishment. I never asked if she attributed her staying power to a will to live or to a fear of dying. The first, however miserable, was at least familiar; the second, presumably, the source of existential dread. I never let on that I had long been ready for her to die, even if she wasn't, and that I wished she'd catch up with me. A terrible thought, but one I suspect that is shared by more people than those willing to say it out loud. In retrospect, how grateful I am that her mind was intact and that I wasn't making life-and-death decisions on her behalf as a health care proxy. I'd have jumped the gun by many months, used that awesome power prematurely, and cheated her of time, however brief, that she obviously still wanted.

Instead, I counted on my mother to tell me when she was ready to go, and she counted on me to help her find a way out, as she knew I'd done once before, for a friend. We had long conspired to make her end-of-life wishes part of the conversation at every family meeting. And in the privacy of my mother's room, without staff or my brother there to hear us, what we regularly discussed was how trapped she felt. Under the "right" set of circumstances, she could refuse heroic medical intervention—like CPR, a ventilator, or a feeding tube—but none was needed or seemed to be on the horizon. If intractable pain required a morphine drip, some sympathetic doctor or nurse might be willing to crank it up—not a criminal act, and known among medical ethicists as the "double effect"—if the purpose was to relieve suffering, with a hastened passing an unintended consequence.

But her heart and lungs were strong. She didn't have cancer. She wasn't even dying, using a disease-based definition. So here we were, my mother and I, wishing she were terminally ill and feeling a bit creepy about it. How many times in those last few months had she commented, "We treat our pets better than we treat people!"

It was a refrain I would later hear over and over from elderly readers of the blog. Unlike my mother, however, these readers rarely admitted to their children how badly they wanted to die, or knew that there were ways to bring about death at the moment of their choosing that were not illegal or horrible and did not require the participation of anyone else. Nor had their adult children, but for one or two, offered suggestions or help. As a rule, the parents said that their children were afraid of that conversation and the children said the reverse. I do not pretend to know who is right. But I do know this: most old people do not want their lives extended beyond reason. They don't want their adult children changing their diapers. They don't want to lose their minds and their memories. Give them the chance to tell you that. Don't try and jolly them out of it. Imagine yourself in their shoes. Love them enough to let them go.

When I described these conversations with my mother to friends, some judged me harshly, others fell eerily silent, and still others were agnostic but amazed. "You *let* her do that?" one asked when my mother decided to stop food and hydration. I mumbled that it wasn't up to me, nor should it be, but I was both stung by the implied rebuke and concerned that she would keep her own mother, whom I'd known since childhood, alive at all costs. Another friend's mother, who had end-stage Alzheimer's, no longer recognized her three children and had already spent ten years in a nursing home. Eventually she would forget how to eat or drink, so others would have to spoon-feed her and hold a cup to her lips. Had my friend and her two siblings even discussed whether this made sense? I didn't ask, and my friend didn't say. Another friend, whose mother died of lung cancer, second-guesses herself about certain life-saving decisions she made along the way, usually when a doctor called midcrisis. Once, the doctor found her on her cell phone as she was driving from New York City to the east end of Long Island, telling her what he proposed to do to save her mother's life and warning of the dire consequences of inaction if she didn't decide that very minute. It's always easier to say yes than no, especially in the heat of an emergency. In retrospect, my friend knows each of these dramatic interventions extended her mother's life only briefly and caused her great suffering. Yet she had discussed none of these split-second contingencies in advance, not with her mother or with her sister.

So why did my mother and I have these difficult conversations so effort-lessly? Could it be because we had an arm's-length relationship? She had always been a distant woman, at least with me, literally recoiling if I tried to hug her. The locket she gave me for high school graduation was inscribed "From Mom & Dad." *From?* What must the jeweler have thought? When

I ended a phone call with "I love you, Ma," her reply was never more than "Uh-huh." She wasn't a big part of my life. Until she was.

Or maybe these conversations came easily because my mother was a woman without obvious emotional attachments, but for my brother, yet with a fierce intelligence, a strong will, a stoic nature, and no patience for self-indulgence. The day I left for college, with my father driving me, we had not completely backed out of the driveway before she had filled the curbside trash cans with my cheerleading uniform, poems I had written, and other cherished possessions, now just clutter to be cleared away. More than thirty years later, in one nursing home conversation, I asked her about her three half- and stepbrothers, whom I knew only vaguely, although two of them lived nearby when Michael and I were children. I struggled to remember their wives' names and am not sure I ever met some of their children, my first cousins. She had long ago lost track of them, she said, and claimed not to know if they were alive or dead. Why did I care? she asked. She seemed to find my curiosity unnatural.

I wanted to let them know that my mother was near death. I wanted them to come visit her if they were alive and to attend her funeral—my wish, not hers. I was tired of enduring all this, just me and Michael, with no relatives. Now, I let the subject drop as I once would not have, mostly out of kindness. I also had a gathering sense that my mother's detachment had become her greatest strength, and that strength made my job of taking care of her easier. She could view her own situation dispassionately—as a problem in need of a solution. She could view me as a smart and capable person, a skilled gatherer of information, and an effective advocate, sufficiently disengaged myself to be willing and able to help her.

Together we had made a plan.

Ours was more or less the same plan that Dr. David M. Eddy and his mother made back in 1994, which he chronicled in a now-famous essay in *The Journal of the American Medical Association* titled "A Conversation with My Mother." Read just about any research paper about voluntarily stopping eating and drinking, or VSED (as it is known in the trade), and there, in the footnotes, will be a reference to Dr. Eddy's account. That essay fulfilled a promise to his eighty-five-year-old mother to "write about this, David. Tell others how well this worked for me. More people might want to know that this way exists. And maybe more physicians will help them find it."

Mrs. Eddy, like so many her age, had seen her health "unravel with amaz-ing speed," her son wrote in the essay. Until that point, she had lived alone in a grand old Greek Revival house in Middlebury, Vermont, next door to another son, passing the time reading large-print books, doing word puz-zles, and watching news and sports on TV. For sure, she had had her share of problems, including depression, now well under control, and a history of serious bowel issues. But none stood in the way of her two daily walks, rain or shine, one to buy the newspaper and the other to the grocery store.

Then her bowel problems worsened, along with a sudden cascade of other health issues: dehydration, anemia, nausea, loss of appetite, itchy skin, irregular heartbeat, a lump in her breast, failing eyesight. Mother and son began talking about "how she could end her life gracefully," a conversa-tion that came easily to both of them. A doctor's widow, Mrs. Eddy "prided herself on being able to deal maturely with the idea of death." Her paper-work was in order—not just a living will but also an organ donor card, to flag her acceptance of the inevitable. She lived in dread of becoming "little more than a blank stare." Her son did not disagree, once he was satisfied that she had "an accurate understanding of her prognosis" and was not in the middle of "a correctable depression or a temporary trough."

To his surprise, during this ongoing conversation, his mother decided to try risky bowel surgery, which could leave her incontinent, half hoping it would kill her. (My mother's attempt at "suicide by doctor," it seemed, wasn't as far-fetched as many thought.) But she survived, and with the worst possible outcome. Too debilitated from the surgery to go home, but well enough to leave the hospital, Mrs. Eddy was discharged to a nursing home. She knew, her son wrote, that "it was very unlikely she would ever be able to take care of herself alone, or walk to the Grand Union." When the doctors agreed, her questions about suicide became more urgent. What were the options, legal and illegal, to end her life even though she had no fatal illnesses, no heroic treatment to refuse or discontinue, and no need for opiates that might hasten death? This was a scenario I knew firsthand, shocking in its familiarity, although it wasn't until many years later that I encountered the Eddys' story.

The year after Dr. Eddy wrote his account, the voters of Oregon narrowly passed, for the first time in U.S. history, a referendum making physician-assisted suicide legal. After several legal challenges, it finally became law in 1997. The vote, by a wide 70–30 margin, permitted physicians to pre-scribe, but not administer, lethal medication to terminally ill people under tight safeguards, which included mental competence, a prognosis of six months or less to live, a second opinion, and a two-week waiting period after the original request. The State Department of Health has tracked the law annually and found—unexpectedly to both advocates and opponents of physician-assisted suicide—that the availability of such an escape may be more important than its actual use, which turns out to be very rare. Across time, with great stability, the legal right has led to 1 in 1,000 deaths per year, while 1 in 50 patients discussed the option with their doctors and 1 in 6 with family members.

These results were cited in Supreme Court briefs when the nation's highest court consolidated two assisted suicide cases, one from New York (involving Dr. Timothy Quill, now the director of palliative care programs at the University of Rochester Medical Center, who had written openly of his own involvement in an assisted suicide in *The New England Journal of Medicine*) and another from California. The Court ruled that there is no constitutional right to a physician-assisted death, sending the highly charged issue back to the states to decide by referendum or legislation. But the Court added that all Americans have the right to good pain management at the end of life, even in doses that could, as a secondary effect, hasten death. The state of Washington joined Oregon in 2008, passing a similar referendum, as did Montana (via the legislative route, and with the threat of a legal challenge); as of this writing, they are the only states that permit or at least do not prosecute the assistance of physicians in dying (as its advocates refer to the process, rather than physician-assisted suicide, the preferred nomenclature among opponents).

That is not to say that doctors everywhere don't help their patients die, in an underground and thus unsupervised and unregulated way. The physician participation estimates range from 1 to 10 percent, without the regulations in Oregon and Washington. (Montana did not legalize physician-assisted suicide but, by state law, outlawed prosecution. Other states are considering variants of legalizing the practice.) Dr. Quill points out that "empirical research" on underground behavior is all but a tautology, since querying doctors on their behavior is asking them to admit to a crime and subjecting themselves, and anyone else present, to prosecution. Prosecutions rarely occur, absent flaunting the crime. Even Jack Kevorkian, who claimed to have participated in at least 130 assisted suicides, was jailed only after he actively killed someone rather than only giving him the means to do it himself. That said, in what Dr. Quill himself calls "imperfect studies," conducted anonymously, he has found that 1 to 2 percent of physicians say they have assisted patients, which is 10 to 20 percent higher than in Oregon. One might say this is another example of denial exacerbating problems, not eliminating them.

"Don't ask, don't tell" is how Dr. Quill refers to the existing state of affairs, and in recent years he has turned his own attention and advocacy to palliative care, which includes pain and symptom management for the patient and psychosocial supports for patient and family, without the hospice requirement that the illness be terminal and, in most cases, that curative treatment be abandoned. "It's more nuanced than I once thought it was," Dr. Quill wrote in a 2008 briefing for the Hastings Center. "The remedies have expanded," and assisted suicide "is not the singular solution." (Dr. Quill's change in focus, largely inspired by the Oregon data, puts his work in line with that of Dr. Diane Meier, at Mount Sinai Medical Center in New York. What people most fear, both agree, is the dying process and not death itself. They rest easier with the assurance that they will not suffer or be abandoned by their physicians.)

Long before Dr. Quill turned his attention to palliative care (which, unlike hospice, is not generally reimbursed by Medicare or by private insurance), he had already written and spoken about VSED as a method for ending one's life legally, without suffering and with the same sense of control, and thus solace, that the possibility of assisted suicide would bring. I interviewed him in the late 1990s, at the time of the Supreme Court case, which is how I knew my mother had this option. Sections of his books were the first I read to her. Then I met with him again after her death, to tell him our story and of his unwitting role in it, and to ask him to explain, in greater detail, what happens physiologically when someone dies this way. My curiosity came partly from the reaction of readers when I wrote about it in the *Times* and on the blog, and of friends who assumed this must be a brutal way to die. Was my mother's death easier than most, I wanted to know, or typical? Why don't more people do it? Is it rare to get a nursing home to support you in this decision?

According to Dr. Quill, my mother's experience was typical in some ways and not in others. The physiology of this kind of death, he told me, was pretty basic and depended on discontinuing liquids, not food, although some scientists have said that discontinuing food releases endorphins and eases the process. Without fluids, Dr. Quill explained, the electrolytes (sodium and potassium) elevate, and the kidneys fail. This is evident in a low-volume but highly concentrated urine. Soon the blood pressure drops. To protect the core organs, the vessels of the extremities contract, making the feet go cool and gray. Breathing becomes irregular, the pulse "thready," or rapid and soft. The patient becomes ever less responsive, and eventually the heart stops. "The technically correct cause of death," Dr. Quill said, "would be kidney failure from dehydration." This manner of death was often uneventful, not that different from a "natural" one with "a beginning, middle, and end," as opposed to the "instantaneous" end of life that comes with an overdose of lethal drugs in an assisted suicide.

Dr. Quill added that the process required supervision because "bad things can happen," including severe dry mouth in the early stages and, occasionally, delirium near the end. The dry mouth can be managed easily with swabs, Dr. Quill said, and the delirium with sedation. In his Hastings Center briefing, Dr. Quill said that VSED was "different from natural loss of interest in food and drink when a person is actively dying" but rather is an "informed decision." It is "only an option [for those] with mental capacity," and can have "unforeseen complications" and thus might wind up "physician supported," not physician assisted. Dr. Quill said that hospices in Rochester, New York, his base, "permitted and supported" VSED, which accounted for 1 percent of their deaths. In Oregon, in 2003, 102 nurses were surveyed who had supervised deaths by voluntary dehydration. The nurses said that using a 1 to 10 rating scale, with 10 being the "best" death, the median for these patients was 8. Hard deaths, 0 to 4 on the scale, were reported by eight of them. Eighty-five percent of the dehydration patients died within fifteen days, according to the nurses whose experience was chronicled by Linda Ganzini, a professor of psychology at the Oregon Heath and Science University, in a 2003 article in *The New England Journal of Medicine.*

Dr. Quill and others said this method of dying is so rare because it is not widely understood. It is mistakenly thought to be horrible when it is not. Unlike assisted suicide or the removal of feeding tubes or ventilators, which lead to immediate deaths, it is a gradual process, Dr. Quill said, "so you know this is your chance to tie up loose ends." Still, most nursing homes discourage it, he said; many of the physicians there are foreign-born and have issues of conscience common to certain cultures and religions, including some in the United States. The medical profession here, Dr. Quill said, remains "judgmental when there is no life support to stop," since that issue has been clearly resolved by court rulings and become commonplace. In other words, doctors have an easier time taking out "artificial" feeding tubes (or ventilators), or not putting them in in the first place, than telling patients that, after careful deliberation, they can stop drinking, or helping them through the process, even if they haven't initiated the conversation.

In our case, no medical professionals ever raised the subject or participated in the private conversations between my mother and me. The first they knew of it was the day she refused hydration. Even the ethicists, who are queasy about medical professionals having even tangential involvement in what could be considered suicide, agree that forcing liquids down someone's throat is an "unwarranted bodily intrusion." In other words, they can't stop you from VSED in a nursing home, but they can make matters uncomfortable and difficult by dissuasion or lack of cooperation. Our circumstances were like perfectly lined-up stars, Dr. Quill said. My mother was not going to die imminently from a lethal disease, but her condition would continue to erode inexorably. She was not dependent on artificial life support that could be withdrawn or withheld. We'd had many conversations and understood what we were getting into. We'd laid out my mother's long-standing end-of-life philosophy so nursing home staff would see this deliberate decision for what it was, not as a depressed impulse. We were in an open-minded environment. And my mother had what Dr. Quill said must have been (as it was) a "strong sense of self, both individually and in terms of ethos.

"If you know [you can do] that, it's a gigantic gift," he told me. "It's kind of radical the first couple of times you think about it. And it requires capacity. You cannot do this by proxy, as you also can't assisted suicide. But to have the knowledge that this is in your hands—that possibility is huge, but not many people are aware of it. It is the same general psychology as assisted suicide. Control is the issue, more than pain: being in charge."

To the Eddys, for sure, it seemed preferable to many other alternatives. Mrs. Eddy and her son had discussed his legal exposure if he provided her with the sedatives (easy for a doctor to come by) to take her own life, and she was offended that the only recourse seemed to be criminal behavior. They had read Derek Humphry's *Final Exit* together, and she was repulsed by the descriptions of a backup system in case someone fell asleep midway through ingesting a fatal dose of pills, involving the plastic bag around the head. At this moment of frustration and indecision, Mrs. Eddy fell ill with pneumonia and was readmitted to the hospital. She reminded everyone there that she was not to be resuscitated under any circumstances. She refused antibiotics and rested a bit easier thinking she would surely die, legally and without criminality or high drama for her son. He could hear the gurgle deep in her throat, once called the death rattle, and found it a relief. But again Mrs. Eddy did not die.

"What else can I do?" she implored him. "Can I stop eating?" He explained that she would need to stop drinking as well, since fasting alone is not effective. On the eve of her eighty-fifth birthday, Mrs. Eddy had one piece of her favorite chocolate, and then the attending physician removed the intravenous line that was keeping her hydrated and wrote an order for medication to control any discomfort she might have as her organs shut down. For four days, with her children at her bedside, Mrs. Eddy reminisced. Proud of her own pluck, she recalled traveling across Africa on her own at the age of seventy and being dumped from a raft into the Snake River in Wyoming at age eighty-two. On the fifth day with no food and water, Dr. Eddy wrote, it was difficult to wake her. On the sixth day, she was unresponsive and breathing unevenly. And then she was gone. Her son described it as a "happy death."

So did Joshua Segar's daughter, Alison, when Segar chose this manner of death at home in Brattleboro, Vermont, in 2007. At the age of eighty-four, he was worn out by the indignities and well aware of the ultimate outcome of Parkinson's disease. Alison had written her father a letter begging him to reconsider once he had made his plans known. After he died, Segar's son, Adrian, on board from the start, was eager to spread the message that his father's had been a peaceful death, carefully planned, and with plenty of time for him to say his goodbyes, so he told the story to a reporter for the *Brattleboro Reformer* who used to be a nurse. In writing the article, the reporter, Richard Davis, turned for commentary to Dr. Ira Byock, who had written extensively on the subject in the *American Journal of Hospice and Palliative Medicine* and elsewhere. Dr. Byock told the newspaper that "after adequate discussion, at some point the patient's choice becomes none of our business." What such men and women tell him, Dr. Byock said, is of "a felt sense of being done. Eating and drinking were no longer relevant to their situation. They were far along in the process of withdrawing and had turned their attention inward or beyond."

•   •   •

My mother's wasn't a bad death. It would take a week, the nursing home staff told us, probably less. It turned out that they had guessed based on the cases they were familiar with, when people died this way by unintended circumstance rather than by design, during end-stage cancer or Alzheimer's, which causes loss of interest, ability, or memory of how to eat or drink. In fact, depending on the health (and perhaps stubbornness) of the person involved, VSED can last as long as three weeks, the textbooks say. Knowing that would have prepared me better psychologically, allowed me to pace myself emotionally. As the days passed, I watched the hands of the clock from my perch in a reclining chair in a corner of my mother's room. They seemed to have stopped moving. She soon became a curiosity, as people stood in her doorway to watch the old lady who would not die. I accused the aides of sneaking her ice chips when my back was turned. I was twitching with impatience. I wanted my mother to hurry up and die and was ashamed to admit it.

Only the rabbi seemed to get it. Indeed, his impatience, knowing my mother's wishes and the inevitable result, matched my own. During our vigil, which seemed without end, two other people died on my mother's floor. One was right next door, an apparently healthy woman whose head simply fell to her chest as she watched soap operas from her wheelchair. I was on the bench outside my mother's room and saw it happen. Summoned from the nurses' station to the dead woman's side, the rabbi raced down the hallway and screeched to a halt at my mother's door. The wrong door, it turned out. He made no effort to hide his disappointment.

"I must have given the angel of death the wrong room number," he said to me.

"Well," I replied, in a comparably lighthearted tone, "go back to your office, call again, and this time give better directions."

My mother had started the process while my brother was on vacation, so I had to call and tell him. He decided to stay in Italy until the end of his vacation, five days hence, as planned. We had some acrimonious back-and-forth about that, but after years of turning it over in my mind, I'm persuaded that my mother timed her exit to coincide with that trip. She knew Michael wouldn't try to dissuade her, but the distress on his face would be obvious. Could she put him through that? And could she go forward in spite of it? As Dr. Quill told me later, this may not be a painful way to die, but it demands great fortitude: "It takes a strong psyche in the early going."

Perhaps my mother concluded that the self-control necessary would be possible only if she didn't have to look at Michael, bereft, at the foot of her bed. She knew what she wanted and how best to get it. Based on what we'd been told about how long it would take, I doubt she imagined she'd still be alive, or only barely, when Michael returned.

But my insight into her exquisite orchestration of this event didn't come until much later. At the time, my rage was directed at Michael, with some residual resentment for Rabbi Hirschhorn, whom my brother had called from Europe to ask if he should come home. The rabbi asked if he felt his business with my mother was completed, whether he thought he would rest easy if she died while he was gone. Michael's answer to both questions— accurate, I think, not rationalizations to avoid returning—was yes. I wondered then, and for years afterward, why the rabbi had left me out of the equation, why he hadn't also asked whether a brother and sister should go through this together, whether Michael belonged at my side even if he felt no pressing need to be at my mother's.

"You and your mother were doing important work," the rabbi said to me much later, and Michael would have interrupted, not helped that. "He would have just been static, noise at a time that begged for silence." That was true. My mother and I were better off alone. Understanding that, albeit belatedly, was sufficient for me to put to rest the long-held feeling that Michael had abandoned me. The time she and I had together, what we learned about each other, and what we were finally able to "say" were more than worth the cost. In retrospect, I admire my mother's understanding of her children's strengths and weaknesses, what each could and couldn't do, and what *she* needed most at this moment of ultimate trial.

Understanding and peacefulness, unfortunately, would not come until much later. My fury at Michael permeated the early days of my mother's intentional dying, as did my dismay at an unanticipated, and very disturbing, turn of events: Eileen found my mother's decision to be incompatible with her Roman Catholic faith. She searched me out one morning, along with my mother's primary aide, a Seventh-Day Adventist, both in tears, to tell me of their crisis of conscience. They were recusing themselves from hands-on care, switching assignments with another excellent RN and aide for the duration. Both would work the other side of the floor and visit my mother frequently throughout the day, but they would not actually swab her dry mouth, apply the low-dose morphine patches that were ordered immediately, or inject the opiates that were later prescribed for discomfort, agitation, or delirium. That Eileen wouldn't be there, in her normal capacity, had never crossed my mind. Indeed, I'd decided against bringing in the hospice team, when that alternative was offered to me, because my mother didn't like strangers around her and I thought the familiar and loved professionals, especially Eileen, would be a balm to her and to me as well.

Reading the legal and ethical literature later, I learned that the reluctant staff had done exactly the right thing. Their responsibility to my mother, and to me, did not include violating their own consciences. But it did include making sure she was properly cared for by comparable professionals and that we understood why and how that would happen. According to Nancy Berlinger, a scholar at the Hastings Center, "conscience clauses" have been common in state and federal statutes, in professional codes of ethics, and in institutional policies since the *Roe v. Wade* Supreme Court abortion ruling in 1973. Medial professionals can "refuse to provide service because of moral or other personal beliefs." But they have an "obligation to minimize disruption in the delivery of care" and to "not abandon" the patient by alerting a superior and colleagues, making a referral to another professional, and "stepping away but not between the patient and another provider." They also must not make patients feel "ashamed or uncomfortable" about their decisions. Eileen did all that, and more, with care and compassion. Six years later (the amount of time Eileen had predicted my mother might otherwise live), she told me over one of our regular lunches that in retrospect she saw the rightness of the decision, given who my mother was and how she had lived her life.

Counselors from Compassion and Choices, an organization that advocates for physician assistance in dying and provides free end-of-life consultations, told me much later that I could have, and probably should have, changed my mind about hospice care, regardless of my original decision. Nobody at the home let me know it was possible to do that or otherwise brought up the subject again, after offering hospice the first day. I was too dazed to even discuss with anyone my distress that Eileen would not be with my mother all the time, let alone think that I could reverse course. I wish someone there had been more cognizant of that and more active in reminding me, more than once, of my options. It seemed, then and now, that it was too much to ask, in a place so dense with medical, social, psychological, and spiritual resources, that in my mother's last days I was expected to be simultaneously daughter, knowledgeable decision-maker, and advocate, without the time or peace to properly say goodbye.

CHAPTER 17

Dying Days

The days, unsurprisingly, were a blur. The very first thing I did after my mother's *N-O-W* was ask that the full team, especially Hannah, the social worker, and a psychiatrist, talk to her when I was not in the room. There was no pretending I hadn't been part of her decision, had arguably even encouraged it. Many experts say that old people choose to end their lives, or say they don't want them extended, not because of their own genuine wishes but to spare their children trouble and expense. We needed to be certain that my mother was doing this for herself, not for me. Clearly, the private conversation satisfied them: I was offered either a recliner in her room or an apartment for visiting relatives on the grounds, so I could be with her, or very close by, for the duration. I spent one night walking the floors of the unfamiliar apartment, with no telephone or cell signal, which frightened me. Then I spent a few nights in the recliner before realizing I would not get through this without some time alone and some sleep in my own bed. I stayed with her from eight a.m. to eight p.m., then went home. Because Lily was on vacation, I hired an overnight aide with one job and one job only: to summon a nurse at any sign of discomfort, since my mother's medication orders permitted opiates or other sedation on demand.

I must have been more frightened and lonely than I admitted, even to myself. My friends, but for one, did not come and keep me company there. They must have assumed it was the right and respectful thing to do (which it wasn't, although I don't doubt they were well intentioned). They might have stayed away out of their own discomfort about being in a nursing home under any circumstances, let alone the ones surrounding my mother's chosen method of dying. The one friend who did come brought lunch, sat with me on the sunny balcony, distracted me with chitchat, told me how brave my mother and I both were, and generally made me feel cared for.

As much as I longed for relatives to share my vigil, not for my mother's sake but for mine, I expected none and thus wasn't disappointed by their absence. Instead, very early on, I called the only close friend my mother had ever had, going back to the 1950s. She was someone who had felt like family to me growing up, when we shared holiday celebrations. Her friendship with my mother was a complicated one but steady through the years, and I couldn't imagine they wouldn't want to say their goodbyes. Kathryn, herself an old woman who shouldn't have been driving, made the trip from Long Island, with her older sister, Virginia, without hesitation. This visit, which I willfully did not warn my mother of in advance, lasted less than five minutes.

I don't know what transpired in the privacy of her room, but my mother booted them out, behaving as ungraciously as one can when unable to talk. I was both mortified and mystified by her rudeness, undone by having asked these two elderly friends to make the pilgrimage, only to have them be treated as they were. For the first time in many weeks, I unraveled, sobbed in their arms when I should have been apologizing for my unfathomably bad judgment in summoning them. What Kathryn and Virginia understood immediately was that my proud mother could not bear being seen in this condition and had had no way of expressing that other than striking out at them. "That was not the way she wanted to be remembered, as a human being transformed and wasted by illness," Kathryn said many years later. "We weren't offended when she repulsed us. She was true to her proud character to the very end." What they also both understood was that my summons had been a call for help. I wanted *them* to take care of *me*. I wanted *somebody* to take care of me. I wanted a mother. "How could you face something like that without support?" Kathryn said in a recent conversation. "It wasn't a small event, which is as it should be."

Since I hadn't figured out yet that Michael's absence, in effect, was my mother's doing, I sought ways to spare her the pain of his not being there.

She was fully conscious, even able to "talk" to me once I'd traded the alphabet board—her hands now swam incomprehensibly over the letters, as if she were a storefront fortune-teller using a Ouija board—for a sheet of cardboard that required her only to point to *yes* or *no*. Her sense of time, however, was way out of whack, and the difference between today and tomorrow meant nothing. So every day I'd tell her that Michael would be back the next day and wasn't that wonderful! After one of these false reassurances, she pushed away the yes-no diagram for the alphabet board. Her hands were tremulous, but she nevertheless made clear contact with each letter, poking out, "Not fair to you." I assumed, but will never know, that she meant my being there without my brother and her being the primary choreographer of that arrangement.

Michael returned on schedule, five days into the process. His arrival, in terms of my mother's attenuated dying, came at just the right moment. In short order my fury was replaced by gratitude that he was around just as things got dicey. My mother, at this point, was showing occasional signs of agitation. I do not think it was pain per se. Still, we were in a constant battle to get her the morphine she'd been promised. The first problem was logistical. The narcotics were in a locked cabinet, and the one employee charged with holding the key was sometimes on break or at lunch or even in the bathroom when I asked for her. Since the medication order had been written so we could have the drug whenever I asked, not at fixed intervals, we solved this problem fairly easily by always requesting it before my mother needed it, often *way* before.

The second problem was trickier. Since my mother couldn't speak, nor was she moaning or writhing, what made us think she needed more morphine? the keeper of the key wanted to know. My answer apparently sounded lame. She would periodically pump her arm in a way I'd never seen before; I had no clue what it meant, but I was taking no chances. Even if it didn't signal physical pain, but rather existential pain or raw terror of what lay on the other side, did that really matter at this point? Not to me. (Dr. Quill in his Hastings Center briefing wrote that "the [VSED] patient's suffering can not be restricted to the physical" and "must include psychological, social, existential and spiritual dimensions." Earlier, in *The Journal of the American Medical Association,* he had declared that the "loss of meaning, dignity and independence" are symptoms no less real than physical pain.)

The challenge of proving that my mother was in sufficient pain—and pain of the kind deemed worthy of relief—and the surprise of Eileen's decision were impediments, although not outright obstacles, to choosing VSED in a nursing home. Both would have been mitigated had I chosen to use the entire hospice team. (The hospice doctor did eventually get minimally involved.) Most of all, I wish someone had reminded me, repeatedly, that I could change my mind at any time.

Without hospice in charge, the regular staff faced a real dilemma. A nursing home is closely regulated by the state in its dispensing of narcotics and may be asked to defend the amount of morphine administered. It took a specialist in palliative care to persuade the staff physicians that they could raise the dosage without risking state sanction or legal liability. Only with that dosage did my mother stop pumping one arm frantically. In addition, a nursing home is staffed by people with widely differing views about end-of-life issues, unlike a hospice program, which attracts like-minded professionals. Religion, cultural background, or personal experience made some of the nurses uneasy about giving the morphine injections. So did affection for someone they had gotten to know over the two years she'd lived there.

Each nurse drew her own conclusion about whether my mother was in pain, or enough pain to justify medication. For days, my brother and I badgered the doctors and nurses to medicate her sufficiently. We cried. We screamed. We threatened to take her home. We went ever higher in the home's hierarchy, risking insult to the people who had cared for her so tenderly. We beeped department heads at all hours, collected cell phone numbers from caller ID, and used them shamelessly.

Outside her room, we huddled with the heads of all the relevant departments. Why did we promise her she would be comfortable if we couldn't deliver? What good was medication on demand if she had to suffer before she got it? And who gets to decide whether she is suffering, we or they? My mother's pumping hand, for example, could be signaling frustration that she could not "say" anything anymore, even on the alphabet board. Maybe it was a reflex, devoid of meaning. Possibly she was rowing herself across the river Styx. Who was to say?

To let my brother and me answer these subjective questions carried its own risk for a nursing home. Unlike many families, we were on the same page, supportive of my mother's decision and grateful that she could make it herself. But in these litigious times, I would not blame the home's authorities if they were afraid we would later sue them, in the muddle of grief.

Once Michael returned home, he was briskly efficient, as always. Whether it was because his was a new face on the scene, because we could again play good cop–bad cop, or simply because these kinds of problems tend to smooth themselves out over time, my mother started getting the medication she needed when she needed it, without my feeling that begging for morphine was my full-time job. Nor did I feel I had to be there every minute of every day, because he and I could take turns. I had lunch in Manhattan with a visiting out-of-town friend. I went to the theater. I had my hair done. My mother was fading but, the nurses said, at a glacial pace.

Until the last two or three days, she was in and out of consciousness. Since hearing is the last sense to go, I talked to her, played music, and sometimes read aloud from whatever I was reading. There was nothing more to do but wait. Michael came less in the last forty-eight hours, not seeing much point in staring down at a woman he assumed to be comatose. I do not mean this as criticism. His is not an uncommon reaction, although I don't want to die alone or attended by strangers, and didn't want my mother to, either. Diana Lubarski, her physical therapist, had months before given me a poem written by a long-dead patient of hers titled "Nursing Home." Among its loveliest lines are these:

> *Move gently here.*
> *The old are not you. Neither sun nor love*
> *Do they await, but that opening door*
> *Permitting departure.*
> *It is not an occasion for interference . . .*
> *This is their time not yours . . .*
> *Their sleep holds the mercy of preparation.*
> *Let it be.*

Lily finally returned from a two-week visit with her mother in South Carolina. Technically it had been a vacation, but really she was doing for free, and out of love, what she did for a living in New York. It was July 22. Her presence from the first would have made everything so much easier for me, since she and I could have worked out some kind of rotation;

instead, when I could no longer bear the twenty-four-hour vigil myself, I had hired a parade of not-very-bright overnight aides. By then Lily was like a member of our family, a comfort to my mother, and to me and to Michael, too. My mother had now gone twelve days without hydration and was totally uncommunicative and unresponsive. I didn't want Lily arriving unprepared for the decisions that had been made and the events that had transpired during her absence. Knowing the agency was perfectly capable of not alerting her (Lily would tell me later that sometimes she showed up for a long-standing case only to find a beloved client had died and her bed had been stripped), I phoned her the night before. Lily took the news in stride. Before her departure, she told me, it had been clear to her what my mother was thinking. Still, before leaving, Lily had begged her to eat. "When I come back, Mrs. Gross, I still want you to be here," she recalled saying. But both of them knew the time was ripe. "Enough is enough," Lily said to me later. "She got tired of suffering. You do after a while. She still had her mind, and she'd decided."

Together, we sat with my mother. The next day, the twenty-third, in the early evening, the nurses finally saw the tell-tale signs of approaching death. My mother's feet were cold to the touch. Her fingers picked at the covers. That was the very warning she had described from her own nursing days. Nobody understood what it meant, she had said, and doctors denied that it even happened or, if it did, that it meant anything. But nurses knew better from being at the bedside of the dying, my mother had told me from the time I was small, and they were rarely if ever wrong.

With these changes, my mother's nurses urged me to go. Some people wait for their loved ones to arrive before they die. Others wait for them to leave. My mother required privacy for this passage. I didn't argue with their wise counsel, although I assumed Lily would stay with her. No, said Josephine, the swing-shift nurse. Given who my mother was, Lily would have to go, too, or she would needlessly linger. And so we departed, together.

Usually, Lily took the bus home to Harlem, but this night I drove her. I'm sure it was because I wanted her company and consolation. The call from Josephine came just as I arrived at my house, at most an hour after Lily and I had left the Hebrew Home. Given the bureaucratic busywork that follows a death, I suspect I was still in the elevator when my mother died. I never asked the time or agonized about not having been there to witness it. I could imagine her final exhale, like one I had heard anytime I'd ever been present at a death, as a friend or a journalist, that last whoosh of life back into the universe. With the news of my mother's death, I matched that outbreath. Mine was a sigh of relief.

On the thirteenth day without food or water, my mother had gotten her wish. She was eighty-eight years old.

The time of my mother's passing, it turns out, was 7:40 p.m. This was according to the infelicitously titled "Discharge Summary" that was among the stacks upon stacks of records of her stay at the Hebrew Home. I was looking for a death certificate when I came upon it, curious if the doctors there who pronounced her dead would tell the truth about how it happened or whether they would avoid raising red flags with the state that they had given their blessing, as it were, to my mother's choice, legal but surely a matter of queasiness for many nursing homes. There was no death certificate in the file, and the "Discharge Summary" does not speak to how she died; rather, it listed her various maladies, diagnosed during her stay at Weill Cornell Medical Center more than a year before, and concluded by saying that "her family requested no further hospitalization and wanted only comfort care with pain control."

My curiosity unsatisfied, and with no death certificate to be found in either my jumble of "Mom documents" or Michael's, I filed for a copy through the City of New York Department of Health. What arrived in the mail had pretty much the same information as a birth certificate but for the "place of disposition"—in other words, the name of the cemetery where she was buried and the date of her burial there. Decades earlier my father's death certificate had an additional section itemizing immediate, secondary, and tertiary causes of death. I found its absence on my mother's odd. Thus began my education into death certificates in general, the lack of useful information on my mother's, and the fact that in New York City, even as her daughter and proxy, the Department of Health had told me all I was ever going to know, at least from them.

It turns out that it's illegal, so to speak, to die of anything but a disease, according to both the Centers for Disease Control and the World Health Organization. Forget about something as exotic as my mother's manner of dying. Even the simple explanation "old age" cannot appear on a death certificate. Neither can "infirmity" or "senescence," according to the CDC handbook on how to properly fill out the forms. Why? These words "have little value for public health or medical research," the agency says on its website. Plus, "age is recorded elsewhere on the [death] certificate." Instead, every death must be attributed to a single disease, which is the immediate cause of death. A second disease is to be cited as the intermediate cause, and a third as the underlying condition. Even in situations "when a number of conditions or multiple organ/system failure resulted in death," the CDC instructs that "the physician, medical examiner or coroner should choose . . . a clear and distinct etiological sequence," a "chain of morbid events."

Here's an example from the CDC online handbook. The cause of death is cardiac arrest, precipitated by a gastric hemorrhage, which in turn was the result of an ulcer. And here's something more challenging to decode. The terminal event was a rupture of the myocardium, caused by acute myocardial infarction, caused by coronary artery thrombosis and underlying atherosclerotic coronary heart disease. It sounds so specific, so orderly, doesn't it? But eighty- and ninety-year-olds don't usually die of one thing. Eventually, as with all machines, the human body simply wears out.

In his remarkable 1994 best seller *How We Die,* Dr. Sherwin B. Nuland rails at the "soulless summary" of the death certificate. "Every octogenarian or nonagenarian must die of a named entity," he writes. Dr. Nuland finds it ridiculous and dishonest that "government statisticians and the scientific clinicians insist that proper names must be applied to sluggish circulation and an antique heart." Being old isn't the same as having a heart attack or cancer. Frail, weak, bedridden old people don't get well, in the permanent sense of the word, ever. "To call a natural process by the name of a disease is the first step in an attempt to cure it and thereby thwart it," he writes. Plus, the "biomedical worldview" distorts what actually happens. Veins and arteries stiffen and narrow. Less blood flows to the brain. Neurons die. Bones get brittle. Tiny strokes leave bigger deficits. Infections have their way once the immune system is shot. Sometimes all of the above happen, usually at least three. So a person in that condition dies. Calling it heart disease or pneumonia or osteoporosis or vascular dementia seems both arbitrary and beside the point. Everything stops working because the time is up and, as Dr. Nuland writes, we are mowed down by a "series of destructive events that involve, by their very nature, the disintegration of the dying person's humanity. . . . The thing that peters out is nothing other than the life force. . . . The very old do not succumb to disease, they implode their way into eternity."

What would it mean to medical science, I wondered, if death certificates described us as dying not of something that could have been treated, and perhaps was, but instead of something inevitable and universally shared? The leading causes of death in 2008 among those sixty-five and over, as the CDC would have it, were (1) heart disease, (2) cancer, (3) stroke, (4) respiratory disease, (5) Alzheimer's disease, (6) diabetes, (7) influenza, (8) kidney disease, (9) accidents, and (10) infection. Can we really pursue new treatments for heart disease or late-onset diabetes among the oldest of the old without also directly addressing the most frequent cause of those conditions: age itself? Age, according to Charles Mobbs, a molecular biologist and professor of neuroscience at Mount Sinai, often causes inflammation (and thus arthritis, atherosclerosis, and Alzheimer's disease), sensory impairments (cataracts and deafness), loss of muscle mass, and endocrine and immune changes (each associated with other diseases). What would it mean for public policy if the leading cause of death among the very old were "the wheels fell off the bicycle"? Would long-term care, its costs and indignities, find a place on the national agenda, as they have not, even in yet another period of hope for health care reform?

Dr. McCullough, author and Dartmouth geriatrician, who shares my views on this subject and Dr. Nuland's, not the CDC's, says government statisticians will not accept "natural causes" on their official documents. He expects "frailty," also forbidden, to become permissible before long, as this once-descriptive, rather than medical, term is increasingly accepted as a "real" syndrome in advanced old age, much as dementia was once considered innocuous senility, not an inexorably fatal disease. Dr. McCullough says that he sometimes gets away with "inanition," meaning the failure to take in enough food and fluid to sustain life, which can happen naturally, as in the case of terminal cancer or Alzheimer's, or by volition, as in cases of VSED.

As for the New York City Department of Health's refusal to provide me with the part of my mother's death certificate that describes the "chain of morbid events," I learned that since 1988 this has been one of the few jurisdictions in the country that, under local public health law, withholds such details. Rosalyn Williams, director of the department's Office of Vital Statistics, explained, "We wanted to get accurate cause-of-death information without the doctor being pressured by the family" to keep anything out of the "legal record." There are a handful of exceptions, including "criminal action," the "official purposes" of a government agency, and a "demonstrated" need for family medical history "otherwise unavailable" and requested by a physician. A daughter's curiosity is nowhere to be found in Public Health Law 4141. An elder care attorney I consulted advised I'd be wasting my money hiring him to file a subpoena, as he had lost many such cases before.

The medical director at the Hebrew Home was more forthcoming. He had a copy of the half of my mother's death certificate that I had been denied. She died, according to that document, of "cardio-pulmonary arrest, what just about everybody 'dies' of," said Dr. Zack Palace. The quotation marks around "dies" were audible in his voice even over the telephone. "If we were to write 'frailty' or 'poor nutritional intake at the end of life' they'd bounce it right back as 'nonspecific.'" Dr. Palace was clearly not trying to hide from our family or the government the cause of my mother's death. "Individually, every family knows when someone just gave up," he said. "Your mother was not the first person to reach that point, and often sensibly so. But it's not reflected in the statistics."

Come morning, I realized, I would no longer have to worry about my mother, advocate for her, or figure out how to do my work and take care of her at the same time. I wouldn't have to pretend composure, for her sake, when my mind was flying every which way. When the phone rang, I wouldn't have to answer it. I wouldn't have to ruminate about my brother and me running out of money paying for private-duty aides. I wouldn't have to coordinate my comings and goings with him and my sister-in-law. This brutally hard job was over at last. Or was it?

First I had to call Michael and inform him that she was dead and begin discussing the funeral details that had not already been taken care of: whether to hire cars beyond the hearse, use a rabbi or conduct the service ourselves, notify the tiny group of people who needed notifying. I told him I was going back to the nursing home to sit with the body until the funeral director took it away. Michael clearly found this unpleasant and unnecessary, but rather than just blurt that out, he asked—sincerely, not combatively—if it was okay if he didn't join me. It was fine, really fine, I told him. Later he would tell me he found the whole ritual "pointless" and said it would have given him "no comfort."

"Men are like that," Lily said, with the wisdom of a long life and a long career. "There's just some stuff they can't do."

The novelist Julia Glass makes the same point in an essay about her own cancer in Nell Casey's anthology *An Uncertain Inheritance: Writers on Caring for Family*. "Like many of his gender, Dennis is uncomfortable with comfort—giving or receiving," Glass writes of her husband. "He would much rather set about, *at once,* solving the problem at hand so that comfort is moot." But all the problems at hand were now moot. Comfort was the only thing left, and that kind of comfort comes more easily to women and has absolutely nothing to do with "setting about" or "solving."

Back at my mother's bedside, I welcomed the undemanding and peaceful occupation of sitting with her body until it was taken away. It reminded me of a practice among the most observant Jews, called sitting *shmira*, fulfilling the holy commandment to keep watch over the dead, who must not be left alone from the moment of death until burial. So sacred is this tradition that for months after the carnage of September 11, in four-hour shifts, Orthodox Jews sat watch over the trucks of human remains, of all religions, from the World Trade Center. While the tradition is a peculiarly Jewish one, Dr. Norman Lamm, president of Yeshiva University, told me he felt the mitzvah, or good deed, reached across denominations. "The idea that you have companionship in death is a very consoling thought, whether you are Jewish or not," he said. Dr. Lamm called "the loving watching of the corpse a very human act" and noted that the *shmira* is the "truest and most sublime" of the 613 mitzvoth "because there can never be reciprocity."

The rabbi was called after hours and joined me in this new, oh-so-brief, and consoling vigil. We talked, mostly sharing stories of my mother's idiosyncratic sense of humor, so off-putting to some people, but her salvation and ultimately mine. He also told me, for about the tenth time, as if explaining what took so long, the parable of the foxes and the vineyards, the animals first eager for the sweet grapes and later no longer interested. And the story about the train at the platform, and the passengers who were eager for departure but were at the mercy of the conductor, who would blow the whistle and leave only in his own time. They were both a personal and a generic reminder about impatience: that people die when they are ready. The words themselves (and his soothing voice) touched me, no matter how many times I had heard the stories, although sometimes I'd tease him that he needed new material.

In my mother's room that night, what happened next, I have no doubt, would have cracked her up, had she been around to witness it. I was choosing clothes to bury her in, as I had for my father thirty years earlier, when

I put in his pocket exact change for the afternoon paper and a subway token. I was so young then and impressed with my own cleverness, and I knew this was a story I could dine out on for decades, as I am still. This time, I prosaically shuffled through my mother's closet, filled with old-lady elastic-waist pants and tops without buttons, now so many sizes too big for her that they'd require clothespins at the back so she wouldn't look like a refugee.

As I considered and rejected outfits, my mother's body was stiffening into rigor mortis. Only then did the rabbi mention (he probably assumed I already knew it) that Jewish law forbids the funeral director to put her dentures back into her mouth, the equivalent of disturbing the body by embalming it or rouging the cheeks, which is also forbidden. My mother was not a vain woman, but she would never appear in public without her teeth. Only after she was semiconscious earlier in the week did she allow me to remove them so she would be more comfortable. Burying her this way was out of the question, I told the rabbi. He looked at me like I'd gone mad, then gently replied that, at this point, I might have to break her jaw to get the dentures in. I needed to take a minute, he said, and figure out if I really wanted to do that. *What difference did it make?* was his unspoken message.

When words came, they were a child's. "She'll kill me," I said to the rabbi, intending to elaborate about how furious my mother would be to go to her final rest toothless.

He cut me off midthought. "She's dead, Jane," he said.

CHAPTER 18

Orphans

I have no idea when someone first said to me, after my mother's death, that I was now an orphan. It was such a peculiar locution, I thought, for a middle-aged woman who had, predictably, outlived her parents. Orphans are street urchins, characters in a Dickens novel, their faces smeared with dirt, searching trash bins for food. They are robbed of the adults in their life prematurely to face the world on their own. If they are lucky, other grown-ups protect them. But they are *children*. Even the dictionary defines them as such. So, no, Michael and I weren't orphans. Still, something about the term resonated with me. Not only were Michael and I different people than we had been before my mother died, we were different in a way we hadn't been when we'd lost our father. It was now just the two of us. We were the grown-ups in charge, of ourselves and each other. That entirely changed the architecture of our family, as I suspect it will yours.

This is a notion I've watched evolve over many years. It has no easy chronology that I can look up in my date books, in my mother's medical records, in a neat period of time bookended by November 15, 2000, when we began the process of moving her from Florida to New York, and July 25, 2003, the day we buried her in New Montefiore Cemetery in

Pinelawn, New York, next to my father. That's 983 days in all, not that I counted them at the time, merely felt them in my weariness, resentment, sadness, and ultimately love. I can count them now, and document, sometimes to the hour, most of what happened during those days. What has happened afterward didn't have a neat beginning and won't have a neat end.

In between, there have been some standout moments: the day of the funeral; the day my brother and I divided up my mother's meager possessions; the day I gave gifts of some of her cherished mementos—needlepoints, her nursing cape, a gargling cup from the camp infirmary—to people who had lovingly cared for her, pretending my sentimentality was actually hers; the first Thanksgiving without her (and others that followed). The first holiday Michael and I spent together because we actually wanted to; the day her tombstone was unveiled, just the two of us there and no religious ceremony; the informal resumption of our "eagle has landed" telephone calls once we'd fled our forced collaboration and come back together, by choice, as loving siblings and trusted friends; the memorial candles I light for my mother every year (and now for my father, too); the pull I feel to the nursing home on special occasions like her birthday rather than to her grave or to our family home.

Perhaps, like beads on a string that together make a necklace, these isolated moments will tell a coherent story of what happens to middle-aged orphans who need to learn a new way of relating to each other. It has less to do with the *and then, and then, and then* of a chronological story. There are no "how to be an orphan" books, and no statistical reports by advocacy groups about who and how many of us there are. Only a paltry collection of journal articles, contemporary fiction, plays, and films is devoted to this underexplored subject, as if the adult sibling relationship were somehow less captivating or important that that of husband and wife, parent and child, or even children themselves when they are children still. When I asked as a blogger for literary suggestions, my readers could provide hardly any.

Yet who I am in regard to Michael, and he to me, without parents, seems crucial in defining us in the world, especially since we are both childless. We are not obligated to each other because of my mother anymore, or even by a lifetime of loyalty, good deeds, or love. We are obligated by the ties of blood, because we were both born and fledged in the same tangled nest of biological, moral, psychological, cultural, and experiential matter that makes us who we are and who we will be until we die. And none of this is quite the same as it was before.

What I saw with me and Michael is that my baggage, if you will, got lighter. Our sibling rivalries became the subject more of humor than of hurt. With both parents gone, what had been was over; each of our relationships with our parents is static, as if set in stone at the times of their deaths. We can look back at it, make sense out of it if that is our style, or put it behind us if we are not of a mind to review and revisit. But no longer did we have to live, in a day-to-day way, in competition over them, or so it seemed to me. The ongoing relationship, the one that would change and grow, stop and start, move forward or backward or nowhere at all, was overnight the one that existed between us.

My mother's funeral was held on a steamy July day. She had often said she did not want a rabbi to officiate. A hired hand we'd never met had done my father's funeral and consistently mispronounced his last name, to all of our unforgiving annoyance. She had also said that funerals were for the living, not for the dead. Michael and I were the living, and we wanted Rabbi Hirschhorn to preside. He spent much of the day before with each of us, separately, asking us for our memories of her, what mattered to us.

The rabbi, in his eulogy, was funny. My mother would have enjoyed that. Our eyes met several times when he told stories that likely didn't amuse some of our guests as much as they did us. He didn't make her sound nice, or easy to get along with, but rather prickly and irreverent and totally her own person, not concerned whether anyone liked her very much. She would have enjoyed that, too. In our house, we didn't suddenly change our tune about people just because they were dead. In my eulogy, I said of her much of what I've said here, totally dry-eyed and within the two-minute limit I'd set for myself. Maybe it seemed cold or overprepared to the tiny gathering of mourners, but my goal was self-control, honesty, dignity, brevity, and some measure of eloquence. Michael, behind me and out of my line of sight at the grave, spoke next, fighting back tears and losing that battle. He didn't seem concerned about whether his words were highly polished. He was real and loving and brief, very brief. My sister-in-law didn't speak but wept openly. She and my mother understood each other.

There was no postfuneral family gathering, the start of the traditional week of mourning, which we eschewed. So at the end of this uniquely exhausting day, after a meal with dear friends, I swam long, cool laps at the village pool and then went home to sleep. I hung around the house all weekend, mindlessly gardening. On Monday I returned to work, sooner than I would have liked, but coiffed, dry-eyed, and efficient. I wanted to write about aged parents and adult children, and I have.

By the time my mother died in 2003, everything she owned fit in two cartons. Never one for sentiment, she would insist, each time she downsized, that we discard, discard, discard, and mostly we did. My brother and I had no interest in the furniture or clothing, so off it went to Goodwill. There were no heirlooms, as our grandparents were poor Eastern European immigrants. The family vault had long ago been emptied of its documents: birth certificates, wills and proxies, deeds to the cemetery plots. We had already laid claim to the photographs, mostly of my father with various famous people. My brother had the sports memorabilia. I had the "good china" and the holiday sterling (which turned out not to be sterling at all). I also had my mother's pearls. My sister-in-law had my mother's engagement ring, a gift on the eve of her marriage to my brother. My mother, of course, had no money left. Michael and I had never expected an inheritance. I'd heard enough horror stories about siblings squabbling over valuable real estate, art, and stock portfolios to be glad about that. Plus, we didn't have to bother putting the will into probate, because there was nothing left behind.

Well, not quite nothing, we discovered weeks after her death, when we spread the contents of two small cardboard boxes on my living room floor. She'd never been sentimental about things, seeing trash where some would see memories. And what a paltry collection of belongings remained, after a long, complicated, and interesting life. There were all the books my brother had written. There was a collection of decorative boxes and some costume jewelry, in a suede pouch I'd given her. There was a poster-size photograph of my father, smiling, which makes him almost unrecognizable. She had kept all the silly cards I'd sent her during her nursing home years. I assumed she'd thrown them away, but instead, unacknowledged, she had clearly treasured them. She had expired chits from winning bingo games that we hadn't had time to redeem at the nursing home store. And we found her wallet, a worn remnant of some designer accessory my brother had given her. It must have cost a bundle. In it was this card and that card—Social

Security, Medicare, library, driver's license, ATM, and AmEx—some her own and some my father's, all these decades later.

And $26: two $10 bills and six singles.

This careful parsing of the money revealed that my mother had recognized our pattern: I would pretend I didn't want whatever it was, unctuously tell Michael he was welcome to it, and then silently fume. Now, by stuffing the wallet with exact change, she'd made my false generosity all but impossible, seen to it that I'd get my fair share of this pittance.

As we emptied the wallet, our routine jabbering stopped. In that rare window of silence, I looked up at Michael with what I hoped was a poker face. He smiled in recognition, then dealt out the money like cards, passing me my $13. We waved the bills in the air. This was our inheritance, split down the middle, and well worth celebrating.

The two cartons, it turned out, were not really all that was left. On the first Thanksgiving without my mother, I decided to stay home quietly by myself, to eat a turkey sandwich off those ugly but much beloved "good dishes" and thus honor her. Then I came upon a small wicker basket of unknown provenance, but clearly hers. Lifting its cover, I found (hiding under her high school yearbook, my birth announcement, and other treasures) the embossed Sarah Lawrence folder, her writings from Alexandra's class that we had attended together a few times, before I left her to the assistance of others and the privacy of doing her own creative work.

The first class had begun with a reading from *The Dead* by James Joyce, the section describing a table groaning under the weight of a fat brown goose and a ham with a paper frill around its shin; side dishes of blancmange, peeled almonds, and Smyrna figs; cut-glass decanters of port and dark sherry; and pyramids of oranges and huge puddings. The students were asked to think back to meals from childhood and to describe the food, the conversation, the rules, and the eating habits of family members. Be as specific as you can, Alex had instructed, and write for ten minutes.

My mother's essay is strange reading in someone else's handwriting, as hearing it read in someone else's voice had been in the classroom. It didn't look familiar, like her shopping lists that even now show up from time to time in a coat I wore back in those days, bringing a gasp of recognition, as if it were yesterday. Still, her "voice" comes through in the writing in fits and starts, telling me both things familiar and things brand-new. "I had a good appetite, and I ate everything," my mother wrote, which remained true almost until the end of her days. In a small town in the distant reaches of upstate New York, her family had had a vegetable garden (I never knew that), and her father's favorite meal was four ears of corn. Her mother was a good cook, she wrote, without mentioning that this was her stepmother, who had treated her so cruelly. (In a later essay titled "Home," she hints at that early unhappiness: "I don't even think about where I lived as a child. I must have blocked it out.")

The essay about childhood meals quickly veers to the eating habits of her husband and children. My father was "fussy." My brother loved veal. "Janie loved nothing," my mother wrote. I stiffened. My eating habits had led to great disharmony in the family that I was not eager to relive, so I skimmed the rest of the essay. There was a funny bit about my mother's golf-ball-hard matzo balls (my preference to this day); they came out that way because of her overzealous rolling and forming rather than a haphazard but more effective approach. Then I came to a sentence more revelatory than anything I'd ever heard my mother say or thought her capable of saying, thinking, or understanding.

The pediatrician had begged my mother to relax about my food issues; as long as I was tall enough to open the refrigerator, I wouldn't starve, he told her. But I was the firstborn child, after three miscarriages and eight months of bedrest. Relax? She learned to relax in time for Michael. "I was a terrible mother," she wrote. "I used to force her to eat and that's really stupid." An apology from the grave.

Another writing exercise of my mother's, the one that Alex remembered years later, was not about food but interpersonal relationships. It showed my mother's sharp eye for detail. The students selected photographs from the collection *The Family of Man,* a photography book culled from the famed 1955 exhibit, curated by Edward Steichen at the Museum of Modern Art. My mother chose a photo of a handsome American soldier embracing a weeping, towheaded boy. At first, my mother wrote, she had assumed this was a picture of a happy postwar reunion. On closer inspection, she saw a rifle pressed to the man's side and revised her narrative. The child must be a stranger, maybe German with his fair hair, perhaps lost in a crowd and looking for his parents. "No father would be holding a gun when hugging his child," my mother wrote. "He must have seen the little boy crying and because he loves children or has children of his own, he hugged the boy and tried to comfort him." Alex was struck by the acuity of the observation. "She'd already given the man a moral character," she said to me. "She was very perceptive and rarely got people wrong."

The essay titled "Character" is about her father, who had come to America from Russia as a sixteen-year-old to avoid being drafted by the czar's army. "He would be so ashamed of me," my mother wrote, "because I'm not going to vote in this next election. He loved his country. He was the best citizen I ever knew." During World War II he had given her savings stamps so she could buy meat and butter when her husband, my father, came home for visits from his Washington-based duty for *Stars and Stripes.* Those savings stamps and coupons also paid for nylon stockings and a black nightgown to wear when she visited him there. My father loved her, she wrote, "because of my sense of humor."

She also wrote of my father's writing career: "My husband was quite famous in his time. He wrote five columns a week and said the only way to write was to paste the seat of your pants to the chair." My brother and I inherited that ability. *Lay bricks,* we would tell each other throughout our working lives, when words didn't come easily. *Type if you can't write.* Long before Michael and I related to each other on any other level, this was our bond. It was the only glue we had until the end of my mother's life, when unwelcome circumstance brought us together. Slight though it seemed, the writing may have been what made the larger connection possible when the time was right. Now, as this Thanksgiving Day turned dark and I kept reading, my mother had joined the fraternity. She wrote of my begging her to take notes during her years in Florida, to put into words the stories she told me when I visited: "My daughter told me if you can say it you can write it."

No change in the architecture of our family is more surprising to me, now that the grown-ups are gone, than the fractured myth that I am my father's child and Michael my mother's. Easy formulations to the contrary, it isn't either/or, as we all believed or pretended; instead, it's and/but.

As a child, I may have been my father's favorite, the one who accompanied him on assignment; went to bat at Miller Huggins Field in Saint Petersburg, Florida, where the Yankees trained in those days; and who practiced my cheerleading routines in the echoey bowels of the old Madison Square Garden while he wrote his columns late into the night. I imagine Michael felt cheated of that, too young to have come along. But it's Michael who is prouder that my father's name was once on the side of a newspaper truck, and it's Michael who looks for and battles injustice, as my father did when that fight meant a burning cross on our front lawn because he championed Branch Rickey's signing of Jackie Robinson. My father would be so proud of Michael. On the other hand, it was always Michael who made my mother laugh; it was his magazine cover stories that were stacked in her room; and he made getting a motorized wheelchair and an assisted speaking device into occasions for mirth, not misery. But I was the one who shared her habit of preparing for the worst, way in advance, and was strong enough to help her die, as she wished. My mother wound up proud of me.

Sometimes I think about losing her just when I found her, the time we could have enjoyed, the terrible waste. I saw a glimmer of what we could have been if we'd paid attention to each other sooner. Then I can hear her saying, *What are you making such a big deal about, Jane?* I'd rather she say, *Oh, sweetheart, better late than never.* But "Oh, sweetheart" wasn't part of my mother's vocabulary, as it isn't part of my brother's. And neither of them has to say "better late than never," because I already know it's true.

Lost and Found

There was only one thing of my mother's that I wanted as she lay dying: a delicate gold Longines watch, circa 1949. It had been a gift to my father, when he was the Yankees' beat writer for the *New York Post,* and was inscribed as follows:

> *To Milton Gross*
> *For Services To Baseball*
> *1949 World Series*
> *Albert B. Chandler*
> *Commissioner*

I don't for one moment recall my mother without that watch on her arm, until deep into her nursing home stay, when her arthritic and eventually paralyzed fingers could no longer work the tiny latch. Then it moved to her night-table drawer, where it remained. I can't recall the moment when she finally offered it to me, an odd gap in memory, given my intense desire to feel its cool touch around my wrist. I took it from the night table and put it on my arm the evening she died, and the pleasure nearly took my breath away.

Then, one terrible day fifteen months later, the watch was gone. It had been on my wrist in the morning, but it was missing at nightfall. I retraced my steps, from home to office to parking garage, to theater to restaurant, on my hands and knees to look under furniture, in elevators, at curbsides, all over the city. I tore apart my car and my house, stripped the bed, emptied drawers. I scoured the streets of my suburban neighborhood, eyes to the ground, along the route where I walk my dog several times a day. I put flyers on lampposts. I filed a police report with the kindly small-town cops.

For weeks I was inconsolable. Often I awoke in the morning to find my thumb and forefinger circling my wrist, as if expecting it to be there. I sometimes actually felt it, a phantom sensation, like amputees report. But as with all things, the intensity of the loss finally passed, and life moved on. And then, years later, something magical happened. I wrote an e-mail to my great friend Esther Fein about it.

FROM: Jane Gross
TO: Esther Fein
Tuesday, 30 Dec. 2008 7:38 p.m.
SUBJECT: Little miracle

Esther,

I found my mother's watch. I'd lost it during the remodel of the 2nd floor of the house and it's taken me this long to work my way thru all the packing boxes. So, on Christmas, I tackled the last 4, a virtuous chore at this hard and lonely time of the year.

I unpacked one box. Unpacked two. Unpacked three. Then I was down to the last one, everything else already either put away or at the curb for garbage pickup. And just as I'm walking the last empty box outside, I see a glint of gold among the paper clips, dried-up rubber bands, crumpled Post-its—the watch, one bracelet link broken but otherwise intact, even telling the right time! What are the odds it would be in the *last* box? And in that very last box, what are the odds it wouldn't end up, unnoticed, in the garbage and ultimately the village dump?

I can't help but remember your great kindness when I lost it, and the wise words about how the phantom sensation of it around my wrist was good enough, given that the watch itself would have meant nothing to me not so many years ago. And my sister-in-law giving me my mother's engagement ring, as a substitute, her greatest kindness to me in twenty years of being married to my brother. And the painters and contractors prowling the neighborhood, during their lunch break, looking for it in the street. And the local cop who came by with his metal detector because I was so sure it had fallen through the gaps in the 150-year-old floorboards. And a neighbor I barely know who prayed, "Dear Saint Anthony, please come around. Something is lost that must be found." And, of course, my yoga teacher who kept saying it would find me . . . but only when I stopped looking.

RESOURCES

Websites often change their addresses, and the smaller organizations appear and disappear, so this listing is likely to be inaccurate as soon as it is published. Should a link no longer work or take you to the wrong place, a Google search for the name of the organization will get you where you want to go, and we will update in later printings or editions.

GOVERNMENT SITES

- *Administration on Aging,* **www.aoa.gov.** An agency of the U.S. Department of Health and Human Services. Fact sheets and statistics on aging, and a searchable nationwide directory for an assortment of caregiving issues, including financial planning, residential options, in-home services, case management, and the law.
- *Centers for Medicare and Medicaid Services,* **www.cms.gov.** Forms and publications to download on enrollment, eligibility, fraud, and much else. A tool for comparing nursing homes, based on the CMS rating system.
- *Eldercare Locator,* **www.eldercare.gov.** A service of the Administration on Aging. Contact information for local agencies and ombudsmen nationwide and for community-based services like transportation, meals, home care, and caregiver support.
- *Family and Medical Leave Act,* **www.dol.gov/esa/whd/fmla/index.htm.** Explanation of the Department of Labor law that provides up to twelve weeks of unpaid leave for eligible employees. Fact sheets and forms.
- *Medicare,* **www.medicare.gov.** All-purpose site. Interactive tools for planning and paying for long-term care and choosing among drug plans. Inspection results, good and bad, for all the nation's skilled nursing facilities.
- *MedlinePlus,* **www.medlineplus.gov.** A collaboration of the National Institutes of Health and the National Library of Medicine. Fact sheets, statistics, policy papers, guidebooks, and articles from a variety of sources on health and disease, drugs and supplements. Videos and tutorials.

- *National Center on Elder Abuse,* www.ncea.aoa.gov. An agency of the Administration on Aging. Statistics, a help hotline, an elder care locator, and local resources.
- *National Institute on Aging,* www.nia.nih.gov. Descriptions of ongoing research on aging. A list of clinical trials seeking participants.
- *Senior Health,* www.nihseniorhealth.gov. A collaboration of the National Institutes of Health and the National Library of Medicine. Authoritative information on all diseases and disorders of old age. Available in both large-type and audio versions.
- *Social Security Administration,* www.ssa.gov. Eligibility, instructions and application forms.

GENERAL INFORMATION AND RESEARCH

- *AARP,* www.aarp.org. A national membership organization whose site provides general information and news about health, retirement, finances, caregiving, and much more, as well as tool kits, downloadable fact sheets and checklists, chatrooms, blogs, videos, resources, and links. Site links to the AARP Public Policy Institute, with research reports, public policy analysis, and current caregiving data.
- *American Society on Aging,* www.asaging.org. Publications, educational opportunities, and other resources. Geared to professionals working with the elderly and their families but often useful for caregivers.
- *Commonwealth Fund,* www.commonwealthfund.org. Private foundation whose research topics include the elderly and Medicare.
- *Family Caregiver Alliance,* www.caregiver.org. Publisher of *Caregiving Policy Digest,* a twice-monthly digest of state and federal news, research, and public policy regarding caregiving. Free e-newsletter subscription.
- *Health Policy Institute at Georgetown University,* www.hpi.georgetown.edu. Public policy reports and research. Its affiliations include the Center on an Aging Society and the Long-Term Care Financing Project.
- *International Longevity Center–USA,* www.ilcusa.org. Research reports, position papers, and conferences.
- *The Joint Commission on Accreditation of Healthcare Organizations,* www.jointcommission.org. Online search engine of accredited hospitals, labs, and nursing homes.
- *Kaiser Family Foundation,* www.kff.org. News on health care reform, Medicare, insurance, state policy, drugs, and more. A variety of PowerPoint tutorials and podcasts.
- *MetLife Foundation,* www.metlife.com. Reports (often in collaboration with AARP and the National Alliance for Caregiving) on the overall state of family caregiving, cost to employers and employees, and the physical and emotional strain of long-distance caregiving.
- *National Association of Area Agencies on Aging,* www.n4a.org. An association of local organizations, each with its own menu of services and areas of expertise.
- *National Council on Aging,* www.ncoa.org. Information, services, and advocacy on a range of subjects that include senior centers, health care reform, benefits, and fall prevention.

· *United Hospital Fund of New York,* **www.uhfnyc.org.** Information on Medicaid, health care finances, aging in place, family caregiving, naturally occurring retirement communities (NORCs), and transitions from one level of care to another.

HOUSING, CARE MANAGEMENT, AND OTHER SERVICES

· *American Health Care Association,* **www.ahca.org.** A federation of fifty state health organizations that represent 12,000 nonprofit and for-profit assisted living facilities, nursing homes, and other providers of services for the elderly.
· *A Place for Mom,* **www.caregivers.com.** Location search for residential options and other elder care services.
· *Arch Respite and Crisis Care Services,* **www.archrespite.org.** Network of respite services, with locator.
· *Assisted Living Federation of America,* **www.alfa.org.** A database of assisted living facilities searchable by location or parent company.
· *Catholic Charities,* **www.catholiccharities.org,** and *Jewish Community Services,* **www .jcsbaltimore.org.** Free or low-cost home care and care management.
· *Cleveland Clinic,* **www.clevelandclinic.org.** Locator for top specialists.
· *Evercare,* **www.evercarehealthplans.com,** and *Home Instead Senior Care,* **www.home instead.com.** For-profit companies with locally owned and operated franchises that provide nonmedical in-home help, such as companions. At **www.caregiverstress.com,** Home Instead has a website for caregivers, with a stress meter, tips, and a series of videos called "Caring for Your Parents: Education for the Family Caregiver."
· *Hebrew Home for the Aged,* **www.hebrewhome.org.** A continuing care retirement community in Riverdale, New York. Its community services division is ElderServe.
· *Jewish Home Life Care,* **www.jewishhome.org.** A nonprofit group of nursing homes in the New York metropolitan region. Care managers and other home care services, at hourly rates.
· *LeadingAge,* **www.aahsa.org.** Formerly called the American Association of Homes and Services for the Aging. An association of nonprofit nursing homes, assisted living centers, continuing care retirement communities, adult day care centers, and the like. Consumer information on senior housing.
· *National Adult Day Services Association,* **www.nadsa.org.** Information about senior centers, day care services, and places to go from nine to five for the aged seeking activities and social contact and family caregivers in need of part-time respite.
· *National Adult Protective Services Association,* **www.apsnetwork.org.** Listing of statewide elder abuse services.
· *National Association of Professional Geriatric Care Managers,* **www.caremanager.org.** A search by location for geriatric care managers who meet association guidelines. Also, guidance on whether this service would be beneficial under individual circumstances.
· *National Association of Senior Move Managers,* **www.nasmm.com.** Professionals to take care of downsizings, relocations, and home modifications for the elderly and their families.

- *National Center for Assisted Living,* **www.ncal.org.** List of state affiliates; consumer guides on choosing, paying for, and preparing for a move, plus research studies.
- *National PACE Association,* **www.npaonline.org.** In some states and communities, an all-inclusive program of medical care, housing assistance, social support, transportation, adult day care, and other services paid for by Medicare and/or Medicaid to keep those eligible for nursing homes in the community.
- *Paraprofessional Healthcare Institute,* **www.phinational.org.** All issues involving so-called direct care workers, primarily home health aides. A separate site, **www.directcare clearinghouse.org,** for locating home care workers.
- *Pioneer Network,* **www.pioneernetwork.net.** A consortium of small nursing homes practicing so-called culture change, or patient-driven care, in a number of areas, including flexible mealtimes and homey design of facilities. Similar work is being done by *Eden Alternative,* **www.edenalt.org,** and the *Green House Project,* **www.thegreenhouse project.org.**
- *SeniorBridge Care,* **www.seniorbridge.com.** A for-profit care management company offering an array of home care services. Nationwide offices.
- *SeniorDecision,* **www.seniordecision.com.** Consumer ratings and reviews of nursing homes, assisted living centers, retirement communities, and home health care agencies.
- *Senior Living Guide,* **www.seniorlivingguide.com.** Search by state and region for all types of senior housing, care managers, lawyers, and more. A glossary of industry jargon.
- *Visiting Nurse Associations of America,* **www.vnaa.org.** Search for home health services nationwide. Suggested questions to ask service providers. Most localities have their own nonprofit organizations of nurses and other home care workers.

CAREGIVING

- *Adult Care,* **www.adult-care.org.** Interactive information about caring for the elderly. Bibliography of books, articles, links.
- *Caregiving.com,* **www.caregiving.com.** Online support groups and a weekly e-mail newsletter, upon request. Other features include "Caregiving Journal," with podcasts and an Internet talk show (both live and archived), and "Caregiver Deals," a frequently updated listing of discounted products.
- *Caring.com,* **www.caring.com.** An all-purpose site with original essays from experts, checklists, how-to guides, a national service directory, support groups, and blogs.
- *Caring Bridge,* **www.caringbridge.org.** A tool for creating a free personal website for family and friends to share information during a loved one's illness.
- *Caring from a Distance,* **www.cfad.org.** Connects caregivers with long-distance services. Founded by siblings caring for an ailing father.
- *Caring Today,* **www.caringtoday.com.** Magazine website.
- *Children of Aging Parents,* **www.caps4caregivers.org.** Support groups, both online and face to face. Newsletter focusing on interpersonal matters like stress among siblings, caregiver depression, and getting through the holidays.

- *Family Caregiver Alliance,* **www.caregiver.org.** Information on a wide range of topics, including how to hire help, hold a family meeting, balance work and caregiving, find important papers, and decide whether parents should move in with an adult child. A locator for programs and services, fact sheets, publications, and discussion groups.
- *Family Caregiving 101,* **www.familycaregiving101.org.** A joint project of the National Alliance for Caregiving and the National Family Caregivers Association. Advice on time management, asking for help, navigating the health care maze, and communicating with insurance companies and hospitals.
- *Get Care,* **www.getcare.com.** A three-step process to assess long-term care options, learn about each type, and then search by location for a variety of services, including Alzheimer's day care, grief support, and respite for a caregiver.
- *Lotsa Helping Hands,* **www.lotsahelpinghands.com.** Site for creating a community of caregivers who can coordinate tasks, like providing meals and running errands. Free computerized calendar.
- *National Alliance for Caregiving,* **www.caregiving.org.** A coalition of organizations with resources for caregivers and professionals. Information on research, legislation, and public policy; reviews of books; videos; and links to other resources.
- *National Family Caregivers Association,* **www.nfcacares.org.** Education, caregiver support, statistics, research and policy reports, tip sheets, first-person accounts, message boards, a newsletter, and an exhaustive resource list.
- *Next Step in Care,* **www.nextstepincare.org.** A United Hospital Fund initiative about transitions from hospital to rehabilitation to home for both professionals and family caregivers. Separate checklists and other materials for each move, in several languages.
- *Rosalynn Carter Institute for Caregiving,* **www.rosalynncarter.org.** Evidence-based research about interventions and best practices for professional and family caregivers.
- *Share the Care,* **www.sharethecare.org.** A system of group caregiving with handbook and forms, to organize friends and neighbors to collaboratively help those who are ill or homebound.
- *Strength for Caring,* **www.strengthforcaring.com.** An all-purpose site from Johnson & Johnson with original articles written by experts, how-to materials, and an online community and resources center with news, publications, and links to other resources.
- *Third Age,* **www.thirdage.com/caregiving.** Articles, expert interviews, quizzes, and discussion boards for caregivers.
- *Today's Caregiver,* **www.caregiver.com.** Magazine with articles on caregiving.

LEGAL AND FINANCIAL

- *American Bar Association,* **www.abanet.org.** A ten-step process, with worksheets, for making end-of-life decisions.
- *Insurance Information Institute,* **www.iii.org.** Information about long-term care insurance, annuities, and Medigap insurance policies.
- *National Academy of Elder Law Attorneys,* **www.naela.com.** Search by location for mem-

bers of the association. Provides questions to ask lawyers about qualifications and areas of expertise, and a wide-ranging resource list for the elderly.

· *National Association of Insurance Commissioners,* **www.naic.org.** Similar to Insurance Information Institute. Fact sheets and shoppers' guides for long-term care insurance, annuities, and Medigap policies.

· *NOLO,* **www.nolo.com.** Do-it-yourself legal advice. Wills, powers of attorney, and other documents.

· *Reverse Mortgages,* **www.reverse.org.** Consumer guide to reverse mortgages, from a non-profit with no ties to the industry.

· *U.S. Living Will Registry,* **www.uslivingwillregistry.com.** Free state-by-state forms. Electronic storage for advance directives, making them available to health care providers via secure Internet. There is a one-time fee, but some health care providers offer the service free or discounted.

END OF LIFE

· *Aging with Dignity,* **www.agingwithdignity.org.** A popular living will that can be downloaded.

· *American Hospice Foundation,* **www.americanhospice.org.** Discussion of many end-of-life issues. Links to a searchable database for hospices.

· *Compassion and Choices,* **www.compassionandchoices.org.** Free counseling for families making end-of-life decisions. Advocacy for state ballot initiatives and legislation to permit physicians to assist in death under specific guidelines.

· *Hospice Foundation of America,* **www.hospicefoundation.org.** Information on end-of-life issues, such as pain management, regulatory issues, statistics, and Patient's Bill of Rights, plus a searchable database for local hospices.

· *National Center to Advance Palliative Care,* **www.capc.org.** Group based at Mount Sinai Medical Center in New York City, to explain and promote palliative care. CAPC's consumer site, **www.getpalliativecare.org**, is a directory of hospitals with palliative care programs, an explanation of how palliative care differs from hospice, an interactive questionnaire to help people decide its appropriateness for them, a state-by-state report card, and videos.

· *National Hospice and Palliative Care Organization,* **www.nhpco.org,** and NHPCO's consumer site, *Caring Connections,* **www.caringinfo.org.** State-by-state advance directive forms, as well as guides on issues related to palliative care, including Medicare coverage and techniques for communicating end-of-life wishes.

· *Palliative doctors,* **www.palliativedoctors.org.** Search by location for providers of palliative care and hospice.

ADVOCACY

- *Center for Medicare Advocacy,* **www.medicareadvocacy.org.** Detailed information about what Medicare covers, how to enroll, and if necessary, how to appeal denial of claims and other abuses.
- *Consumer Consortium on Assisted Living,* **www.ccal.org.** Consumer-based organization promoting needs, rights, and protections for residents and caregivers.
- *Medicare Rights Center,* **www.medicarerights.org.** A tutorial on how Medicare works. Links to the Kaiser Family Foundation's "Medicare 101." A hotline for questions and complaints.
- *National Citizens' Coalition for Nursing Home Reform,* **www.nccnhr.org.** A membership organization of long-term care ombudsmen, legal service providers, religious groups, unions, concerned homes, and family and resident councils. A consumer guide to choosing a nursing home, information on regulatory policy and legislation, and fact sheets on residents' rights, the use of restraints, and the "culture change" movement.
- *National Senior Citizens Law Center,* **www.nsclc.org.** Litigation and other assistance for low-income elderly in areas including Medicare, Medicaid, the Americans with Disabilities Act, nursing homes, pension rights, and Social Security.
- *Service Employees International Union,* **www.sciu.org.** Representation for home health care workers.

ALZHEIMER'S DISEASE

- *Alzheimer's Association,* **www.alz.org.** Information about the disease, links to community resources, and a twenty-four-hour help line. Local chapters all over the country, each with a website, like New York's, **www.alznyc.org,** which includes information on local clinical trials, support groups, and special programs for early-onset disease.
- *Big Tree Murphy,* **www.bigtreemurphy.com.** Heart-warming advice to caregivers from a rehabilitation counselor who retired to care for her husband.
- *Fisher Center for Alzheimer's Research Foundation,* **www.alzinfo.org.** Information about current research, plus an online community with chatrooms, message boards, and a resource database.
- *Hearthstone Alzheimer Care,* **www.thehearth.org.** Small units for dementia patients located within existing senior living facilities, run according to principles similar to the "culture change" movement in nursing homes, founded by an early practitioner of non-pharmaceutical treatment for dementia.
- *Leeza's Place,* **www.leezasplace.org.** A growing network of community gathering places and resource centers, founded by the television performer Leeza Gibbons, for caregivers of people with dementia. Each location—in Florida, California, Illinois, and Texas—is run by a "care advocate" who assists families as the disease advances. Free on-site lectures, support groups, meditation classes, and other group events.

· *This Caring Home,* **www.thiscaringhome.org.** Information on best practices and home safety from experts at Weill Cornell Medical College. Multimedia site includes videos, animations, photographs, and reviews of products. A simple mouse click over each room in the house shows research-based solutions to safety and daily care issues.

OTHER DISEASES

· *American Cancer Society,* **www.cancer.org.**
· *American Heart Association,* **www.heart.org.**
· *American Lung Association,* **www.lungusa.org.**
· *American Parkinson Disease Association,* **www.apdaparkinson.org.**
· *American Stroke Association,* **www.strokeassociation.org.**
· *Cancer Care,* **www.cancercare.org.**
· *Lighthouse International,* **www.lighthouse.org.**
· *National Multiple Sclerosis Society,* **www.nationalmssociety.org.**
· *People Living with Cancer,* **www.plwc.org.**

AGING IN PLACE

· *Beacon Hill Village,* **www.beaconhillvillage.org.** The first such "village," in Beacon Hill in Boston. Members pay dues. A salaried "concierge" and staff vet, hire, and dispatch requested service providers, like carpenters and physical therapists, to individuals' homes. Beacon Hill Village created and sold a manual on its business model, and there are now more than fifty clones. All can be found, with links to individual websites, at the Village to Village Network, **www.vtvnetwork.org.**
· *Caring Collaborative,* **www.ttncaringcollaborative.org.** The Transition Network's New York City–based pilot program that organizes members living in the same zip code to help one another during illness, based on a time-bank system. The umbrella organization, **www.thetransitionnetwork.org,** for women past fifty who are moving from work to retirement, has expanded to several cities nationwide and intends the same for this project, in which an hour spent running errands for someone, for example, can be exchanged for an hour of transportation or a companion for a doctor's appointment.

MISCELLANEOUS

· *American Medical Association,* **www.ama-assn.org.** "Physician's Guide to Assessing and Counseling Older Drivers."
· *Benefits,* **www.benefitscheckup.org.** A service of the National Council on Aging, **www.ncoa.org,** to determine eligibility for more than one thousand benefit programs that help pay for medications, health care, utilities, and so forth.
· *Home Care America,* **www.homecareamerica.com.** Products for sale.

· *Home Modification,* **www.homemods.org.** Advice on home renovation from the University of Southern California.
· *NeedyMeds,* **www.needymeds.org.** Information on how to find assistance programs.
· *RXAssist,* **www.rxassist.org.** Patient assistance on obtaining free or low-cost drugs from pharmaceutical companies.
· *Senior Driving Safety,* **www.seniordrivers.org.** A service of the American Automobile Association that helps the elderly assess their driving skills, remediate when it is safe to keep driving, and find ways to get places when they no longer can drive.

ACKNOWLEDGMENTS

A book has only one author, responsible for its accuracy and honesty, but many loving and knowledgeable hearts and hands that help bring it to life.

In this case, first and foremost, are Kathy Robbins, my agent at The Robbins Office, and Jonathan Segal, my editor at Knopf, who waited thirty years for me to find the courage to leave the comfort zone of daily journalism for the unfamiliar, daunting, and lonely world of book writing. Kathy and her able staff, especially Mike Gillespie, held my hand every emotional step of the way, helped shape every chapter, read every word, and made sure a novice book writer had the finest guide possible through the unfamiliar shoals of the publishing business. Jon, an editor of intelligence and precision, saved me from excesses that would have taxed the reader's patience and detracted from the practical value of this book. He protected me from myself more times than I can say. He was unsparing, giving the lie to the notion that thorough editing is a lost art, and he provided a first-time author the rare opportunity to be published by Knopf. My thanks also go to his assistant, Joey McGarvey, and to Ellen Feldman, Michelle Somers, and Gabrielle Brooks.

It was *The New York Times* that gave me twenty-nine years to stretch myself to my limits at America's greatest newspaper and, in my final years there, to explore the demographic and emotional intersection of aging parents and their adult children, both in the pages of the paper and in a blog. The stories would not have been possible without the abiding support of my immediate editor, Barbara Graustark, who never said no when I said, "Trust me, it'll work." Barbara fought to get the stories into the paper, forced me to think more rigorously than I otherwise would have, and all but channeled my voice when the time came to actually edit four years' worth of words on the subject. She is as gifted an editor of narrative journalism, and as dear a friend, as I have ever had. The blog that came later was inspired by Jonathan Landman, who was my editor and mentor at the *Times* in too many iterations to list. Thanks for the blog's creation also go to William Schmidt, who authorized its cost once I was no longer on staff; Mike Mason, its producer; Laura Chang, editor of Science Times; and Rich Meislin, supporter and technical wizard. I am also indebted to the three executive editors who most nurtured my career at the *Times*: Bill Keller, Joe Lelyveld, and Max Frankel, and to many department heads, none more than Soma Golden-Behr. Also at the *Times*, James Estrin was for many years my photographer, sidekick, amateur psychologist, and trusted friend.

Next are the wonderful people at the Hebrew Home for the Aged in Riverdale who cared for my mother (as well as for me and my brother, Michael). They include Dan Reingold, the home's director; Eileen Dunnion, head nurse on my mother's floor; Hannah Curry, her social worker; Diana Lubarski, her physical therapist; Lily Ford, her private-duty aide; Rabbi Simon Hirschhorn; and Alexandra Soiseth (from Sarah Lawrence College), her creative writing teacher at the home. All participated in this book, as well, by refreshing, amplifying, and correcting my memories. The home also provided me with complete medical, nursing, and financial records of my mother's time there. Others involved in our family's experience, who also spoke with me during the writing of this book and provided me with medical, financial, and legal records, are Gregg Weiss and Peter Strauss, both elder care lawyers; Claudia Fine, then a principal at the care management agency Fine, Newcombe & Winsby (now SeniorBridge); Barbara Clark, then a social work supervisor at the smaller agency; Dr. Mark Bilsky, neurosurgeon at Memorial Sloan-Kettering; and Dr. Lori Saltzman, my mother's internist for a brief period. The management who had been in charge of the Meadowview assisted living facility during my mother's stay were no longer there, but I was brought up to date by their successors.

After my mother's death, I met far too many experts on geriatrics and caregiving to list here, but several shared with me, over the course of many years, huge swaths of time and expertise, and some read portions of this book in manuscript form for technical accuracy. While far from a complete list, the ones to whom I am most grateful are Carol Levine, at the United Hospital Fund; Dr. Dennis McCullough, at Dartmouth College; Dr. Timothy Quill, at the University of Rochester; Patricia Mulvey, at Jewish Home Life Care; and Drs. Rosanne Leipzig, Audrey Chun, Patricia Bloom, and Diane Meier at the Mount Sinai School of Medicine. I also had the rare opportunity to learn from many experts in bioethics at the Hastings Center in Garrison, New York. Thanks to the kindness of Mary Crowley, the center's director of communications, I spent three months there as journalist in residence, enjoying access to their library, views of the Hudson River, and restorative and intellectually stimulating staff lunches and hikes.

Last, but indispensable, are the friends who talked me off the ledge when I wanted to quit, read portions of the manuscript (and in one case line-edited every word), and otherwise believed in me. In alphabetical order, they are Ann Bancroft, the late Barry Blumberg, Katherine Grande Campbell, Jim Estrin, Esther Fein, Elizabeth Felber, Peter and Claire Filippelli, Michael Fuchs, Barbara Graustark, Isabel Gulden, Ellen Hendrickx, Bob Hermann, Jon Landman, Maria Benedetta LoBalbo, Barbara Lorber, Jim Matison, Lucille Matison, Jerry Pritchett, Joyce Purnick, Frieda and Jason Rabinovitz, Jonathan Rabinovitz, Deirdre Roney, the late Jill Schehr Sacks, Liza and Ali Sacks, Judith Schwartzstein, Janny Scott, Dr. Leatrice Simpson, Lenna Warner, Hilma Wolitzer, and Aaron Woodin.

Literally at my side through the writing was my dog, Henry. On my shoulder, whispering encouragement, although long dead, was my friend and *Times* colleague Bob Reinhold. With me, too, always, was my late father, Milton Gross, who founded the "family business." My brother, Michael, to whom this book is dedicated, and his wife, Barbara, talked me into writing it. Michael then guided me through the publishing process as only a career book author could, and read and generously signed off on every word regarding our family. What I owe him is boundless.

But my most profound gratitude goes to my mother, who taught me, in the last years of her life, everything there is to know about good sense and courage. She set an example for graceful old age and dying that will be hard to live up to, and gave me the opportunity to get to know her.

INDEX

AARP, 116, 178, 222–8, 277–8
absence, leaves of, 116, 118–19, 224
absenteeism, 116–17
accidents, 229, 308
accountants, 166, 232–3
acute care, 150, 202, 204, 207
advocacy resources, 329
aging in place, 43, 82, 244, 247
   resources for, 330
agitation, 146, 153, 206, 249, 273, 302
aides, 79, 97, 163–7, 225
   agency, 10, 164–5, 224, 235, 255, 264,
     305
   at appointments, 64, 147, 152–5, 165
   of Bloom's patients, 152–5, 165
   E. Gross's firing of, 96
   at Hebrew Home, 138, 190, 196, 206,
     234–5, 298, 300, 304–5
   home care, 10, 28, 63, 149, 150, 153, 164–7,
     223–4, 233, 235, 237, 263, 267
   live-in, 46–7, 51, 86, 90, 255, 264–5
   at Meadowview, 89, 93, 101
   Medicaid and, 87, 263–5
   nonagency, 10, 164, 165, 167
   non-English-speaking, 64, 147, 164
AIDS epidemic, 115
alphabet board, 276, 286, 287, 302
Alzheimer's disease, 66, 104, 137, 150, 154,
     193, 204, 249, 273–6, 289, 308
   Bloom's patients with, 152–6
   caregivers and, 224, 225
   driving and, 227, 230
   at Hebrew Home, 138, 169, 206, 242
   resources for, 329–30
   restraints and, 136

testing for, 158
   see also cognititve impairment; dementia
ambulances, 35–6, 48, 68, 133
ambulance workers, 34
ambulettes, 125, 126, 128
American Association of Homes and
   Services for the Aging (AAHSA), *see*
   LeadingAge
American Geriatric Society, 104
American Medical Association, 227, 228
   recommendations on driving, 228
anesthesiologists, 64, 65
annuities, 218
antidepressants, 143
anxiety, 26, 104, 278
   of author, 32, 38, 73, 86, 92
   of E. Gross, 72, 73, 85, 97, 107, 111, 143,
     144
appetite, loss of, 141, 154, 155, 291
appointments, medical, 61–4, 73, 146–7, 226
   accompanying a parent to, 61–3, 64, 71,
     147, 223
   of Bloom, 152–7
   follow-up, 130
   time required for, 54, 63, 64, 147–8, 152
Aricept, 159
Armstrong, Carol, 249
Armstrong, Jim, 249
arthritis, 17, 18, 22, 61, 173, 280, 308
assets, 27, 28
   Medicaid and, 255–6
"assignment of benefits" form, 212
assisted living communities, 8, 22, 26–52,
     77, 81, 86, 150, 202, 224, 226, 244, 246,
     263

A NOTE ABOUT THE AUTHOR

Jane Gross was a reporter for *Sports Illustrated* and *Newsday* before joining *The New York Times* in 1978 as a reporter and national correspondent. Since 2008 she has written for the *Times* on a freelance basis. She launched and wrote a blog for the *Times* called *The New Old Age,* to which she still contributes. She has taught in the graduate programs at the University of California, Berkeley and at Columbia University, and was the recipient of a John S. Knight Fellowship. She lives in Westchester County, New York.

A NOTE ON THE TYPE

This book was set in Minion, a typeface produced by the Adobe Corporation specifically for the Macintosh personal computer, and released in 1990. Designed by Robert Slimbach, Minion combines the classic characteristics of old-style faces with the full complement of weights required for modern typesetting.

Composed by Creative Graphics, Allentown, Pennsylvania

Printed and bound by Berryville Graphics, Berryville, Virginia

Designed by Maggie Hinders